Italian Gothic
Horror Films,
1980–1989

Italian Gothic
Horror Films,
1980–1989

Roberto Curti

McFarland & Company, Inc., Publishers
Jefferson, North Carolina

ISBN (print) 978-1-4766-7243-4
ISBN (ebook) 978-1-4766-3524-8

LIBRARY OF CONGRESS CATALOGUING DATA ARE AVAILABLE

BRITISH LIBRARY CATALOGUING DATA ARE AVAILABLE

Front cover: Italian lobby card for the 1981 film *Murder Obsession*,
featuring a screaming Anita Strindberg

Printed in the United States of America

*McFarland & Company, Inc., Publishers
Box 611, Jefferson, North Carolina 28640
www.mcfarlandpub.com*

To Cristina, my light half.

Acknowledgments

My most sincere thanks go to the following, who in one way or another contributed to the making of this book: Mark Thompson Ashworth, Enzo Boetani, Ricky Caruso, Davide Cavaciocchi, Francesco Cesari, Brigitte Christensen, Luigi Cozzi, Michele De Angelis, Pierpaolo De Sanctis, Alessio Di Rocco, Christoph Draxtra, Steve Fenton, Jacqueline Freda, Mario and Roderick Gauci, Julian Grainger, Troy Howarth, Peter Jilmstad, Frank Lafond, Stefano Loparco, Leandro Lucchetti, Fabio Melelli, Domenico Monetti, Antonio José Navarro, Chris Orgelt (BIFFF), Stefano Patrizi, Alberto Pezzotta, Roberto Poppi, Fabio Pucci, Luca Servini, Pete Tombs, David C. Tucker, Davide Vincenti.

Table of Contents

Introduction

"World champions!"

On July 11, 1982, Italy won the 12th edition of the FIFA Soccer World Cup, defeating West Germany 3–1 during the final match at the "Santiago Bernabeu" stadium in Madrid, Spain. Almost 37 million Italians were watching TV on that night, and as the referee blew the final whistle the nation exploded in a collective exultation, while TV commentator Nando Martellini shouted, over and over, *"Campioni del mondo!"* ("World champions!"). It was more than just a victory: it was a collective catharsis, and not only because soccer was (and still is) Italy's most popular sport. The Soccer World Cup came as a symbolic revival, marking the end of one of the darkest periods in Italian history.

After the kidnapping of premier (and leader of the Democrazia Cristiana party) Aldo Moro on March 16, 1978, at the hands of the terrorist group Brigate Rosse (Red Brigades), the whole nation had fallen into a state of shock. The ensuing 55 days of Moro's imprisonment, the exhausting negotiations, the letters written by the premier to government leaders, his family and the Pope, and Moro's dramatic photographs in his cell sent to the newspapers by the Brigate Rosse had marked the eruption of death on the political scene. Death and politics had become one and the same: a grim, terrible spectacle which had invaded every single minute in the media, day after day. All this had climaxed on May 9, with the finding of Moro's lifeless body, executed by his kidnappers after a summary "trial" and

riddled with eleven gun and machine-gun bullets, stuffed in the trunk of a red Renault parked in the very center of Rome.

Aldo Moro's killing marked the beginning of the end for the Red Brigades and other terrorist groups. It generated a widespread sense of revulsion in public opinion, and many defections from the ranks of these groups. The BR and other groups performed more violent acts, with 29 victims in 1978, 22 in 1979 and 30 in 1980. But the terrorists were becoming more isolated, and with the contributions of the so-called *"pentiti"* (repentants) the BR columns were dismantled.[1] But Moro's death was the deflagration that started a chain reaction of political events, such as the resigning of the President of the Republic Giovanni Leone on June 15, 1978, and the Communist Party losing 4 percent of votes in the June 1979 elections—marking a negative trend for the first time since 1948—and abandoning its strategy of "historic compromise," that is, the plans of a government in convergence with Democrazia Cristiana in name of a greater political good (to which Moro was also favorable: not by chance, his body was found in a road symbolically equidistant from the Democrazia Cristiana and Partito Comunista Italiano headquarters). Finally, in mid–October 1980 a long and massive strike at Turin's FIAT automobile plant (which had started after the company's announcement that it would lay off some 14,000 employees due to the market for cars being in recession) came to an unexpected end with 40,000 FIAT employees marching through the streets of Turin and demanding their right to go back to work. It was, as the *Washington Post* noted, "the ultimate repudiation of both their own union leadership and, of course, the Communists."[2]

After the collective commitment of 1968, the social struggles and their degeneration, which gave way to the "Years of Lead" (1973–1980), characterized by the violent confrontation between the State and the militant terrorist groups, ordinary people were losing touch with politics. The disengagement (or "political reflux") led to the refusal of ideologies and parties and the rise of neoliberal ideas. The discovery in 1981 of the subversive pseudo–Masonic Lodge Propaganda Due (or P2) didn't improve upon this widespread distrust. A clandestine far-right organization led by Licio Gelli, P2 counted among its members some of Italy's most powerful individuals (politicians, industrialists, military leaders, et cetera). Its plans for a "Democratic Rebirth" encompassed corruption, murder and assorted crimes (including, possibly, a participation in the 1980 explosion at the Bologna train station, which killed 85 people and wounded more than 200), and were aimed at the control of mass media, suppression of trade unions, and the radical rewriting of the Italian Constitution in order to favor a totalitarian State.

The P2 scandal further weakened the nation's political conscience. A "silent majority" came to the fore, and the new decade marked the return from the public to the private sphere: Italians were rediscovering consumerism, and the advent of private TV networks gave new impulse to frivolities, advertising, and all things revolving around pure and simple entertainment. Italy's 1982 soccer triumph (with the new President of the Republic, ex-partisan Sandro Pertini, watching the game on the stands of the Madrid stadium, significantly representing the whole of Italy) became the coronation of all that—and more. After a decade of blood and bullets, people wanted to smile. Even more,

they wanted to purchase cars, clothes, jewels and other expensive status symbols, eat and drink in fashionable restaurants. Consumerism had become a way to elevate oneself above his or her social status and feel like a member of the elite. The climate was favorable for the advent to power of another political force. In 1983, the rise of PSI (Italian Socialist Party) and Bettino Craxi's designation as prime minister was the coronation marking such an era.

Milan, the economic center of this new trend, the design and finance capital, was nicknamed "*la Milano da bere*" (drinking Milan) for its excesses—cash, cocktails, cocaine—and Silvio Berlusconi was its undisputed emperor. Already a successful entrepreneur who had founded his empire on construction with the building of the residential neighborhood of Milano Due (Milan Two) in the late 1960s, Berlusconi had entered the world of communication and television as early as 1973, when he set up a small cable television company named TeleMilano, originally limited to service the Milano Due area, which later evolved into Canale 5, Italy's first national private TV station. Between 1980 and 1984 Berlusconi (a P2 member, incidentally) expanded his broadcasting empire by absorbing the competitors and becoming the monopolist in the TV market with his company Fininvest: in 1982 he bought Italia 1 from the Rusconi family, and two years later he acquired Rete 4 from Mondadori. In 1984 he owned the three major networks outside RAI, each targeted at a specific audience (general, young, female/elderly). The constant violation of the laws on the part of Berlusconi's channels prompted the magistrate to forcibly obscure them, but Craxi, Berlusconi's close friend, was the right man in the right place, and he came to his aid. Between October 1984 and June 1985, the Socialist premier favored the development of Berlusconi's TV empire with the so-called "*decreti Berlusconi*" ("Berlusconi decrees"), which made this system "temporarily" legal. It wasn't until 1990 that a new law (the so-called "*Legge Mammì*") consolidated what Craxi's decrees had established, making Berlusconi the most powerful man in Italy.

Death Smiles at the Murderer, or: Cinema vs. Television

The number of spectators, venues and films distributed theatrically can provide an idea of the quick death of Italian cinema throughout the decades. In 1970, there had been 525 million moviegoers; in 1980 the number had decreased dramatically to 241.8 million. In 1990, there would be only 90 million. Meanwhile, the *seconda* and *terza visione* venues—second-run and third-run cinemas, located in the outskirts of cities and small towns respectively—were gradually closing down, engulfed in the red-light circuit or simply dismantled to make room for banks, megastores and bingo halls, cutting short the commercial life of B-movies. The 11,560 theaters (of which 6,929 were "industrial venues" while the rest comprised parish cinemas, cultural associations, and so on) active in 1970 were reduced to 8,453 in 1980 (of which 5,336 were industrial venues) and 3,923 in 1990 (with 2,519 industrial venues). The percentage of first run theaters on the market, which was a very low in 1970, at just 1.6 percent, became 92 percent in 1980, and 94 percent in 1990.[3] This indicated that there was no longer room for the "*mercato di profondità*" (deep market), which allowed most genre films a long period (years) of commercial exploitation before their withdrawal from distribution. Many films were distributed only regionally, such as those aimed at southern audiences, and rarely if ever arrived in big cities, while others opened directly in the second-run and third-run circuit. These were the first victims of the muted market conditions, as they were not granted a commercial theatrical run any longer.

In fact, the number of films distributed theatrically dropped dramatically. In the 1969–1970 season there were 587 releases, in 1979–80 there were 480, and in 1989–90 the number decreased again to 376. In the early 1980s, the hardcore porn market had been an illusory oasis for some, but by the end of the decade, home video (with movies being distributed not only in video shops, but in newsstands as well, often at cut-rate prices) had almost completely consumed that area too. The rise of home video in the mid–1980s meant that some titles found a second commercial life: Lucio Fulci's films, for instance, were among the most rented in video stores.

Newspapers announced "*Berlusconi a capofitto nel cinema*"[4] ("Berlusconi dives headlong into cinema") in July 1986, reporting the news of the TV mogul's massive entry in the movie business through a deal between Reteitalia—a subsidiary of the Fininvest holding owned by Berlusconi, founded in 1979 and devoted to producing and purchasing films and TV programs—and one of the country's major distribution companies, Medusa. At first Reteitalia was fully engaged in foreign TV acquisitions, submitting Italian audiences to a steady diet of American TV shows, from *The Dukes of Hazzard* to *The Jeffersons*, but Berlusconi's plans rapidly expanded to cinema. The company began purchasing the "*diritti d'antenna*" (broadcasting rights) in 1983 by paying huge sums in advance to producers, a system which soon replaced the "guaranteed minimum" advanced by distributors for the theatrical release: Nanni Moretti's *Bianca*, released in February 1984, had been the first motion picture officially co-produced by Reteitalia. In 1986, with 70 to 80 billion *lire* invested, Berlusconi had become Italy's biggest film producer. That same year Reteitalia acquired 49 percent of Medusa. The year 1988 opened with Berlusconi's company taking control of the Cannon cinema chain in Italy, which consisted of 50 theaters,[5] and resulted in Berlusconi owning or operating 300 theaters across the country. Then, in October of the same year, Reteitalia—who already owned other distribution companies, namely Orion-Cdi, Cidif, DMV and other minor ones—acquired 100 percent of Medusa. "Now we are a major European company," Berlusconi exulted.[6] In March 1989 Reteitalia cut a deal with Mario and Vittorio Cecchi Gori, the owners of the Cecchi Gori distribution group, to create a new company devoted to producing and distributing films in the Italian market.[7] Born with an ambitious investment of 250 billion *lire*, Penta Film—described triumphally as a "full cycle company which carries a movie from production to theatrical distribution, and then from the theaters to the living room, that is the home video"[8]—acquired a key position on the market, both theatrical and home video.

RAI (the national broadcasting company) had been co-producing films since 1963, but its output grew after the notorious law 103 (April 14, 1975), which acknowledged its economic monopoly on television (while admitting the legitimacy of local television networks) and urged the company to set up "a specific structure dedicated to the production of films, in financial co-participation with Italian or foreign companies." Over the years, RAI was devoted to financing mostly cultural-oriented products, sometimes shot in dual versions: a feature-length film for cinema release, and an extended cut for a two-part airing on prime time a few months after the theatrical run.

Federico Fellini, Ermanno Olmi, Michelangelo Antonioni, Marco Bellocchio, the Taviani brothers were among the *auteurs* who benefited from RAI's financing, but the choice of titles produced by the company remained spotty, awkwardly blending committed projects and forgettable ones, with the inner logic likely being simply that of political intervention. In the words of scriptwriter Tonino Guerra, in the corridors of RAI, "one can detect too much the smell of the politicians who are behind the executives. And this

is a shame … we need competent people … it sucks walking across those corridors and sniffing all this political smell instead of having someone in charge who truly knows about spectacle and culture."[9] It goes without saying that genre films were barely represented—a few exceptions being Roberto Faenza's *Copkiller*, Giorgio Bontempi's *Notturno* and Antonio Margheriti's *Il mondo di Yor* (all 1983), and Duccio Tessari's *Tex e il signore degli abissi* (1985). As for the Gothic and horror genre, the only significant titles financed by RAI were Pupi Avati's remarkable zombie yarn *Zeder* (1983), which turned out to be a box-office disappointment, and Alberto Abruzzese and Achille Pisanti's virtually unseen political vampire allegory, *Anemia*, quickly shelved after an inauspicious screening at the 1986 Venice Film Festival.

Reteitalia took quite a different direction with its productions. Besides a bunch of art-house titles which would grant the company a cultural legitimacy rather than big profits (including works by Marco Ferreri and Marco Bellocchio), its offerings featured a prevalence of comedies and genre films—often co-produced with existing companies such as Luciano Martino's Dania Film—aimed at younger audiences, including *gialli*, horror and Gothic films, such as Lamberto Bava's *Morirai a mezzanotte* (1986) and *Le foto di Gioia* (1987), Marcello Avallone's *Spettri* (1987) and *Maya* (1989), *Pathos—Segreta inquietudine* (1988, Piccio Raffanini), *Nosferatu a Venezia* (1988, Augusto Caminito), *Il nido del ragno* (1988, Gianfranco Giagni) and Michele Soavi's *La chiesa* (1989). In turn, RAI struck a deal with producers Mario and Vittorio Cecchi Gori to invest more in genre cinema: among the titles co-produced by this new venture there was Dario Argento's *Opera* (1987).

But the massive presence on the market of Reteitalia and RAI meant the Italian movie industry would gradually set out to make films aimed more and more at a television audience, with easily understandable consequences: tamer products, devoid of the sexual and violent excesses of the past. Censorship raised its head again, too. Whereas in the 1970s it had been the magistrates who seized those films judged "obscene" (a practice which reached its peak in the early 1980s with a mass seizure of hardcore film all over the Italian territory), during the decade a number of committees, associations and other guardians of the public moral appeared, watching over the impressionable minors and influencing the board of censors. Meanwhile several representative and groundbreaking *auteurs* had disappeared (think of Pasolini, for instance) and the weight of television had become decisive. In turn, censorship changed, in part, its focus by giving more attention to "fears and preoccupations that come out of psychologists' environments, mostly toward the spreading of violence, because sex seems to be less important for them."[10] Moreover, political agendas were submitted to commercial ones: while judging a movie, the main issue was its final destination—television.[11]

This would lead to the 1990 Mammì law, which severely limited the TV airing of films, by forbidding to broadcast films with a V.M.18 rating and relegating those with a V.M.14 rating after 10:30 p.m. A movie had to be certified for all audiences to be aired on prime time, which led to a massive resubmitting of old films that had been rated V.M.14 and V.M.18 to the rating boards, in order to obtain a new screening certificate after several cuts. In fact, it was a powerful weapon of barely disguised censorship, and a much more effective one than there had ever been.

There Will Be Blood...

All this heavily influenced Italian cinema in general, and the Gothic and horror movie genre in particular. It's no surprise, then, that comedy became by far the most profitable genre of the decade and engulfed

most of the mainstream. Audiences wanted to laugh, and the likes of Renato Pozzetto, Paolo Villaggio, Adriano Celentano, Enrico Montesano and Johnny Dorelli meant surefire box-office hits, which sometimes—as was the case with *Mia moglie è una strega* (1980, Castellano & Pipolo) starring Pozzetto and Eleonora Giorgi, *Bollenti spiriti* (1981, Giorgio Capitani), starring Dorelli and Gloria Guida, or the Paolo Villaggio vehicle *Fracchia contro Dracula* (1985, Neri Parenti)—borrowed plots and ideas from old fantasy classics. It was an attempt to give new blood to an industry experiencing a nonstop hemorrhage of moviegoers.

Italian locandina for *Bollenti spiriti* (1981, Giorgio Capitani), one of several Italian comedies of the early 1980s which borrowed plots and ideas from old fantasy classics.

As for the horror genre, the decade started with a big-budget production, Dario Argento's *Inferno* (1980), which however failed to become a trend-setter, and in April of that year the death of Mario Bava and the feature film debut of his son Lamberto (*Macabro*, co-scripted and produced by Pupi Avati) marked a symbolic turn for Italian fantastic cinema. Meanwhile the old glories stepped aside or headed toward different genres. Riccardo Freda managed to direct one last motion picture, the low-budget *Murder Obsession* (1981), while Antonio Margheriti, after the Vietnam War/cannibal film hybrid *Apocalypse domani* (1980), for most of the decade stuck to more profitable products—namely war yarns and adventure flicks, *Raiders of the Lost Ark*–style—aimed to please foreign audiences, after the Western and the *poliziotteschi* had dried up.[12]

It was precisely abroad that Lucio Fulci established himself as Italy's most prominent horror film director in the early 1980s. Between 1980 and 1983, following the success of *Zombi 2* (1979), the director helmed a handful of titles that offered an original take on Gothic themes, with the notable exception of the ultra-violent *giallo*, *Lo squartatore di New York* (1982), and were distributed abroad with some success. Fulci's original aesthetics of fear and violence attracted the interest of French critics, who called him "poet of the macabre," but in Italy, despite the commercial success of some of his films, he was perceived as a B-filmmaker.

Fulci's Gothic tales, which sported literary influences (from Lovecraft to Henry James) in addition to the cinematic ones, were liberally imbued with conspicuous gore. Others followed the same thread with plenty of gruesome graphic deaths, mutilations, disembowelments and gallons of hemoglobin spread before the camera. This was the case with the zombie subgenre following Fulci's exploit, with the likes of Marino Girolami's *Zombi Holocaust* (1980), Bruno Mattei and Claudio Fragasso's *Virus*

(1980) and Andrea Bianchi's *Le notti del terrore* (1981)—the latter produced by Gabriele Crisanti, who also gave the world the mind-numbing *Patrick vive ancora* (1980), a rip-off of Richard Franklin's 1978 film *Patrick* (a surprise hit in Italy, where it was released with a new score by Goblin) plus a little bit of Cornell Woolrich's novel *Rendezvous in Black* thrown in for good measure. Also in the game were Luigi Cozzi (the *Invasion of the Body Snatchers*–inspired *Contamination*, 1980), Umberto Lenzi (*Incubo sulla città contaminata*, 1980, as well as the gory non-horror cannibal adventure diptych *Mangiati vivi!*, 1980, and *Cannibal Ferox*, 1981, following Ruggero Deodato's controversial *Cannibal Holocaust*, 1980) and Aristide Massaccesi (*Antropophagus*, 1980, and *Rosso sangue*, 1982). These films had little if any Gothic blood in them, but plenty of blood nonetheless: they are noteworthy principally as a testimony to the last fireworks of Italian extreme cinema.

Dario Argento's directing and producing output during the decade certified him as the Italian "Master of Horror" (as per the title of a 1991 Luigi Cozzi documentary), a commercially successful name brand that was to Italian cinema what Ferrari was to cars, or Armani to high fashion. Argento produced Lamberto Bava's two *Dèmoni* films—*Dèmoni* (1985) and *Dèmoni 2 … l'incubo ritorna* (1986)—which introduced the type of sophisticated special effects that would rival American horror films and launched Sergio Stivaletti as Italy's answer to renowned U.S. special makeup effects artists such as Rick Baker and Rob Bottin. Their box-office success seemed to indicate there was a mainstream market for reasonably budgeted, technically polished horror films.

On the other hand, the relationship between horror and the small screen was far from idyllic. Lamberto Bava's *giallo*, *La casa con la scala nel buio* (1983), originally devised for TV, was released theatrically not least because of its graphic violent scenes, and the same happened with Bava's *Morirai a mezzan-*

otte. Most notably, Argento's controversial appearance as special guest in the TV show *Giallo* (October 1987–January 1988, Rai Due), where he introduced a series of gory short films he directed, "*Gli incubi di Dario Argento*" (Dario Argento's Nightmares), caused a controversy, with many protests on the part of spectators. In 1986 Reteitalia commissioned the making of several Gothic and horror TV movies, hoping to intercept those audiences who rented horror videos and followed late-night broadcasts of old and recent films alike. Lamberto Bava was recruited to direct the four films in the "*Brivido giallo*" series, and so were Lucio Fulci and Umberto Lenzi for a similar project named "*Le case maledette.*" The results were far from satisfying, and, most of all, they proved that TV execs were willing to allow the genre on the small screen only in an overly diluted form, as shown by the bland "*Brivido giallo,*" but there was no room for the uncompromising, over-the-top gore of "*Le case maledette.*"

The ill-fated destiny of made-for-TV Gothic and horror films reflects the illusory well-being of a nation living above its possibilities. In 1982 Italy had emerged from a period of recession and would undergo a constant expansion that had economists refer to "a second Italian economic miracle" after the early 1960s' boom. But it would end abruptly with the international recession of the early 1990s. Similarly, the dreams of grandeur of Italian horror—exemplified by Augusto Caminito's *Nosferatu a Venezia*, an ambitious sequel to Werner Herzog's 1979 film, starring Klaus Kinski, which turned out to be a commercial and artistic disaster—were reduced by the end of the decade to hit-and-run productions designed for home video, such as the series of films produced on a shoestring budget by Luigi Nannerini and Antonino Lucidi and were distributed

under the misleading label "*Lucio Fulci presenta*" ("Lucio Fulci Presents").

As for Fulci himself, his severe health issues were only one of the causes that resulted in his transition from "poet of the macabre" to his decidedly less impressive low-budget output of the late 1980s, with such works as his horror comeback *Aenigma* (1987)—not a Gothic film by any means, but another *Patrick* rip-off mixed with references varying from *Carrie* (1976) to Patricia Highsmith's short story *The Snail Watcher*—and the ill-fated *Zombi 3* (1988), both let down by mediocre scripts, bad actors and shoestring budgets. Lamberto Bava, who had seemed to be on the verge of becoming second fiddle to Argento as Italy's most commercially successful horror filmmaker, eventually chose the path of television, with questionable results. The brightest promise of Italian horror seemed to

French lobby card for *Quella villa accanto al cimitero* (1981), one of the films that earned Lucio Fulci the definition of "poet of the macabre" from French critics.

be the talented Michele Soavi, whose transition from low-budget (*Deliria*, 1987) to the Argento factory (*La chiesa*) crowned him as the next big thing in the genre.

However, it was becoming harder and harder for debuting filmmakers to find financing for their work. Some opted for help from the state through Article 28 of the 1965 Italian law on cinema, which had instituted a fund to finance films "of national cultural interest," but the results were little-seen products that barely surfaced in theaters (*La casa del buon ritorno*, 1986, Beppe Cino), not to mention that their "cultural interest" was debatable to say the least, as with the abysmal *La croce dalle 7 pietre* (1987, Marco Antonio Andolfi). But relying on state support meant that genre projects (popular products, hence not culturally relevant in the common opinion) were mostly cut out. As for Reteitalia's approximations to the horror genre, the box-office results proved disappointing, while RAI's investments in young filmmakers would "offer study material to some willing cultural scholar,"[13] to quote film historian Paolo Mereghetti, for their often inexplicable choices, with obscure and scarcely attractive titles that sank to well-deserved oblivion.

Throughout the decade, small companies such as Aristide Massaccesi's Filmirage kept producing low-budget horror pictures aimed at foreign markets and gave debuting filmmakers a chance to make their bones. A new generation of directors surfaced, namely Michele Soavi, Fabrizio Laurenti, Claudio Lattanzi and Andrea Marfori, but there were also young independent, underground filmmakers who tried their hand at the horror genre, such as Giovanni Arduino and Andrea Lioy (*My Lovely Burnt Brother and His Squashed Brain*, 1988), and the Milanese Fabio Salerno, who made several interesting Super8 and 16mm short films characterized by heavy cinephile references, screened at specialized festivals.[14] But, as shown by such works as the Gothic-oriented *Streghe* (1989, Alessandro Capone),

the important thing to many was to disguise their national identity, in a chameleon-like game that went in the opposite direction than the gory excesses of the early decade. Once the motto was to stand out, to exceed, to exaggerate; now, it was to dissimulate.

The Changing Faces of Italian Gothic

The main characteristics and figures of Italian Gothic cinema can often be found under a very different light in the films made during the 1980s. Take the witch, for instance: the evil seductress, the temptress, the driving narrative of the genre since the days of *La maschera del demonio* (1960), is in turn seduced by the present-day commodities and becomes a benevolent housewife who takes care of her wealthy husband in *Mia moglie è una strega*, an example of comedy feeding vampirically on the genre's clichés and depriving them of their primal essence. On the other hand, *La casa 4—Witchcraft* (1988, Fabrizio Laurenti) or *Il bosco 1* (1988, Andrea Marfori) revisited the seductive witch within a context inspired by Sam Raimi's *The Evil Dead* (1981) and the new wave of gory American horror films. Throughout the decade, the most interesting take on the figure of the female sorceress in all its subversive essence was Marco Bellocchio's *La visione del sabba* (1988). Though not a Gothic horror movie per se—and therefore not included in this volume—it is nevertheless an intriguing look at sexuality and the battle of the sexes in today's society by way of psychoanalytic symbols and evocative dream sequences set in the 16th century, which reprises one of the Gothic's main tropes in an original and thought-provoking way. Bellocchio uses the theme of sorcery to explore the idea of an irreducible feminine, in the story of a psychiatrist (choreographer/dancer Daniel Ezralow) who is called to examine a delusional young woman (Beatrice Dalle): she claims to be a

350-year-old witch and almost killed a man who had sexually assaulted her. Likewise, the film employs the fantastic, by mixing past and present, reality and dream, realism and fantasy in the very same shot—and sometimes with extraordinary visual inventions—to tell the protagonist's escape from the "mediocrity of reason," as one critic called it.

With its complex, thought-provoking vision of woman as an order-shaking element in a male-oriented society—a notion in tune with Bellocchio's work of the period: see also his "scandalous" 1986 film *Il diavolo in corpo*—*La visione del sabba* pointed indirectly at the depiction of woman as an object of desire, which had been relaunched by television and the media, although in safer and more glamorous terms than the run toward sex of the previous decade(s). Bellocchio's film had what most Gothic films made during the decade lacked— eroticism, either explicit or not. Still, the blending of hardcore porn with Gothic and/or supernatural themes had produced a few notable hybrids in the early 1980s, which attempted to include sex scenes within a proper narrative frame, namely Alberto Cavallone's surreal *Blow Job (Soffio erotico)* (1980) and Mario Bianchi's *La bimba di Satana* (1983), a remake of *Malabimba* (1979, Andrea Bianchi).[15] On the other hand, the Piero Regnoli–scripted *Malombra* (1984, Bruno Gaburro), a loose adaptation of Antonio Fogazzaro's novel which had inspired one of Italy's proto–Gothic films, Mario Soldati's *Malombra* (1942), sported hardly any Gothic elements, and turned out to be a glamorous soft-porn tailor-made for the voluptuous starlet Paola Senatore, in the wake of the trend of erotic period films spawned by Tinto Brass' *La chiave* (1983). But, as the decade went on, the "adult" elements were discarded.

Classical Gothic was usually revisited within the context of spoofs (such as *Fracchia contro Dracula*), while the politically committed approach to the genre that had proven so fruitful in the past had virtually disappeared: *Anemia* was a less than remarkable exception. Similarly, the attempt at exploring an Italian flavor of the genre resulted in very few and often obscure films, as was the case with Giorgio Cavedon's downbeat ghost story *Ombre* (1980), with Pupi Avati's *Zeder* standing out as a startlingly original achievement. As proven by the diffusion of Gothic and horror films via home video, the genre had been adopted

Marco Bellocchio's *La visione del sabba* (1988) reprises one of the Gothic's main tropes (the seductive witch) for an intriguing look at sexuality and the battle of the sexes in today's society.

by a different and much younger audience—teenagers who purchased popular horror comics such as *Dylan Dog* and watched horror movie marathons on TV. Dario Argento understood it well: his 1985 *giallo, Phenomena*, and the *Dèmoni* diptych were aimed at a public who listened to Iron Maiden or Mötley Crüe, a generation of film buffs who could savor the cinephile homages and would also buy the soundtrack albums.

Postmodernist Gothic evolved from the mélange of references in the films scripted by Dardano Sacchetti for Lucio Fulci, which stuck to the habit of borrowing themes and ideas and reworking them in a different way (often, it must be added, with impressive results), to the open homage and self-referentiality of *Dèmoni* and especially Soavi's *La chiesa*, Italy's most self-conscious and coherent postmodernist horror movie of the decade. Other, less impressive examples were the self-conscious *Anemia*, which amply displayed its makers' elitist approach, and Fulvio Wetzl's feature length debut, *Rorret* (1988), about a psycho cinema owner (Lou Castel) who screens only horror films and picks his female victims among the most impressionable in the audience; he then attempts to have them revive traumatic fears in real life. The premise partly recalls *Fade to Black* (1980, Vernon Zimmerman), *Anguish* (1987, Bigas Luna) and of course Michael Powell's *Peeping Tom* (1960), and Wetzl is remarkably bold in recreating key scenes from no less than three Hitchcock films: *Psycho* (which becomes *Blood in the Shower*, directed by a "Graham Sutherland" but replete with Bernard Herrmann's music score), *Strangers on a Train* and *Dial M for Murder*. But the theoretical discourse about cinema seems to have been lifted from some not-too-bright film student's thesis, and the only thing more awkward than the acting is the concept that a movie theater that specialized in horror films would attract enough spectators to survive in late 1980s Italy.

NOTES

1. See Paul Ginsborg, *A History of Contemporary Italy. Society and Politics 1943–1988* (London: Penguin UK, 1990).
2. "The End of the Fiat Strike," *Washington Post*, October 29, 1980.
3. See Barbara Corsi, *Con qualche dollaro in meno. Storia economica del cinema italiano* (Rome: Editori riuniti, 2001), 124–129.
4. "Berlusconi a capofitto nel cinema," *La Stampa*, July 17, 1986.
5. Gian Guido Oliva, "Berlusconi: 'L'87? È andato così," *Corriere della Sera*, January 5, 1988.
6. Paolo Calcagno, "Siamo una major europea," *Corriere della Sera*, October 28, 1988.
7. P.Ca. [Paolo Calcagno], "Patto Berlusconi—Cecchi Gori," *Corriere della Sera*, March 8, 1989.
8. Maurizio Porro, "Berlusconi e Cecchi Gori: la Penta Film è in orbita," *Corriere della Sera*, October 25, 1989.
9. Tonino Guerra, quoted in Franca Faldini and Goffredo Fofi (eds.), *Il cinema italiano d'oggi, 1970–1984* (Milan: Mondadori, 1984), 393.
10. Domenico Liggeri, *Mani di forbice. La censura cinematografica in Italia* (Alessandria: Falsopiano, 1997), 183.
11. Which explains such paradoxical episodes as a deputy prosecutor envisaging the crime of "complicity in obscene spectacle" for the members of the rating board who had classified *9½ Weeks* (1986, Adrian Lyne) with only a V.M. 14 rating, allowing it to be broadcast at prime time in December 1987 on Canale 5.
12. Margheriti returned to the science fiction/horror genre with *Alien degli abissi* (1989).
13. Paolo Mereghetti, "Piccoli film crescono (1976–1998)," in Alberto Barbera (ed.), *Cavalcarono insieme. 50 anni di cinema e televisione in Italia* (Milan: Mondadori Electa, 2004), 37.
14. Born in 1965, Salerno made his first short film, *Spirit*, at 14. Several more followed: *Cadaveri* (1982), *Extra sensoria* (1985), *Vampiri* (1986, presented at Cattolica's Mystfest), *Mezzanotte* (1986, predating *Hellraiser*), *Arpie* (1987) and *Oltretomba* (1987). In 1990 Salerno directed the 16mm feature film *Notte profonda* (1990), which cost only 11 million *lire*, followed by another short, *L'altra dimensione* (1993). He committed suicide in 1993, at just 29 years old.
15. The same cannot be said about other porn films with sparse horrific and supernatural elements, sketchily inserted between one graphic sex scene and the next. This is the case with *Orgasmo esotico* (1982, Mario Siciliano, as "Lee Castle"), in which Sonia Bennett plays a witch who puts her deadly spell on the other characters, including Marina Hedman (credited as Marina Lotar), resulting in assorted deaths and in Hedman turning up as a zombie to perform one last fellatio. In the circular ending it is revealed to be a dream ... or maybe not? However, Siciliano's direction is so dire that one never cares about the plot, but the sex scenes are even more boring. *Nera ... calda ... e dolce* (1987, A.P. Spinelli [Alessandro Perrella]) is a rip-off of Jonas Middleton's golden age classic *Through the Looking Glass* (1976), starring future porn star Rocco Siffredi as a malevolent sex phantom who lures the heroine (Marie-Christine Veroda, credited as "Jennifer O'Naeale") into sex escapades, including a particularly unpleasant climax involving a close encounter with a horse.

A Note on the Entries

This volume lists all the films produced and released in Italy between 1980 and 1989 that in my view can be defined as "Gothic" (according to the analysis included in my previous volume *Italian Gothic Horror Films, 1957–1969*, on pages 3 to 9, and continued in my *1970–1979* volume), or have prominent Gothic elements and themes to them. The entries include spoofs, hardcore films or modern-day riffs on classic themes and characters (the ghost story, the werewolf, the vampire). Each entry is listed according to its first official screening or theatrical release date instead of its filming or its submission to the rating board. This led to the exclusion of such titles as Lamberto Bava's made-for-TV remake of *La maschera del demonio* and Luigi Cozzi's *The Black Cat* (a.k.a. *De Profundis*) which are dated 1989 on the IMDb but were in fact screened or released later: *La maschera del demonio* premiered in June 1990 at Rome's Fantafestival, whereas Cozzi's film was shot over a period of time between spring and fall of 1989 and is copyrighted 1990 in the credits. Its video premiere took place even later, in June 1991.

As with the previous volumes, I did not include Spanish majority co-productions directed by Spanish filmmakers, such as *Estigma* (1980, José Ramón Larraz), which was not even released theatrically in Italy. On the other hand, I opted to include two films that were filmed abroad and financed with foreign money but helmed by Italian directors. Damiano Damiani's *Amityville II: The Possession* (1982) was produced by an Italian mogul,

Dino De Laurentiis, who had relocated his production company overseas for financial reasons, and developed from an original script by Dardano Sacchetti, possibly the most active scriptwriter in the genre during the decade. As for the werewolf movie *Monster Dog*, a.k.a. *Leviatán* (1985), listed in official sources as an out-and-out Spanish production (but financed by the Dutch producer Eduard Sarlui with his company Continental Motion Pictures), it was filmed in Spain by genre specialist Claudio Fragasso, who also scripted it.

Each entry features a comprehensive crew and cast list, based on the film's opening and closing credits. Uncredited extras are also listed, if noteworthy. Please note that on some occasions the Italian crew and cast members adopted English pseudonyms: whenever possible, I included the participants' real names after their Anglo-Saxon aliases. Also featured are filming locations, running time, screening certificate (Visa) number, release dates, Italian box-office grosses, alternate titles; a brief synopsis; and an essay on the film, often with the inclusion of little-known or never-before-seen data regarding production history and assorted trivia. As for filming dates, whenever possible I included the official ones as reported in the Public Cinematographic Register in Rome, but bear in mind that this official source, although very valuable, is not 100 percent reliable, as sometimes the dates registered don't correspond to the actual ones (see, for instance, the case of Argento's *Inferno*). Still, it is useful to date a movie's production properly.

Unlike previous decades, box-office grosses were sometimes problematic to find, due to the lack of proper sources (such as Maurizio Baroni's invaluable *Platea in piedi* volumes, which stop at 1979) or sometimes the unreliability of data. I have taken advantage of various sources, including Roberto Poppi's *Dizionario del cinema italiano. I film dal 1980 al 1989* and, starting from 1985, the issues of the monthly magazine *Ciak si gira* with the list of the year's top 100 box-office films, but for some of the more obscure titles the grosses were not available.

The entries are listed under their original Italian title, followed by the English title (referring to the U.S. theatrical or video release) in brackets and italics. If there was no English language release, a literal translation is included, but not set in italics. Please keep in mind that the films are mentioned throughout the text under their original Italian title, for instance *Quella villa accanto al cimitero*, not *The House by the Cemetery*.

The book features two appendices. The first covers direct-to-video releases, namely the eight films of the series "*I maestri del thriller*" (a.k.a. "*Lucio Fulci presenta*"), which were never submitted to the rating board and didn't receive any certificate for theatrical re-lease. Some of these titles fall flatly into the Gothic genre, while others feature minor or sparse Gothic elements, so I have decided to discuss them in a comprehensive essay for the sake of explaining their common production history and their main traits and themes, while giving much more room to those that have proper Gothic qualities. The second appendix covers Gothic made-for-TV films, with two series produced by Reteitalia during the decade, namely "*Brivido giallo*" (consisting of four films directed by Lamberto Bava) and "*Le case maledette*" (four films directed by Lucio Fulci and Umberto Lenzi). In both appendices, the entries are arranged in chronological order, according to their shooting dates; for "*Brivido giallo*," they are arranged based upon their original air date.

The information bits provided throughout the text are the result of thorough research from a variety of sources such as academic texts and essays and other assorted material (interviews with filmmakers, producers and actors, old newspaper articles and reviews, ministerial papers and archives). Whenever possible, I located and consulted the original scripts deposited at the Luigi Chiarini Library of the Centro Sperimentale di Cinematografia (CSC) in Rome.

Abbreviations

The following abbreviations are used in the credits list for each entry

Crew

AC: Assistant camera; ACO: Costume assistant; ACON: Assistant continuity; AD: Assistant director; AE: Assistant editor; AMU: Assistant makeup; APD: Production design assistant; ArtD: Art director; ASD: Assistant set designer; B: Boom man; BB: Best boy; C: Camera; ChEl: Chief electrician; CHOR: Choreographer; CO: Costumes; CON: Continuity; D: directed by; DialD: Dialogue coach/dialogue director; DOP: Director of photography; DubD: Dubbing director; E: Editor; El: Electrician; GA: Gaffer; Hair: Hairdresser; KG: Key grip; LT: Lighting technician; M: Music; MA: Master of arms; Mix: Sound mixer; MU: Makeup; OE: Optical effects; PD: Production designer; PrA: Press attache; PrM: Property master; S: Story; 2ndAD: 2nd Assistant director; SC: Screenplay; SD: Set decoration/set dresser; SE: Special effects; SO: Sound; SOE: Special sound effects; SP: Still photographer; SPFX: Special make-up effects; SS: Script supervisor/Script girl; STC: Stunt Coordinator; SVFX: Special visual effects; W: Wardrobe/Seamstress.

Production

ADM: Administrator; AP: Associate producer; EP: Executive producer; GM: General manager; PA: Production assistant; PAcc: Production Accountant; PCo: Production Coordinator; PM: Production manager; PR: Production runner; PROD: Produced by; PPS: Post-Production supervisor; PS: Production supervisor; PSe: Production secretary; PSeA: Production secretary assistant; UM: Unit manager; UP: Unit publicist.

Italian Gothic Horror Films, 1980–1989

The films are listed alphabetically within each year.
Notes are given at the end of each entry.

1980

Blow Job (Soffio erotico) (Blow Job—Erotic Whiff)

D: Alberto Cavallone. *S and SC*: Alberto Cavallone; *DOP*: Maurizio Centini; *M*: Ubaldo Continiello; *E*: Alberto Cavallone; *AD*: Michelangelo Pepe; *AC*: Carlo Marotti; *ChEl*: Armando Dramis; *El*: Costante Martinelli, Aldo Gentili; *KG*: Gaetano Barbera; *G*: Aldo Negretti; *MU*: Silvana Petri; *SO*: Pietro Spadoni; *SS*: Emilio Taliano. Cast: Danilo Micheli (Stefano Vicinelli), Anna Massarelli (Diana), Anna Bruna Cazzato (Angela), Mirella Venturini (Sibilla), Valerio Isidori (Alphonse), Antonio Mea (Hotel Concierge); *uncredited*: Martial Boschero (Hotel Customer), Guya Lauri Filzi (Woman at Party), Hassen Jabar (Masked Party Guest), Pauline Teutscher (Suicidal Woman). *PROD*: Martial Boschero for Anna Cinematografica [and Pietro Belpedio, uncredited, for Distribuzione Cinematografica 513]; *PM*: Martial Boschero; *PSe*: Maria Ludovica Bologna. *Country*: Italy. Filmed in Riolo Terme, Ravenna and Cesena, Italy. *Running time*: 80 minutes (m. 2190). Visa n. 74774 (5.17.1980); *Rating*: V.M.18. *Release dates*: 5.17.1980 (Italy), 6.25.1984 (Spain); *Distribution*: Distribuzione Cinematografica 513. *Domestic gross*: 425,371,000 *lire*. *Also known as*: Blow Job—Dolce lingua (Italy, alternate title); *Blow Job (Trabajo de absorción)* (Spain).

Stefano and Diana, two young and penniless actors, flee from a hotel without paying the bill, taking advantage of a woman's suicide. Later, at a racetrack, they meet a scarred older woman, Countess Angela, who helps Stefano pick a winning horse. In return she asks them for a ride to her villa in the countryside because she wants Stefano to help her "pass the gate." During the trip they meet some surreal characters, including a biker whose head looks like a skull. At the villa, a sinister-looking butler named Alphonse awaits them. Strange things ensue: Angela puts a spell on Diana, who becomes ill; Stefano goes looking for a doctor and meets a young, beautiful woman named Sibilla, who gives him a magic powder to cure Diana. The Countess and Diana leave Stefano alone in the villa and go to a ball; in the middle of the night, Sibilla comes out of a mirror and takes Stefano to a cave where she hypnotizes him, and they make love. Then Stefano finds himself again in the villa, in the middle of an inexplicable ritual which turns into an orgy: Diana, seemingly in a hypnotic trance, dances with the guests in turn, regardless of him. The mysterious biker shows up and turns out to be a woman with a skull mask; she starts a primitive tribal dance, and all those she passes by drop dead, until she and Diana are the only ones left in the room. Diana becomes mad at Stefano and falls out of a window. Stefano is left alone with Angela: she and Sibilla are one and the same, a powerful witch who absorbs her lovers' energy in order to reincarnate into a new body. Stefano confronts and apparently destroys them by shattering the huge mirror in the salon. Then he suddenly finds himself back at the hotel. The woman who has committed suicide is revealed to be Diana. Amidst the

15

crowd, Stefano glimpses Sibilla and Alphonse, staring at him…

Always a controversial filmmaker, who had managed to cut for himself a niche as a singular *auteur* whose works blended eroticism, politics (especially Third World-related themes) and experimental film style, by the late 1970s Alberto Cavallone[1] had made the transition between erotic cinema to hardcore porn. "It is a deliberately pornographic film, but with a political content. A movie about violence as a means of communication and knowledge in a repressive society." This is how he announced *Blue Movie* (1978), labeling it as "Italy's first hard-core film…. The characters discuss like in a progressive comic book, shoot, copulate and sodomize, kill and ejaculate in a mixture where everything is dream. The only reality is sex, with its functions pushed to the extreme."[2] But his choice was also dictated by the rapidly shrinking market, and the impossibility to mount the projects he wanted to make (such as *Dream*, a violent rape-and-revenge tale set entirely in a department store). Even though his films—most notably *Spell—Dolce mattatoio*, 1977—were advertised as Italy's answer to Walerian Borowczyk and Dušan Makavejev, there was little or no room for him as an independent director who worked outside Rome.

Following *Blue Movie*, Cavallone split his activity as a filmmaker into two. On the one hand, he worked on television, returning to his origins as a documentarist with the reportage *Dentro e fuori la classe*, broadcast in three parts (respectively titled *Io sono … capisci?*, *Boh!* and *Il pezzo di carta*) on Rai Uno from November 27 to December 12, 1979, to very positive reviews.[3] Parallel to that, he was now fully dabbling in hardcore porn.

Shot during the Summer of 1979[4] with the working title *La strega nuda* (The Naked Witch),[5] *Blow Job* was an extremely rushed production, officially financed by Martial Boschero's company Anna Cinematografica but in fact produced by Pietro Belpedio, one of the pioneers of Italian porn with his company Distribuzione Cinematografica 513. Boschero—the brother of actress Dominique Boschero and one of Cavallone's closer collaborators—had a cameo as a customer at the hotel in one of the early scenes. Filming took place almost entirely in a villa near Riolo Terme, in North-East Italy, near the city of Faenza. Belpedio recalled that the villa belonged to a dirty old man, who gave it almost for free to the production but asked to be on set when the explicit sex scenes were shot. The extreme poverty shows throughout the film, shot on a shoestring and harmed by inadequate actors, especially the bovine-looking Dario Micheli. Yet the result is strangely fascinating, and certainly doesn't deserve the crass contempt (and lack of critical depth) reserved to it by some biased historians of Italian porn.

The director's mystical and esoteric interests are well in evidence here. The story is spiced with literary references that vary from Carlos Castaneda's writings to Aldous Huxley's 1954 essay on drugs, *The Doors of Perception*. As the director explained, "the whole film was focused on the possibility of escaping from our own bodies, by modifying sensorial perceptions through the use of drugs or self-concentration." *Blue Movie* conveyed a stark, grim and matter-of-fact view on the contemporary world, in which consumerism leads to alienation and madness; *Blow Job*, on the other hand, is a metaphysical and elusive, even escapist fantasy which nevertheless exudes the same pessimistic feel. Significantly, at one point Sibilla says: "The world is tired, its end is near, people have lost the will to live…."

Dialogue was never Cavallone's biggest asset, and such lines as, "I don't know what got me today, I feel like a bitch in heat" are definitely not Shakespeare. But the protagonists' words convey the director's disconsolate vision of the present and link the film to his previous works. Whereas *Blue Movie* was about a world smothered by commodities such as Coca-Cola and Marlboro cigarettes, the characters in *Blow Job* cannot see beyond the merely phenomenal vision that today's consumerist society has instilled in them, and discuss even death in down-to-earth, materialistic terms. In the early scenes, set in a cheap hotel, we meet the protagonists, two young, penniless actors, Stefano (Micheli) and Diana (Anna Massarelli), who see a woman throw herself out of a window from the room above. Their reaction is telling: "We are made of guts, of dampish matter," Stefano comments, cynically comparing the dead woman on the floor to "an overturned bowl of spaghetti with lots of sauce." Thus, when the witch talks about a "key" to "open a gate," referring to a threshold to another dimension, Stefano and Diana can only interpret her words literally, unaware of their real significance, because, as Sibilla tells Stefano: "You, like all the others, refuse to see beyond the images of your eyes…." They are empty, desperately void inside: it's no surprise that Stefano confesses: "I have many air bubbles in my head…. Many white air bubbles." But *Blow Job*'s ordinary, squalid everyday world proves permeable to forces and presences beyond our comprehension. Magic is all around us, as are doors (and mirrors, like in *Inferno*) to other dimensions.

Blow Job is the closest the director came to making a proper horror movie: at times, it almost looks like a live-action version of one of the adults-only comics made in the 1970s, such as *Oltretomba* or *Storie Blu*. Cavallone's take on the main themes of Italian Gothic—the haunted house, the warped space/time continuity, the gullible male hero, the duality between animate and inanimate—is imbued with the director's literary and cinephile tastes, with at times striking results. The recurring character of the skull-masked biker echoes Jean Cocteau's *Orphée* (1950), and the plot itself is basically a reworking of Cocteau's film, from which it also reprises some central ideas, namely the characters crossing a mirror which acts like a boundary between this world and the afterlife. The one-eyed witch and her scarred butler Alphonse recall the princess played by Maria Casarés and her enigmatic chauffeur Heurtebise (François Périer), while Stefano and Diana are modern-day versions of Orphée and Eurydice. The seductress (and bisexual) witch literally splits into two to put the man under her spell, as had happened in Damiano Damiani's *La strega in amore* (1966),[6] and Cavallone was likely familiar with Carlos Fuentes' novel *Aura* which had inspired Damiani's film. Moreover, the dual appearance of the witch—played by two very different actresses—pays homage to Buñuel's *Cet obscur objet du desir* (1977). The actress playing the countess, Anna Bruna Cazzato, is characterized as a mature dark lady, and wears a make-up that has the left side of her face crossed by a deep scar and without an eye—a mutilation she hides behind huge dark glasses and hats that recall the titular diva in Billy Wilder's *Fedora* (1978). It is a yin/yang image of beauty and horror, seduction and repulsion that recalls the character played by Barbara Steele in *Amanti d'oltretomba* (1965, Mario Caiano). Her butler Alphonse (Valerio Isidori, in a role devised for Luciano Rossi) is similarly scarred, all over the *right* side of his face, as if to underline a link between them, a subterranean complementarity. On the other hand, Mirella Venturini's Sibilla is a young hippie woman who exudes an earthier, sunny sexuality, yet equally mystical and mysterious.

The result at times recalls Jean Rollin's films—take the sequence where Sibilla emerges from the bathroom mirror and leads Stefano away in the night, which has the same striking naivety as the grandfather clock scene in *Le frisson des vampires* (1970). Cavallone was especially proud of the ensuing sequence where the witch brings Stefano to a cave and makes him drink a magic potion, especially the 360° shots following Sibilla from the man's point of view, as she moves in circles around him like a predator and then hypnotizes him with snake-like moves. Other parts are definitely less successful: the ball sequence in the darkened hall, with the enigmatic participants carrying torches while dancing a waltz and Alphonse directing a spotlight on them, and Stefano vainly trying to catch Diana, looks like an excerpt from some threadbare avant-garde experimental oddity. It soon degenerates into a confused orgy whose participants are masked and made up like birds and animals. The scene gives a measure of the inner duality of Cavallone's cinema, always striving to overcome its limits but ultimately unable to fulfill its ambitions, wavering between remarkable visual intuitions and slapdashness.

All this concurs to form a shaky, one-of-a-kind concoction that blends atmospheric *fantastique*, elusive symbols, pretentious dialogue, bouts of tasteless H.G. Lewis-style gore (concentrated in the aftermath of the suicide scene) and explicit sex. In a late interview the director denied that *Blow Job* featured any graphic sex scenes except for "one simulated [*sic*] blow job,"[7] but this claim was refuted by other participants in the film. A hardcore version was filmed, and the cast features three uncredited performers who would work again in Cavallone's hardcore films: the Dutch Pauline Teutscher (the girl who commits suicide) and the Italian Guya Lauri Filzi, plus the Lebanese actor Hassan Jabar. The latter two appeared in the orgy scene.

Blow Job was first rejected by the rating board on February 23, 1980, after Cavallone refused to perform the cuts that had been requested,[8] for a total of 3 minutes and 16 seconds. In May 1980, in appeal, he eventually obliged, and the movie was given the censorship certificate with a V.M. 18 rating, on the condition that the title be accompanied by the subtitle *Soffio erotico* (Erotic Whiff), which the board—evidently not too familiar with English lingo—

assumed was "the title's contextual and faithful translation into Italian," as requested by the implementing regulation to the 1962 law on censorship (D.P.R. 2029, 11.11.1963). However, the blatantly allusive posters bore the more explicit subtitle *Dolce lingua* (Sweet Tongue), and featured the image of an open female mouth, a sight which undoubtedly helped the film's commercial success. *Blow Job* performed well in Italy and was also released in Spain: it premiered in Madrid in June 1984, in the hardcore version, as *Blow Job (Trabajo de absorción)*, to poor box-office.

The director's next film was *La gemella erotica (Due gocce d'acqua)* (The Erotic Twin—Dead Ringers), a disappointingly bland erotic thriller (shot in hardcore version as well) featuring among others Teutscher and Filzi, which retained none of *Blow Job*'s weird fascination. Facing severe economic problems, in the early Summer of 1981 Cavallone accepted to direct another hardcore porn for Boschero and Belpedio. He ended up making three, very weird ones—*Baby Sitter* (also known as *Il nano erotico*), *Pat, una donna particolare*, and *... e il terzo gode*—which he signed under the pseudonym Baron Corvo.

NOTES

1. For an in-depth analysis of Cavallone's work, see Roberto Curti, *Mavericks of Italian Cinema. Eight Unorthodox Filmmakers. 1940s–2000s* (Jefferson NC: McFarland, 2018), 28–63.

2. "Spogliandosi discutono," *Corriere della Sera*, August 12, 1977.

3. *Dentro e fuori la classe* depicted an ordinary day in three schools from different parts of the nation—respectively a technical institute in Genoa, a lyceum in Rome and an agrarian institute in Cosenza—with interviews with the students. Cavallone shot over 45,000 meters of film, without any pre-existing script, and granting total freedom of expression to the interviewees to preserve spontaneity. It was a return to his early days, which explored with an uncommon sensibility the world of teenagers at school, their problems, the relationship with their parents, their dreams (or lack thereof) for the future. The documentary was characterized by a singular pessimism: as a critic noted, "it seems there are no wishes, nor ideals, ambitions or fights to share." G.B., "Quegli studenti ghettizzati...," *Corriere della Sera*, November 27, 1979.

4. According to the Public Cinematographic Register, shooting started on August 16, 1979.

5. The 19-page outline and the 199-page script deposited at Rome's CSC are titled *La strega*.

6. For an in-depth analysis of Damiani's film, see Roberto Curti, *Italian Gothic Horror Films, 1957–1969* (Jefferson NC: McFarland, 2015), 171–176.

7. Davide Pulici and Manlio Gomarasca, "Il dolce mattatoio. Incontro con Alberto Cavallone," *Nocturno Cinema* #4, September 1997, 54.

8. Namely, as reported in the ministerial papers: "1) Sexual intercourse in the opening scene: the bit in which the man's member is seen and the part in which the woman is astride the man; 2) Lesbian scene on the sofa: the whole part in which Diana is masturbating Angela; 3) Scene of the coupling in the bathroom, heavy shortening; 4) Cave scene: the bit in which the erect member of the man is seen, shortening of the scene in which the woman licks the man; 5) Mating *more pecorum* during the orgy."

Inferno (Hell)

D: Dario Argento. *S and SC*: Dario Argento; *DOP*: Romano Albani (Technicolor, Technovision); *M*: Keith Emerson, arranged by Emerson and Salmon, conducted by Godfrey Salmon; *E*: Franco Fraticelli; *ArtD*: Giuseppe Bassan; *SD*: Francesco Cuppini, Maurizio Garrone; *CO*: Massimo Lentini; *MU*: Pierantonio Mencacci; *Hair*: Luciana Maria Costanzi, Giancarlo De Leonardis; *AD*: Lamberto Bava; *2ndAD*: Andrea Piazzesi; *SVFX*: Mario Bava, Pino Leoni; *C*: Idelmo Simonelli (*underwater sequence*: Gianlorenzo Battaglia); *SE*: Germano Natali; *SOE*: Luciano Anzellotti, Massimo Anzellotti; *SOE editor*: Attilio Gizzi; *Sound engineer*: Francesco Groppioni; *B*: Giancarlo Laurenzi; *Mix*: Romano Pampaloni; *KG*: Agostino Pascarella; *GA*: Alberto Altibrandi; *SP*: Francesco Bellomo; *SS*: Maria Serena Canevari; *AC*: Michele Picciaredda, Stefano Ricciotti; *SO*: Mario Dallimonti; *DialD*: Neil Robinson; *W*: Berta Berti; *AsstArtD*: Davide Bassan; *AsstSD*: Massimo Garrone; *Set painters*: Giorgio Palomba, Mauro Tiberi; *AE*: Piero Bozza. *Cast*: Leigh McCloskey (Mark Elliot), Irene Miracle (Rose Elliot), Eleonora Giorgi (Sara), Daria Nicolodi (Elise Delong Valadler) Sacha Pitoeff (Kazanian), Alida Valli (Carol), Veronica Lazar (The Nurse), Gabriele Lavia (Carlo), Feodor Chaliapin, Jr. (Prof. Arnold/Varelli), Leopoldo Mastelloni (John the Butler), Ania Pieroni (Musical Student), James Fleetwood (Cook), Rosario Rigutini (Man), Ryan Hilliard (Shadow), Paolo Paoloni (Music Teacher), Fulvio Mingozzi (Cab Driver), Luigi Lodoli (Bookbinder), Rodolfo Lodi (Old Man in library); *uncredited*: Lamberto Bava (Passer-by in New York), Andrea Piazzesi (Passer-by in New York). *PROD*: Claudio Argento for Produzioni Intersound (Rome); *EP*: Salvatore Argento, Guglielmo Garroni; *PM*: Andrew Garroni, Angelo Iacono; *UM*: Cesare Jacolucci; *PA*: Anna Maria Galvinelli, Saverio Mangogna, Michela Prodan; *PAcc*: Carlo Du Bois, Ferdinando Caputo, Carla Menicocci, Egle Friggeri;

New York production services: William Lustig. *Unit publicist*: Enrico Lucherini, Walter Afford. *ADM*: Solly V. Bianco. *Country*: Italy. Filmed in New York and at De Paolis In.Ci.R. Studios and R.P.A. Elios Studios (Rome). *Running time*: 106 minutes (m. 2896). Visa n. 74729 (2.8.1980); *Rating*: V.M.14. *Release dates*: 2.8.1980 (Italy), 4.16.1980 (France), 6.1.1980 (Spain), 9.12.1980 (West Germany), 9.13.1980 (Japan), 9.1980 (UK), 8.15.1986 (USA); *Distribution*: 20th Century–Fox. *Domestic gross*: 1,331,763,000 *lire. Also known as*: Horror Infernal—Feuertanz der Zombies (West Germany).

New York. Rose, a young poetess, discovers from a book she borrowed from elderly antique dealer Mr. Kazanian that the building where she lives is one of three houses—the other ones being located in Freiburg and Rome—built by an architect named Varelli for the Three Mothers, supernatural entities who have the power of life and death upon humanity. Rose writes a letter to her brother Mark, a music student at the Rome conservatory, telling him about her discovery. However, the letter is stolen by Mark's girlfriend Sara, who soon meets a horrible death together with a casual acquaintance, a man named Carlo. Meanwhile, in New York, Rose is horribly murdered too. Upon learning of his sister's death, Mark takes a plane to New York to investigate. He settles in Rose's apartment and meets the other tenants, who include an elderly wheelchair-bound professor and his nurse, the drug-addicted countess Elise and her servants Carol and John. More gruesome deaths ensue, including Kazanian's death during a moon eclipse. Eventually Mark finds the solution to the mystery and comes face to face with the elusive Varelli…

The impulse had become irresistible. There was only one answer to the fury that tortured him. The production of *Suspiria*, his most ambitious and elaborate film, had psychologically drained Dario Argento, and the end of his relationship with Daria Nicolodi had marked him deeply. He was the father of two daughters, who were away from him. He was young, rich and famous, but he wasn't happy. At that time, as he recalled in his memoir, he had been often tempted by the thought of suicide. He had even barricaded himself in his hotel suite on the top floor of the Grand Hotel Flora, in Rome's via Veneto, moving a wardrobe and a table against the French window so that, when the impulse of throwing himself into the void grabbed him in the middle of the night, it would be impossible to quench it.[1]

Then, one day Argento realized he was healed. Around the same time Daria Nicolodi resurfaced in his life, and what followed was the most satisfying period in his career, with *Suspiria* opening overseas to enthusiastic audiences (among them, a young Stephen King, who would mention the maggot scene in his 1981 essay *Danse Macabre*) and becoming a worldwide hit. It even inspired some foreign epigones, namely Norman J. Warren's *Terror* (1978) and Richard Marquand's *The Legacy* (1978), two movies which explicitly borrowed from Argento's work—and, in case of Warren's film, the British director acknowledged it in interviews.

Before he started working on his next picture, Argento decided to take a long break, taking advantage of a promotional tour in the States: this resulted in his association with George A. Romero, with the Italian director co-producing *Dawn of the Dead* (1978). Argento liked America so much that he not only chose to set his next movie there (something he already had in mind since he finished *Suspiria*[2]) but he moved to New York to complete the script for what he would later label as "one of the most mysterious projects in my career"[3]: the second part of his esoteric journey in the world of alchemy. As with the previous film, the title would be composed of only one word, a universal one which recalled Medieval images: *Inferno*.[4] Daria Nicolodi had a part in the writing, even though this time she only devised the basic storyline: "At the beginning I didn't want to have anything to do with it, after all the shocks and injustices of *Suspiria*…. But they kept telling me that I was the only one who could write a similar story, and in fact there were not many people well versed in the matter in Italy. So, I accepted, also because I had the whole story already in my head. I wrote it and as a reward I got a beautiful trip in the Caribbean."[5]

Then Argento set out to pen the script, in utter isolation in his beloved hotel rooms. The result of several months' work was a 267-page screenplay, divided into 99 scenes described in minute details, including set elements and camera movements. Dardano Sacchetti was called in for a last-minute, uncredited job as consultant:

It was a friendly collaboration, but completely irrelevant. Dario had been working on the script for six or seven months. He had just finished it. He was about to start shooting and, as it happens when you finish a work, he had some doubts. His father and his brother called me and asked me if I could spend some days with Dario and be his sparring-partner, so to speak. The pact was that I could ask all the money I wanted, but I wouldn't sign the script, whatever may happen. I read the script and for a week I spent seven to eight hours a day with Dario, in a hotel … he told me his doubts, we talked about them, and eventually Dario became convinced that the script was all right as it was, except for one scene. We discussed some changes, but when Dario rewrote it he only changed a marginal detail—nothing more. So, for a week I gave Dario my professional availability … but there is nothing of mine in the film.[6]

Filming started in Spring 1979, on a budget of 3 million dollars. Argento had cut a deal with Twentieth-Century Fox, who had had an unexpected hit with *Suspiria*, and the company secured worldwide distribution rights to his new film. First, the director and his crew moved to New York to shoot some exteriors and the Central Park scene and faced many issues due to the union laws. Then, on May 21, 1979, shooting began in Rome for a total of 14 weeks, at the De Paolis In.Ci.R. Studios and R.P.A. Elios studios (where the façade of Rose's palace was built). The Public Cinematographic Register in Rome reports April 16 as the official beginning of shooting, but a more plausible start date for the U.S. shoot seems to be May 7, 1979. Claudio Argento and others claimed that the New York shooting went on for "two weeks, ten days, something like that"[7] and articles of the period mentioned that filming in New York had lasted two weeks.[8]

The newspapers gave ample coverage to the making,[9] and highlighted the film's complexity and high budget, which made it a "horror *kolossal*"—the French-German term *colossal*, or *kolossal*, being a typical expression used in Italy to label big-budget movies, and accordingly Argento was rather intimidated at first by the complex production machine.[10] Moreover, the many special effects took lots of time and money. The director had even considered shooting some scenes with electronic cameras (as Antonioni would do with the 1980 made-for-TV movie *Il mistero di Oberwald*, with Luciano Tovoli as d.o.p.), but eventually he changed his mind as the results were unsatisfactory[11]; some scenes included in the script were discarded because of technical reasons.

Argento put together a cast that included Leigh McCloskey (cast after James Woods, his first choice for the lead, backed out to shoot *The Onion Field*), Irene Miracle (chosen for her past as a professional swimmer, which would help her perform a long scene underwater), Sacha Pitoeff (of *L'année dernière à Marienbad* fame), plus faces seen in his previous works (Daria Nicolodi, Alida Valli and Gabriele Lavia) and new ones, such as Eleonora Giorgi and Leopoldo Mastelloni, and the Romanian Veronica Lazar, Adolfo Celi's wife. The casting choices were also telling about Argento's status as one of the country's most popular filmmakers: Lavia, in his first movie role in five years, was by then one of Italy's most noted stage actors,[12] and Giorgi's presence was widely publicized in the Italian press. The blonde actress (then the wife of producer Angelo Rizzoli) was at the top of her game at the box-office, dividing herself between *auteur* films (*Dimenticare Venezia*, 1979, by Franco Brusati) and commercial cinema (*Mani di velluto*, 1979, alongside Adriano Celentano). But the film didn't have a strong lead for the American market: McCloskey had worked almost exclusively on TV, and his main claim to fame had been Tom Kotani's *The Bermuda Depths* (1978)—not exactly an earth-shattering title.

Reportedly, Argento kept the ending a secret for his cast as well: Giorgi told the press that the last page of her script bore the line "You will know the ending when we shoot it."[13] The actress' claims must be taken with a grain of salt, given that her character is killed off way before the climax. But Veronica Lazar confirmed that she learned about the true nature of her character only near the end of the shoot. It was typical of Argento to take precautions in order not to give away too much of the plot, so as to maintain his reputation for unpredictable twist endings. Speaking of which, when *Suspiria* came out, in Milan there were some amusing attempts at boycotting it: an unknown hand had written in spray under the posters the line "THE MURDERER IS THE HEADMISTRESS"—a laughable attempt at a spoiler if there was one. Argento was amused by the fact, and often recalled the anecdote in interviews and in his memoir as well.[14]

Suspiria had been Argento's "first act of murder" toward the genre that he had perfected, the *giallo*, and after breaking "the most deep-rooted taboo" he had found himself experiencing "not guilt, not anxiety or fear, but freedom." Indeed, freedom is *Inferno*'s most evident trait, thematically and stylistically. In contrast to *Suspiria*'s relatively straightforward narrative, *Inferno* adopts a more volatile approach. "It is as if it was an ensemble of stories which slip into one another," he wrote. "Over the course of the narration the characters take a direction and then suddenly the viewers realize that whoever they thought was the protagonist is actually a marginal figure, and the story changes shape under their very eyes."[15] Rather than a homage to *Psycho*—to which the unexpected early death of Rose (Miracle) has been compared—this narrative scheme brings to mind Luis Buñuel's *Le fantôme de la liberté* (1974), which had utilized a similarly episodic framework.

Such freedom of approach is exemplified in the film's most abstract scene, where we get to see Death at work, portrayed as a child's game, before Carlo (Lavia) and Sara's (Giorgi) murders. A hand cuts out the heads of four childish human figures on black paper, and a series of deceases (human and animal) ensue, within the space of a few seconds. The rhythmic montage, which recalls the opening scene of *Macchie solari* (1975, Armando Crispino), riffs on the Soviet montage theory—which Argento had employed in a satiric way in *Le cinque giornate* (1973)—by connecting apparently disconnected images by analogy, and thus emphasizing their common denominator: death. It's a stunning variation on the myth of the Parcae (or Fates), the female personifications of destiny who controlled the metaphorical thread of life of every being: Clotho spun the thread, Lachesis measured it, Atropos cut it short with her shears, choosing how and when someone would die.

The scene was longer in the script, and described as follows:

> While the music acts as an accompaniment, rhythmic as well, a series of 7 scenes start. They will be very brief, 3 seconds each. And the camera will fly over the images as if on the run, so as to appear as an aerial flight over a series of episodes.
>
> 1. The moon, up in the sky, is obscured by a huge black cloud. The black cloud fills the screen. It's shaken by a blinding white lightning. The camera flies against the lightning. More bouts of lightning cross the sky. The screen turns white, while it looks as if the camera has thrown itself in the middle of the lightning bolt and…
> 2. Three cats mew and brawl in a corner of the courtyard.
> 3. A big green lizard with a triangular mouth has caught a moth bigger than it, which struggles as it is being savaged.

> 4. A flight at crazy velocity (either shot at a very low number of frames a second or removing frames during printing) on some roofs and streets in the city.
> 5. Panning shot from above a bed. A woman is lying on it. Next to her, two or three people. Halfway through the panning shot, the woman arches her back, stiffens, and dies. But the camera is already going away.
> 6. A girl is putting her neck into a noose. She jumps into the void, hanging herself.
> 7. Very fast zoom in on the facade of the building where Sara lives.[16]

Argento filmed only part of it, cancelling some shots (#1, #2, #4, and #5) because, according to d.o.p. Romano Albani, "they didn't fit with the scene, they weren't useful."[17] Yet the director regretted not having shot #1, which he described as "the POV shot of a lightning bolt which starts from the top of the clouds and hits the city,"[18] a decision forced by the special effects he had to work with not being up to the idea.

Never one to lose a chance to play with his public image, Argento stressed *Inferno*'s unconventional structure in interviews by claiming that it was "difficult to understand even for me, the author, to the point that during the shoot I often have to reread the script in order to clear up my mind."[19] When asked about the film's theme, he replied: "My movie wants to explore and find the key of the big secrets of life and death."[20]

As in *Suspiria*, Argento reconnects with the world of fairy tales. The director himself acknowledged this, referring to his film as "a thrilling fairy tale." Not only does the sequence where Sara ventures into the basement of the library—only to find a menacing, ogre-ish figure intent on cooking something presumably unhealthy and most certainly horrible (a magic potion? an unfortunate human victim?) in a boiling cauldron—hark back to typical fairy tale cliché, but Argento admitted that the fate of Sara herself references *Sleeping Beauty*: "[she] pricks her finger, and in that precise moment she enters a sort of parallel world—enchanted and haunted—from where she will never come back."[21]

Dream—or nightmare—is *Inferno*'s driving force. Characters behave according to a dreamlike logic and find themselves in nightmarish situations. The film's oneiric quality is best summed up by the surreal sequence—shot in a water tank at the De Paolis studios with Gianlorenzo Battaglia as cameraman—in which Rose dives into a small pool where she lost her key,

Italian lobby card for Dario Argento's *Inferno* (1980), depicting one of the film's surreal highlights: Rose (Irene Miracle) diving into an underwater room underneath her building and discovering a fascinating yet deadly submerged world.

only to find herself in a huge underwater room, fully furnished and replete with a rotten corpse which pops up unexpectedly, changing the tone of the scene from wonder to horror. Argento likely got the inspiration from Jean Cocteau's *Orphée*, although another antecedent is the sequence in *Caltiki il mostro immortale* (1959, Riccardo Freda, Mario Bava) in which Bob (Daniele Vargas) dives into a pool inside a cave and discovers human remains on its bottom. Albani complained that the scene didn't come out as striking as it could have been, for the water was rather too muddy due to the underwater shoot, the fake dust on the submerged furniture and so on. He asked Argento to reshoot it the following day, but the director was immovable.[22] Despite these imperfections, Argento's development of the scene is something extraordinarily beautiful, and its manipulation of Cartesian space is exemplary.

The sequence makes a pair with the exploration of the tunnel under the floor undertaken by Mark (McCloskey). These are surfaces and volumes that *could not* and *should not* exist, doors of (unprecedented) perception that allow

for unusual areas and geometries to emerge. Perhaps Argento was thinking of Aldous Huxley and Carlos Castaneda's works on the subject of altered and enhanced perception through drugs? With its fleeting image of a calm sea, Mark's dream—another last-minute addition absent in the script—is another puzzling moment that defies narrative logic. Is it a symbolic moment, depicting Mark's subconscious? Or merely an abstract parenthesis in which Argento's imagination runs loose, free from the limits of storytelling?

In this absurd universe where actions, events and especially deaths are connected to each other according to a logic that escapes rationality but cannot be attributed to chance, the Fantastic element comes from the "visionary destruction of any established order, which recomposes itself only in the unity of measurement of the single shot"[23] Or, as Kim Newman put it, "every sequence is a meticulously orchestrated mini-symphony of camera movement, stylized lighting, sound effects, music and found objects…. Argento makes ordinary events mysterious, exciting, erotic or horrifying. Previously, the murders in Argento's films … have all been set-pieces. *Inferno* is all set pieces, and thus all of a piece."[24]

Argento had chosen New York because it would offer "a poetic setting" to his movie, but what appears in *Inferno* is the director's ideal vision of the Big Apple: a depopulated night city, a surrealistic, almost abstract vision, even more so if one thinks that Rose's apartment building was actually an invention on the part of the production designer—even though inspired by an existing edifice, namely St. Walburg's Academy, a Roman Catholic school for girls in the Late Gothic Revival style built by the architect John W. Kearney and completed in 1913.[25] The concept the director had for New York in the film is best explained by a scene he had devised but eventually discarded and never shot, similar in tone to the one about "death at work": an unknown hand (possibly Mater Tenebrarum's) picks up a crystal ball with a tiny miniature of the Manhattan skyline in it, and starts shaking it, causing a thunderstorm. The image recalls the beginning of *Citizen Kane* (1941), with Charles Foster Kane's hand dropping the crystal ball; and like Kane's "Rosebud," *Inferno*'s New York is a child's memory, or perhaps a child's dream—not a real city.

But Argento's Rome was an unorthodox vision too, not unlike the visual mosaics of different cities he put together in his previous films. The Rome setting is relegated to a few scenes shot at the so-called "*Quartiere Coppedé*" (Coppedé district)—not an actual district, though, but a group of buildings in the Trieste district in a mixture of Liberty, Art Déco and references to Greek, Gothic, Baroque and Medieval art. It was designed in early 1900 by architect and sculptor Gino Coppedé, a visionary just like Varelli who left the project incomplete on his death in 1927. The exterior of the library where Sara ventures is actually the same building as the one seen in *La ragazza che sapeva troppo* (1963, Mario Bava) and *Il profumo della signora in nero* (1974, Francesco Barilli).

The link with the director's previous film is given precisely by buildings, and not just because both pictures end with one of them on fire. Expanding the barely sketched myth of *Suspiria*, Argento (and Nicolodi) imagined the existence of three "palaces of evil" designed and built by an alchemist/architect whose very name recalls the elusive alchemist Fulcanelli, for three "Mothers" whose names were again lifted from Thomas De Quincey's 1845 book *Suspiria de Profundis*. The buildings were actually thresholds to Hell—a concept not dissimilar from *The Sentinel* (1977, Michael Winner), but developed in a strikingly original way. Even more than in *Suspiria*, the house as architectural emanation of evil has a central importance in the story. The three houses are not only "the repository of all [the Mothers'] secrets" but have a life of their own, and their humanization is made explicit in a line of dialogue. "This building has become my body, its bricks my cells, its passageways my veins, and its horror my very heart," Varelli's voice confesses: a baroque extremism of Shirley Jackson's Hill House or, even more appropriately, Richard Matheson's Hell House.

To give this dreamlike world of cries and whispers its own lights and shadows, the director concocted a rigid and original color scheme with his director of photography Romano Albani, formerly Luciano Tovoli's assistant. Argento wanted *Inferno* to have a different look than *Suspiria*, but just as striking. This time the dominating colors would be violet, lavender blue (or periwinkle) and raspberry. "I only wanted two basic colors, all the tones of blue and pink—and so it was," Albani explained. "There is only one red spot in the film, in the library scene, when someone calls Giorgi with a mysterious voice…. Dario was very happy, very enthusiastic about this choice: 'Yes, yes, let's not make it a kaleidoscope like *Suspiria*, let's make something different.'"[26] Even the blood was not red, but dark blue, almost black, as in the scene of Rose's death by guillotine.

Some elements pay explicit reference to *Suspiria*, namely the taxi ride in the rain (the cab driver is even played the same actor, Fulvio Mingozzi, whom Argento cast as a "lucky charm" in all of his films up to *Phenomena*), the presence of Alida Valli, and the architectural ornaments of the New York building. Another element of continuity is the nod to melodrama, in the blend of music and scenic action. The choice of Keith Emerson—writing his first film score—confirmed the director's idea of "making a rock opera … a film for young people."[27] Argento was as much a rock star figure as Emerson was, and both knew and appreciated each other's work. In a way, having him on board was the fulfillment of an old dream, as the director claimed he had been toying with the idea of working with Emerson, Lake & Palmer since the days of *4 mosche di velluto grigio* (1971).

With its wild reimagining of Giuseppe Verdi's opera chorus *Va, pensiero* (from the third act of the 1842 opera *Nabucco*) as a 5/4, keyboard-driven Prog-Rock extravaganza to accompany the scene of Sara's taxi ride, the former ELP member gave the movie a soundscape in tune with the type of music to which Italian twenty-somethings were listening: in 1980, British progressive rock was still the most popular subgenre among them, as certified by such music magazines as *Ciao 2001*, and Punk was looked at with diffidence by many. Moreover, the blond keyboardist had become a household name even among general audiences, after his appearance in the closing credits of the popular (and unconventional) TV show *Odeon. Tutto quanto fa spettacolo* (broadcast from December 1976 to April 1978) as a ragtime-era pianist playing rearranged versions of *Honky Tonk Train Blues* and *Maple Leaf Rag*. Argento was deeply impressed by Emerson's approach: "He composed the music practically on the spot. He sat before the screen, behind a keyboard, and he played while we screened the film back and forth. He had the projection stop, wrote on his music paper, and then started again. I have never seen anyone do this."[28]

Even though Argento pushed the pedal on the gore in *Inferno*, the results are rather different from *Suspiria*. The most gruesome moments waver between outrageousness and black-humored mockery, even more unabashed than the odd verbal joke ("Have you ever heard of the Three Sisters?" "Do you mean those black singers?"), and even more biting in a movie so dark and pessimistic. The murder of Carlo, with its masterful use of diegetic music, sound and words, manages to take the viewers off-guard and works as the perfect "boo" moment. As he leaves to check the electricity generator, the lights in Sara's apartment come and go, as does *Va, pensiero* which was playing in the background. At a certain point he stops answering to Sara's questions, and the frightened girl follows him to the storage room. For a few seconds the audience is left with a doubt: is Carlo an agent of evil? Is he going to jump out and kill Sara? Or is he already dead? Then we hear Carlo's voice again, calm, reassuring and almost joking: nothing bad has happened to him. And then, in that split-second—an impossibly brief gap for anything to happen—the man appears again, with a long knife stuck in his neck. The use of timing here is arbitrary as it is unfair, but it achieves the desired result.

The sequence in Central Park, with Kazanian attacked by rats, goes even further. Argento builds the suspense with an almost unbearable sadistic crescendo, with the invalid man falling into the pool of water (originally Kazanian was to have two wooden legs, which he would lose in the muddy lake) and lying there at the mercy of the rodents, screaming in pain for help. In the distance, a hot dog vendor[29] hears the screams, notices the elderly man in danger, throws away his cap, grabs a hatchet and starts running toward him. The build-up, aided by Emerson silent movie-like piano score, is irresistible, and the shot-by-shot construction of the scene seems to hint that Kazanian is going to be saved at the last minute. But then, surprise: the apparent savior turns out to be an agent of Hell, and with a few well-placed strokes in the neck he finishes poor Kazanian (the hand was that of assistant director Lamberto Bava, who managed to get a convincing performance out of the imbibed Pitoeff). It is a blatant joke which "openly ratifies the playful unpredictability of death"[30] at the expense of the audience, who are treated to a macabre gag when they least expected it. It is almost the grim reversal of *Suspiria*'s elaborate symphonies of death, although the scene was originally even more complex in the script, with the agonizing Kazanian glimpsing a Charon-like figure coming out of the sewer tunnel, on a boat, amidst the fog. The boat scene was ultimately discarded because, as Albani explained, the water in the lake was too shallow. Another grotesque gory scene, cut from the final edit, was the death of John the butler (Mastelloni), who is strangled with a curtain rope, so violently that his eyes pop out as if he was a living Tex Avery cartoon (always true to himself, Argento handled the rope personally, holding it so tight around the actor's neck that Mastelloni collapsed).[31] In the finished film we only get to see the aftermath of the scene, with Carol discovering John's disfigured body, but it's never clear how that happened.

All these scenes have in common the use of crude, sometimes rudimentary weapons (butcher's knives, hatchets, an ersatz guillotine in Rose's death scene) which sometimes are replaced by animals acting as agents of evil. Felines, in particular, are ubiquitous. A horde of cats assault Elise (Nicolodi) in what remains the film's weakest death scene, with Bava Jr. and his assistant Andrea Piazzesi throwing felines at the actress' stand in—Maurizio Garrone[32]—just like

Aristide Massaccesi had done over Luciano Rossi's face on the set of *La morte ha sorriso all'assassino* (1973); and Kazanian is so obsessed by cats that he captures them and takes them to the lake to drown them, with gruesome results. Originally Argento had devised a scene depicting a rabid cat in a courtyard, with white foam dribbling from its open mouth, which would serve as a counterpart to the antique dealer's death. Thousands of rodents were imported from China for the scene, and a lot of them escaped, hid in the studios and bred. "They're still there, after over 30 years! Our rats!" Claudio Argento quipped.[33]

Animals (a key presence in Argento's oeuvre since the very beginning) are everywhere in the film—living or dead, killing or being killed, embalmed or portrayed in *objets d'art*. They reflect their human counterparts' actions or status (such as the caged bird in Elise's apartment), but they are also the keys to unveil alchemic mysteries that are denied to humans. The script's opening even included a shot of a row of ants disappearing into a hole in the floor in Rose's apartment, hinting at the secret passage "underneath the soles of [her] shoes" which is the final key to solve the mystery in Varelli's book. By following the insects, Mark will reach the architect's secret apartment: the affinity between the hero/heroine and the insects will become central in *Phenomena* and will be reprised in the epilogue of *Opera*.

As with *Suspiria*, the main characters are artists, sensitive souls who can see and feel beyond the ordinary world. Suzy was a dancer, Rose is a poetess, and Mark[34] is a musicologist. Rose has a sense of smell so developed that she can feel the sickly sweet smell that is typical of the infernal buildings described by Varelli, and which people mistakenly attribute to a "cookie factory" nearby (sweetness as a tempting trap is again a nod to fairy tales—think of the marzipan house in *Hansel and Gretel*), and Mark is as weak as any young romantic hero—pale, sickly and subject to fainting: an impulsive, ineffectual lead. At first, he and his sister even communicate by way of letters,[35] as if they belonged in another era. Like Suzy and her unfortunate schoolmates before them, they, too, are overgrown, asexual children, bodies in the splendor of youth whose vital forces are absorbed through magic spells and potions, and who are preyed upon by elderly people like Varelli. The same can be said about Countess Elise,[36] diaphanous, feverish and weak like a modern-day version of De Quincey's opium eater.

The script elaborated on the idea of old creatures praying on the young: in an unfilmed scene near the beginning, while on her way to the mailbox, Rose was to meet a 40-year-old woman in a black cloak, who suddenly, and almost subliminally, turned into an old hag. The Three Mothers are described by Varelli as "wicked stepmothers, incapable of creating life," queen bees who bewitch men and deprive them of their will, as they did with the architect—who will show up as an impotent figure on a wheelchair, at the mercy of his nurse/lover/wicked stepmother (Lazar). It's an image which recalls the ending of Alberto Lattuada's black comedy *Venga a prendere il caffè da noi* (1970), starring Ugo Tognazzi as a middle-aged man who settles in the house of three wealthy spinsters (Francesca Romana Coluzzi, Milena Vukotic, Angela Goodwin) and sets out to seduce them, only to end up in a wheelchair after suffering a stroke, served and revered, but in fact dominated, and sexually defused, by the three queen bees. In this sense, Argento's film can well be considered a horrific take on this type of grotesque comedy centered on vampiric female figures—see also Marco Ferreri's *Una storia moderna—L'ape regina* (1963)—and not surprisingly it doesn't feature proper male figures besides the boyish Mark: the other men in the film are either elderly and/or crippled (Varelli, Kazanian) or sexually ambiguous (John the butler), and the only one portrayed as heterosexual and sexually active (Carlo) is dispatched within a handful of minutes.

In the conservatory scene, Mark notices a stunning-looking young woman caressing a cat in her lap, who stares at him intently and makes him dizzy. Romano Albani's lighting singles her out in the room, as if struck by a (not-so) divine light—almost a blasphemous version of a Renaissance Madonna. Unlike *Suspiria*, here Argento depicts a seductive sorceress who captivates the male and puts a spell on him, one of the archetypes of Italian Gothic horror. According to Daria Nicolodi, the woman is *not* one of the Three Mothers: "She was a witch. She couldn't have been Mater Lachrymarum because the Mater is Death. She was rather an emanation, in that moment very visible and seductive, as so very often Death has been portrayed."[37] This otherworldly appearance, however, is not just Argento's cinephile homage to *Bell Book and Candle* (1958, Richard Quine), whose most iconic image featured Kim Novak holding a Siamese cat; it is also an interesting key to penetrate the author's approach to the female universe at a time where Italy was experiencing the rise of the feminist movement, portrayed in controversial terms on the screen. Fellini, in the contemporaneous *La città delle donne* (1980), had his alter ego Marcello Mastroianni tried and condemned by a court of liberated feminists.

In *Inferno*, the mysterious witch is played by Ania Pieroni, then the lover of politician (and future prime minister) Bettino Craxi: a ravishing young woman who displays an aggressive, somehow vulgar beauty (pouty lips, heavily made-up eyes, bright red lipstick) and who is lighted like a glamorous diva. Argento would cast her again in *Tenebre* as the kleptomaniac who becomes the murderer's first victim, but first we had seen her, defiant and provoking, put a much earthier spell upon another man (Enio Girolami), using her sexuality like a credit card. In these two images of seduction, embodied by the same woman, one can perhaps see the director's problematic vision of womanhood in the 1980s. Argento had already depicted a feminist type, Gianna Brezzi, in ambiguous terms in *Profondo rosso* (1975), where she proved a much stronger presence than the ineffectual hero, but also a sinister, suspicious character who could as well have been the murderer. In his following film he would portray liberated women either as expressions of evil or as the victims of a mad moralizer. Whereas *Tenebre*—populated by Lolita-esque nymphs, buxom lesbians, real-life transsexuals and *femmes fatales* in shades and red shoes—represented an explosion of unbridled and predatory sexuality in Argento's cinema, in *Inferno* sexuality is either denied, repressed or alluded to in a sinister manner, most notably in the couple portrayed by Alida Valli and Leopoldo Mastelloni, who seemingly have an ambiguous relationship—even more puzzling since Mastelloni is a controversial and openly gay stage actor, notorious for his provocative behavior, while Valli here portrays a masculine, stern woman. It was Nicolodi who convinced Argento to cast her friend Mastelloni, with whom she had acted in the TV movie *Tre ore dopo le nozze*, directed by Ugo Gregoretti. "I managed to have Leopoldo in *Inferno*, whereas Dario absolutely didn't want him, because he said, 'No, I don't want a gay butler!' But eventually, after many tortures, he succeeded in making him stop wiggling and walk straight."[38]

Ultimately, such ambivalence is echoed in the poster, which features a sinister skull with female lips emerging from the darkness, and which recalls Asa's face magically rejuvenated in *La maschera del demonio* (1960). It is an image of sexuality and death with few equals in the realm of Italian horror, and further underlines the director's complex look at the eros/thanatos duality.

Inferno marked Argento's professional encounter with Mario and Lamberto Bava. Mario took care of some special optical effects, painting *maquettes* and concocting other trick shots: as recounted by Tim Lucas,[39] the elderly master created some cityscape views by way of milk cartons covered with photographs, as well as a sculpture that augmented Rose's apartment building, which is set on fire in the climax. Bava also took care of the special effects for the final appearance of Death—a scene which incidentally recalls a moment in *6 donne per l'assassino* (1964), in which Tao-Li (Claude Dantes) advances toward

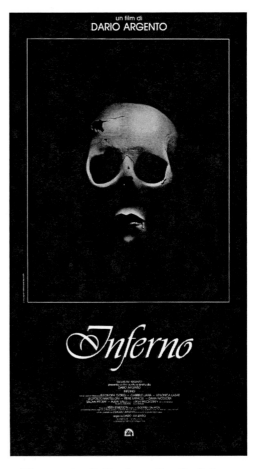

The stunning Italian *locandina* for *Inferno*.

the camera, before being revealed as a reflection in a mirror—by way of lights and a semi-transparent mirror. The script featured a somewhat different climax, with Death portrayed not as a hooded skeleton (a less than convincing moment, actually) but as a monstrous fleshless figure, with eyes emerging from the orbits and exposed teeth. Other special effects in the scene were discarded, making it less powerful than it had been devised on paper, and a bit underwhelming compared to *Suspiria*'s climax. Lamberto was the assistant director, and he and Dario developed a strong bond, which resulted in Bava Jr. working again as a.d. on *Tenebre* and Argento producing his two *Dèmoni* films.

The Bava connection can be stretched further. With its *ronde* of gory knife murders, always suspended between the truculent and the ridiculous, *Inferno* recalls the overexcited chain reaction of *Reazione a catena* (1971), of which at times it seems a supernatural remake of sorts. During a memorable sequence in *La frusta e il corpo* (1963) Bava's camera displayed the director's disinterest toward the story, by cutting from two characters discussing a key plot point to a vase of red roses, thus turning the viewer's attention from their words to the visual elements surrounding them. Here Argento does something similar in the scene where Elise explains to Mark the myth of the "Three Mothers": the camera moves away from them and, mimicking the wobbling motion of a sound wave, it approaches the air ducts from where the sounds propagate in the heart of the building; Elise's voice becomes confused and unintelligible, and the audience is denied vital bits of information. The only thing left to do is let oneself be carried away by the mere flow of images. However, the scene is not a hint of the author's disregard for the narrative, but rather the sign of a rhapsodic, whimsical inspiration, which leaves behind narrative logic in favor of visual expression.

And, indeed, *Inferno* is, in Argento's words, "full of riddles that will be left mostly unexplained"[40] as well as of alchemical and esoteric references, from the homage to Gurdjeff (the celebrative plate which signals his stay in the New York building[41]) to the presence of the four natural elements. Water (the descent of Rose into the flooded room, the rain that accompanies Sara's taxi ride, the murder of Kazanian in the lake); Air (the nauseating smell that pervades the areas around the houses, the irruption of the invisible presence in the university hall, the sound of the voices carried as a flow into the conduits of the building); Earth (the reference to the mystery key "under the soles of your shoes," and the tendency to "sink into the magma ... and the brute matter. Everything points downwards, toward the lowest, the invisible, and what is hidden 'below'"[42]); Fire (the cauldron and the flames in the basement of the library, the final conflagration).

But, above all, the film conveys the idea of books as carriers of an occult and exclusive knowledge. Varelli's opening monologue mentions the rule of *silentium*, "silence," which alchemists vow not to break, in order not to upset profane minds with their secrets. Argento—with the amiable complicity of De Quincey—recreates his own surrogate of the *Necronomicon*, but he also centers an entire sequence on the theft of a book that will cost Sara's life, and makes one of the main characters an antique book dealer, who is given one of the picture's key lines of dialogue: "The only true mystery is that our lives are governed by dead people." In some other director's film this could be read as a political statement; here it expresses a deeper, philosophical truth: our very life is governed by books, which contain nothing but the words and thoughts and dreams of dead people speaking to us from another age. (In the script, Argento wanted to emphasize the concept by having Varelli's voice rising slowly in volume in the opening scene, as if coming from far, far away in the past and gradually approaching the viewer).

The characters of *Inferno* spend their time reading, translating, and thinking over a cultural heritage that opens up an unsuspected view of the world. They read books in Latin, the language of enigmas to be weighed and interpreted. (In the same year, Umberto Eco published his best-selling period mystery *Il nome della rosa*, set in the Middle Ages and with a riddle in Latin playing a central role in the plot.) It is as if our fathers had delivered to us an opaque vision of the world: a cataract, a veil destined to be torn from the opening of the "third eye." However, awareness does not lead to superior wisdom, but rather to the astonished contemplation of the horror that rules our lives, as in the ineffable triumph of Death that ends the film.

Inferno was released in Italy on February 7, 1980, to mixed reviews. Film critic Giovanni Grazzini, in the *Corriere della Sera*, labeled it as a "fine butchery," and even though he praised Argento's direction, he judged the result as mannerist and even boring, dismissing the emphasis on gore as follows: "One wonders whether to force the viewers to look away from the screen and bring them to the point of throwing up is a merit to be proud of."[43] Tullio Kezich complained: "Despite a few effective moments, and a few sequences of true Fantastic cinema, there are too many counterparts of gloomy banality, as well as concessions to the brutal tastes of audiences already contaminated by the aesthetics of hooliganism."[44]

During filming, Argento pointed out that the film was "the second part in a trilogy on modern alchemy"[45] started with *Suspiria*, which he would complete the following year, but he soon abandoned the idea. The main reason was the underwhelming box-office grosses. The initial response was enthusiastic: reportedly, on the night of the premiere in Rome, the theater owner (producer Peppino Amati) had to give back 500 tickets because the venue was packed full, with people even sitting on the floor, while in Turin, on the Sunday of its release, the film grossed the astonishing sum of 24 million *lire*.[46] But after the initial enthusiasm, audiences were gradually disappointed by Argento's switch toward out-and-out supernatural horror. Daria Nicolodi recalled that people told her, "You have been Argento's ruin, we followed him until *Profondo rosso* but afterwards one can't understand anything anymore."[47] The film was a good success, however, and ended up at the fourteenth place among the season's top-grossers, and eighth among Italian releases of the year.[48] In this respect, it was topped by seven comedies—such as Pasquale Festa Campanile's *Qua la mano*, Castellano & Pipolo's *Mani di velluto* and Maurizio Nichetti's debut *Ratataplan*—which gives an idea of the commercial path taken by Italian cinema of the period.

Inferno was released theatrically all over Europe[49] and even in Japan, where Argento was enjoying a huge cult. The response overseas was disappointing, though. 20th Century–Fox did not commit to a wide theatrical release, and the film was shelved for five years. It had a brief theatrical release and played for one week in a New

Japanese poster for *Inferno*, featuring a collage of the most frightening bits.

York venue in August 1986,[50] and a couple of months later it was released to home video on the subsidiary Key Video label. When asked about it by Maitland McDonagh, Argento said he didn't know the reason why,[51] but in his memoir he mentions that after the premiere Fox's head Sherry Lansing told him she didn't like the movie's narrative structure at all.[52] In the end, *Inferno*'s biggest virtue—freedom—turned out to be its commercial ruin in the States.

Argento's next project, *Oltre la morte*—an 80-page treatment about a cannibalistic spree set among the homeless in New York—was rejected by Dino De Laurentiis and then the manuscript mysteriously got lost. Soon the director moved to a more traditional project, at least on paper: *Sotto gli occhi dell'assassino*, a *giallo* inspired by autobiographical events, namely an anonymous phone caller who called himself "The Great Punisher" and made death threats during Argento's stay in Los Angeles.[53] It eventually became *Tenebre*, his most violent and grim film to date, and one of his very best.

Throughout the 1980s Argento sporadically returned to Gothic themes. After turning his *gialli* into neo-Gothic works with the unconditional opening to the irrational, with *Phenomena* he took the reverse path, bringing back the many *fantastique* and fairy tale-related ideas to a logical explanation: the monster of the castle is a deformed child, the frightening *matres* of the previous films are replaced by a real mother, but no less terrifying. At the same time, the director reshaped his approach to cinema and remodeled its aesthetics, with an operation of rejuvenation aimed at the teenage public. Whereas movies such as *Profondo rosso*, *Suspiria* and *Inferno* were aimed at young adults, *Phenomena* is a *giallo* rereading of *Suspiria* in a teen-oriented key, which assimilates the language of music videos and includes excerpts of heavy metal tracks used as an auditory counterpoint to the gruesome scenes on screen. On the other hand, the emphasis on the maternal nature that can either lead to madness or perdition or otherwise give salvation, embraces an escapist Neo-Romanticism with vague New Age traits. A similar approach returns in the epilogue of *Opera*, an unofficial rendition of *The Phantom of the Opera* in which the director expresses once again his passion for melodrama and tries to make opposing tensions coexist—a *giallo* plot and a drive toward the irrational—in a precarious stylistic and narrative balance.

Argento resumed the myth of the Three Mothers in 2007, with the third chapter in the trilogy, *La terza madre*.

NOTES

1. Dario Argento, *Paura* (Turin: Einaudi, 2014), 216.

2. *Ibid.*, 213.

3. *Ibid.*, 230.

4. Around the same time, Salvatore Samperi was preparing a film to be titled *Inferno*, loosely inspired by Dante's poem and set in the present day. The script, written by Samperi, Giorgio Basile and Gianfranco Manfredi, was in the director's own words a mixture between *Hellzapoppin'* and *It's a Mad, Mad, Mad, Mad World*, with strong political overtones, "a journey in the confusion of today's world, especially in the left and ultra-left, also conceived as an excursion in various film genres—Western, *giallo*, romantic, etc." Lamberto Antonelli, "*Ombre rosse*, Marx e Guevara nell'*Inferno* visto da Samperi," *La Stampa*, January 26, 1979. Eventually Samperi (who had thought of Roberto Benigni for the role of Dante) abandoned the overly costly project and made the 1950s revivalist comedy *Liquirizia* instead.

5. Davide Pulici and Marco Cacioppo, "Daria Nicolodi:

6. Dardano Sacchetti interviewed, in www.davinotti. com (http://www.davinotti.com/index.php?option=com_content&task=view&id=61&Itemid=79).

7. Manlio Gomarasca and Davide Pulici, "I testimoni," in Gomarasca and Pulici (eds.) *Le tre madri*, 44.

8. "After two weeks' shooting in New York, the crew of *Inferno*, written and directed by Dario Argento, has returned to Rome to shoot the interior scenes, which will last 14 weeks." [not signed] "Kolossal dell'orrore di Dario Argento," *La Stampa*, May 24, 1979.

9. For instance, a piece published on May 23 in the *Corriere della Sera* wrote: "For four consecutive nights, at New York's Central Park, there has been a simulated moon eclipse … those nights the moon got dark at every take of the movie *Inferno*, which director Dario Argento has been shooting in America for some days." Franco Occhiuzzi, "Un inferno tutto d'Argento," *Corriere della Sera*, May 23, 1979.

10. Gomarasca and Pulici, "I testimoni," 44.

11. Paolo Mereghetti, "Dario Argento: per fare paura ha usato anche Verdi," *Corriere d'Informazione*, March 6, 1980.

12. On his part, Lavia has been adamant: "Certain horror films by Dario Argento, *Profondo rosso*, *Inferno* … have become cult movies, but I did them only for money. I was paid well, and an actor doesn't have a fixed salary...." Emilia Costantini, "Gabriele Lavia. Sono innamorato dalle elementari," *Corriere della Sera*, October 13, 2017.

13. Maurizio Porro, "La Giorgi in un viaggio di ricordi," *Corriere della Sera*, April 13, 1979; Adele Ferrari, "Eleonora Giorgi: 'Sono meno infantile e molto più felice,'" *Corriere d'Informazione*, May 2, 1979.

14. Argento, *Paura*, 218.

15. *Ibid.*, 230.

16. Excerpt taken from Davide Pulici, "*Inferno*: dalla sceneggiatura al film," in Gomarasca and Pulici (eds.) *Le tre madri*, 37.

17. Gomarasca and Pulici, "I testimoni," 45.

18. Fabio Maiello, *Dario Argento. Confessioni di un maestro dell'horror* (Milan: Alacran, 2007), 126.

19. "Un brivido che si chiama Argento," *Corriere della Sera*, June 10, 1979.

20. Occhiuzzi, "Un inferno tutto d'Argento."

21. Argento, *Paura*, 231.

22. Gomarasca and Pulici, "I testimoni," 44.

23. Roberto Pugliese, *Dario Argento* (Milan: Editrice Il Castoro, [1986] 2011), 66.

24. Kim Newman, *Nightmare Movies* (London: Bloomsbury, [1988] 2011), 147.

25. See Rachael Nisbet, "Rose Elliot's Apartment Building in *Inferno*," in http://hypnoticcrescendos.blogspot.it/2018/03/rose-elliots-apartment-building-in.html.

26. Gomarasca and Pulici, "I testimoni," 44.

27. Mereghetti, "Dario Argento: per fare paura ha usato anche Verdi."

28. Daniele Costantini and Francesco Dal Bosco, *Nuovo cinema inferno. L'opera di Dario Argento* (Parma: Pratiche Editrice, 1997), 84.

29. Played by James Fleetwood, a bass singer whom Argento had seen in Alban Berg's *Lulu* directed by Roman Polanski and conducted by Christopher Keene, which caused a controversy at Spoleto's Festival of Two Worlds, in 1974. Occhiuzzi, "Nasce in America l'inferno di Argento."

nostra signora degli orrori," in Manlio Gomarasca and Davide Pulici (eds.) *Le tre madri. Guida alla trilogia di Dario Argento. Nocturno Dossier* #64, November 2007, 14–15.

30. Pugliese, *Dario Argento*, 68.

31. Maiello, *Dario Argento*, 137.

32. Garrone, the animal trainer for the film, also replaced Sacha Pitoeff for some shots, since the rats had started biting the actor for real. Gomarasca and Pulici, "I testimoni," 49.

33. *Ibid.*, 44.

34. Mark Davis—not Elliot—in the script.

35. Whereas, in a blatant inconsistency, their phone call from New York to Rome, takes place with no apparent time zone differences.

36. Elisa Taylor Ursi—not Elise Delong Valadler—in the script.

37. Pulici and Cacioppo, "Daria Nicolodi: nostra signora degli orrori," 15.

38. *Ibid.*

39. Tim Lucas, *Mario Bava. All the Colors of the Dark* (Cincinnati, OH: Video Watchdog, 2007), 1009–1019.

40. Argento, *Paura*, 231. See, for instance, the recurring element of glass objects which the characters inadvertently smash to pieces shortly before their own violent demise.

41. The detail, absent in the script, acts as a symmetrical element with *Suspiria* (where on the façade of the Tanz Academy we had seen a plate celebrating Erasmus of Rotterdam's stay).

42. Pugliese, *Dario Argento*, 65.

43. Giovanni Grazzini, "Pregiata macelleria," *Corriere della Sera*, February 8, 1980.

44. Tullio Kezich, *Il nuovissimo Millefilm. Cinque anni al cinema, 1977–1982* (Milan: Mondadori, 1983), 201.

45. "Un brivido che si chiama Argento."

46. Mereghetti, "Dario Argento: per fare paura ha usato anche Verdi."

47. Pulici and Cacioppo, "Daria Nicolodi: nostra signora degli orrori," 15.

48. The box-office data of about a billion and a half *lire* refer to the grosses in the first-run theaters of the 16 "*capozona*" cities (Ancona, Bari, Bologna, Cagliari, Catania, Florence, Genoa, Messina, Milan, Naples, Padua, Palermo, Rome, Turin, Trieste, Venice), that is, the major cities included in the "Borsa Film" in the *Giornale dello Spettacolo*. As for the overall grosses, according to Franco Montini, *Inferno* grossed 4,1 billion *lire* overall. Franco Montini, "La fortuna al box office," in Vito Zagarrio (ed.), *Argento vivo. Il cinema di Dario Argento tra genere e autorialità* (Venice: Marsilio, 2008), 66.

49. According to the official ministerial data, it was seen by 215,412 spectators and grossed an amount corresponding to 188,816 Euro. (http://infoicaa.mecd.es/CatalogoICAA/Peliculas/Detalle?Pelicula=539451).

50. Nina Danton, "*Inferno*: mythic horror tale," *New York Times*, August 15, 1986.

51. "I don't know why. It's a mystery. It's incredible, working with the studios. Every stupid person arrives with an opinion; they start every sentence with, 'For me…' And I don't care what they think, I don't care about 'For you…' That's not the way I work." Maitland McDonagh, *Broken Mirrors/Broken Minds. The Dark Dreams of Dario Argento* (London: Sun Tavern Fields, 1991), 236.

52. Argento, *Paura*, 231.

53. *Ibid.*, 238.

Macabro (*Macabre*, a.k.a. *The Frozen Terror*)

D: Lamberto Bava. *S and SC*: Pupi Avati, Roberto Gandus, Lamberto Bava, Antonio Avati; *DOP*: Franco Delli Colli (Kodak, Telecolor); *M*: Ubaldo Continiello (Ed. Gipsy); *E*: Piera Gabutti; *ArtD*: Katia Dottori; *CO*: Katia Dottori, Gian Franco Basile (for Bernice Stegers); *MU*: Alfonso Cioffi; *AD*: Rosanna Rocchi Bava; *SE*: Antonio Corridori, Angelo Mattei; *C*: Antonio Schiavo Lena; *AC*: Gianni Modica Canfarelli; *AE*: Carlo D'Alessandro; *AsstD*: Dario Amadei; *SO*: Gianni Zampagni; *SOE*: Luciano Anzellotti, Massimo Anzellotti; *ChEl*: Michele Pellegrini; *KG*: Mario Pizzi; *Generator Operator*: Roberto Cuccoli. *Cast*: Bernice Stegers (Jane Baker), Stanko Molnar (Robert Duval), Veronica Zinny (Lucy Baker), Roberto Posse (Fred Kellerman), Ferdinando Orlandi (Mr. Wells), Fernando Pannullo (Leslie Baker), Elisa Kadigia Bove (Sally). *PROD*: Gianni Minervini and Antonio Avati for A.M.A. Film (Rome); *PM*: Gianni Amadei; *PS*: Alessandro Vivarelli; *PSe*: Rosa Mercurio; *PA*: Francesco Gesualdi; *ADM*: Raffaello Forti; *Cashier*: Fiorella Bologna. *Country*: Italy. Filmed in Gardone Riviera (Brescia, Lombardy) and Crespi d'Adda (Bergamo, Lombardy) and on location in New Orleans. *Running time*: 89 minutes (m. 2448). Visa n. 74887 (3.27.1980); *Rating*: V.M.14. *Release dates*: 4.17.1980 (Italy), 10.14.1980 (Spain), 5.13.1981 (France), 11.27.1981 (West Germany), 10.28.1983 (USA; Canada); *Distribution*: Medusa Distribuzione (Italy), Les Filmes Jacques Leitienne (France), Cinefrance (West Germany), FVI (USA). *Domestic gross*: approx. 560,000,000 *lire*. *Also known as*: *The Frozen Terror* (USA), *Baiser macabre* (France), *Macabro—Die Küsse der Jane Baxter* (West Germany).

Note: the song "Jane in Love" is performed by Gil Ventura (E.M.I. records)

New Orleans. Jane Baker, a married woman with two children, has an affair with another man, Fred Kellerman. When her elder daughter Lucy discovers it, she drowns her little brother in the bathtub and then calls her mother for help. While Jane and Fred are driving home, they have a terrible car accident in which the man is decapitated. One year later, Jane moves to the place where she used to meet her lover. The house is owned by a blind young man, Robert Duval, who lives alone with his elderly mother. Robert, who is in love with Jane, starts hearing weird noises coming from the woman's apartment, and decides to investigate. Little by little, he discovers a horrible truth: Jane keeps Fred's severed head in the fridge and uses it as a sex fetish…

"Why don't you pay us a visit?" the man on

the other end of the line asked. "We have an offer for you, you know?" When Lamberto Bava was summoned to the office of the Avati brothers, sometime in Summer 1979, he was an experienced assistant director. At 35, he had learned the craft with his father, whom he assisted since the mid–1960s, and had worked with the likes of Aristide Massaccesi (on *Sollazzevoli storie di mogli gaudenti e mariti penitenti*, 1972, and *Pugni, pirati e karaté*, 1973), Mario Lanfranchi (on *Il bacio*, 1974) and Ruggero Deodato (on *Ultimo mondo cannibale*, 1977, *L'ultimo sapore dell'aria*, 1978, and *Cannibal Holocaust*, to be released early in 1980), and he had just finished working with Dario Argento on *Inferno*. "I was very happy, and told myself, 'Gee, how I'd like to be Pupi Avati's assistant…'"[1]

At Avati's office, Pupi and Antonio showed him an American newspaper clip about a woman who had killed her lover and kept his head in the fridge. "Will it be Pupi's next film?" Bava asked. "No, we'd like *you* to make it!" Within a week, Lamberto, the Avatis and Roberto Gandus had written a 15-page treatment, and while Antonio Avati attempted to involve Medusa in the financing, Bava Jr. went back to the U.S. with Argento to do some reshoots for *Inferno*, as some of the footage presented technical defects.[2] While he was overseas, Antonio Avati called him: Medusa had greenlit the project. Six weeks later, in November,[3] Lamberto Bava was shooting his first film as a director.

The genesis and making of *Macabro* were very quick, as was typical of low-budget projects. The script was cranked out in 15 days,[4] and filming lasted for four weeks. There was no interference whatsoever from the Avatis, not even in the choice of the actors. The female lead, in the director's words, "had to be not really beautiful, and about 40 years old,"[5] and the Liverpool-born Bernice Stegers, who in that period was in Italy, acting in Fellini's *La città delle donne*, seemed perfect for the role of Jane Baker. Bava chose the Croatian Stanko Molnar over Michele Soavi for the role of the blind landlord Robert Duval, who becomes suspicious of the strange goings-on in his house. On the set, the debuting director didn't feel the same inadequacy as Pupi Avati had while directing *Balsamus*. "I had my wife Rosanna with me as my assistant. I slept wonderfully the night before, and on my first day on the set I completed 28 shots, urging the crew, 'Come on, come on, come on!' They asked me, 'Why, how many movies have you done?!?'"[6]

Even though the theme of necrophilia recalls two milestones of Italian Gothic such as Riccardo Freda's *L'orribile segreto del Dr. Hichcock* (1962) and Mario Bava's *Lisa e il diavolo* (1973), *Macabro* depicts a pathological case that has nothing to do with the grand excesses of tradition. It is indeed macabre, as the title suggests, but also squalid and repellent, closer to the antics later depicted graphically in *Nekromantik* (1987, Jörg Buttgereit) than to the delirious, dreamlike mood of Freda and Bava's films. Moreover, *Macabro* develops the Gothic tale no longer in a mythical dimension, but in a domestic one, as with *Shock* (1977). In a way, the film can be also seen as a late appendix and, in some respects, a compendium of themes explored in the "Female Gothic" works of the previous decade,[7] but the mentally unstable Jane Baker recalls Daria Nicolodi's character in the 1977 film rather than the disturbed ladies (in black or white) played by Mimsy Farmer (*Il profumo della signora in nero*) or Florinda Bolkan (*Le orme*, 1975). She is a very different kind of heroine than we were used to meeting in the classic Gothic film: not particularly attractive, a bit vulgar-looking, Jane is a disturbed housewife who finds solace in adultery and will be haunted by the memory of her deceased lover. The theme of the "forbidden room" which hides a dark sexual secret, typical Gothic fare (see Cynthia's attempts to sneak into her husband's quarters in *L'orribile segreto del Dr. Hichcock*), is also developed in a non-glamorous, matter-of-fact manner. Almost all the film takes place in the suburban villa where Jane used to meet with her lover, anxiety arises from everyday situations, and horror is concealed in the household object par excellence, the fridge.

If *Macabro* lacks the sparse oneiric and surreal elements of *Shock*, it nonetheless retains a similar look and directorial restraint. This could be a point in favor of the thesis that *Shock* was in equal parts the work of Lamberto as Mario, but the similarities can be traced back to the scripts, which Bava Jr. co-authored and which carry a trace of his different sensibility.

For me, in *Macabro*, fear comes from the inside: the anxieties, frustrations, all the psychological disorders. I want everyone to be able to identify with my characters, because if they were unreal, that would show on screen…. It is not a coincidence [that both stories are similar] because it interests me a lot to take a family which at the beginning is normal and perturb it, to create a Fantastic-themed tale from there. In people's eyes, family is what they can and have that is most normal, logical and real.[8]

Visually, the film retains the same ordinary quality, as the director shoots the story in a matter-of-fact, unspectacular way: the fatal car accident near the beginning, for instance, consists of just two shots, the broken windshield and Jane screaming. Bava worked with d.o.p Franco Delli Colli, a regular collaborator on Avati's films, who used old lamps and projectors to obtain diffuse, intimate lighting: a very different atmosphere than the one normally associated with the genre.

Macabro plays cruelly with the voyeurism of the audience, who is presented a case of sexual obsession (a woman keeps the head of the deceased lover in the freezer and uses it as an erotic fetish) that can only be depicted through imagination. Soon viewers find themselves in a similar position as the blind Robert Duval—unable to see what is going on, and gradually bound to imagine the worst. The character of the blind man—a keen variation on the blind helpless heroine as seen in such films as *Wait Until Dark* (1967, Terence Young) and *Blind Terror* (1971, Richard Fleischer)—brings to unsettling extremes the weak male figure, another staple of Italian Gothic. Not only is Duval—who repairs music instruments but *can't play them*, a symbolic hint at his ineffectiveness—totally inadequate as a hero, literally groping in the dark from beginning to end, but he is utterly helpless and vulnerable. In the early scenes we see his elderly mother take care of him like a child, giving him a bath—and, even more humiliating for him, under Jane's distressed look. The sight of a grown woman helping a man as if he was a boy, with its emasculating implications, recalls not only Mino Guerrini's morbid Gothic yarn *Il terzo occhio* (1966), but also such grotesque classics such as Ferreri's *La Grande bouffe* (1973) and Luciano Salce's underrated *Alla mia cara mamma nel giorno del suo compleanno* (1974), where the image of the mother bathing her grown child was pushed to mocking, black-humored extremes. Later, it will be Jane who will meet Robert while taking a bath, in an even more humiliating reversal which further underlines the man's sexual frustration.

Lamberto Bava's debut has indeed a noticeable grotesque quality to it, possibly an element introduced in the script by Avati, whose films often featured weak, ineffective male figures, from the impotent dwarf in *Balsamus l'uomo di Satana* (1970) to the dysfunctional all-male family in *Le strelle nel fosso* (1979).[9] The duality of eros/thanatos and the theme of the *amour fou* that obsesses Jane are also developed with an eye on the grotesque akin to Avati's films: see, for instance, the small altar in the woman's bedroom, which evokes Henry James' story *The Altar of the Dead* and François Truffaut's film adapted from it, *La chambre verte* (1978). Avati's contribution to the script extended also to the depiction of the dysfunctional Baker family, particularly with the relationship between Jane and her malevolent daughter Lucy (Veronica Zinny). In one of the early scenes Lucy is seen drowning her little brother in the bathtub out of spite for her mother's affair, and during the story she proves she has the same vein of madness as Jane, even cooking a nasty meal for her and Robert in a memorable dinner scene which fuels the violent ending. Lucy's delusions for a "perfect" family reunited (that is, her mother coming back home with her dad, to an ideal but impossible idyllic marriage), no matter what the cost, make her a disturbing little psycho, and a haunting addition to the gallery of neurotic children in Italian cinema of the period, well-played by the 13-year-old Zinny (Victoria's daughter and Karl Zinny's sister).

Bava wisely keeps the gore down to a minimum. As the director recalled, "the violence had been played down intentionally because Avati's production hadn't wanted to be excessive in any way, otherwise the story might have deteriorated into bad taste eroticism, and so we set all our story by the tension and the slow, relentless pace of the drama."[10] *Macabro* is a tale played on ambiguity, which builds anxiety through reticence. Is the subjective shot that traverses the house at night a supernatural presence evoked by Jane (after all we are in New Orleans, perhaps America's most "magical" city)? Or is it a product of the woman's disturbed imagination? Such an ambiguity is protracted until the very end. For the whole movie, we are convinced that Jane is just a crazy delusional woman, who performs repulsive sex acts with a surrogate of her dead lover; but, as Robert discovers in the frightening epilogue, things are not as simple as they seem, and the truth is even more harrowing and absurd. Bava claimed it was his idea to end the film with a last-minute shock twist, and the sudden leap into the *fantastique* is a truly memorable moment, which spins the cards in the very last shot. A payoff at the limit of self-sabotage, it goes in the opposite direction to the rational *denouements* of the pseudo-narrative puzzles of so much Gothic literature and cinema: rather, it recalls in tone the mocking and grim endings in Mario Bava's cinema.

A good part of *Macabro*'s weird fascination relies on its subdued use of locations. Except for a few scenes in New Orleans, accomplished in just four days (such as the exterior shots of the main location, Duval's two-story house), most of the film was shot in Northern Italy, namely in Gardone Riviera, near Salò, on the Lake Garda, in the villa once owned by Mussolini's lover Claretta Petacci. But the outstanding opening title image, set in a monumental, creepy cemetery dominated by a ziggurat-like mausoleum which sets the tone for a story in which the living a re dominated by the dead, was shot in Crespi d'Adda, an industrial village near Bergamo built in the last quarter of the 19th century by the Crespi family, owners of textile factories, which has become a UNESCO site.[11] Bava shot a brief sequence there with Bernice Stegers visiting a grave. "The sky was grey, a little fine rain was falling, which gave a formidable atmosphere," the director recalled, "but I must say that Franco Delli Colli added his own personal touch, and tried something new with lots of filters, because I wanted a very dusky coloring."[12] The score, by Ubaldo Continiello (who had written the music for *La Venere d'Ille*), is also peculiar, and blends classical passages with jazzy saxophone and harmonica-driven parts, more rhythmic and aggressive, which are typical of the Louisiana setting.

Mario Bava had no input on the film. When his son gave him the script to read, he refused to give him any suggestion: "It's your movie, make it the way you want to!" He saw the rough cut in late January 1980. "Now I can rest in peace," he told Lamberto.[13] Three months later he was gone.

Macabro was submitted to the rating board in late March 1980 to obtain a screening certificate. The Board invited the producers to "lighten" (i.e., trim) the scene in which Jane kisses the dead man's head on the bed. The cut (of 4.20 meters, that is about 8 seconds) was performed immediately, and the committee gave the film a V.M.14 rating. Released with an apt tagline ("*il film che ha terrorizzato anche Dario Argento*," the film which frightened even Dario

Argento) and an eerie stylized poster featuring a broken doll's head from which a pool of blood has come out (the red making a stark contrast on the black and white composition), *Macabro* received good press reviews. It proved also a commercial success. As Bava recalled, "a week after the film's release, Minervini told me it was the first Avati production that made any money."[14]

The film was also screened at the Sitges Film Festival in Catalunya in October 1980, prior to its distribution in Spain,[15] and at the 10th "Festival international du film fantastique et de science-fiction" in Paris, to good response. When interviewed in *L'Écran fantastique* Bava announced that his next film would be *Gnomi*,

Macabro (1980), Lamberto Bava's film debut, came out in Italy with the tagline "*Il film che ha terrorizzato anche Dario Argento*" (the film which frightened even Dario Argento), hinting at new heights in horror (courtesy Luca Servini).

a grotesque story set in a small building inside a city (possibly Vienna or Trieste) where strange events occur. Eventually the inhabitants find out that the top floor, apparently vacant, is inhabited by gnomes. The building is gradually deteriorating, with humidity, moss and plants growing everywhere, as the little creatures are recreating their favorite microclimate, and are planning to turn the whole city into a forest. The gnomes are good to gentle and kind souls, while they kill those who are bad and selfish. In the end, only few tenants survive the carnage, and must adapt to the gnomes' way of life and rules. Bava had written the script with Roberto Gandus and Alessandro Parenzo, and the movie was to be produced by Vides. But the project would cost too much, and Bava sent the script overseas to several U.S. companies, including Steven Spielberg's Amblin, hoping to find an American co-producer, but to no avail. *Gnomi* was eventually dropped, but in 1984 Joe Dante's *Gremlins* came out, which Bava claimed had many similarities with his script[16] (although judging from the brief synopsis the director told *L'Écran fantastique* it doesn't seem so).

Eventually, despite the good critical and commercial results of his film debut, Lamberto Bava had to stay at home without working for a whole year, due to family matters. It was Dario Argento who helped him recover his professional path by hiring him as his a.d. on *Tenebre*. Bava returned to directing with *La casa con la scala nel buio*, scripted by Dardano Sacchetti and Elisa Briganti and produced by Luciano Martino, a violent *giallo* with some Gothic references—including an impressive opening sequence which reprised the same concept from which Sacchetti's own script for *Quella villa accanto al cimitero* was born—set in a modern-day version of the Gothic haunted house: the story revolves around a young composer (Andrea Occhipinti) who rents an isolated villa to write the score for a horror film, only to find out that the elusive tenant before him (a mysterious girl named Linda) might be the maniac who slashes Bruno's female neighbors in graphically gory ways. Born as a made-for-TV project, it eventually found theatrical distribution due to its graphic violence.

NOTES

1. Manlio Gomarasca, "Intervista a Lamberto Bava," in *Genealogia del delitto. Il cinema di Mario e Lamberto Bava. Nocturno Dossier #24*, July 2004, 37.

2. Gomarasca and Pulici, "I testimoni," 49.

3. According to the Public Cinematographic Register, filming started on November 19, 1979.

4. Alain Schlockoff and Robert Schlockoff, "Entretien avec Lamberto Bava," *L'Écran fantastique #16*, January 1981, 14–15.

5. *Ibid.*, 15. ·

6. *Ibid.*

7. See Curti, *Italian Gothic Horror Films, 1970–1979*, 4.

8. A. Schlockoff and R. Schlockoff, "Entretien avec Lamberto Bava," 14.

9. See Curti, *Italian Gothic Horror Films, 1970–1979*, 9–14, and 214–217.

10. Luca M. Palmerini and Gaetano Mistretta, *Spaghetti Nightmares* (Rome: M&P Edizioni, 1996), 37.

11. Bava had planned to shoot another project in Crespi d'Adda: *I ritornanti*, the story of a group of teenagers who undergo a series of extreme trials to prove their courage and defy death, getting close to a point of no return. One day a girl goes too far and seemingly dies, only to return from death a little while later. But in fact, it is not she who has returned from the other side, but someone (or something) else…. Bava wanted Crespi d'Adda to pass off as an American college: he had completed location scouting and was ready to shoot, but the project never took off.

12. A. Schlockoff and R. Schlockoff, "Entretien avec Lamberto Bava," 14.

13. Lucas, *Mario Bava. All the Colors of the Dark*, 1025.

14. Gomarasca, "Intervista a Lamberto Bava," 38.

15. According to the official ministerial data, it was seen by 177,037 spectators and grossed an amount corresponding to about 146,595 Euro. (http://infoicaa.mecd.es/Catalogo ICAA/Peliculas/Detalle?Pelicula=559451).

16. "But, I assure you, I have been told a couple of years ago that Joe Dante had this Italian script in his hands, translated into English, with drawings, how to make them [gnomes]; lots of work had been done. Funny enough, there is not much difference between *Gremlins* and *Gnomi*. However, nowadays I'm pleased, because it means that surely what we think, that we are not inferior to them, is true." Alberto Morsiani, "Conversazione con Lamberto Bava," in Alberto Morsiani (ed.), *Rosso italiano (1977/1987). Sequenze #7*, March 1988, 57.

Il medium (The Medium)

D: Silvio Amadio. *S*: Silvio Amadio; *SC*: Claudio Fragasso, Tonino [Antonio] Cucca, Silvio Amadio; *DOP*: Maurizio Salvatori (Eastmancolor, Telecolor); *M*: Roberto Pregadio (Ed. Nazionalmusic); *E*: Silvio Amadio; *PD, CO*: Elio Micheli; *AD*: Mauro Paravano; *AE*: Marina Candidi; *SO*: Alberto Salvatori; *C*: Giancarlo Granatelli; *AC*: Renato Palmieri; *MU*: Angelo Roncaioli; *Hair*: Galileo Mandini; *W*: Renata Renzi; *SS*: Romana Pietrostefani. *Cast*: Vincent Mannari Jr. [Guido Mannari] (Paul Robbins), Sherry Buchanan (Laura), Stefano Mastrogirolamo (Alan), Martine Brochard (Daniela), Nicoletta Amadio (Anita, the Psychic), Achille Brunini [Brugnini] (Vanni, the Doctor), Vincenzo Ferro (Benedetti, Daniela's husband), Mirko Ellis [Mirko Korcinsky] (Anita's Husband), Andrea Aureli (Berto, the Gardener), Paolo De Manincor (Bersani), Loris Zanchi (Prof. Albitzen), Salvatore Martino, Philippe Leroy (Prof. Power). *PROD*: Ars Nova Cooperativa S.r.l. (Rome); *PM*: Augusto Silvestrini; *PS*: Marco Kustermann; *PSe*: Nicola Princigalli. *Country*: Italy. Filmed at Palatino Studios (Rome). *Running time*: 89 minutes (m. 2441). Visa n. 74452 (12.7.1979); *Rating*: V.M.14. *Release date*: 3.10.1980 (Italy); *Distribution*: Regional. *Domestic gross*: approx.15,000,000 *lire*.

Note: painting by Agostino De Romanis.

American composer Paul Robbins moves to Rome with his ten-year-old son Alan to work on his new dodecaphonic opera. Robbins, a widower, hires the young Laura to look after Alan, but soon the boy starts acting in a weird way, and mentions an imaginary playmate whom only he can see, a black-haired woman dressed in white. Weird events take place: Robbins is attacked by a ferocious dog, a mysterious female voice is recorded on his tapes, and he is perturbed by a painting given to him by Daniela, the wife of the art director with whom he is working for his new opera. Things turn even worse, as Alan seems to be possessed by a malevolent entity. Upon advice of a doctor friend, Robbins summons a noted psychic, Professor Power, who solves the mystery. It turns out that Daniela, a powerful psychic, is seeking revenge against Robbins, who years earlier had provoked her sister Eleonora's death. The two psychics confront each other during two séances that take places simultaneously at Robbins and Daniela's house, and the outcome will be surprising...

Released marginally in early 1980 and immediately disappearing into oblivion, *Il medium* represented the culmination of Silvio Amadio's interest in the occult, which the director had developed thanks to his friendship with art director-turned-filmmaker Demofilo Fidani, the mind behind many low-budget Italian Westerns.

Compared to his work as a film director, in fact, Fidani's activity as a medium proved much more successful. Through his "*Circolo di spiritualisti*" (Circle of Spiritualists) he became a well-respected figure in the world of esoterism and wrote some books on the topic, including *Il medium esce dal mistero*, published in 1986 and graced by a testimony by Amadio himself. "We had started gathering as a permanent group interested in the phenomena of Spiritism around you, a psychic with most unique powers, in the early 1970s; we met on a rigorous weekly basis,

on Friday nights, after dinner, at your place,"[1] Amadio wrote. The participants—Fidani and his partner Mila Valenza Vitelli, Amadio and his wife Gabriella, Roman lawyer Roberto Castaldi, Fidani's brother Arturo and Mila's son Paolo—used to record the séances with tape recorders and microphones. They closed doors and windows and sat in the dark, waiting for their guide spirits to manifest. "We know it is not possible for us to understand some concepts, at least until we will remain in a material state," the director added, recalling the "crass laughs of our friends whenever we discussed and mentioned the earthly concepts of time and space." Among the otherworldly visitors that manifested during the séances, as Amadio recalled, once there was even Pope John XXIII.

There is little doubt that *Il medium* was conceived as a sincere homage to Fidani, on whom Prof. Power, the titular savant played by Philippe Leroy, seems to have been patterned. In a scene, the psychic lectures about the survival of the spirit after death ("The spiritual world belongs to a distinct dimension from our time and space") and the permanence of evil in the afterlife, linked with the least evolved spirits ("We cannot and mustn't approach the spiritual world without a deep moral preparation"), with words very similar to those later used by Fidani in his book.

The film's genesis benefited from the director's adherence to the subject matter. As scriptwriter Claudio Fragasso told *Fangoria*, "Silvio Amadio came to me with an actual medium and told me that the dead had told them I should write the script [laughs]! And so I began to write this story with the direct inspiration of the dead."[2] According to Fragasso, this was the first script he wrote, even before *Pronto ad uccidere* (a.k.a. *Meet Him and Die*, 1976, Franco Prosperi), and in fact a scenario with the same title is registered at Rome's SIAE offices and dated October 14, 1975, although it is credited to Massimo Franciosa and Luisa Montagnana. However, it took a few years before the movie went into production: shooting started on May 7, 1979.[3] But it was too late for such a story to find an audience.

Often labeled as a horror film, *Il medium* is in fact a supernatural drama, a ghost story of sorts which deals with some Gothic staples such as the return of the past, the perturbing portrait, the seemingly haunted house. The story has some points in common with the domestic apocalypse of Bava's *Shock*—here as well a kid turns against a parent, by way of a supernatural presence looking for revenge—and the idea of it revolving around a dodecaphonic composer is a singular variation on the theme of artistic sensibility, which makes Gothic heroes more receptive to the manifestations of the supernatural. The musician's open-minded approach to composition—the twelve-tone technique overcomes the limits of writing in a key—might be compared to a psychic's approach to reality, that is, going beyond the limits of everyday reality and experience.

But the odd interesting detail (the composer working on his music, which allows for a weird electronic score by Roberto Pregadio) fail to make up for poor characterization and bad dialogue, not to mention a banally moral punchline ("Evil always backfires against those who do it"). The direction is flat, and the story moves at an excruciatingly slow pace. The horrific bits are limited to a mild dog attack which is poles apart from a similar scene in *Suspiria*, and the few supposedly eerie moments fail to generate much interest: laughter arises from a burning painting, a mysterious voice is inexplicably recorded on the musician's tapes, and Prof. Power shows up unexpectedly at the protagonist's house—we will soon discover that it is a phenomenon of bilocation, as the psychic has the ability of being in two different places at the same time—and saves him from a deadly trap concocted by his son.

The cast is wasted. Martine Brochard drinks her J&B and tries to look malevolent, and Philippe Leroy sleepwalks through his guest star role with stoic resignation. Mannari (seen in Brass' *Caligula*) hides, so to speak, behind a transparent pseudonym. Brochard had little or no recollection of the film: "I only remember that it all seemed very homemade, and I had a very cold relationship with Amadio. I did my stuff and 'Thanks and goodbye.'"[4]

Amadio's next, and last, film was the soapy melodrama *Il carabiniere* (1981), starring Fabio Testi and Massimo Ranieri, loosely based on a popular Neapolitan *sceneggiata*.

NOTES

1. "Lettera del regista Silvio Amadio," in Demofilo Fidani, *Il medium esce dal mistero* (Trento: Luigi Reverdito Editore, 1986), 180.

2. Howard Berger, "Claudio Fragasso's Gore Wars," *Fangoria* #163, June 1997, 56.

3. According to the Public Cinematographic Register.

4. Stefano Ippoliti and Matteo Norcini, "Una favola chiamata cinema. Intervista a Martine Brochard," *Cine70 e dintorni* #6, 2004, 36.

Mia moglie è una strega (My Wife Is a Witch)

D: Castellano & Pipolo [Franco Castellano, Giuseppe Moccia]. *S*: Laura Toscano, Franco Marotta; *SC*: Castellano & Pipolo, Laura Toscano, Franco Marotta; *DOP*: Alfio Contini (Technospes); *M*: Detto Mariano (Ed. Slalom); *E*: Antonio Siciliano; *PD*: Bruno Amalfitano; *CO*: Luca Sabatelli; *AD*: Alessandro Metz; *MU*: Nilo Iacoponi, Walter Cossu; *Hair*: Paolo Franceschi, Corrado Cristofori; *SS*: Vittoria Vigorelli; *PDA*: Gualtiero Caprara; *C*: Sandro Tamborra; *AC*: Sandro Grossi; *2ndAC*: Francesco Damiani; *SO*: Benito Alchimede; *B*: Marco De Biase; *SE*: Antonio Corridori; *AE*: Giancarlo Morelli, Andrea Caterini; *KG*: Giancarlo Rocchetti; *ChEl*: Antonio Leurini; *PROP*: Vittorio Troiani; *W*: Maura Zuccherofino, Clara Fratarcangeli; *Mix*: Romano Checcacci; *Chor*: Renato Greco; *SP*: Giuseppe Botteghi. *Cast*: Renato Pozzetto (Cardinal Emilio Altieri, Pope Clement X; Emilio Altieri) Eleonora Giorgi (Finnicella), Helmut Berger (Asmodeus), Lia Tanzi (Tania Grisanti), Enrico Papa (Roberto), Renzo Rinaldi (Emilio's collaborator), Stefano Varriale, Sandro Ghiani (Emilio's collaborator), Anna Cucinotta (Witch), Dino Fassio (Police Commissioner), Raimondo Penne, Ferdinando Paone (Engineer), Rita Caldana (Emilio's secretary), John Stacy (Hotel concierge in Paris), Sonia Otero (Apollonia), Sveva Altieri (Witch), Gianni Olivieri, Geoffrey Copleston (Man who picks up invitation cards), Fulvio Mingozzi (Emilio's collaborator), Vittorio De Bisogno (Shareholder), Guadalupe Barrera (Balsarina); *uncredited*: Jimmy il Fenomeno [Luigi Origene Soffrano] (Waiter at Disco), Serena Grandi (Witch), Shôko Nakahara (Magañara), Nazzareno Natale (Cab driver), Franca Scagnetti (Housemaid). *PROD*: Mario Cecchi Gori and Vittorio Cecchi Gori for Capital Films. *GM*: Luciano Luna; *UM*: Francesco Giorgi; *PS*: Gianni Stellitano; *PSe*: Paolo Giorgi; *PSeA*: Luigi Lagrasta; *ADM*: Mario Lupi, Giulio Cestari; *Press attache*: Lucherini—Ghergo. *Country*: Italy. Filmed at De Paolis In.Ci.R. Studios (Rome). *Running time*: 88 minutes (m. 2438). Visa n. 75767 (10.23.1980); *Rating*: all audiences. *Release date*: 12.1.1980 (Italy); *Distribution*: Cineriz. *Domestic gross*: 1,835,662,000 lire. *Also known as*: *Mi mujer es una bruja* (Spain),

Geliebte Hexe (West Germany), *Meine Frau ist eine Hexe* (West Germany—home video).

Notes: The song "Magic" is sung by Eleonora Giorgi; Helmut Berger is dubbed by Sergio Di Stefano.

In 1656, in Rome, a witch named Finnicella is condemned to the stake by Cardinal Altieri, soon to become Pope Clement X. Her demon lover Asmodeus makes her return to life three hundred years later, in 1980, so that she can get revenge on Emilio Altieri, a distant descendant of her torturer. At first Finnicella tries to make Emilio fall in love with her and then punish him when he least expects it. But when Emilio finally leaves his fiancée Tania and vows love to her, Finnicella realizes she loves him too, and abandons her revenge. But during the couple's honeymoon in Paris, Asmodeus, disguised as a waiter, enters Emilio's room and shoots Finnicella, framing him for murder. The man is arrested, but Finnicella, with a ploy, manages to trap Asmodeus, forcing him to bring her back to life and save Emilio.

In the merry euphoria of the early 1980s, while the other genres languished, it was comedy which kept the Italian movie industry afloat. The top grossing movies were those starring Paolo Villaggio, Renato Pozzetto, Adriano Celentano, Enrico Montesano, Johnny Dorelli, and the plots were safer, tamer versions of the erotic farces of the Seventies: the gradual toning down of nudity and salaciousness was the consequence of the need to secure an "all audiences" rating and capture a wider public.

The Gothic and its tropes became one of the favorite sources for scriptwriters to build their sketchy plots around the comedians' gags. After the Paolo Villaggio vehicle *Dottor Jekyll e gentile signora* (1979, Steno), it was Renato Pozzetto's turn to star in a comedy with mild Fantastic overtones. Since his beginnings in the mid–1960s in an on-stage comedy duo with Aurelio "Cochi" Ponzoni, aptly named Cochi & Renato, Pozzetto had specialized in an absurdist kind of humor, replete with nonsense monologues with a surreal feel. Following Cochi & Renato's TV appearances of the early 1970s, Pozzetto's staring, dazed looks and naive characterizations had turned him into one of the most popular Italian comedians of the decade. Whereas in the previous years he had often starred in nonconformist works—such as *Sturmtruppen* (1976, Salvatore Samperi), based on the comic strip of the same name, or his own directorial debut *Saxophone* (1978)—Pozzetto's

output in the 1980s was decidedly uneven and far more conventional, in tune with the growing tendency of Italian comedy.

Shot in the late Spring of 1980,[1] *Mia moglie è una strega*, the actor's fourth starring role of the year, was a far cry from *Sono fotogenico* (also 1980), Dino Risi's biting satire on the movie business, where Pozzetto had given one of his best performances as a naive man who dreams of becoming a film star, only to discover the squalid world of the movie industry. The story for *Mia moglie è una strega* was basically a remake of René Clair's classic 1942 comedy *I Married a Witch*, starring Veronica Lake and Fredric March. The similarities were already evident during filming, despite directors Franco Castellano and Giuseppe Moccia (a.k.a. Castellano & Pipolo) claiming otherwise: "René Clair's film has nothing to do with ours … it is not a remake, a rip-off or a retelling. Let's say that René Clair is a reference point, one that served as inspiration. Our film rather tries to revive an American trend of the *fantastique*, which goes from *Mary Poppins* to *The Love Bug*."[2] The newspaper *La Stampa* even published a one-page article on the shooting with pictures of Giorgi, Veronica Lake and Kim Novak, which even referenced another supernatural comedy as a direct influence, *Bell Book and Candle*.[3] Still, the credits pay no reference to either film. Taking inspiration from classic Hollywood fare without acknowledging it was not an uncommon occurrence for Italian comedies of the period: a couple of successful Paolo Villaggio vehicles, *Fracchia la belva umana* (1981) and *Sogni mostruosamente proibiti* (1982), were respectively uncredited remakes of *The Whole Town's Talking* (1935, John Ford) and *The Secret Life of Walter Mitty* (1947, Norman Z. McLeod), adapted to Villaggio's screen persona. Similarly, *Mia moglie è una strega* featured several verbal gags which echoed Pozzetto's repertoire. As Pipolo revealed years later, "Renato was very skeptical about that film. He did it because he had a contract and so he had to do it, moreover … he hadn't chosen us, so he found himself a bit stuck in it."[4]

The film pairs Pozzetto with the then 27-year-old Eleonora Giorgi, at the top of her popularity in Italy: the previous year the ravishing blonde actress had married publisher Angelo Rizzoli, the head of distribution company Cineriz, which had a key role in her rise to the top of the box-office (the couple would split in 1984, after Rizzoli's involvement in the infamous

Italian lobby card for *Mia moglie è una strega* (1980, Castellano & Pipolo), featuring Helmut Berger (left) as the devil Asmodeus, Eleonora Giorgi (center) and Renato Pozzetto. The film was basically an uncredited remake of René Clair's classic 1942 comedy *I Married a Witch*.

P2 scandal). As the titular witch Finnicella, Giorgi (who also sings a disco tune named *Magic*, featured during the end credits) vows revenge on the inquisitor who betrayed her trust and sent her at the stake: she returns to life 333 years, 33 months and 33 days later, after her ashes have been discovered during the excavations for the Rome underground (a nice touch that links the film to such works as Fellini's *Roma* and the Gothic TV series *Il segno del comando*). Predictably, she falls for the descendant of her enemy, Emilio, a meek and not-too-bright stockbroker who is about to get married with another woman, and proceeds to ruin his life (*à la Bringing Up Baby*) with her constant seduction attempts.

The opening scene, with several witches (including an uncredited Serena Grandi) performing a Sabbath amid a cemeterial set complete with owls, bats and hanging dolls, is exemplary in the way it recycles the Gothic paraphernalia into material worthy of a Saturday night TV ballet. The result is not that different from the infamous opening of Pier Carpi's *Un'ombra nell'ombra* (1979). A dungeon scene

ensues, with Finnicella the witch being flogged by an inquisitor, but *La maschera del demonio* this ain't, and the expected face to face between Finnicella (scantily dressed but not nearly as provoking as her screen predecessors of the past two decades) and Cardinal Altieri (Pozzetto, donning a long curly wig and musketeer mustache) is a by-the-numbers moment played for a cheap punchline: "If you confess I'll be clement," he promises, and after Finnicella has confessed he immediately orders her to be burnt at the stake. "But you promised you'd be clement," she protests. "In fact, tomorrow I'll be elected pope, with the name Clement the Tenth," is the reply. Apart from the odd historian in the venue, it is unlikely that the wordplay elicited many laughs amid the audience. The filmmakers were clearly more at ease with the contemporary part of the story, but the sloppiness of the *mise-en-scène* gives an idea of the careless way these products were cranked out. Overall, the movie is slapdash and haphazardly shot, with the lack of care typical of many commercial films of the period, including below-par special effects and indifferent camerawork. Product placement is, as always, conspicuous, with Pozzetto repeatedly displaying to the camera a packet of Muratti Ambassador cigarettes.

Throughout the story, the *fantastique* becomes fodder for gags *à la Bewitched*, with Finnicella working up all kinds of magic tricks to seduce Emilio, until the inevitable happy ending. "We tell fairytales, clean stories, funny, and good for everyone—young, old, children, soldiers,"[5] the directors claimed, the reference to soldiers being significant as they were among the most assiduous audience of adults-only (or V.M.18) films. Even Pozzetto was careful to distance *Mia moglie è una strega* from the erotic comedies arena: "It is funny and relaxing without resorting to vulgarity, profanity or risqué situations."[6] In fact, there is no trace of nudity and the occasional satiric punchlines are mild, with the predictable reference to the feminist movement and their slogan "*Tremate! Tremate! Le streghe son tornate!*" (Shake! Shake! The Witches are back!). Feminists must not have been pleased with Castellano & Pipolo's story: the moral of the tale is not only that richness equals happiness (with Emilio becoming a millionaire after selling his shares in a disastrous oil company), but that a quiet family life is just what a wild and independent woman needs to be fully realized. In the epilogue, Emilio shares his wife's magical powers, getting home from work atop an electric broom, and the whole family—husband, wife and three children—sit at the table while Finnicella's fellow witches, who have become their maids and housekeepers, clean the house and serve them dinner.

Some gags are mildly funny, mainly because of Pozzetto's whimsical delivery and taste for the surreal, such as the actor atop a car that drives by itself, or him watching a rerun of *Casablanca* on TV with Finnicella popping up in the place of Ingrid Bergman. Others, like a disco scene where the actor launches into a frantic dance, fare worse. A bored-looking Helmut Berger is the requisite guest star, as the haughty devil Asmodeus, who pops up every now and then in the film under various disguises (a cop, a waiter, an orchestra director) in a manner akin to Edmund Purdom in Paolo Lombardo's trashy sex-horror flick *L'amante del demonio* (1972)—not that anyone noticed, anyway—and finally gets his comeuppance via a guillotine after being tricked by Finnicella. Before he is decapitated (offscreen) he comments: "Women know always better than the devil."

Mia moglie è una strega—which according to the directors cost about 800 million *lire*[7]—was a huge box-office hit, ending up 7th among the season's top-grossing films (Kubrick's *The Shining* was at 10th place), in a list dominated by Italian comedies. The directors refused to make a sequel,[8] and their next film, *Asso* (1981), starring Adriano Celentano and Edwige Fenech, was another comedy with supernatural elements—this time borrowed from *A Guy Named Joe* (1943), *Here Comes Mr. Jordan* (1941) and its remake *Heaven Can Wait* (1978)—about a master card cheater who returns as a ghost to help his widow find a new husband.

NOTES

1. According to the Public Cinematographic Register shooting started on May 19th.
2. Paolo Cervone, "Una 'strega' innamorata nella fiaba degli anni '80," *Corriere della Sera*, July 4, 1980.
3. Lamberto Antonelli, "Terzo matrimonio per la strega," *Stampa Sera*, August 26, 1980.
4. Andrea Pergolari, *La fabbrica del riso* (Rome: Unmondoaparte, 2004), 321.
5. Antonelli, "Terzo matrimonio per la strega."
6. *Ibid.*
7. Franca Faldini and Goffredo Fofi (eds.), *Il cinema italiano d'oggi, 1970–1984 raccontato dai suoi protagonisti* (Milan: Mondadori, 1984), 316.
8. *Ibid.*, 322.

Ombre (Shadows)

D: Giorgio Cavedon. S and SC: Giorgio Cavedon; *DOP*: Erico Menczer (Eastmancolor, LV-Luciano Vittori); *M*: Maurizio Sangineto (Ed. Melodi); *E*: Maria Grazia Dell'Ara; *ArtD*: Giorgio Luppi; *AD*: Massimo Guglielmi; *C*: Luigi Bernardini; *AC*: Ercole Visconti; *SS*: Nora Monsellato; *SO*: Ivo Morbidelli; *B*: Luciano Locatelli; *AsstArtD*: Anna Maria Zerri; *MU*: Giuliana De Carli; *Hair*: Roberto Magnani; *KG*: Giovanni Carbonera; *ChEl*: Domenico Cavaliere; *Mix*: Danilo Moroni; *SOE*: Italo Cameracanna; *Cast*: Lou Castel [Ulv Quarzéll] (Renato), Monica Guerritore (Monica), Laura Belli (Susanna Schumann), Carlo Bagno (Monica's Father), Antonio Guidi (Schumann, Susanna's Father), Elisabetta Odino (Monica, the Child), Mita Medici [Patrizia Vistarini] (Patrizia), Auretta Gay (Elena), Ugo Bologna (Professor at Hospital), Roberto Tiraboschi (Hippie), Lorenzo Logli (Monica's Stepfather), Riccardo Gavagna, Elena Borgo, Luca Torraca (Doctor); *uncredited*: Edy Angelillo (Girl in Disco). *PROD*: CTP Cineteleproduzioni (Milan); *PM*: Pierluigi Ottina; *PS*: Gaetano Carottini; *PSe*: Riccardo Pintus; *ADM*: Maria Cannoni. *Country*: Italy. Filmed on location in Milan and at Icet-De Paolis Studios (Milan). *Running time*: 96 minutes (m. 2650). Visa n. 75223 (5.30.1980); *Rating*: all audiences. *Release date*: 6.26.1980 (Italy); *Distribution*: Eurocopfilms. *Domestic gross*: 1,695,000 *lire*.

Notes: Paintings by Carlo Jacono; the song "Black Out" is sung by Heather Parisi.

Milan. Renato, a painter, wanders gloomily around the city and recalls his doomed love story with Monica. The girl had moved from the country to the city, and rented an attic previously occupied by an old painter who had been found dead there. Renato, estranged from his pregnant and rich wife Susanna, had fallen for her, but Monica was very sick. Before she died, she gave Renato a painting, a portrait of the old painter, who was actually Monica's grandfather. An evil soul obsessed with occultism and tarots, he had used the girl as a medium to paint his own portrait from the beyond. After Monica's death, Renato had moved to the decrepit attic, and became obsessed with the painting. Susanna convinced him to sell it for a large sum, but Renato found himself unable to paint any longer. Renato desperately tries to turn himself into a medium for Monica from the afterlife. He locks himself in the attic, until one day Susanna's father comes to tell him that his daughter has given birth to a baby...

Giorgio Cavedon (1930–2001) was an eclectic personality who crossed the various threads of Italian popular culture for several decades, dabbling in literature, music, comics, and cinema. His name is commonly linked to the adults-only comics he wrote with Renzo Barbieri, starting with *Isabella*, which in 1966 represented Italy's first openly erotic *fumetto*. An accomplished jazz musician and a member of the Milan College Jazz Society, Cavedon had also ambitions to be a filmmaker. In 1953 he shot his first 16mm documentary, and the following year he screened the experimental short film *Arturo* at the Cannes Film Festival. Over the years Cavedon resurfaced sporadically in the movie business: he was Renato Dall'Ara's assistant on the interesting *Scano Boa* (1960), and in 1965 he directed an episode of the comedy anthology *I soldi*, starring Enrico Maria Salerno and Catherine Spaak.

Published from April 1966 to October 1976, for a total of 263 issues, *Isabella* convinced Cavedon to stick to the comics business, although he wrote the script for the movie adaptation directed by Bruno Corbucci, *Isabella duchessa dei diavoli* (a.k.a. *Ms. Stiletto*, 1969). With their company Erregi, later Ediperiodici, Barbieri and Cavedon created many successful erotic pocket comics, such as *Jacula, Lucrezia, Messalina, Lucifera, Jungla, Hessa, De Sade*, before parting ways in 1972, when Barbieri created Edifumetto, which became Ediperiodici's biggest competitor in the adults-only comics market throughout the decade.

Despite his successful activity with Ediperiodici, Cavedon did not give up his passion, and by the late Seventies he returned behind the camera on what would represent his only feature film as director. Shooting took place entirely in Milan; it started on July 9, 1979,[1] with the working titles *Autoritratto* (Self-Portrait)[2] and *Ritratto di un fantasma* (Portrait of a Ghost),[3] and lasted through the months of July and August; by the time filming was near completion, however, the title had already been changed into the definitive one, *Ombre* (Shadows).[4] As the director specified, it referred to the shadows "of the world of a young artist in the district of Brera, a world populated with hopes and disillusions; the ones in which a girl doomed to die struggles; and the ones which upset the human mind in the illusory search for a truth that no longer exists."[5]

Cavedon was understandably vague about the true nature of his film, which newspapers described as a melodrama in the vein of *Love Story* (1970).[6] In fact, it is an eerie ghost story which unrolls in flashbacks, blending present and past events. It reprises elements in vogue in the 1970s, such as the interest in parapsychology, and its bleak plot recalls one of the many adult comics Cavedon scripted—devoid of nudity and gore, that is. *Ombre* is surprisingly understated, at a time where extreme violence and sex were the norm: Cavedon was attempting to make an old-style horror story, leaving aside shocks and scares and aiming for subtlety, and focusing on such themes as the need for artistic creation and the ultimate inescapability of fate.

The director's own script plays with Gothic's traditional imagery: the doomed artist, the evil portrait, a menace from the past, the thin boundaries between this world and the afterlife, a circular conception of life where past events are doomed to repeat themselves over and over. Despite the many literary references, from M.R. James to Poe (a cat seems to be a medium between the dead artist and the one who will take his place), what sets apart *Ombre* from many Gothic tales with similar plots is precisely the contemporary Milanese setting, which gives the supernatural angle a realistic backdrop. As Giulio Questi did in *Arcana* (1972), Cavedon manages to convey the feel of obscure forces working subtly in an everyday reality, just beneath the surface: even children's chalk drawings on the asphalt take on a sinister meaning.

In the opening sequences we see Monica take a tramway to the outskirts of the city, to the Navigli district and its canals, and move to one of those big condos that housed hundreds of families, mostly immigrants, depicted in such films as *Rocco e i suoi fratelli* (1960, Luchino Visconti). The squalid, claustrophobic attic where she and then Renato move to is a prosaic but no less perturbing variation of the dilapidated Gothic castles which feed on their inhabitants' primal fears and retain the malevolent presence of their previous occupants. Perhaps the director had in mind the building where the doomed Trelkovsky goes to live in Roman Polanski's stunning adaptation of Roland Topor's novel, *Le locataire*, a.k.a. *The Tenant* (1976). On top of that, Cavedon has his lonely protagonist wander around the city, juxtaposing his discouraged meditations with sinister architectural glimpses of Milan, from the imposing caryatids at the Central railway station (built during the Fascist regime) to Giorgio De Chirico's surreal 1973 open-air fountain sculpture "*I bagni misteriosi*" ("The Mysterious Baths"),[7] giving the impression of the big city as a vampire which deprives its inhabitants of the will to live.

In a way, *Ombre* could also be read as a metaphorical meditation on the loss of the 1968 ideals. In a flashback we first meet Renato intent on working on a huge mural painting, together with a group of hippie artists; in the scenes set in the present, the mural looks dilapidated and ruined beyond repair. Likewise, Renato betrays his ideals of artistic purity and finds (ephemeral) notoriety by selling someone else's work and pretending it is his own. Cavedon carries the story coherently to its grim yet logical denouement, with a punchline that plays like a variation on the ending of Luigi Comencini's black comedy *Lo scopone scientifico* (1972), where rat poison also played a key role.

The direction attempts to be stylish, with some impressive images (Renato and Monica meeting on opposite sides of a palace with glass walls, as if on opposite sides of an aquarium) and ample use of comic book-style shots, such as freeze frames and details of faces, hands and objects. Cavedon even pays homage to *L'Année dernière à Marienbad* in the scene at the Sempione park, where the camera tracks laterally and discovers the two lovers standing motionless while kissing by a tree, and here and there he comes up with suitably eerie images, such as the little girl playing hopscotch in the courtyard. He is immensely aided by Erico Menczer's top-notch cinematography, characterized by the ample use of *flou* and striking transitions from light to darkness, and by Maurizio Sangineto's score, which mixes "eerie synthesizer droolings and splintering guitar chords."[8]

For all its qualities, though, *Ombre* is badly flawed. The insistent use of voice-over soon becomes tiresome and heavy-handed ("I have remained alone on this useless life's stage," Renato mutters, while wandering on … an empty stage), the story feels stretched despite the intriguing flashback structure, and the characters are so sketchy and perfunctory that it is hard to care about them. In addition to that, despite a pair of capable leads such as Lou Castel and Monica Guerritore, the performances are hardly convincing. Monica's melodramatic death scene seems lifted from some worthless tearjerker, and Castel—by then in a career-low stretch, with titles such as *L'osceno desiderio* (1978) and *Suor omicidi* (1979)—looks uninterested. His performance becomes downright embarrassing in the scene at a disco where Renato gets drunk after selling the portrait Monica had entrusted to him, and dances frantically to the sound of a Heather Parisi song.

Nevertheless, *Ombre* remains a rather interesting oddity, not least because of the participation of personalities from the artistic world, such as Carlo Jacono (one of Italy's most famous illustrators, and the official cover artist of the *Gialli Mondadori* from 1950 to 1986), who provided the eerie portrait at the center of the story, and Roberto Tiraboschi (who subsequently became a renowned writer and scriptwriter), who plays a small role. Some sources credit Mario Caiano as co-director, but the information is groundless: Caiano himself never mentioned his participation to the film, and Castel has been adamant that Cavedon was the film's only director.[9]

Despite a reasonable amount of publicity, *Ombre*—advertised as "a young film for young people"—failed to attract any audience: reportedly, it ended up with only 565 tickets sold and closed after just a week. Critics were tepid, too: "Cavedon's direction … moves among the story's twists and certain inconsistencies in the script with mixed results. If on one hand he goes for effect with naïve and elementary tricks … on the other he takes advantage, thanks also to Erico Menczer's photography, of some rather unseen glimpses of old Milan,"[10] wrote the *Corriere della Sera*, blaming also the story's excessively slow pacing. After such a commercial debacle, Cavedon never directed another picture.

NOTES

1. "Primo ciak del film *Autoritratto* a Milano," *L'Unità*, July 10, 1979. The start date is confirmed by Rome's Public Cinematographic Register as well.

2. "Opera prima con 'star' a Brera," *La Stampa*, August 8, 1979.

3. Sandro Liberali, "Io tanti flirt? Prego, solo amori," *Corriere dell'informazione*, July 18, 1979 (interview with Mita Medici); Franca Morotti, "La mia vita? Tanta rabbia e voglia di pattinare," *Corriere dell'informazione*, July 30, 1979.

4. See Anonymous, "Un'altra troupe 'gira' in autobus con fantasmi e gatto parapsicologo," *Corriere della Sera*, August 18, 1979.

5. Rossella Dallò, "Comincia con la fine di un amore la carriera di un giovane regista," *L'Unità*, August 13, 1979.

6. *Ibid.*

7. Placed in the Sempione park in 1973 as part of the "Art-City Contact" project for Milan's XV Triennale, "*I bagni misteriosi*" is considered by many to be Giorgio De Chirico's greatest sculpture. Made from Vicenza stone, the installation is composed of eight elements placed in a large sinuous pool: two torsos, a dark-haired man and a blond one; a Swan whose outline recalls a floating boat at the amusement park; a multicolored fish and a colored beach ball; a trampoline; a real cabin for swimmers with wind flags; and a fountainhead. Part of the floor of the pool, in yellow ochre, is decorated with a parquet motif that recalls the movement of waves. As the artist explained, "the idea for the "Mysterious baths" fountain came to me while I was in a house whose floor had been polished with wax. I saw a man walking ahead of me whose legs were reflected on the floor. I had the impression that he could have sunk, like in a pool. That he could move and swim. So, I imagined strange pools with men immersed in that sort of water parquet, who moved and played and sometimes even stopped to converse with other men who were outside of the pavement pool." The representation of enigmatic characters immersed in water is a theme that was dear to the Surrealist artist and one that he would come back to repeatedly during his career.

8. Mark [Thompson] Ashworth, "Ombre," *Delirium* #3, 1995, p. 37.

9. Lou Castel, interviewed by Pierpaolo De Sanctis. De Sanctis is the author of an excellent documentary on the actor, *A pugni chiusi* (2016).

10. L.A. [Leonardo Autera], "Mansarda popolata di ombre," *Corriere della Sera*, June 29, 1980.

Paura nella città dei morti viventi (City of the Living Dead, a.k.a. *Gates of Hell*)

D: Lucio Fulci. *S and SC*: Lucio Fulci, Dardano Sacchetti; *DOP*: Sergio Salvati (LV-Luciano Vittori); *M*: Fabio Frizzi, conducted by the author (Ed. Flipper); *E*: Vincenzo Tomassi; *PD, CO*: Antonello Geleng; *MU*: Franco Rufini; *AMU*: Rosario Prestopino; *Hair*: Luciano Vito; *AD*: Roberto Giandalia [*2ndAD*: Michele Soavi, uncredited]; *SD*: Giacomo Calò Corducci; *ASD*: Ovidio Taito; *ACO*: Luciana Morosetti; *SO*: Ugo Celani, Marco Streccioni; *B*: Eros Giustini; *Mix*: Bruno Moreal; *SE*: Gino De Rossi; *C*: Roberto Forges Davanzati; *AC*: Maurizio Lucchini; *AE*: Armando Pace, Pietro Tomassi; *ChEl*: Roberto Belli; *KG*: Giancarlo Serravalli; *SP*: Giorgio Garibaldi Schwarze; *STC*: Nazzareno Cardinali; *Stunts*: Don Ruffin; *SS*: Rita Agostini, Donatella Botti. *Cast*: Christopher George (Peter Bell), Katherine [Catriona] Mac-Coll (Mary Woodhouse), Carlo De Mejo (Gerry), Antonella Interlenghi (Emily Robbins), Giovanni Lombardo Radice (Bob), Daniela Doria [Daniela Cormio] (Rosie Kelvin), Fabrizio Jovine (Father William Thomas), Luca Paisner [Luca Venantini] (John-John Robbins), Michele Soavi (Tommy Fisher), Venantino Venantini (Mr. Ross), Enzo D'Ausilio (Sheriff Russell's Deputy), Adelaide Aste (Theresa), Luciano Rossi (Policeman in apartment), Robert Sampson (Sheriff Russell), Janet Agren (Sandra); *uncredited*: Omero Capanna (Burning zombie), Lucio Fulci (Dr. John Thompson), Michael Gaunt (Gravedigger), Perry Pirkanen (Blond Gravedigger), James Sampson (James McLuhan, Séance member), Martin Sorrentino (Sgt. Clay), Robert E. Werner (Policeman outside apartment building). *PROD*: Dania Film, Medusa Distribuzione, National Cinematografica (Rome); *GM*: Giovanni Masini; *EP*: Renato Jaboni (in the U.S.: Robert Warner); *UM*: Gianfranco Coduti; *PSe*: Franco Galizi; *PSeA*: Alfredo Fornacini. *Country*: Italy. Filmed on location in Savannah (Georgia), New York City and at De Paolis In.Ci.R. Studios (Rome). *Running time*: 93 minutes (m. 2497). Visa n. 75480 (8.7.1980); *Rating*: V.M.18. *Release dates*: 8.11.1980 (Italy), 9.11.1980 (West Germany), 12.10.1980 (France), 11.12.1980 (Spain), 5.7.1982 (UK), 4.8.1983 (USA). *Distribution*: Medusa Distribuzione. *Domestic gross*: 985,238,798 *lire*. Also known as: *Frayeurs* (France), *Miedo en la ciudad de los muertos vivientes* (Spain), *Ein Zombie hing am Glock-*

enseil; Ein Toter hing am Glockenseil; Eine Leiche hing am Glockenseil (West Germany).

In the small town of Dunwich, Reverend William Thomas commits suicide by hanging himself from a tree in the local cemetery. Meanwhile, during a séance in New York, a psychic named Mary Woodhouse has a vision of Thomas's suicide and of its terrifying consequences. Then Mary falls apparently dead, and the police authorize the burial. But the woman is still alive, and it is only for the providential intervention of a journalist, Peter Bell, who heard her scream in the coffin, that she escapes a horrible end. In Dunwich the dead come out of their graves and kill the inhabitants. Mary realizes that her vision predicts the events described in the book of Enoch, and the suicide of Father Thomas marks the beginning of the invasion of the Earth by the dead. The prophecy will come true on the night of Hallowmas. She and Peter leave for Dunwich, where they meet a young psychoanalyst, Gerry. Together, they set out to find Father Thomas's grave and destroy it, which is the only way to stop the dead. They penetrate the cemetery crypt, but find themselves in a dungeon populated with living corpses...

The commercial success of his first horror film, *Zombi 2*—a project he had been entrusted with after Enzo G. Castellari had backed out, which grossed over a billion and a half *lire* at the Italian box-office—revived Lucio Fulci's career and injected him with much-needed enthusiasm after the difficult phase of the late 1970s, characterized by professional and personal issues. The director was determined to seize the moment, sticking to the horror genre, and soon he started working on a new script with Dardano Sacchetti. "After *Zombi 2* turned out a big box-office hit, Fulci called me and said, 'A Sacché, you'll see, they'll stand in line at our door...!' But for six months nothing happened, and we had our story ready in the drawer,"[1] the scriptwriter recalled. If *Zombi 2*, a script Fulci hadn't anything to do with, tried to insert some elements of the Gothic tradition into the story—most notably, the ghost ship entering New York city *à la Nosferatu*, and the character of the mad doctor played by Richard Johnson—the new story would delve deep into the genre.

Involving a producer was not an easy task. Fulci didn't want to work with *Zombi 2*'s Fabrizio De Angelis, whom he called "The Cobra" (in the meantime, De Angelis was busy concocting another zombie movie, *Zombi Holocaust*, directed by Marino Girolami), but nobody wanted to ac-

Italian locandina for *Paura nella città dei morti viventi* (1980), Lucio Fulci's first Gothic film of the 1980s.

cept the risk. Horror had never been (and would never be) a genre much loved by Italian producers. Eventually Fulci managed to convince his friend Renato Jaboni of Medusa Distribuzione, who accepted rather reluctantly and got on board Luciano Martino and Mino Loy's company Dania and National Cinematografica (with a 40 percent and 25 percent quote, respectively).

The project was greenlit while Fulci was still shooting his grim action movie *Luca il contrabbandiere* (1980), and he went to work on the film—tentatively titled *La paura*—right away, leaving his a.d. Roberto Giandalia in Naples to put the finishing touches to *Luca il* contrabbandiere.[2] The tentative cast—which featured Tisa Farrow as Mary, Fiamma Maglione as Sandra, Monica Scattini as Rose, Aldo Barberito as Father Thomas and Robert Kerman as Ross—was mostly dropped in favor of more commercially palatable names, such as the American

Christopher George and the French Janet Agren. George's performance as the nosy cigar-chomping reporter Peter Bell had the acid-tongued director nickname him "the dog with the cigar" on set,[3] and the relationship between the two was always turbulent during filming. Giovanni Lombardo Radice was cast at the expense of Michele Soavi as Bob, a role he was initially supposed to play with a fake hump. Soavi, who hanged around on the set, in production designer Massimo Antonello Geleng's words, as "half-actor, half-under assistant,"[4] was finally cast as Tommy. The female lead was a 26-year-old British actress, Catriona MacColl, a former dancer who had had her first important role in Jacques Demy's film version of *Lady Oscar* (1979); she would become Fulci's own version of Hitchcock's trademark "blonde in peril" character for this and two subsequent horror films, ...*E tu vivrai nel terrore! L'aldilà* and *Quella villa accanto al cimitero*. The director himself appeared in one of his trademark cameos, as a coroner in one of the early scenes. Weird-looking character actor Luciano Rossi can be seen in the same scene, in one of his last screen appearances, as a cop.

Shooting started in April 1980[5] and went on for eight weeks, with six weeks of exteriors filmed on location in Savannah, Georgia, and two weeks in Rome at the De Paolis studios for the special effects scenes. The choice of Savannah—a quiet, happy-looking and decidedly un–Gothic town—was dictated by economic reasons (there would be no issues with unions regarding shooting with foreign cast and crew members). But Fulci and d.o.p. Sergio Salvati turned the place into a ghost town of sorts, with plenty of eerie lights and dry ice as well as many scenes shot at night. The De Paolis shooting involved the infamous sequence in which the protagonists are attacked by a swarm of maggots, filmed with two wind machines and 10 kilograms of living fly larvae. The scene caused a notorious incident on the set: someone from the crew, exasperated by the smell, played a nasty joke on Fulci, putting a handful of maggots in his sack of pipe tobacco. Unaware of this, the director charged his pipe and only after several puffs did he realize what he was smoking, which led to a tantrum on the set. In later years, Fulci even ironically hypothesized that his subsequent illness might have been caused by this episode[6]: in late 1985, he underwent heart surgery after suffering a ventricular aneurysm, and contracted viral hepatitis which degenerated into cirrhosis of the liver.

The movie was eventually released in August 1980 as *Paura nella città dei morti viventi* to cash in on the zombie cycle. Yet, even though it dealt again with zombies, the story moved in quite a different direction from other films of the period, such as *Zombi Holocaust* and Bruno Mattei and Claudio Fragasso's *Virus*. Girolami's film—released in the States in 1983 in a re-edited version as *Doctor Butcher, M.D.*, with additional footage from an unfinished anthology film titled *Tales to Rip Your Heart Out*—was a slapdash reread of *Zombi 2*, with added elements from the controversial cannibal subgenre, proving the makers' attempt to have it both ways. On its part, *Virus* (known overseas as *Hell of the Living Dead*) kept pedantically close to the Romero blueprint, to the point of featuring a quartet of gun-crazy SWAT members and recycling excerpts from Goblin's score. While also bowing to the cannibal subgenre—via stock footage from the Japanese documentary *Zankoku hitokui tairiku*, released in Italy in 1974 as *Nuova Guinea, l'isola dei cannibali*—Mattei and Fragasso even squeezed in a clumsy political message between a gory scene and the next: Fragasso's story envisioned a secret operation to solve overpopulation in Third World countries by having people prey on each other via a lethal chemical (a nod to Romero's *The Crazies*) which turns them into cannibal zombies. The plan goes horribly wrong after a leak contaminates the staff of workers in a secret chemical research facility, turning them into flesh-hungry living dead, and the plague quickly spreads throughout the world.

Both *Zombi Holocaust* and *Virus* are utterly devoid of supernatural elements, and seemingly uninterested in exploring the zombie angle other than for its shock value. Fulci and Sacchetti, on the other hand, aim at a visionary, apocalyptic fresco rooted in the Gothic tradition, which focuses on the theme of the "return of the past" and centers on the character of an evil revenant, a Catholic priest called Father Thomas. The film even includes references to the Gothic literary and film tradition, including the work of Edgar Allan Poe, reprising the theme of premature burial which was already at the core of *Sette note in nero* (1977), and H.P. Lovecraft. Such is the name of the town where the horrific events took place, Dunwich, a nod to Lovecraft's celebrated short story *The Dunwich Horror*. "Fulci had just reread Lovecraft; he wanted to make a movie with that very atmosphere. He was taking his first steps in the horror genre and felt more secure within the comfortable walls of classic literature,"[7] Sacchetti pointed out.

However, the name Dunwich does not appear in Sacchetti's original 34-page story. *La paura*[8]—incidentally, the same tentative title as Mario Bava's horror trilogy which eventually became *I tre volti della paura* (a.k.a. *Black Sabbath*, 1963)—is set in a village called Salem and is sensibly different from the finished film. The first part includes the suicide of Father Thomas, the séance, Mary Woodhouse's apparent death and premature burial, and Mary and reporter Peter Bell teaming up; but the story features a different ending set in a cemetery and then in a church where Father Thomas hanged himself. *La paura* features some different characters as well: Gerry the psychoanalyst teams up with a writer named Mike, who is nowhere to be found in the film (where it is basically replaced by Sandra, a new character absent in the story); a homeless man named Woody turns up only to be devoured by cats and reappear later as a zombie. Moreover, Sacchetti's early concept explores more convincingly the homicidal madness of the villagers: in a scene, John-John's parents kill each other with a knife and an iron before their little son's eyes, and later they will turn up as zombies. The original story also introduces the recurring presence of swarms of flies as an embodiment of evil in the places where evil manifests itself, another bow to the Gothic tradition which in the film is substituted by the "maggot rain" scene, in a nod to *Suspiria*.

Some interesting ideas in *La paura* were either dropped or just fleetingly mentioned in the movie. Namely, the notion that Father Thomas was "the last descendant of one of the 19 women put on trial for witchcraft in 1692 in Salem," and the suggestion that the village where the story takes place may have been founded on the ruins of old Salem, and therefore shall be punished for its sins. Likewise, mention of a "Book of Enoch" (a non-canonical Jewish religious work going back to 4000 BC) is passingly made in the film in the post-séance scene but then forgotten, whereas Sacchetti's story came full circle with a final surprise twist which mentioned Enoch. These ideas appear to have already been discarded in the 223-page draft of the script deposited at Rome's Centro Sperimentale di Cinematografia (CSC) on February 11, 1980, and at the Public Cinematographic Register on February 22, 1980, credited solely to Sacchetti and still titled *La paura*. However, this as well displays

several important differences from the finished film, which hint at radical last-minute changes.

For a film characterized by abundant blood and graphic violence, *Paura nella città dei morti viventi* immediately strikes for its gloomy, otherworldly mood, another element which links it to the Gothic tradition. Fulci is at his best when he suggests the atmosphere of dread and decay that pervades the damned city of Dunwich—incidentally, despite claims in the film that Dunwich is located in the East Coast, the vegetation looks typically Southern. The choice of the setting marks a neat departure from the standard look and mood of Italian Gothic, characterized by the use of Italian villas and manors such as Castle Piccolomini in Balsorano, which resulted in a recurring, familiar microcosm. In fact, Fulci's Gothic films aim at an international look without coming off as awkward; in the meantime, they redesign the coordinates of the genre's imagery.

This approach is immediately evident in the opening scene, which depicts Father Thomas' (Fabrizio Jovine) blasphemous suicidal act with an uncommon visual force, as the camera follows him wandering in the cemetery via a somewhat shaky, insecure long take which nevertheless conveys a powerful sense of disorientation and dread. Then Fulci cuts to the New York séance, depicted in elegant camera movements that wrap around the participants from behind semi-transparent curtains. The juxtaposition not only hints at a link between the two events, but immediately sabotages the notions of time and space by showing a deep and unfathomable connection between the living and the dead.

A damned soul who returns to take his revenge on the living, staring at his soon-to-be victims and thus "passing" the curse onto them (Fulci's fixation with close-ups of eyes is in evidence here), the undead Father Thomas is one of many revenant figures in Italian Gothic, but significantly one of the few *male* ones: think of Iavutich in *La maschera del demonio*, Dr. Hauff in *5 tombe per un medium* (1965, Massimo Pupillo), Uriah in *Contronatura* (1969, Antonio Margheriti). Moreover, he is a priest who hanged himself: a nod to Judas Iscariot's demise which introduces a subtle anti–Catholic element, thus departing radically from the voodoo-related mood of *Zombi 2*, and linking the film to Fulci's previous work, most notably *Non si sevizia un paperino* (1972), which also featured a priest as a source of evil. The Catholic doctrine and imagery becomes associated with damnation instead of salvation: the opening scene features an inscription on a gravestone ("The soul that pines for eternity shall outspan death") which in retrospect sounds like a bitter parody of the Gospel's "promise of eternity," and Father Thomas smearing Emily's face with a disgusting substance filled with living worms looks like a perverted rendition of the baptism ceremony.

Sacchetti's script hints at another key Gothic element, the return of the repressed: the underground crypt where the climax takes place, hidden *behind* Father Thomas' gravestone, looks like a dark half, a parallel world nourished by the sins of the living which lies in wait to rise to the surface and take its revenge at the opportune moment (the memory of the hidden passage behind the fireplace in *La maschera del demonio* comes to mind). The film connects even deeper to the Gothic tradition by way of another typical element of the genre, the séance. As Mary, MacColl plays a psychic heroine with many traits in common to *Sette note in nero*'s Virginia Ducci, a damsel-in-distress who remains basically powerless throughout the movie—a Cassandra of sorts who predicts terrible ruin but cannot do anything to stop it. Her fragility, which makes her a "dweller of the twilight void," a link between two worlds, is best expressed in the premature burial scene by the pictorial image of the flower petal which falls from the rose on Mary's chest, after a feeble breath emanates from the young woman's lungs, revealing that she is, indeed, still alive. It is moments like this (already described in detail in the script, it must be added, yet beautifully rendered on screen) which illustrate the measure of Fulci's sensibility and care toward the genre.

Characterizations are kept to a minimum—Emily (Antonella Interlenghi) is barely introduced before she is mercilessly dispatched, only to return later as a zombie—and often hint at sexual repression. Gerry (Carlo De Mejo) is a psychoanalyst (not Fulci's favorite profession by far) who we assume is hopelessly in love with the beautiful Sandra (Agren), who in turn is introduced while discussing her incestuous desires toward her father. Bob the village idiot—introduced via an impressive exterior shot outside his abode—keeps an inflatable sex doll in his shack and is said to be literally a son of a bitch (being retarded, he is also among the first to experience paranormal visions of the impending apocalyptic events), while Rosie (Daniela Doria)

and Tommy are dispatched while making out in their car. Here, the link between "forbidden" sex and punishment becomes blatant, and the infamous moment in which Rosie starts crying tears of blood makes for yet another subtly blasphemous image, possibly inspired by *Messiah of Evil* (1973) but with a more direct significance for Italian audiences, as it refers to the Catholic "miracles" of the bleeding Virgin Mary statues (such as the Madonna Addolorata in Giampilieri, Sicily).

But the story also has its share of flaws, which look more like the result of unconvincing tampering with the original concept than an attempt at a dreamlike mood. Rather than as a coherent whole, the action proceeds in fits and starts, with bizarre non sequiturs such as the column of fire that appears in the New York apartment where the séance has taken place, perhaps a remnant of the original concept of linking the living dead plague to the Salem witches. On the other hand, the gory and suspenseful set-pieces sometimes barely make sense themselves, as with the case of the appearance of the elderly dead woman in Sandra's house.

Despite its budgetary shortcomings (which called for several cost-cutting choices, such as the same night-time shots of Dunwich repeated throughout the movie) and a cast that is not up to the task (except for MacColl and Lombardo Radice, that is), Fulci develops suspense with a commanding knowledge of the medium. This leads to some show-stopping moments such as the scene in which Peter saves Mary from premature burial: here the thrills come not only from the race against time, but by the fact that the savior might actually harm the woman he is trying to rescue, as the reporter goes at the coffin with a pickaxe whose edge penetrates inches from Mary's eye. It must be noted that Sacchetti's script features only one pickaxe blow, while Fulci *triplicates* them, like a Russian roulette with three bullets. As gratuitous and preposterous as it may be, it remains a top-notch sequence, which not only reprises the likes of Dreyer's *Vampyr*, Corman's *The Tomb of Ligeia* and Freda's *L'orribile segreto del dr. Hichcock* in a refreshing way, but also plays with Fulci's own oeuvre, from *Sette note in nero* to the splinter-in-the-pupil scene of *Zombi* 2.[9] In turn it would become a classic, openly quoted by Quentin Tarantino in *Kill Bill: Vol. 2*.[10]

The director is immensely aided by Fabio Frizzi's score. The composer had already collab-

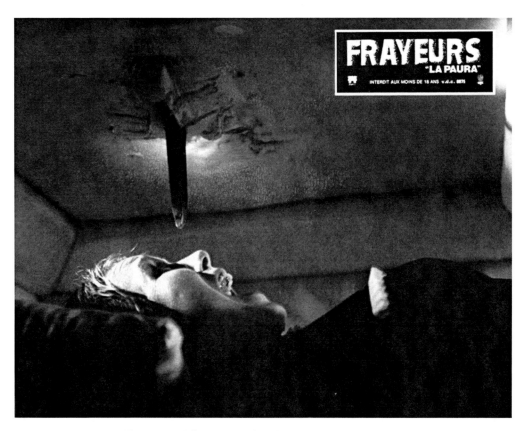

Mary (Catriona McCall) is rescued from the coffin where she was buried alive in a French lobby card for *Paura nella città dei morti viventi*.

orated with Fulci on several films since the mid–Seventies, including *Sette note in nero* and *Zombi 2*, and his work in *Paura della città dei morti viventi* ranks among his best: the unorthodox choice of instruments—such as the jangling, arpeggioing acoustic guitars in the track appropriately titled *Irrealtà di suoni* (Unreality of Sounds), or the Mellotron in *Apoteosi del mistero* (Apotheosis of Mystery)—enhances the film's dreamlike, irrational mood. Frizzi was particularly satisfied with the use of the Mellotron to convey a feeling of dread: "I was born musically at the time of the great success of The Beatles and The Rolling Stones. I knew that they had used the Mellotron (the harmonizing flutes in *The Fool on the Hill*, for instance, were a Mellotron). I inquired if I could find one in Rome, rented it and learned how to play it. The best zombie voices you can find on the planet."[11] Frizzi would reuse *Apoteosi del mistero* with some variations in his scores for *...E tu vivrai nel terrore! L'aldilà* and *Un gatto nel cervello* (1990).

These atmospheric scenes rub shoulders

with gross moments of gore (with special make-up effects by Franco Rufini and Rosario Prestopino[12]) which seem only too preoccupied to shock and disgust the viewer. Interestingly, the film's most celebrated graphic horror moments are not included in the original story nor in the CSC script. The scene with Rosie and Tommy in the car is absent in the former, which features the bit where Woody is devoured by cats in a rubbish dump instead. It can be found in the CSC draft, yet, it climaxes in a decidedly different way. After witnessing the ghastly appearance of the dead priest, the two teenagers try to drive away, but their car won't start; maggots start falling from the sky like rain, covering the windshield and windows and obscuring their sight. The vehicle is surrounded by zombies and, in a Romero-inspired image, "dozens of livid, fleshless arms penetrate inside the car," before the script cuts abruptly to another scene. There is no trace whatsoever of the scene's highlight, the infamous intestine barfing bit, which seems to have been a last-minute addition.

Bob's death, the film's most infamous gory highlight, is also quite different from the original story and the CSC script draft. Here, after Bob is discovered by Ann's father, he manages to escape, but the man shoots him in the leg and blows up his knee. The badly injured Bob is surrounded by the villagers, who tie his leg to a car's fender and drag him around. One of the boy's legs gets stuck, and the scene climaxes in the gruesome sight of Bob being graphically quartered like in a medieval ordeal, before the eyes of his torturers. Incidentally, the same scene was described in a very similar way in Sacchetti's original story: the only difference is that Bob is not shot by Ann's father, but stabbed in the leg by a little girl. In its early conception, the sequence was even closer in tone to the lynching of the *maciara* (Florinda Bolkan) at the hands of the villagers in *Non si sevizia un paperino*. It was possibly dropped due to budgetary reasons and replaced by a simpler (although even more shocking) version, in which the meek, retarded Bob has his skull drilled from side to side by the jealous father (Venantino Venantini) of the girl he was hanging out with. According to Geleng this was Sacchetti's idea.[13]

Finally, in the CSC script the zombies don't squash their victims' skulls but simply bite them (offscreen, in Sandra's case), and poor Peter Bell ends up with his throat ripped open by Sandra. The living dead's different *modus operandi* is one of the film's most significant departures from the subgenre's canon: Fulci's zombies are not driven by a pathological hunger, but by a punishing rage, which doesn't aim at the consumption of the bodies, but at the destruction of the minds.

This latter change further proves the director's willingness to detach from the Romero-inspired mayhem and follow a different approach to graphic violence. In his later horror films, however, Fulci would perfect the mixture of subtle atmosphere and over-the-top gore with much more convincing results: here, the recurring images of zombies squeezing the brains out of their unfortunate victims as if they were ripe grapefruits are shoddy and unimpressive. Even the much-discussed scene of Daniela Doria's character barfing up her own intestines doesn't live up to its fame, coming off as enthusiastic but slapdash, and perhaps more in tune with some Hong Kong oddities as, say, *Centipede horror* (1982, Keith Li), due to the actress' willingness to actually barf baby veal intestines on camera for the first part of the scene before the special effects guys turn up with a rather unconvincing replica of Doria's face.

As Fulci once claimed, "what I am really scared of are TV news. My nightmares, or Argento's, are imaginary. Whereas TV news show real nightmares lived daily by real people."[14] Not surprisingly, the film's most infamous gory highlight, Bob's atrocious death, leaves any supernatural implication aside. Fulci described it as "a cry I wanted to launch against a certain type of fascism."[15] It is an astonishing portrayal of human evil, as opposed to the ghostly curse that forms the movie's core: an act of gratuitous, extreme violence, symbolically directed to the same body part as the zombies' attacks, the brain—and therefore by extension to free, individual and independent thought. It implies not just unspeakable horrors that are far more terrifying than any revenant in the film (namely, a father's unspoken incestuous desires, a nod to Fulci's own version of *Beatrice Cenci* as well as to Sandra's early monologue in the film about incest), but also a grim meditation on the state of modern society, where savage fury and hatred are barely concealed under a façade of civilized behavior, and are pushing to come loose at any minute in the form of violent repression at the expense of the weak and the marginalized. The revolt of the undead takes in turn the form of a generational revenge: once she returns from the dead, Emily slaughters her parents, and the teenage zombies (Rosie, Bob, Tommy) assault the squalid bar where the middle-aged locals spend their time idling, chatting and drinking. But all this is barely and incoherently sketched, so much so that the living dead suddenly materialize out of nowhere and disappear likewise. Fulci and Sacchetti's following collaborations would result in much tighter scripts.

Paura nella città dei morti viventi climaxes with an extended "good vs. evil" confrontation set in a huge underground catacomb riddled with skeletons, an impressive set-piece built by Geleng at the De Paolis studios. Fulci and Sacchetti would reprise and improve upon the idea of an underground hell, a parallel world of sorts, for *...E tu vivrai nel terrore! L'aldilà*. The result is quite impressive, and the director was presumably very happy to get rid of his annoying leading man by having him dispatched by the zombies, thus promoting Carlo De Mejo's Gerry as the savant hero. But Sacchetti's early story envisioned quite a different denouement, with a sting in the tail. After dispatching Father

Thomas and apparently delivering the place from evil, Mary and Gerry walk away in a snowy landscape. She explains to him that he was the only one who could stop evil, because the spirit of Enoch is inside him. Then, suddenly, her voice and feature change, "her eyes become evil, and before Gerry can do anything she bites him savagely on the throat. Red drops of blood fall on the snow, while in Mary's eyes a smile of black triumph appears." Such a grim ending reconnected to the tradition of the Italian Gothic, with the leading lady turning into a primary force of evil (see *La maschera del demonio, I Wurdalak,* even *Estratto dagli archivi segreti della polizia di una capitale europea*) and gave sense to the references to the Book of Enoch which are lost on the screen.

Whereas the CSC script draft for *La paura* ends as follows. Just as Mary and Gerry return to the surface, they meet John-John, the little kid who is one of the few survivors of the zombie plague. "The kid runs toward them and hugs them." The End. But the film features an unexpected coda instead. Mary and Gerry's relieved faces turn into weird grimaces and the image of the kid running toward the camera suddenly slows down, freezes and cracks into a thousand pieces, accompanied by Mary's screams and the ominous sound of thunder. Black screen, end credits. This abrupt closure—decided at the eleventh hour in post-production, upon the suggestion of the editor, Vincenzo Tomassi, who noticed a sudden change of expression on De Mejo and MacColl's face near the end of the take—is both infuriating and chilling, as it arbitrarily denies any trace of a happy ending. Such a final act of annihilation and an anarchic stab at conventions is perfectly in tune with Fulci's approach to cinema, which he self-described as being a "terrorist of genres.... I'm working inside the genre, but every now and then I ignite a bomb that attempts to make the genre explode."[16] Which is exactly the case here.

Paura nella città dei morti viventi was released in Italy with a predictable V.M.18 rating, to somewhat disappointing box-office grosses of slightly less than a billion *lire,* despite a memorable press campaign: the ads featured a laughable gimmick worthy of William Castle, a warning by a "Prof. Sven Cuzak," primary of the "III Cardiology Clinic at Houston University": "... and therefore I discourage the vision of the film *Paura nella città dei morti viventi* to subjects suffering of cardiocirculatory imbalances: the strong emotions aroused by the viewing could cause considerable damage to the entire vascular system."

Critics were ambivalent toward the film. The *Corriere della Sera*'s reviewer, Giovanna Grassi, wrote ironically that "lately Lucio Fulci seems to have been ensnared by some malevolent living dead,"[17] adding that "the passage from *giallo* to horror, blow by blow, seems to harm Fulci, who relies on truculent effects and orgies of blood and gruesome murders in his attempt to relaunch Italian Fantastic cinema." The reviewer dismissed it as "incoherent and stretched beyond measure" and complained about its lack of atmosphere and bad acting, even though it praised Lombardo Radice's acting and Frizzi's score.

On the other hand, *La Stampa* hailed the film as "a *grand guignol* with class" and gave it a surprisingly positive, if rather patronizing review:

> Until now, Lucio Fulci's 20-year-old film career had dissipated amid "popular" products, appreciated by the less demanding audiences and mistreated or neglected by the critics. They were light efforts, either starring Franchi & Ingrassia or belonging to the sexy thread (*Una sull'altra*) or the Italian thriller (*Non si sevizia un paperino*).
>
> With *Paura nella città dei morti viventi*, Fulci seemingly wants us to forgive his earlier slips into bad taste, vulgarity and an often-inattentive routine. He has made a movie which, although not recommended for easily impressionable viewers, is the sign of a reached expressive maturity.... The story has an engrossing pace. It is a succession of events that progressively create a nightmarish atmosphere, and Fulci, like a great puppeteer, pulls the strings, at times even allowing himself some figurative preciousness. His film ends up becoming a true *grand guignol* spectacle, with the bloody and gruesome scenes typical of the genre.[18]

It was a sign the director was starting to earn critical recognition in his home country that went beyond the usual bias toward horror films. Soon the younger critics, such as Claudio Carabba, would openly praise his work, giving way to a gradual critical reevaluation.

The film was distributed theatrically all over Europe, including the Netherlands, Spain,[19] Portugal and West Germany. The German edit was sensibly shorter, as the distribution company Alemannia/Arabella removed about ten minutes of expository and dialogues scenes to make the story faster, although the violent scenes were left uncut. It was a huge box-office hit. On the other hand, the U.K. theatrical version, passed by the BBFC on December 10, 1981, was cut by one minute by the distributor Eagle Films, to remove the drill sequence.[20] In Great Britain, the film (and its director) found one of its staunchest defenders, *Starburst*'s Alan Jones, who praised its "claustrophobic atmosphere full of menace" and called Fulci "a master of … manipulation…. At this stage in the game his talent cannot be called merely accidental."[21] *Film and Filming*'s Julian Petley drew a favorable comparison, calling the film "reminiscent of Tourneur … in its greater reliance on the power of suggestion, its crepuscular air and its conjuration of a nightmarish Other World out of simple everyday reality."[22] But most critics were not impressed, to put it mildly, even more so on the other side of the Atlantic.

Released in the United States in May 1983, Fulci's film was originally advertised as *Twilight of the Dead* but, following a cease and desist order on the part of United Film Distribution Company, the U.S. theatrical distributor (Motion Picture Marketing) pulled poster and prints and released the movie with the title *The Gates of Hell*. Reviews were generally scathing ("No one with any hope of being entertained should waste their time or money to see it"[23]) if not downright offensive:

> When I want to see a badly dubbed idiotic Italian cheapie, I'll take Steve Reeves, thanks. I will not—willingly—take something like *The Gates of Hell*, a badly dubbed, idiotic sleaze fest with nothing to offer but an abundance of filmed animal innards. The only interesting aspect is watching the mostly European cast try to adjust their Continental cadences to director Lucio Fulci's muddled vision of Middle America—sort of a heartland smothered in mozzarella.[24]

In West Germany, *Paura nella città dei morti viventi* became the target of a notorious press campaign after the broadcasting in June 1984 of the sensationalist TV reportage *Mama, Papa, Zombie—Horror für den Hausgebrauch* on the channel ZDF. The 45-minute film, directed by Claus Bienfait, denounced it as an exemplary case of the ultra-violent movies available to minors in the home video market: in fact, the German motion picture rating system, FSK, only examined theatrical releases, whereas videos could be borrowed virtually by people of all ages. Rather than a documentary, *Mama, Papa, Zombie* was closer in concept to a *Mondo movie*, as

it featured several patently fake interviews (among the interviewees were 6-year-old kids reciting lines they had obviously memorized, such as "If nobody is decapitated, a movie is boring"), interspersed with gory footage from horror films—including titles such as *Mother's Day* (1980, Charles Kaufman) and *Mangiati vivi!*—commented by a teacher who warned her students' parents of the impending danger represented by horror videotapes. Some of the most violent scenes in Fulci's film were included.

Mama, Papa, Zombie triggered a wave of seizures against horror videos which marked a turn of the screw in the history of German film censorship. In the early 1980s, the German distributors had had a rather unusual freedom, and such titles as *L'aldilà*, *Maniac* and *Cannibal Ferox* were released theatrically uncut, but after *Mama, Papa, Zombie* all this ended abruptly. Fulci's film was banned and prints of the 1983 German Euro Video VHS *Ein Zombie hing am Glockenseil* (A Zombie Hung on the Bell Rope)—running 80 minutes and 36 seconds—were confiscated by order of the District Court of Munich dated July 11, 1986. An abridged version, *Ein Toter hing am Glockenseil* (A Dead Body Hung on the Bell Rope), running 75 minutes and 40 seconds, was released in 1988 on the GM-Vilm label: it was missing complete dialogue sequences and most of the gore (the vomit scene was only hinted at, but part of the drilling scene was still visible, namely the bit when the drill comes out of the victim's head). This too was banned and confiscated by order of the District Court of Munich dated May 26, 1988. A third, slightly more trimmed version, *Eine Leiche hing am Glockenseil* (A Corpse Hung on the Bell Rope) also on the GM-Vilm label, came out in 1991 and was banned by order of the District Court of Munich dated January 5, 2001. A fourth, *Ein Kadaver hing am Glockenseil*, was finally released with an FSK-16 certificate.

France, as it had happened with Riccardo Freda and Mario Bava, was the country that embraced more enthusiastically Fulci as an *auteur*. One of the key moments in his career was *Paura nella città dei morti viventi*'s screening at the 10th "Festival international du film fantastique et de science-fiction" in Paris (as *Frayeurs*),[25] where it was given the "Grand Prix du Public" (the audience award). Fulci used to recall with great pride an episode that happened after the screening: a girl in a wheelchair approached him from the audience and thanked him "for the horrors that you made me experience during the film. They made me feel free. Not like in the outside world."[26] An anecdote which summarizes perfectly the director's concept of the horror film as a cathartic shock.

The bi-monthly magazine *L'Écran fantastique* gave ample coverage to the film. A raving one-page review (with stills from Lombardo Radice's death scene) called it a "definitive film [on zombies] after which it will be useless to revisit the same subject matter, and which ranks Lucio Fulci among the best craftsmen of a certain branch of the *fantastique*."[27] On the same issue, the magazine's editor-in-chief Robert Schlockoff conducted a four-page interview with the director, which consecrated him as "the new master of horror." At over 50 years old, Lucio Fulci had become Italy's "poet of the macabre."

NOTES

1. Dardano Sacchetti interviewed, in www.davinotti.com (http://www.davinotti.com/index.php?option=com_content&task=view&id=70)

2. Paolo Albiero and Giacomo Cacciatore, *Il terrorista dei generi. Tutto il cinema di Lucio Fulci—Seconda edizione aggiornata* (Palermo: Leima, 2015), 251.

3. *Ibid.*, 254.

4. *Ibid.*, 257.

5. According to the Public Cinematographic Register, shooting started on March 24, but the date (reported to the register for bureaucratic purposes) shall likely be postponed by a few weeks.

6. Michele Romagnoli, *L'occhio del testimone* (Bologna: Granata Press, 1992), 41.

7. Sacchetti interviewed, in www.davinotti.com.

8. The original story is summarized and discussed in Manlio Gomarasca and Davide Pulici, "La paura dell'aldilà," *Nocturno Cinema* #115, March 2012, 66–69.

9. The scene features porn actor Michael Gaunt (born Michael J. Dattorre) as one of the gravediggers. The other one is the blond Perry Pirkanen, one of the leads in Deodato's *Cannibal Holocaust* and Lenzi's *Cannibal Ferox*.

10. Besides the premature burial scene in *Kill Bill: Vol. 2*, Tarantino included another passing reference to Fulci's film in *Kill Bill: Vol. 1*, when Gogo Yubari (Chiaki Kuriyama) dies crying tears of blood.

11. Alessandro Tordini, *Così nuda così violenta. Enciclopedia della musica nei mondi neri del cinema italiano* (Rome: Arcana, 2012), 205.

12. Unlike what some sources state, Gino and Giannetto De Rossi and Maurizio Trani did *not* work on the special effects for the film, save for Giannetto De Rossi's uncredited help (he took a cast of Giovanni Lombardo Radice's head) for the skull-drilling scene.

13. Albiero and Cacciatore, *Il terrorista dei generi*, 257.

14. John Martin, "Lucio Fulci: L'Edgar Poe du 7ème art," *L'Écran fantastique* #149, May 1996, 28–34.

15. Robert Schlockoff, "Entretien avec Lucio Fulci," *L'Écran fantastique* #16, January 1981, 20.

16. Marcello Garofalo and Antonietta De Lillo, "Il cinema del dubbio. Intervista a Lucio Fulci," in Manlio Gomarasca and Davide Pulici (eds.), *L'opera al nero. Il cinema di Lucio Fulci. Nocturno Dossier #3*, September 2002, 18.

17. G.Gs. [Giovanna Grassi], "Con gli zombies nella città sconvolta," *Corriere della Sera*, August 25, 1980.

18. O.G., "Terribili morti resuscitano e uccidono nel *grand guignol* (con classe) di Fulci," *La Stampa*, August 17, 1980.

19. According to the official ministerial data, it was seen by 185,556 spectators and grossed an amount corresponding to 177,061 Euro (http://infoicaa.mecd.es/CatalogoICAA/Peliculas/Detalle?Pelicula=580551).

20. The same version was released on video before 1984. Subsequently, when it was submitted to the BBFC for a video certificate, further cuts were made to eliminate Daniela Doria's intestinal vomit scene and the brain squashing bits, for a total of 2 minutes and 21 seconds. The film later passed uncut in 2001.

21. Alan Jones, *Starburst* #48, 1982.

22. Julian Petley, "City of the Living Dead," *Films and Filming* #333, June 1982.

23. Dick Fleming, *The Daily Times*, Salisbury, Maryland, September 11, 1983.

24. Eleanor Ringel, *The Atlanta Constitution*, September 19, 1983.

25. Other Italian films screened in competition the festival were *Apocalypse domani*, *Contamination*, *Macabro*, and Ugo Tognazzi's dystopian drama *I viaggiatori della sera*. Fulci's *Sette note in nero* was screened out of competition, together with Argento's *Profondo rosso*.

26. Romagnoli, *L'occhio del testimone*, 24.

27. Pierre Gires, "Frayeurs," *L'Écran fantastique* #16, January 1981, 17.

1981

L'altro Inferno (*The Other Hell*, a.k.a. *The Guardian of Hell*)

D: Stefan Oblowsky [Bruno Mattei] [and Claudio Fragasso, uncredited]. S: Bruno Mattei, Claudio Fragasso; SC: Claudio Fragasso; DOP: Giuseppe Berardini (LV-Luciano Vittori); M: Goblin (Ed. Grandi firme della canzone/Bixio C.E.M.S.A.); E: Liliana Serra; AD: Maurizio Tanfani; MU: Giuseppe Ferranti; Hair: Maria Teresa Carrera; ACO: Claudio Bissattini; APD: Francesco Raffa; C: Sergio Melaranci; AC: Luca Odevaine; W: Elda Chinellato; KG: Mario Boccanegra; ChEl: Roberto Roberti; SP: Domenico Cattarinich; SO: Paolo Picchi; Mix: Danilo Moroni,

Luigi Di Fiore. *Cast*: Franca Stoppi (Mother Vincenza), Carlo De Mejo (Father Valerio), Francesca Carmeno (Elisa), Susan Forget [Susanna Fargetta] (Sister Rosaria), Frank Garfeeld [Franco Garofalo] (Boris), Paola Montenero (Sister Assunta), Sandy Samuel [Daniela Samueli] (Catatonic Nun), Andrew Ray [Andrea Aureli] (Father Inardo); *uncredited*: Dolores Calò (Nun), Tom Felleghy (The Cardinal), Simone Mattioli (Priest), Pupita Lea Scuderoni (Nun). *PROD*: Arcangelo Picchi for Cinemec Produzione S.r.l.; *PS*: Silvio Colecchia; *PSe*: Giovanna Quadrini; *ADM*: Pierluigi Tarabusi. *Country*: Italy. Filmed at Convento di Santa Priscilla (Rome), Cimitero delle Fontanelle (Naples) and Icet De Paolis studios (Milan). *Running time*: 94 minutes (m. 2582); theatrical version: 88 minutes. Visa n. 75322 (7.23.1980); *Rating*: V.M.18. *Release dates*: 1.22.1981 (Italy), 10.2.1981 (France), 12.4.1981 (UK), 5.17.1983 (Spain), 9.6.1985 (USA). *Distribution*: Accord Cinematografica. *Domestic gross*: n.a. *Also known as*: *Terror en el convento* (Spain), *L'autre enfer*; *Le couvent infernal* (France).

Note: the tracks *Dottor Frankestein, Notte, Le cascate di Viridiana* are taken from the Goblin LPs "Roller" and "Il fantastico viaggio del bagarozzo Mark."

Strange and frightening things are happening at a convent headed by the stern Mother Vincenza: necromancy rituals take place in the vaults, and mysterious deaths ensue. The Mother Superior calls an exorcist, Father Inardo, who in turn asks the help of a younger priest, Father Valerio. As the latter finds out, the convent is inhabited by an elusive presence, a young woman who falls in love with him. After witnessing more horrible murders, and escaping death himself, Father Valerio discovers that the young woman, Elisa, is Mother Vincenza's illegitimate daughter, and was disfigured at an early age after being thrown into a hot cauldron by a nun. Elisa, who has strong telekinetic powers, was exploited by Mother Vincenza, who used her to dispatch all those who learned about her secret. Now that he knows the truth, Father Valerio too becomes the target of Mother Vincenza's fury...

Shot in six weeks, at the same time, on the same location and with part of the same cast as *La vera storia della monaca di Monza* (1980), *L'altro Inferno* offers a good example of Bruno Mattei's approach to filmmaking and his working methods. He explained that "*La Monaca* was outsourced by [distributor] Stefano Film. Practically, we were the executive producers. There

had to be a profit on the budget and I suggested we invest it in a second movie, which would be 100% ours. And so, we reinvested the profit on *L'altro Inferno*. We shot them both in parallel. When you shoot two movies in one, the saving is substantial."[1]

La vera storia della monaca di Monza was an erotic retelling of the story of the Nun of Monza, included in Alessandro Manzoni's 1827 novel *I promessi sposi* (a.k.a. *The Betrothed*), along the lines of the so-called "nunsploitation" thread which included such titles as *Interno di un convento* (1978, Walerian Borowczyk) and *Immagini di un convento* (1979, Joe D'Amato [Aristide Massaccesi]). *L'altro Inferno* was instead conceived and marketed as a rip-off of *Inferno*, to the point that the title font in the opening credits is roughly the same as Argento's film.

Shooting took place at a convent built in the 1920s, above the ancient Roman catacombs of Santa Priscilla, with Fragasso acting as a *de facto* second unit director, if not even more, according to his own words.

> Upstairs, Bruno was shooting *La vera storia della monaca di Monza*, which was the "A" movie, so to speak, whereas in the vaults I was shooting the "B" movie, *L'altro Inferno*.... In fact, there was a real interchange because the actors were the same and so they moved from one set to the other, going upstairs and downstairs depending on the film in which they were requested to act. In short, they were two movies tangled together ... you know, sometimes I had to go upstairs where Bruno was shooting to "steal" cans of film! I needed it to finish my movie, and often I borrowed other material secretly. I was given very little, he had everything.[2]

If we take Fragasso's words for granted, then, the process was the same as other movies the duo made together, namely the W.I.P. diptych *Violenza in un carcere femminile* (1982) and *Blade Violent* (1983), and the Westerns *Bianco Apache* (1986) and *Scalps* (1986). On the other hand, Mattei always maintained that Fragasso was always an assistant director on these, and nothing more.

That said, the analogies between *L'altro Inferno* and its model are limited to the title and some visuals or situations, which is understandable. According to Rome's Public Cinematographic Register, filming started on October 23, 1979, and lasted through October and November, when very little was known about Argento's film besides its title and some set stills. Most notably, *Inferno*'s alchemist's lair is reprised, albeit in a

Italian lobby card for *L'altro Inferno* (1981). Note the use of a similar font as Argento's film.

minor key, in the scenes set in the necromancer's lab (filmed, according to Mattei, inside Villa Mussolini, in an old shack all repainted in black and silver). The sight of a boiling cauldron becomes also the link to the solution of the mystery, evoked by a childish drawing *à la Profondo rosso*; the moment where Father Valerio (Carlo De Mejo) notices a crazy nun combing her hair in front of a mirror recalls the scene of the spell in *Suspiria*; Franco Garofalo's repellent caretaker Boris behaves toward animals with the same cruelty as Kazanian, killing a cat for no reason (and decapitating a rooster, in one of those lousy bits of animal cruelty not uncommon in Italian films of the period) and as a comeuppance he ends up with his throat ripped apart by his own dog like the pianist (Flavio Bucci) in *Suspiria*. On top of that, here and there Mattei and Fragasso try to color the scene with schemes akin to those seen in Argento's 1977 film, as far as their scarce budget would allow. Finally, the score features ample extracts from two Goblin albums, *Roller* (1976) and *Il fantastico viaggio del bagarozzo Mark* (1978): the music scarcely blends with the visuals, and often feels like a

botched job. As Fragasso recalled, "we called Goblin because they were very fashionable, and asked them to write the music. But they asked for a lot of money, and we got a deal being able to obtain the possibility of using stock music with a few modifications done specifically for the film."[3] Mattei's explanation was simpler: "I am very good friends with Carlo Bixio, who was their music publisher, and he gave me all the music I wanted...."[4]

Besides the odd Argento reference, the story—concocted by Mattei and Fragasso, with the latter penning the script by himself—draws primarily from other sources, namely, as Mattei admitted, William Friedkin's 1973 classic *The Exorcist* ("It was a time when it still had an impact"), Brian De Palma's *Carrie* and Richard Franklin's *Patrick*. The latter had been a surprise hit in Italy, thanks also to an aggressive distribution campaign and the replacing of Brian May's soundtrack with music by Goblin (like Dario Argento had done with Romero's *Martin*, released in Italy as *Wampyr*), and spawned an explicit sequel/rip-off, *Patrick vive ancora*. Elisa, the disfigured girl with telekinetic powers who may well be the Devil's daughter, is a mixture of the characters in De Palma and Franklin's films, and her confrontation with her mother, played with crazed relish by Franca Stoppi, reprises *Carrie*'s climax almost to the letter. Finally, not to leave any stone unturned, a little zombie movie touch was added toward the ending for good measure.

The script blends the various borrowings into a weird mystery plot, where one is never sure whether the horrible events are the result of the devil at play or are conducted by a devilish but human presence. In this sense, the film's best scene is the one where the investigator, Father Vincenzo, listens to the confession of an unknown woman (who we later learn is Elisa) who tells him she is in love with him, and barely escapes an attempt on his life, as a mysterious hand drives a knife through the confessional. The priest runs out, only to find himself in the middle of the morning mass, with all the nuns singing in a choir in church; he turns back to the confessional, and sees the knife still vibrating in the wood—a moment rendered with an elegant change of focus which is one of the film's few attempts at stylish direction.

Making use of a Gothic staple as the convent location (but with barely any nod to the literary tradition of Ann Radcliffe and Matthew Lewis, for that matter), Fragasso and Mattei draw heavily from Catholic-related themes such as sin and sexual repression, and play with religion and blasphemy in a way not unlike the popular serial novels of the late 1800 and early 1900 (with a nod to Manzoni's story as well). This prompted the newspaper *La Stampa* to pair *L'altro Inferno* with William Peter Blatty's directorial debut *The Ninth Configuration* (1980), released in Italy around the same time, labeling the two films as "fantatheological" in an article titled "*Crisi mistica dell'horror-cinema*" ("Mystical crisis of horror cinema").[5] Curiously, in the interview with Franca Stoppi that accompanied the piece, and which described her as an ex-mannequin-turned actress, *L'altro Inferno* was mistakenly mentioned as Stoppi's debut—whereas she had debuted in 1976, in Dino Risi's *Telefoni bianchi*, and had played one of the main roles in *Buio omega* (1979). The actress didn't correct the interviewer. "'Were you satisfied with making your film debut in the role of a nun, in a story which mixes parapsychology and horror?' 'Every chance is good to make a debut, provided that the character offers a minimum of opportunity to give one's best.'"[6]

Stoppi and Franco Garofalo bring a demented intensity to their roles, whereas porn actress Sandy Samuel (a.k.a. Daniela Samueli) pops up in a non-speaking part as a nun gone crazy, but she does not take her clothes off. Carlo De Mejo looks rather uncomfortable as the alcoholic Father Vincenzo, who records his soliloquies on a video camera and comes across the solution by way of some sort of "telepathic broadcast" not unlike the one experienced by the protagonists in John Carpenter's *Prince of Darkness* (1987), in one of the script's most bizarre twists. As for Paola Montenero, she appears only in the pre-credit sequence set in the convent's vaults and delivers a monologue which reaches new heights in trash ("The genitals are a door to evil! The vagina, the uterus, the womb … the labyrinth that leads to hell … the devil's tools…"). The scene, barely related to the rest of the film, was performed by Montenero (who played a role in *La vera storia della monaca di Monza* but was not cast in *L'altro Inferno*) as a personal favor to Mattei.[7]

On top of that, the few gore scenes are cheap and crude: in the prologue, Montenero starts an anatomy lesson on a dead female body by sticking a scalpel in the corpse's crotch, and then rips the ovaries from her womb with her bare hands. But the low budget severely undermines the makers' efforts: when Elisa's disfigured face is finally revealed, Pino Ferrante's make-up is so poor that it looks like the actress has smeared her mouth with peanut butter. Another embarrassing moment is the flashback where the newborn Elisa is thrown into a boiling pot by the Mother Superior, on paper a truly shocking moment that shows how far Italian cinema could venture in terms of sheer cinematic excess. It was Fragasso's daughter, three months old at the time, who had the honor of playing the Devil's infant offspring: "The baby was quiet while she was in her mother's arms, but as soon as Franca Stoppi picked her up she started crying. So, I had to repeat the scene many times, until eventually she fell asleep and I could film her quietly. Luckily, I had already done a close-up of her blue eyes, like those of the character as an adult."[8] Of course, the child was replaced by a baby doll for the scene's climax, as no viewer will fail to notice.

Predictably, the film was given a V.M.18 rating, but the running time indicated in the official papers differs from the version released in theaters, amounting to about 94 minutes instead of

88. Mattei signed it as "Stefan Oblowsky," the same a.k.a. as in *La vera storia della monaca di Monza*, where the Eastern European sounding surname was supposed to recall such masters of erotic cinema as Borowczyk.[9]

Even though the screening certificate dated July 1980, *L'altro Inferno* was released in Italy only the following year to poor business, signaling that the blatant filiation to Argento's original was not enough to guarantee commercial success, and that, most of all, unlike a decade earlier with the many *gialli* with animal-related titles, it was not possible to build a *filone* based on Argento's Gothics. Times were changing, and audiences were looking for a different type of horror film, with more convincing special effects and better production values: *L'altro Inferno* was openly derided by the audience when screened at the Trieste Film Festival. However, it was sold in Spain[10] and France and over the years it became something of a cult film. It even surfaced theatrically in the U.S., in the mid–1980s, as *The Guardian of Hell*.

Mattei and Fragasso's next venture was the gory zombie film *Virus*, released in Spain in November 1980 and in Italy in August 1981.

NOTES

1. Manlio Gomarasca and Davide Pulici, "Intervista a Bruno Mattei," in Manlio Gomarasca and Davide Pulici (eds.), *Il sopravvissuto. Guida al cinema di Bruno Mattei. Nocturno Dossier* #45, April 2006, 16.
2. Federico Caddeo and Laurent Lopéré, "Passion devoreuse," *Mad Movies* #175, May 2005, p. 72.
3. *Ibid.*
4. Gomarasca and Pulici, "Intervista a Bruno Mattei," 16.
5. Lamberto Antonelli, "Crisi mistica dell'horror-cinema," *La Stampa*, January 9, 1981.
6. Lamberto Antonelli, "L'ex mannequin si fa suora," *La Stampa*, January 9, 1981.
7. Gomarasca and Pulici, "Intervista a Bruno Mattei," 16.
8. Caddeo and Lopéré, "Passion devoreuse."
9. "Probably a pseudonym," cautiously conceded the reviewer in *Corriere della Sera* before slaughtering the film, noting that "in these Italian subproducts we have now reached the point, with a procedure akin to pornographic flicks, that the plot had been reduced to less than an accessory to a series—almost uninterupted and senseless—of gory effects." L.A. [Leonardo Autera], "L'orrore entra in convento," *Corriere della Sera*, July 13, 1981.
10. According to the official ministerial data, it was seen by 65,398 spectators and grossed an amount corresponding to 71,096 Euro. (http://infoicaa.mecd.es/CatalogoICAA/Peliculas/Detalle?Pelicula=240382). It must be noted that the Icaa catalog dates the Spanish release to May 17, 1983, and not July 1, 1981 (as IMDb does).

Black Cat (Gatto nero) (*The Black Cat*)

D: Lucio Fulci. *S*: Biagio Proietti, based on the short story by Edgar Allan Poe; *SC*: Biagio Proietti, Lucio Fulci; *DOP*: Sergio Salvati (Technovision—Eastmancolor, Telecolor); *M*: Pino Donaggio, conducted by Natale Massara (Ed. Zita); *E*: Vincenzo Tomassi; *PD*: Francesco Calabrese; *ArtD*: Massimo Antonello Geleng; *CO*: Massimo Lentini; *2ndUD*: Roberto Giandalia; *AD*: Victor Tourjansky, David Del Bufalo; *C*: Franco Bruni, Roberto Forges Davanzati; *AC*: Maurizio Lucchini; *MU*: Franco Di Girolamo; *AMU*: Rosario Prestopino; *Hair*: Maria Pia Crapanzano; *SP*: Gianfranco Massa; *SO*: Ugo Celani; *B*: Eros Giustini; *1stAE*: Rita Antonelli; *2ndAE*: Pietro Tomassi; *SE*: Paolo Ricci; *SOE*: Fernando Caso, Alvaro Gramigna; *MA/STC*: Nazzareno Cardinali; *ChEl*: Alfredo Fedeli; *KG*: Ennio Brizzolari; *W*: Palmina Tacconi; *SS*: Daniela Tonti. *Cast*: Patrick Magee (Prof. Robert Miles), Mimsy Farmer (Jill Trevers), David Warbeck (Inspector Gorley), Al Cliver [Pierluigi Conti] (Sgt. Wilson), Dagmar Lassander (Lilian Grayson), Bruno Corazzari (Ferguson), Geoffrey Copleston (Inspector Flynn), Daniela Doria [Daniela Cormio] (Maureen Grayson), Vito Passeri (Warehouse Watchman). *PROD*: Giulio Sbarigia for Selenia Cinematografica S.r.l. (Rome); *PM*: Ennio Onorati; *GM*: Renato Angiolini; *UM*: Antonio Da Padova, Tommaso Pantano; *ADM*: Adalberto Spadoni. *Country*: Italy. Filmed on location in England (West Wycombe, Hambledon) and at RPA—Elios, Cine International and De Paolis In.Ci.R. Studios (Rome). *Running time*: 92 minutes (m. 2513). Visa n. 76321 (3.9.1981); *Rating*: V.M.14. *Release dates*: 4.4.1981 (Italy), 1.7.1982 (Netherlands), 5.14.1982 (Norway), 3.9.1983 (France), 2.10.1984 (USA); *Distribution*: Italian International Film (Italy); World Northal (USA). *Domestic gross*: 433,967,662 *lire. Also known as*: *I kattens klør* (Norway), *Le chat noir* (France), *El gato negro* (Spain).

In a small village in the English countryside, solitary researcher Robert Miles spends his days in the company of a black cat, recording the voices of the dead. One after the other, the villagers die in strange and gruesome ways: a young man loses his life in a car accident; two young lovers, Maureen and Stan, are asphyxiated in the railroad car where they had been looking for some intimacy; Ferguson, the local drunkard, falls to his death from a scaffold, and Maureen's mother Lilian dies in the fire that engulfs her house. Inspector Gorley of Scotland Yard realizes that all these deaths have something in common and he begins to investigate. A young American photographer named Jill has found a cat's footprints near many of the bodies and starts suspecting that Miles has something to do with the crimes. When Gorley remains victim of a strange accident and news of his death spreads, Jill decides to continue investigations alone…

"I hate cats. They are ingratiating animals, they think only about themselves and they are sly."[1] Lucio Fulcio didn't hide his dislike for felines, and even titled one of his films *Un gatto nel cervello* (A Cat in the Brain) to depict his on-screen alter ego's descent into madness. Moreover, he often employed animals as a subject or object of horror, from the infamous dog vivisection scene and the bats attack in *Una lucertola con la pelle di donna* (a.k.a. *A Lizard in a Woman's Skin*, 1971) to the suffocated cat in *La casa nel tempo*. That said, one might think that *Black Cat* was born as a personal project, a way to dig into the director's own obsessions and make a movie about men and animals the way Mario Bava would have done (as in *Reazione a catena*, 1971). Truth is, as Fulci himself admitted, *Black Cat* was a work-for-hire assignment—or, to be more precise, a favor to a producer friend, Giulio Sbarigia.

Of course, Fulci loved Edgar Allan Poe. But he was also very well aware that the 1843 short story *The Black Cat* was quite difficult to adapt into a feature length film, being more apt for a short or an anthology, as in Roger Corman's *Tales of Terror* (1962) or Dario Argento's episode in *Due occhi diabolici* (1990). Previous adaptations had been very loose, and sometimes the source wasn't even mentioned, as in the Ernesto Gastaldi-scripted thriller *Il tuo vizio è una stanza chiusa e solo io ne ho la chiave* (1972, Sergio Martino). Usually, they retained only the basic elements of the story and the final twist, in which the narrator finds out, much to his horror, that he has buried alive his hated cat together with the body of the woman he has assassinated. But sometimes all that was left of the original was the title, and a black cat wandering around in some scenes, as in Edgar G. Ulmer's outstanding 1934 film of the same name.

Fulci got to work on a pre-existing script, penned by Biagio Proietti. After his work on the TV mini-series *I racconti fantastici di Edgar Allan Poe* (1979, Daniele D'Anza),[2] Proietti had been summoned by Sbarigia to write a movie based on Poe's work. As the scriptwriter explained,

I moved away from the original story … because it wasn't very cinematic. Since one of my interests was the relationship with one's sixth sense—even though I don't believe in it, I'm fascinated by it from a narrative point of view—I invented this character with paranormal powers, who is in touch with the unearthly world, and we inserted this Poe thing in it … the black cat was evil, the executor of his occult desires; there was a split between good, that is, what he did consciously, and evil, which was his subconscious.[3]

Proietti's interpretation is admittedly offbeat but close to the original core. Poe's *The Black Cat* is a story about crime and punishment, as many of the Baltimore-based writer's works; but unlike Dostoyevsky, Poe's tales had guilt and remorse turn into paranoid, horrific elements which allowed the writer to meditate on the inner nature of human evil, and Poe's feline was a projection of the man's darkest impulses, hidden and barely disguised, which eventually come to the fore and give away his real nature. Sbarigia had Fulci in mind as the director from the start, and the story was close to the filmmaker's world.

What interested me in this tale was to comment on the relationship between a man and a cat, with the latter being like the man's inner house. The two characters are identical, even though the cat is to win: for the cat may be cruel, but after all he is only the judge, the conscience of this man. The man hates the cat, but, like in the story, he can't kill him, because how could one kill his own sick and tortured soul? Impossible. We often try to kill off our bad conscience, to no avail.[4]

The director liked Proietti's script and suggested some changes and additions (such as the fire scene, possibly a homage to Corman), and Fulvio Lucisano's distribution company I.I.F. granted a substantial advance. At first, according to *Variety*, the film was to be an Italian/British co-production, with Sbarigia teaming up with none other than Harry Alan Towers, and shooting was to take place in Canada. Towers even claimed that he and Sbarigia were going to co-produce a series of Poe adaptations "with a Northern American look and with Italian visual quality."[5] But eventually Towers backed out and Sbarigia carried out the project alone.

According to Rome's Public Cinematographic Register, filming started on July 28, 1980[6] with the working title *Il gatto nero di Park Lane* and lasted eight weeks, mostly in England (Miles' house was located in the suburbs of London), with only one scene filmed in Rome, the man falling to his death on a bed of spikes, shot in an abandoned furnace. A couple of years earlier, on *Alien* (1979), Ridley Scott and his crew had gone to a great deal of trouble to shoot the scenes featuring Jonesy, the crew's cat, and had to employ four felines during filming. Fulci claimed that he opted for a more practical solution: an animatronic cat was built for the scenes that required specific movements, while a second unit headed by Roberto Giandalia and cameraman Roberto Forges Davanzati shot 7,000 meters of film, studying every possible movement of a real feline.[7] According to Sergio Salvati, however, five cats were employed, and each had a specific ability. It was Giandalia who shot the impressive credit sequence.

The casting of Patrick Magee came after a series of refusals. Fulci's first choice for Professor Miles was Peter Cushing: the British actor was sent the script in May 1980, and, as film scholar David Miller notes, "he meticulously annotated it with costume requirements and instructions to himself on his performance ('Play Miles oddly. Slightly mad to start with')."[8] But his observations—such as the necessity of a vet to be "standing by" when filming scenes involving the cat, so as to avoid any cruelty to animals—also provide a likely reason why he eventually backed out. Fulci's reputation as a director specialized in gory horror films must have played a part in the decision as well … unless Cushing was still haunted by the memory of the laughably bad *The Uncanny*, another horror movie about feline revenge he shot in 1977. The *Variety* article mentioned Donald Pleasence as the lead, who allegedly demanded too much money,[9] then Richard Johnson (in what would have been his second teaming with the director after *Zombi 2*) was briefly considered too. Eventually Fulci settled for Magee, whom he had admired on stage in London, playing Faust.

The British actor, whose notorious bad temper had become aggravated by his drinking problem, proved very difficult to work with, as the director admitted. Fulci's d.o.p. Sergio Salvati was adamant that Magee was constantly drunk on set: he was still effective for the role, but somewhat slow to work with, and Fulci—who spoke little English, and was notoriously cruel to actors he didn't like—had a field day teasing him with a whole array of nasty Italian expressions.[10] As for the director, in an interview he

The stylized American poster for Lucio Fulci's *Black Cat* (1981).

even claimed to have beaten his lead, after Magee had sexually harassed the script girl.[11] *Black Cat* was one of Magee's last movie roles. Around the same time, he appeared in another offbeat Gothic adaptation, Walerian Borowczyk's *Docteur Jekyll et les femmes* (1981), before his untimely death in August 1982, at only 60.

The trio of leads was completed by Mimsy Farmer and David Warbeck (in his first Fulci film), and the cast included also the director's regular Al Cliver (in a secondary role as a bumbling country cop), Bruno Corazzari, Fulci's favorite victim Daniela Doria, and ex-sexy starlet Dagmar Lassander. Cliver recalled the director's mocking attitude towards the latter: "I remember that at a certain point we had to shoot a scene where Lassander had to get off a motorboat and walk away quickly.… Dagmar started wiggling exuberantly, and Fulci yelled on the megaphone: 'Ms. Lassander, this is a horror movie, not an erotic flick!'"[12] For her part, the actress called Fulci a very difficult director to work with. He demanded absurd things from the actors. In *Black Cat* there was a scene with a fire, and he wanted me to run through the flames and come out a door. I pointed out to him that if the door didn't open, I'd be trapped amid the flames. In reply, he started yelling like mad. We shot the scene and what I had foreseen duly happened. Not only the door didn't open, but it fell on me.... Anyway, it wasn't Lucio's fault. The problem was that he asked actors to do things that were dangerous even for an expert stuntman.[13]

The theme of communicating with the beyond through scientific devices recalls partly Richard Matheson's 1971 novel *Hell House* and pushes the film toward territories akin to Pupi Avati's *Zeder*, with a scientist obsessed with the afterlife and the possibility of explaining its mysteries by way of technical measurements. But the presence of the British thesp adds an odd note, as it recalls Samuel Beckett's one-act play *Krapp's Last Tape*, which had been written specifically for him in 1957. In Beckett's play, Magee played the 69-year-old titular character, who records his daily life events, thoughts and moods on tape, and meditates on the meaning (or lack thereof) of his existence. In Fulci's film, he looks like an embittered and imbibed version of Krapp, clinging to his tape recorder and immersed in the voices he hears, isolated and emarginated from the living and morbidly attached to the world of the dead.

Had Fulci and Proietti played their riff on Poe's tale as a one-character story about a man's vengeance against humanity, the result would have been much more convincing. Instead, the bland mystery plot, which includes a predictable series of violent deaths, is too repetitive to be involving. Moreover, the contrast between Miles and Jill (the latter, being a photographer, is therefore attached to a vision of life where only visible facts and events matter) is mechanical and supported by throwaway dialogue, thus failing to convey the necessary tension and dread. On top of that, as noted by some critics, "the essence of Poe's story, the relationship between the man and the animal—exclusive, obsessive and belonging to the realm of the Fantastic—fades; and the priceless ambiguity between real events and the projection of the subconscious, which was the true matrix of terror, disappears."[14]

Dubbing director Pino Colizzi, who also took care of the Italian dialogue, recalled that often during post-production he had to fix plot holes together with editor Vincenzo Tomassi:

The scripts for those films were very poor and often things didn't add up, and since I took care of the dialogue I had to fix them … the dialogue writer doesn't meet the scriptwriter. He starts working afterwards, when the film is finished, and when things don't add up, a scene or a detail are missing, he must find a solution and ask the editor, "Do you have a bit when, say, he runs and goes to the phone?" If Tomassi had it, we were good, or else I'd call Fulci, who often would still be on the set: "Lucio, I need you to shoot a bit where we see this and that." And he, invariably, replied: "Don't break my balls, what d'ya need that for? What are ya goin' to do with it?" But then he shot it, we developed it and edited it.... Sometimes, when we were screening [the rough cut] Lucio didn't know why a certain thing was happening. He asked, "What's going on? Why does that guy go over there?" … This, because many parts of the scripts were unbelievable, moreover when filming he often took detours from it.[15]

Colizzi refers to the scene where the young Maureen (Daniela Doria) and her boyfriend sneak into a refrigerating cell by the lake (which had been turned into a bachelor flat by the local boat caretaker!) to make love, only to find themselves locked inside and die asphyxiated, which fails to make much sense even after the dialogue changes in post-production. But other things are left unexplained: who and how made Jill's photos disappear? What is the function of the scene in which her house is invaded by spirits and her bed levitates, besides aping *The Exorcist*? Fulci himself was dismissive about the latter scene when interviewed in the Italian newspaper *L'Unità* about the special effects industry in Italy: "It did not fit in with the style of the film, I know, but it was imposed by the producer. He said that 'it fitted in well.'"[16]

Perhaps even more than Fulci's other works of the period, *Black Cat* is a display of technique, with the camera dollying and tracking around Professor Miles' house, and the director indulging in his trademark close-ups of eyes—here both human and feline—aided by Sergio Salvati's excellent scope cinematography. As Proietti noted, "What Lucio did really well were the things I was most worried about, that is the actual things the cat did in the film. The murders: he opened doors, ran, attacked, jumped, scratched.... Lucio exasperated them, in a positive sense. When scripting the movie, I had skipped these parts because I was afraid they wouldn't be able to shoot them in a convincing way."[17] Fulci even filmed subjective shots at ground level from the cat's point of view, as Argento would later do in *Due occhi diabolici*, an effect achieved by building a rudimentary Steadicam surrogate as the production couldn't afford hiring one: a sort of a wooden suitcase with the camera placed inside it.

Black Cat recalls Fulci's previous works in many ways. The cemetery scenes and the overall description of the village suggest the grim mood of *Paura nella città dei morti viventi*, while the sequence in which Jill is attacked by bats echoes *Una lucertola con la pelle di donna*, and the one in which Ferguson (Bruno Corazzari) falls to his death onto some construction spikes recalls Gabriele Ferzetti's deadly fall in the church scene in *Sette note in nero*. Fulci had already paid homage to one of Poe's most perturbing themes— imprisonment and premature burial—in the 1977 film; and he had also offered a stunning variation on the theme in one of *Paura nella città dei morti viventi*'s most memorable scenes. The climax, with Gorley destroying the wall behind which Jill has been buried alive with a pickaxe, is a combination of both earlier films, with the camera zooming alternatively on the pickaxe and on Miles' face.

This time, however, the director didn't resort to delirious over-the-top gore. According to Proietti, "he understood that if he put offal in the movie he would ruin it," but perhaps it was also Sbarigia who wanted to avoid a V.M.18 rating. In fact, *Black Cat (Gatto nero)*—the full Italian title included "the title's contextual and faithful translation into Italian," as requested by the law—was passed with a V.M.14 rating after a small cut (3,80 meters) in the scene where the dead lovers' rotten bodies are found covered with rats in the refrigerating cell, and premiered in Italy on August 4th, in a venue in Jesolo (Venice). The critics were rather kind with it, perhaps more because of the lack of gory excesses than for the Poe connection,[18] but Italian box-office grosses were below expectations, barely over 430 million *lire*. Foreign sales were satisfying, though, resulting in theatrical releases in several European countries (Netherlands, Norway, France, England) and overseas.

Black Cat was screened in competition at the 11th "Festival international du film fantastique et de science-fiction" in Paris, together with *Quella villa accanto al cimitero*, and gained ample coverage in *L'Écran fantastique*. In the festival chronicles, Pierre Gires labeled it "a mellower Fulci which has favorably surprised those who saw him only as the painter of innominable

horrors risen from the grave to devour the living."[19] In his in-depth review of the film in the same issue, future film director Christophe Gans praised it with much more conviction than he reserved to *L'aldilà*. Calling *Black Cat* a "very devious and camouflaged" remake of *Paura nella città dei morti viventi*, Gans described it as "an exercise in style, revealing of the director's favorite techniques. The pleasure we can take in this spectacle, a true visual feast, is therefore all on the surface as the director's proceedings are exacerbated by the reference to Edgar A. Poe." In discussing Fulci's visual choices, the French critic pointed out the use of crane shots, noting how "fear grasps the characters with the speed of a soaring camera, a Damocles' sword suddenly brandished on their heads. Whereas American directors insist on making the crane movement the coarse representation of a release and, even more, of a "happy end," Fulci infuses this mania with a malevolent dimension."[20]

Years later, however, Fulci himself dismissed the result as "a weak film, except for Donaggio's music, even though it's got very good actors…. We all failed with *The Black Cat*, even Argento."[21] His next directorial job would see the director teaming again with Fabrizio De Angelis' Fulvia Film with the outstanding ...*E tu vivrai nel terrore! L'aldilà*.

NOTES

1. Romagnoli, *L'occhio del testimone*, 21.
2. For an analysis of D'Anza's mini-series, see Curti, *Italian Gothic Horror Films, 1970–1979*, 224–225.
3. Albiero and Cacciatore, *Il terrorista dei generi*, 265.
4. Robert Schlockoff, "Entretien avec Lucio Fulci," *L'Écran fantastique* #22, January 1982, 11.
5. *Variety*, June 4, 1980, quoted in Stephen Thrower, *Beyond Terror. The Films of Lucio Fulci* (Godalming, Surrey: FAB Press, [1999] 2016), 221.
6. Albiero and Cacciatore report different dates, from August 11 to early October 1980 (Albiero and Cacciatore, *Il terrorista dei generi*, 267), while Stephen Thrower reports the starting date as August 4 (Thrower, *Beyond Terror*, 220). The film was reported as finished by *Variety* on October 15, 1980.
7. Schlokoff, "Entretien avec Lucio Fulci" (1982), 10.
8. David Miller, *The Complete Peter Cushing* (Richmond, Surrey: Reynolds & Hearn, 2005), 161.
9. Albiero and Cacciatore, *Il terrorista dei generi*, 267. Other sources suggest a schedule conflict with David Hemmings' *The Treasure of the Yankee Zephyr* (1981).
10. Albiero and Cacciatore, *Il terrorista dei generi*, 444.
11. Garofalo and De Lillo, "Il cinema del dubbio. Intervista a Lucio Fulci," 18.
12. Manlio Gomarasca. "Saprofito. Intervista con Al Cliver," *Nocturno Cinema* #3, June 1997, 58.
13. Igor Molino Padovan, Giorgio Navarro and Luca

Rea, "Dagmar Lassander, il rosso segno della bellezza," *Amarcord* #13, May-June 1998, 21.

14. Kezich, *Il nuovissimo millefilm*, 60.

15. Albiero and Cacciatore, *Il terrorista dei generi*, 268.

16. Michele Anselmi, "Mostri con l'anima," *L'Unità*, May 1, 1982.

17. Albiero and Cacciatore, *Il terrorista dei generi*, 269.

18. "Even though it abuses Poe's name and tells a rather different story from the title, the film is not devoid of suggestion. Well-shot, set, photographed and edited with care." a.v. [Aldo Viganò], "Gatto nero e scienziato folle nell'horror di Fulci da Poe," *La Stampa*, June 5, 1981.

19. Pierre Gires, "Onzième anniversaire du Festival de Paris," *L'Écran fantastique* #22, January 1982, 4.

20. Christophe Gans, "Les deux nouveaux films de Lucio Fulci," *L'Écran fantastique* #21, November 1981, 59.

21. Garofalo and De Lillo, "Il cinema del dubbio. Intervista a Lucio Fulci," 18.

Bollenti spiriti (Hot Spirits)

D: Giorgio Capitani. *S and SC*: Franco Marotta, Laura Toscano; *DOP*: Silvano Ippoliti (Technovision, LV-Luciano Vittori); *M*: Piero Umiliani (Ed. Ameuropa International Negritella), *E*: Sergio Montanari; *ArtD, CO*: Ezio Altieri; *AD*: Marzio Casa; *SS*: Lucilla Clementelli; *C*: Enrico Sasso; *AC*: Andrea Sabatello; *2ndAC*: Luigi Conversi; *SP*: Roberto Nicosia Vinci; *Press attache*: Naria Rühle; *ACO*: Tiziana Mancini; *APD*: Massimo Spano; *MU*: Giulio Mastrantonio, Pier Antonio Mecacci; *Hair*: Maria Teresa Corridoni, Patrizia Corridoni; *AE*: Carlo Bartolucci; *2ndAE*: Carlo D'Alessandro; *SO*: Claudio Maielli; *B*: Stefano Zito; *W*: Marisa Vivarelli Cherubini, Bertilla Silvestrini; *KG*: Renato Cinti, Sergio Profili; *ChEl*: Marcello Cardarelli; *Mix*: Danilo Moroni. *Cast*: Johnny Dorelli [Giorgio Guidi] (Count Giovanni degli Uberti/Guiscardo), Gloria Guida (Marta Sartori), Alessandro Haber (Dr. Vittorio Cavalletti Spada LL.D.), Lia Tanzi (Nicole Steiner), Adriana Russo (Chambermaid), Lory Del Santo (Lilli, the Call Girl), Francesca Romana Coluzzi (Station Attendant), Geoffrey Copleston (Dr. Eric Steiner), Roberto Della Casa (Antonio, the Waiter), Giorgio Gobbi (Postman), Corrado Olmi (Doctor); *uncredited*: Bruno Alias (Guest), Erminio Bianchi Fasani (Guest), Angelo Boscariol (Worker), Rossana Canghiari (Guest), Eolo Capritti (Donor), Carlo Cartier (Electrician), Enrico Cesaretti (Guest), Raffaele Di Mario (Guest), Lionello Pio Di Savoia (Giovanni), Tom Felleghy (Donor), Giulio Massimini (Waiter), Vittorio Ripamonti (Guest), Maria Tedeschi (Amelia Bordon), Pietro Zardini (Old Station Attendant). *PROD*: Silvio Clementelli, Anna Maria Alementelli for Clesi Cinematografica, Italian International Film (Rome); *PM*: Marcello Crescenzi; *PS*: Guido De Laurentiis, Enzo Nigro; *PSe*: Roberto Cartocci; *PSeA*: Pietro Proietti; *ADM*: Maurizio Nobili. *Country*: Italy. Filmed at the Castle Piccolomini in Balsorano, and at De Paolis In.Ci.R. Studios (Rome). *Running time*: 92 minutes (m. 2634). Visa n. 77444 (12.23.1981); *Rating*: all audiences. *Release date*: 12.30.1981 (Italy); *Distribution*: D.L.F. *Domestic gross*: approx.765,000,000 *lire. Also known as*: *Qui c'est ce mec?* (France), *He, Geister!* (West Germany), *The Ghost Who Loves Sex* (Philippines), *Forróvérű kísértet* (Hungary).

Count Giovanni degli Uberti, a nobleman close to financial collapse, inherits a magnificent castle from his uncle Ubezio. A Swiss company is ready to buy the manor from him for two billion lire and turn it into a luxury hotel, but there is a problem: Giovanni is not the only heir, but he shares the property with a young nurse named Marta, who has been bequeathed 10 percent of it. With the aid of his lawyer, Vittorio concocts a scheme to have Marta sell him her share thus enabling the sale of the castle. But he finds out that the family manor is inhabited by the ghost of his ancestor Guiscardo, who died a virgin 300 years earlier, and that Guiscardo's soul cannot find peace unless he finally makes love to a woman. A series of misunderstanding ensue, because Guiscardo is a dead ringer for Giovanni, and the two are often mistaken for one another. The plot thickens when Giovanni finds out that his lover, Nicole, is the wife of the Swiss entrepreneur he is about to meet during a party at the castle. What is more, when he meets the beautiful Marta, Giovanni falls in love with her...

After the commercial success of the amiable sophisticated comedies *Aragosta a colazione* (1979) and *Odio le bionde* (1980) both starring Enrico Montesano, producer Silvio Clementelli asked scriptwriters Laura Toscano and Franco Marotta to write another comedy script for director Giorgio Capitani. Born in 1927, Capitani had started directing in the 1950s: after a handful of tear-jerking melodramas, he soon turned to comedies, with appreciable results, even though his best film was perhaps the grim Western *Ognuno per sé* (a.k.a. *The Ruthless Four*, 1968), written by Fernando di Leo and starring Van Heflin, Gilbert Roland, Klaus Kinski, and George Hilton. But it was with *Aragosta a colazione* that the director had shown his skills in the French-style *pochade* based on misunderstandings and slapstick gags, with a rather different structure than most Italian comedies of the period, less vulgar and relying on pitch-perfect comic timing rather than verbal jokes.

A vehicle for the popular singer-turned-actor Johnny Dorelli, *Bollenti spiriti* relies on a mild supernatural-tinged plot, like other comedies of the period. The story, which revolves around a haunted castle inherited by a bankrupt nobleman, draws from the typical genre clichés and owes a lot to René Clair's *The Ghost Goes West* (1935). It is also similar to both *C'è un fantasma nel mio letto* (1981) and *La casa stregata* (1982), for it features a ghost with strong sexual needs, who is condemned by a secular curse to wander in the family castle until he mates with a living partner. But Guiscardo (Dorelli, in an amusing wig) is a stuttering, nerdy wimp who doesn't know how to seduce a woman (and, being dead for 300 years, doesn't even know what panties are).

The theme of the *Doppelgänger* is also played for laughs, as Guiscardo continuously takes his descendant Giovanni's place with humorous results: the sexual innuendoes—such as when Giovanni mistakes the other heir Marta (Guida) for a hooker he has called in order to release his ancestor from his pains—are spiced with a moderate number of double-entendres, and Gloria Guida doesn't have any nude scenes, unlike the sexy Lory Del Santo. The latter, as the hooker, spends much of her brief screen time wearing only her panties (which she tells Guiscardo she will take off in exchange for "dough" … resulting in yet another misunderstanding). It all climaxes in a lengthy party scene (which basically reprises those seen in Capitani's previous comedies scripted by Marotta and Toscano) where all kinds of slapstick ensue before the expected happy ending.

The result is *déjà-vu* but nonetheless amusing. The breezy script keeps the movie afloat with misunderstandings galore, and the typical Gothic setting and elements, complete with trapdoors and secret passages, are employed for laughter with pleasant results. As Toscano explained, "the misunderstandings were brought to their extreme consequences, for the ghost, his appearances and disappearances gave an infinity of possibilities to the story. But in all our stories there is always a realistic starting point. That is, the protagonist is forced by necessity to move along in the story. It's never gratuitous. And I think this gives strength to the script, even though the plot is rather thin."[1] Toscano openly acknowledged the René Clair influence: "That's the type of comedy I love so much. Clair in my opinion is such a great director. He was not what I would call a model, but surely his work as a filmmaker influenced our choices in the script."[2]

As for Capitani's direction, it is very precise and always at the service of the performers and the gags, with an admirable levity throughout. The *Corriere della Sera* film critic Giovanni Grazzini praised the director and suggested an illustrious comparison term: "Choosing as model the American Stanley Donen, Capitani pursues honorably his project of helming Italian comedies that, for their svelte rhythm and graceful touch, make paradox pleasant and give levity to farce."[3]

The director is also aided by Johnny Dorelli's comedy skills. An accomplished singer, Dorelli had evolved from his early TV appearances to the movies, first with spoofs such as *Arriva Dorellik!* (1967, Steno), before moving on to more committed roles, most notably in *Pane e cioccolata* (1974, Franco Brusati), alongside Nino Manfredi—where he played an Italian businessman in Switzerland who goes bankrupt and commits suicide—and as the ruthless reporter who investigates a serial killer, only to find out a most shocking truth, in Luigi Zampa's underrated *Il mostro* (1977). *Bollenti spirit* was the first movie that paired Dorelli with Gloria Guida, who would soon become his wife: the two actors had met on the stage comedy *Accendiamo la lampada* (1979), and their union would result in Guida giving up acting after their next film together, *Sesso e volentieri* (1982, Dino Risi). The chemistry between the two leads is all too evident, and the gorgeous actress has at least one memorable scene when, at a gas station, she is given to replay the iconic moment in *The Seven Year Itch* (1955) when Marilyn Monroe's skirt is blown upwards. As usual in productions of the era, product placement is massive and aggressive: Dorelli smokes Merit cigarettes and drinks Amaro Ramazzotti (which he advertised on television during that period).

Bollenti spiriti was a decent box-office success, although perhaps not as much as its makers expected. It ended up at the 42nd place among the season's top-grossers. Capitani's next film was a bizarre comedy about terrorism, *Teste di quoio* (also 1981), starring Christian De Sica, George Hilton and Philippe Leroy, among others, which was a flop. By the end of the decade, after a handful more nondescript works, Capitani started working steadily for the small screen.

NOTES

1. Pergolari, *La fabbrica del riso*, 376.
2. *Ibid.*, 377.
3. G. Gr. [Giovanni Grazzini], "Johnny Dorelli beffato dal fantasma galante," *Corriere della Sera*, January 23, 1982.

C'è un fantasma nel mio letto (There Is a Ghost in My Bed)

D: Claudio De Molinis [Claudio Giorgiutti]. *S*: Claudio Simonelli; *SC*: Luis María Delgado, Jesús Rodriguez Folgar; *DOP*: Raúl Pérez Cubero (Fujicolor, Staco Film); *M*: Piero Umiliani (Ed. Nazionalmusic); *E*: Giorgio [Jorge] Serralonga; *PD*: Gonzalo García Flaño; *SD*: Vittorio Ferrero; *CO*: Susanna Micozzi; *MU*: Marisa Marconi; *SO*: Pietro Spadoni; *SE*: Mario Bernardo; *Stunts*: Franco Maria Salamon; *C*: Emilio Loffredo, Giuseppe Tinelli; *AC*: Giovanni Mozzillo, Adriano Mancori; *SP*: Enzo Savino; *AE*: Roberto Savoca; *SS*: Paola Colonna. *Cast*: Lilli Carati [Ileana Caravati] (Adelaide Ferretti), Renzo Montagnani (Baron Sir Archibald Trenton), Vincenzo Crocitti (Camillo Fumagalli), Vanessa Hidalgo (The Countess), Guerrino Crivello (Angus), Alejandra Grepi (Maryanne, the Innkeeper's wife), Giacomo Assandri (Terence, the Innkeeper), Luciana Turina (Josephina, the Cook). *PROD*: Telecinema 80 (Rome), Victory Film (Madrid); *PM*: Mauro Ruspantini; *PS*: Fabio Calderoni; *PSe*: Maria Ludovica Bologna. *Country*: Italy/Spain. Filmed at Castle Piccolomini in Balsorano (L'Aquila) and at De Paolis In.Ci.R. Studios (Rome). *Running time*: 94 minutes (m. 2564). Visa n. 76446 (3.28.1981); *Rating*: V.M.18. *Release dates*: 4.3.1981 (Italy); 11.28.1981 (Spain), 2.12.1982 (Portugal), 3.25.1983 (France); *Distribution*: Cinedaf. *Domestic gross*: n.a. Also known as: *Hay un fantasma en mi cama* (Spain), *Y a-t-il un fantome dans mon lit?* (France), *Um Fantasma na Minha Cama* (Portugal).

Note: in the Spanish version, the characters played by Crocitti and Carati are renamed respectively Malcolm and Ruth.

Two Italian newlyweds on their honeymoon in Scotland, Camillo and Adelaide, cannot find an accommodation for the night. Because of the fog, they end up lost in the countryside near an ancient castle. They spend the night in the manor, but the place is haunted by the spirit of the old Baron of Black Castle, an unrepentant womanizer in life. Assisted by his loyal servant Angus, by way of potions, sleeping pills and various tricks, the Baron replaces the naive Camillo in bed and has his way with the unsuspecting bride, until in turn he is duped by Angus and relocated to the gallery of portraits of his ancestors.

A late addiction to the erotic farces in vogue in the mid-to-late 1970s, *C'è un fantasma nel mio letto* was produced with an eye to the Spanish market, where the demand for eroticism was constantly growing after the death of Francisco Franco, in the so-called *destape* period. The film employs a basic variation of the haunted house routine, which must have come out straight from some cheap adults-only comic book. When interviewed during shooting, director Claudio De Molinis mentioned René Clair's *The Ghost Goes West*—which provided the inspiration for *Bollenti spiriti* as well—as an influence: "Recently, with *Mia moglie è una*

Italian poster for *C'è un fantasma nel mio letto* (1981), a bland erotic farce with fantasy elements starring Lilli Carati and Renzo Montagnani.

strega, our producers drew from another film by the great French director, *I Married a Witch,* and achieved considerable commercial results. We did a very similar operation, modernizing the story so as to make it more in tune with the audience's mentality and our actors' characteristics."[1]

Truth be told, however, there is very little of Clair's film in the script (credited to Luis María Delgado and Jesús R. Folgar for quota purposes but possibly the work solely of Giovanni Simonelli). On the other hand, the opening pretext is virtually the same as *The Rocky Horror Picture Show,* but, instead of an oversexed alien, the two innocent newlyweds (looking forward to consummating their marriage after a five-year platonic betrothal) end up in the hands of a lubricious ghost. Which gives way to the expected plethora of misunderstandings, sight gags and double-entendres, and characters moving around frantically in the familiar Piccolomini Castle in Balsorano, posing as a Scottish one.

As expected the film did good business in Spain,[2] whereas in Italy it passed almost unnoticed, despite its popular leads. Montagnani and Crocitti were two regulars of Italian erotic farce, and Crocitti also co-starred in another Spanish sex comedy of the period, José Larraz's *Polvos mágicos* (1979), alongside Carmen Villani. As the Countess, the charming Vanessa Hidalgo is underused, compared to her starring turn in Larraz's over-the-top erotic horror *Los ritos sexuales del diablo* (a.k.a. *Black Candles,* 1982), made shortly after this. As for De Molinis (real name Claudio Giorgiutti), this was his sixth and final film as a director, in a body of work that also comprised the cheap crime story *L'unica legge in cui credo* (1976) and the grim drama *Candido erotico* (1978, also starring Lilli Carati).

Despite the occasional cultured reference— Montagnani's character quoting 14th century poet Francesco Petrarca and Giuseppe Verdi's opera *Don Carlos*—the script is hopelessly poor and repetitive, littered with paper-thin characters (the ugly and naive groom, the sexy bride, the jealous innkeeper and his buxom wife, the sexcrazed cook) mumbling such lines as "That is not an ass, that is pure gold!" Montagnani and Crocitti ham it up as if there was no tomorrow, but the material they are given to work with is so threadbare, and De Molinis's direction is so ham-fisted and haphazard, with plenty of silent movie-style speeded-up sequences pitifully trying to make up for the lack of fun, that the whole affair soon becomes insufferable, It all climaxes in a (again) speeded-up threesome accompanied by the final overture of Rossini's opera *Guglielmo Tell,* with Crocitti's character yelling like Tarzan in the midst of the erotic frenzy. *A Clockwork Orange* this is not, unfortunately.

The movie relies mostly on the lead actress' nude scenes to keep the viewer interested, and Carati amply displays her body to the camera. After ending up second at the 1974 "Miss Italy" beauty contest, the gorgeous actress seemed on her way to a bright film career, and soon became one of the most popular starlets of the period, thanks to such titles as Stelvio Massi's action flick *Poliziotto sprint* (1977, starring Maurizio Merli), Fernando di Leo's controversial *Avere vent'anni* (1978, co-starring Gloria Guida), Pasquale Festa Campanile's *Il corpo della ragassa* (1979) and *Qua la mano,* the latter alongside Adriano Celentano.

In the early 1980s, however, Carati's career was already on the verge of decline, due to her heroin and cocaine abuse—an open secret in the film business, which resulted in her being marginalized. During the promotional tour for *C'è un fantasma nel mio letto* the actress infamously appeared on Rai Uno's popular Sunday talk show *TG L'una* in an overtly altered state, giving confused answers to her interviewer; the other guest was, of all people, Karl Heinz Stockhausen. Soon after, she suffered a serious car crash which resulted in a long absence from the screen. Carati would return to the movies only three years later, appearing in Luciano Odorisio's comedy *Magic Moments* (1984), and between 1985 and 1986 she starred in four erotic flicks directed by Aristide Massaccesi before giving in to hardcore porn, the quickest way to obtain the money she needed to finance her drug addiction.

Carati starred in five porn movies shot between 1987 and 1988, which marked the end of her film career. In May 1988 she was arrested for possession of heroin, and attempted suicide for the first time; she would try to kill herself again the following year, during a bout of depression in the midst of a rehab program. Eventually, though, Lilli re-emerged from the abyss, as she herself recalled in the 1994 documentary *Lilli, una vita da eroina* (Lilli, a Heroin[e]'s Life). She died in 2014, of brain cancer.

Notes

1. "Cronache dal piccolo e grande schermo—Fantasma a letto," *Stampa Sera,* 22 December 1980.

2. According to the official ministerial data, it was seen by 278,918 spectators and grossed an amount corresponding to 266,885 Euro. (http://infoicaa.mecd.es/CatalogoICAA/Peliculas/Detalle?Pelicula=105680).

...E tu vivrai nel terrore! L'aldilà (The Beyond, a.k.a. 7 Doors of Death)

D: Lucio Fulci. S: Dardano Sacchetti; SC: Dardano Sacchetti, Giorgio Mariuzzo, Lucio Fulci; DOP: Sergio Salvati (Technicolor); M: Fabio Frizzi (Ed. Deaf) [U.S. version: Walter E. Sear]; E: Vincenzo Tomassi; PD, CO: Massimo Lentini; SPFX: Giannetto De Rossi; MU: Giannetto De Rossi, Maurizio Trani; SE: Germano Natali; Hair: Luciana Palombi; AD: Roberto Giandalia; C: Franco Bruni; AC: Maurizio Lucchini; AE: Armando Pace, Pietro Tomassi; SP: Alberto Corchi; KG: Lamberto Del Bene; ChEl: Alfredo Fedeli; SD: Alfredo D'Angelo; PrM: Rodolfo Ruzza; PrMAsst: Franco Rinaldi; SO: Ugo Celani; SOE: Enzo Diliberto; B: Eros Giustini; Mix: Bruno Moreal; STC: Nazzareno Cardinali; SS: Rita Agostini. Cast: Katherine [Catriona] MacColl (Liza Merrill), David Warbeck (Dr. John McCabe), Sarah Keller [Cinzia Monreale] (Emily), Antoine Saint-John (Zweick), Veronica Lazar (Martha), Al Cliver [Pierluigi Conti] (Prof. Harris), Michele Mirabella (Martin Avery), Giampaolo Saccarola (Arthur), Laura De Marchi (Mary Ann); uncredited: Calogero Azzaretto (Zombie at Hospital), Lucio Fulci (Librarian), Tonino Pulci (Joe), Anthony Flees (Larry), Maria Pia Marsala (Jill), Giovanni De Nava (Zweick—zombie), Roberto Dell'Acqua (Glass-smashing Zombie), Gilberto Galimberti (Zombie), Amedeo Salamon (Zombie at Hospital), Sergio Salvati (Mob Member). PROD: Fabrizio De Angelis for Fulvia Film (Rome). UM: Tullio Lullo; AsstUM: Fabrizio De Martino. Country: Italy. Filmed on location in Louisiana and at De Paolis In.Ci.R. Studios (Rome). Running time: 87 minutes (m. 2355). Visa n. 76406 (3.20.1981); Rating: V.M.18. Release dates: 4.22.1981 (West Germany), 4.29.1981 (Italy), 7.11.1981 (Hong Kong), 8.27.1981 (UK), 10.14.1981 (France), 10.14.1981 (Spain), 3.11.1983 (USA). Distribution: Medusa Distribuzione. Domestic gross: 747,615,662 lire. Also known as: L'au-delà (France); El mas allá (Spain; Argentina; Uruguay); Über dem Jenseits; Die Geisterstadt der Zombies (Germany); Las siete puertas del infierno (Mexico); Woodoo—raedslernes hotel (Denmark).

Louisiana, 1927. A painter, Zweick, who lives in the "Seven Doors" Hotel, is lynched by an angry mob who suspects him of witchcraft. Meanwhile a local girl, Emily, reads a mysterious book and finds out that the hotel is built atop one of the doors to Hell. 1981. Liza Merrill takes possession of the dilapidated hotel and sets out to renovate it with the help of Martha and her husband Arthur, but a series of gruesome accidents result in the death of a worker and of the plumber, Joe. Moreover, a decomposed body is found in the hotel basement. At the hospital, Dr. John McCabe and his colleague Harris study the mysterious corpse, but more horrible events ensue, as Joe's wife dies mysteriously in the anatomy room. Liza makes acquaintance with a blind girl, Emily, who tells her the story of the cursed hotel. Liza's friend Martin, who supervises the works on the hotel, goes to the library to study its planimetry, but meets a grisly fate. Martha and Emily too are horribly murdered. Liza and McCabe take refuge at the hospital, but the place has been invaded by zombies. They manage to escape but end up inexplicably in the hotel basement, and find themselves in the beyond, a deserted land populated by the dead...

When Fabrizio De Angelis came up with the title L'aldilà (The Beyond) for Lucio Fulci's next film, he knew he had a winner on his hands. He managed to obtain a pre-financing on the part of foreign investors based on the title alone—which in fact was the only thing he had, since there was not even a script to begin with. But cranking out a screenplay wouldn't be a problem for Dardano Sacchetti, who duly obliged within the usual 10/15 days. Shooting started in October 1980[1] and lasted for eight weeks. As with his previous horror films, the crew moved overseas, this time to Louisiana. In a 1984 interview, Fulci claimed that the budget was 580 million lire,[2] half as much as what De Angelis declared. For the second time, the director cast Catriona MacColl (although his first choice for the role would have been Tisa Farrow, as he told Robert Schockloff in L'Écran fantastique[3]) and David Warbeck, with whom he had got along very well on Black Cat. Originally the cast was to include Venantino Venantini (as Joe the plumber) and Ivan Rassimov (Prof. Harris), but the roles went respectively to Fulci's friend Tonino Pulci, a stage director who would turn up again in a small role in Manhattan Baby, and Pierluigi Conti, a.k.a. Al Cliver, better known to Fulci as "Tufus." Stefania Casini was originally to play Emily, but refused, not least because she would have to wear painful contact lenses in all her scenes. The painter, Zweick, was played by the French Antoine Saint-John, who was replaced during shooting by Giovanni De Nava (as Zweick's "zombified" version).

Sacchetti claimed that his main source of inspiration was Henry James' novel *The Turn of the Screw*, but the Henry James connection applies much more convincingly to his next film with Fulci, *Quella villa accanto al cimitero*. A clearer influence was again given by Lovecraft's myths, filtered through the work of Clark Ashton Smith, who mentioned the "Book of Eibon" in his stories—Eibon being a fictional sorcerer first mentioned in the short story *The Door to Saturn*. Even more than in *Paura nella città dei morti viventi*, the story draws from a typical Gothic theme—the haunted house—and revisits it in a personal way, with a complex layering of references and borrowings. In this sense, the main cinematic references are blatant: Michael Winner's *The Sentinel*, Argento's *Suspiria* and *Inferno*, Kubrick's *The Shining* (the latter quoted almost literally with the bell for room 36 ringing out of the blue).[4]

When speaking to his biographer Michele Romagnoli, Fulci claimed that he "regularly noticed afterwards" the "borrowings" from other films in Sacchetti's scripts. But in the case of *L'aldilà* this can be ruled out. In the past, the director had had an argument with Dario Argento regarding *Zombi 2*, which the latter labeled as a *Dawn of the Dead* rip-off: Fulci reportedly wrote his colleague a letter in which he listed twelve zombie films made in the 1930s and 1940s, even before Jacques Tourneur's *I Walked with a Zombie*. On *L'aldilà* he was well aware of the similarities with Argento's work, with which his own had in common not just the presence of actress Veronica Lazar. According to script supervisor Rita Agostini, "while shooting, Lucio made references to *Inferno*, and he didn't have anything good to say about it ... undoubtedly *L'aldilà* started from an idea similar to *Inferno*, but he wanted to make a much better film."[5]

But in interviews of the period Fulci referred to other and more illustrious models. When speaking with *L'Écran fantastique*'s Robert Schlockoff, he mentioned Jean-Paul Sartre's famous 1944 existential play *Huis clos* (a.k.a. *No Exit*), which depicts the afterlife as a hotel room, with three characters punished by being locked into it together for eternity. But the Italian director name-dropped another, no less prestigious and certainly more surprising source

of inspiration, the work of French dramatist Antonin Artaud, the inventor of the so-called "theater of cruelty," based on signs, screams and body language instead of words.

> To me, it's an absolute Artaudian film. I personally met Antonin Artaud, he looked at me with his crazy eyes, 30 years ago. My idea was to make an absolute film, with all the horrors of the world. It's a film without a story: a house, some people and the dead returning from the beyond, there is no logic inside the movie, which is just a series of images.... I had studied Artaud a lot before he became trendy again in Italy: *L'aldilà*, like most of those I made, is a homage to Artaud's concept, besides, horror becomes such when one is aware of it, which justifies the presence of atrocious scenes in my film. The viewer is always aware of the horror of these images, this to reply to those people who speak of gratuitousness regarding my movies. There is always a value judgement in my films about such horror, since the viewer is always terrified, thus always in reaction against the very existence of these crimes.[6]

Fulci's passing mention of Artaud's work being "trendy again in Italy" must not pass unnoticed: in June 1981 the Ateneo theater in Rome had hosted "Progetto Artaud," a retrospective on the author on the 33th anniversary of his death, which featured stage plays, exhibitions and screening of the films in which Artaud had played acting roles, including Carl Theodor Dreyer's *La passion de Joanne d'Arc* (1928) to Fritz Lang's *Liliom* (1934). Fulci's reference to Artaud was most likely an attempt on his part to assert the authorial quality of his work by leaning on a respected yet unorthodox cultural model. The foundations of such a claim were shaky, since the notion of cruelty in Artaud (intended as "catharsis") was very different from the one displayed in Fulci's horror films, and it is unlikely to say the least that the director ever met him, although he was familiar with his work (one of Artaud's plays, *Les Cenci*, dealt with the story of Beatrice Cenci, which Fulci had filmed in 1969). But it didn't matter: as a famous line from *The Man Who Shot Liberty Valance* says, "When the fact becomes legend, print the legend." To Fulci, name-dropping Artaud was not just a smart way to reply to those who still considered him as a middle-aged hack who ripped off Argento. It was also an intellectual joke at the expense of those critics who barely knew who Artaud was, and wouldn't—or rather, couldn't—object anything to such a prestigious and specific reference.

The core of *L'aldilà* is the notion of the "haunted house"—or rather, of the "terrible house" as labeled by Robin Wood.[7] The "Seven Doors" hotel is a living, rotting organism whose viscera hide unspeakable secrets and forgotten horrors. In its last screen appearance, ghastly silhouettes show up behind its windows as the only two humans left alive flee from it, certifying the victory of the dead over the living—an iconic Gothic image, and one that certifies Fulci's visual command over the movie, regardless of the low budget. His camera prowls, spies and dollies all over the place restlessly, never stopping for a moment, a curious and possibly unearthly presence itself. But whereas Argento's palaces of horrors are magnificent and multicolored Art déco buildings, Fulci's "terrible house" is a decadent and decaying construction, and if *Inferno's* underwater chamber is a fascinating, spellbinding place where the heroine can swim as an explorer in a lost cave beneath the sea, *L'aldilà's* is a half-flooded, filthy dark basement which plumbers try in vain to repair. Overall, the comparison works symbolically as the difference between "A" and "B" cinema, high and low budget, *auteur* and exploitation. Moreover, *Inferno's* palaces are located in the center of the Western world, whereas Fulci's hotel is in the swamps of Louisiana, a sweaty, humid place which looks like the American counterpart of the Southern Italy landscapes seen in *Non si sevizia un paperino* and hosts a similarly intolerant and violent population.

The Argento connection is also evident in a couple of death scenes, namely those of the blind Emily devoured by her dog—a blatant replica of Flavio Bucci's killing in *Suspiria* (animals become agents of evil, in the spider sequence as well)—and Al Cliver's unfortunate character receiving a deadly rain of glass fragments all over his face, a scaled-down reworking of *Suspiria's* opening murder. But the death sequences in *L'aldilà* go far beyond the cold symphonies of horror orchestrated by Argento, which have a geometrical, ballet-like quality. Fulci goes for the jugular, with a savagery that outdoes anything seen in horror cinema in that period, including the almost pornographic excesses of Gabriele Crisanti-produced gorefests such as *Giallo a Venezia* (1979) and *Patrick vive ancora*. The infamous sight of the little girl's skull cracked open by a gunshot—an act of barbaric cruelty if ever there was one—is among the most extreme acts of violence committed to

celluloid, and yet it conveys a surreal fascination.

But the most impressive set piece has to be the opening scene, which depicts another of Fulci's harrowing looks at the dark core of humanity, the torture, crucifixion and disfigurement of Zweick.[8] As with Florinda Bolkan's *maciara*, the painter—emaciated, feverishly working on his painting, with Fulci's camera isolating his eyes shining in the dark in close-up—is a Christ-like victim, who undergoes a similar ordeal: the peasants hit him with heavy chains on the face, shoulder and chest, ripping his flesh open. Then, in a barbaric mockery of the crucifixion, they drive long nails through his wrists before the final act of cruelty—disfiguring him with lime (with a subjective shot of the corrosive material thrown directly at the camera). For a movie about the horrors of the beyond, *L'aldilà* puts immediately clear that human ones are no less atrocious.

Far from being a pedestrian rendition of the sadistic nastiness that characterized the sex-horror comics of the period, Fulci's visions of death have a terrible yet poetic quality to them, which makes them even more incisive (albeit a couple of scenes, namely the spider attack and Al Cliver's demise, look less than perfect due to below-par special effects). Zweick's disfigurement by lime, with the living flesh melting before the unflinching camera's eye, is not just a chilling reminder of human cruelty, but also a reflection on the expiration of all things human, destined to corrosion, decay, destruction. For a director who repeatedly expressed his horror toward time, there is nothing more horrific than to graphically portray the passing of time via its destructive, implacable action. In Fulci's world view, time equals horror, and in *L'aldilà* the equation is even more surprising than in other works where it is more explicit (as in *La casa nel tempo*).

Eyes, the recipient of horror in Fulci's universe, here are blinded, eaten or gouged out, an act of cruelty which paradoxically becomes an act of supernatural mercy in the finale, when Liza and McCabe are spared the sight of the never-ending extradimensional barren land they are doomed to inhabit for eternity. Rather than being punished for daring too much, they are saved from one last, inconceivable horror, whose essence can be glimpsed only via the filter of art. Whereas Argento's Varelli is an architect, a creator of ordinate shapes and figures who attempted to enclose evil inside a rational-looking, geometrical prison (only to become a prisoner

The frightening sight of the decomposed body of the painter Zweick (Giovanni De Nava) in a West German lobby card for Lucio Fulci's ...*E tu vivrai nel terrore! L'aldilà* (1981).

of his own creation, that is), *L'aldilà*'s Zweick is a painter, a visionary artist whose works are the only way to approach the unspeakable darkness of the universe. Likewise, Fulci's film rejects geometry in favor of a free-form approach which, if on one hand mimics *Inferno*'s rejection of a standard narrative structure, on the other distances itself from Argento's cold, almost mathematical world of horror.

The genesis and evolution of *L'aldilà*, from the first draft to the finished film, is fascinating, and offers more than a few surprises. In fact, Sacchetti's original story was quite different from the script deposited at Rome's CSC and dated August 25, 1980,[9] about a month and a half before shooting began. Originally, in fact, *L'aldilà* was about a man named Arthur McCabe who returns to his family home with his wife Mary, his 12-year-old son Billy and a nephew, Michael, who is a talented young painter. Rumors abound that the house is haunted by a mysterious, ghastly tenant. A plumber called to fix a water leak disappears in the basement; then his body is found together with the rotting corpse of a young man. A female doctor, Liza Merrill, dis-

covers something strange about the second body, but a fire destroys the hospital's anatomy room, halting her investigation. Meanwhile, Michael discovers a secret locked room in the attic, filled with strange old books, including the *Necronomicon* and the Book of Eibon. He finds out that the mysterious tenant was capable of calling up the dead and opening the doors of the beyond, in order to gain immortality. Michael and Liza try to escape to the town, but the place has been taken over by the dead.

Besides the interesting differences regarding the protagonists, this summary shows how Sacchetti's story was closer to classical Gothic stereotypes—the family mansion, the mysterious presence, the secret room—and apparently more canonically structured. The finished script introduced new characters, such as the painter Zweick, liberally changed the protagonists (Liza becomes the owner of the hotel, McCabe is the local doctor), and radically redesigned the opening and the ending.[10]

Fulci's first Italian biography, *L'occhio del testimone*, published in 1992, included several dismissive quotes on the director's part toward the scriptwriter. While discussing *L'aldilà*, Fulci claimed: "Let's forget Sacchetti's story and part of the script, which were just a few pages long and all ripped off from other films."[11] Such a harsh statement, however, was very likely driven by the director's tense relationship with his ex-collaborator, characterized by many arguments over the years. In the case of *L'aldilà*, Sacchetti's script deposited at Rome's CSC is 162 pages long, so the claim is unsubstantiated. But again, a summary of the script shows that it differs considerably from the film, too.

As in *Paura nella città dei morti viventi*, the setting is New England, in the imaginary town of Fullwich (note the affinity with Dunwich). The prologue is set on October 31, 1921, at the "Seven Doors" hotel: the bell of room 36 rings, a young girl named Millie goes upstairs to check and is horribly murdered by the mysterious tenant, Sweick [*sic*], who gouges her eyes out with his hand, "dry and clawlike, red like bare flesh." (The theme of zombies gouging out the eyes is a leitmotif throughout the script) There is no trace of the astonishing act of gratuitous violence that opens the film, the torture and murder of the painter Zweick by a horde of peasants, added later to the story by Fulci.

The CSC script then cuts to October 30, 1980. The early scenes are more or less similar to the ones in the film—Liza Merrill renovating the hotel with the help of Martha and Arthur, the murder of Joe the plumber (who has his arm ripped off in addition to his eyes gouged out), the discovery of a decomposed corpse in the basement, Liza meeting Emily along the road and the introduction of Dr. McCabe and Harris, studying the corpse's brainwaves. However, several differences stand out, starting with the setting (according to production designer Massimo Lentini, the choice of Louisiana was dictated by practical needs). The blind Emily is not an ambiguous, ghostlike presence but a real woman, Harris is much older than McCabe, and the villagers are hostile toward Liza. On top of that, a couple of murder scenes that take place at the hospital involve two characters absent from the film, a nurse named Katia and a priest, Father Francis, who are killed in the anatomy room by the mysterious body (the nurse suffers from extended bleeding from her nose, ears, and mouth, a nod to a notorious scene in *Paura nella città dei morti viventi*).

The Book of Eibon appears only on page 75 of the CSC script, when Liza finds it in room 36. Before that, Emily had told her about the events that took place 60 years earlier, when all the people at the hotel disappeared mysteriously, possibly murdered by Sweick. When she enters the room, Liza finds it in a state of ruin, with moldy walls, insects and larvae. Her vision of Sweick is impressively different: "The man is nailed with open arms and legs to the bathroom wall. One of his hands detaches from the nail that pierced it and with a cry he sticks a long knife into his own heart." When McCabe shows up and explores the room, it is sensibly different from what it first was: Sweick's body is missing, as in the film, and so is the Book of Eibon which Liza glimpsed. It is McCabe who goes to the library to look for it, but to no avail; after he's gone, the female librarian, Tracy, climbs a staircase to pick up the Book of Eibon from the highest shelf, and suffers the same fate as Martin Avery (a character absent from the CSC script) in the film: death by spiders. Martha's murder in room 36 is also virtually identical to the one in the film (but the woman has her eyes gouged out by Joe, instead of being pierced against a long nail on the wall).

It is Emily who gives McCabe the book of Eibon. The doctor takes it to the hospital, where he is joined by Dr. Harris. The latter's wife Anne receives a visit from the late Father Francis, now a living dead: she tries to escape by jumping from the window, but the zombie grabs her in mid-air by the hair. Meanwhile, nurse Katia grabs Anne by the legs from below, and pulls. In a grotesquely spectacular death, the poor woman, torn between two opposite forces, is literally scalped alive.

While McCabe finds out in the Book of Eibon a cryptic sentence about "how to open the door on the night of All Saints," Liza is alone in the hotel, which suddenly comes alive. "A suffocated cry is heard, then a throttled shout. A crackly music, as if from a nickelodeon, covers all the previous noises. Candles light in candlesticks and electric lights turn off."

Following Emily's death scene, identical as in the film, John arrives at the hotel to pick up Liza. He explains: "The man in room 36 had discovered that the door was in the hotel. He tried to open it, but they prevented him from doing it. They erased all traces. Then, 60 years later, without knowing it, Joe opened a breach.... Liza, we must close it." "But what? I don't understand!" Liza objects. "The door! The door that unites the world of the living and that of the dead."

The passage underlines the more conventional tone of Sacchetti's script, which attempts to give an articulate explanation to the story's gruesome events—namely, Joe opening a breach while trying to fix the water leak, thus opening a passage between this world and the beyond. Moreover, McCabe behaves as a standard hero, with his intention to close the door to the beyond. In the film, not only Liza and McCabe are clueless, but Joe's responsibility in disclosing the door to the beyond is never developed.

McCabe and Liza go down in the basement and eventually arrive at the breach. "McCabe rests both his hands on the wall. The hands touch the wall. A flash. A blinding flash bedazzles McCabe and Liza. The wall breaks open with a deafening rumble. Then, silence. And darkness." A skeletal figure appears: Peter Sweick. They are now in the beyond. "A spectral light. A dry, dusty land." The dead come back to life...

The two protagonists run upstairs, only to find all the other zombie characters (Emil, Arthur, Jo, Martha) in the hotel lodge. They manage to escape and reach the hospital, but the first person they find, Dr. Harris, has also turned into a living dead. Other zombies show up and surround them. With a gun "borrowed" from a gun shop nearby, McCabe blows several zombies to smithereens, and he and Liza drive away in the night. On the road they notice an apparently empty amusement park, its lights shining in the night, and stop by. But the place is not empty at all: the eerie image of a wagon coming out of the tunnel of love, with zombies on it, stands out. Soon the park is filled with zombies. McCabe and Liza run away, "and they run, and run, and run. But all the directions are blocked. Then, suddenly, they find themselves in front of a huge mirror, and only then we get to see their images. They are the images of two dead people. Liza screams. Her scream echoes, long and endless." In the final image, the amusement park lights turn off, and darkness engulfs everything. A final line on the screen says "...*e iniziò il regno dell'aldilà*" (...and thus began the realm of the beyond).

The CSC script's ending, close to Sacchetti's original story, is characterized by an explicitly symbolic content, with the amusement park representing life in the scriptwriter's own words,[12] and has a similar tone to the definitive one, plus an explicit nod to Lovecraft's celebrated short story *The Outsider* (in which the narrator finally becomes aware of being a dead revenant when

he gets to see his image reflected in a mirror and touches its "cold and unyielding surface of polished glass") and possibly to Ray Bradbury's *Something Wicked This Way Comes*. It was effective, but evidently too expensive to work on the budget the director had to make do with. It also shares light on the vexed question of the zombie climax, often labeled as a last-minute addition to please the German distributor Alemannia/Arabella, who had had a huge commercial success with *Paura nella città dei morti viventi* and therefore granted an advance on Fulci's next zombie film. The director himself, in an interview published in the January 1981 issue of *L'Écran fantastique*, seemed to deny the presence of proper zombies in the film: "*L'aldilà* is a tale of mystery where the dead are at the core of the story, but they are not "aggressive" dead as in *Zombi 2*. They do some things, but totally dependent from the story, whose theme is very metaphysical but with some horror in it."[13] According to Sacchetti, in fact, "originally the movie had a different ending, without the zombies (it's not true that the Germans wanted it, that ending was inserted by Fulci and the producer as a guarantee to sell the film in certain markets) and the real ending was in a strange place, a sort of dead zone, all white, similar to the one, all red, hypothesized by David Lynch in *Twin Peaks*."[14] But this could only refer to a primeval draft, prior to both the aforementioned storyline and the CSC script, which both feature the living dead taking over; the latter includes plenty of graphic gore in the manner of George A. Romero.

Overall, the polishing done by Fulci and Giorgio Mariuzzo enhanced the ambiguous elements of the story and discarded the most conventional ones. The choice of making Emily a ghostly presence who traverses decades to warn the protagonist of horrible events to come, gives her early appearance on the bridge—a startling moment where the Louisiana location dramatically enhances the film—an otherworldly feel. This can also be said about the beautiful scene in which Emily leaves the hotel in a hurry, and Liza realizes she hasn't heard her steps, a moment rendered by the director with the repeated slow-motion sight of the blind girl running away in utter silence. As in *Quella villa accanto al cimitero*, this leads to inconsistencies (if Emily is a ghost, how could she be slaughtered by her dog?) which only add to the story's fascination. But the director's strongest choice was the new opening sequence, which brings to the story a savage drive.

Regarding the narrative structure of *L'aldilà*, Fulci had claimed that he wanted to "make a movie about all the horrors of the world," while Sacchetti commented that it "was somewhat thinner, without frills in the plot, and deliberately so because it wanted to be a nightmare of emotions."[15] In fact, the rhapsodic storyline isn't particularly thin compared to *Paura nella città dei morti viventi*. But what is interesting is the abrupt juxtaposition of the ultraviolent set pieces with mundane scenes that go nowhere, plot-wise. Take, for instance, the transition between the morgue scene with the death of Joe's wife and Liza and McCabe chatting and flirting in the bar, to the sound of a jazz combo, sharing their uninteresting life stories while sipping drinks, another moment not to be found in Sacchetti's script and one of the film's very best scenes. On the one hand, we have the savage eruptions of violence; on the other, the unbearable lightness of existence, where time passes by immutable and implacable.

Whereas the CSC script takes place within the course of a couple of days and climaxes on the night of All Saints, the film has a more relaxed approach. But *L'aldilà* is no less daring than the Gothic horror films of the 1960s, such as *Danza macabra* (1964) or *Operazione paura* (1966), which liberally played with the notion of time. The perception of space is misleading as well: as Martin Avery discovers, the actual planimetry of the hotel is different from the official one, while Liza and Bob have very different perceptions of Emily's house (which to McCabe appears as a dilapidated ruin, whereas the woman sees it as a cozy colonial house). And the climax plays with space and dimension with the same puzzling results as an Escher drawing.

In *Inferno* the final passage to another dimension is a mirror from which Death emerges, triumphant, into our reality, which it (or rather, she) dominates. In Fulci, the transition happens in the opposite direction (between this world and the beyond) and takes place abruptly and arbitrarily. John and Liza, escaping from the morgue, find themselves in the basement of the "Seven Doors" hotel, and from there within the surrealistic beyond depicted in Zweick's painting. It's a passage almost as daring as the celebrated sequence in *Operazione paura* in which Giacomo Rossi Stuart's character follows his own double through a series of rooms which all look the same. Unsettled by the sight of his own self facing him, he leans against a wall, on a cobweb-covered painting which portrays the villa ... only to find himself trapped in a huge web, *outside* the villa (...or *inside* the painting?). Here, Liza and John find themselves in an apparently three-dimensional space which defies the ordinary notions of tridimensionality: when they turn back, they see the very same landscape that was in front of them, limitless and immutable, with no spatial coordinates to rely upon. It is one final act of horror that pushes *L'aldilà* into the realm of pure abstract *fantastique*, leaving aside the zombies, the gore, the gruesome murder scenes and the obscure events that preceded it. The final line—"*E ora affronterai il mare delle tenebre, e ciò che in esso vi è di esplorabile*" (And you will face the sea of darkness, and all therein that may be explored)—and the eruption of Fabio Frizzi's score (featuring the participation of Goblin members Agostino Marangolo and Maurizio Guarini), with its Latin chants, rolling drums and its operatic almost, almost ecclesiastical intensity, makes it a truly unforgettable moment.

As MacColl commented,

> I love the final scene in which we arrive in the world of the dead, which was very poetic. I remember it was the last scene we shot, and as usual Fabrizio [De Angelis] was standing there, looking at his watch. It was a few days before Christmas.... I don't know why they saved that scene for last, perhaps the set piece was a bit difficult to build.... I just wanted to finish the movie and run home for the holidays, and I was very worried about the contact lenses. They were made specifically for us, and nowadays they'd be totally different, but then they were hard and painful to wear.... I later found out that the bodies in that scene were not professional extras, but mostly homeless men who did the scene in exchange for a bottle of wine or something.[16]

The final, nihilistic *coup de théâtre* cemented Fulci's cult status abroad and won the hearts of the younger Italian film critics, such as Claudio Carabba, of the newspaper *Il Giornale*.[17] Carabba's appreciation for Fulci caused a sort of chain reaction: veteran film critic Tullio Kezich, in turn, in an otherwise condescending review which underlined the film's "banal content and gory bad taste," noted its "effective and even elegant filmic style."[18] When he was reported the news that *Positif* and other French magazines had started praising the director, renowned militant critic Lino Miccichè allegedly blurted: "For goodness' sake, now let's not start revaluating

Fulci too!"[19] Such a stance was comprehensible, at a time when the gap between different generations of critics was bringing new attention to the works of filmmakers who had been previously overlooked, if not ignored, such as Riccardo Freda and Raffaello Matarazzo. In France the situation was similar, with the young critics of the specialized press (such as *L'Écran fantastique*) treating the film with far more attention than the ones writing for highbrow magazines. *La Revue du cinéma* was particularly scathing, calling *L'aldilà* an example of "vomitive cinema," blaming the "non-existent scenario … male acting at the limit of nullity and frightfully pompous music," and adding: "Nevertheless, the worst thing seems to be the director's blatant lack of imagination, as he simply picks up ideas here and there from his fellow directors."[20]

L'Écran fantastique devoted ample space to the film, but this time the response was rather less favorable than earlier. In a five-page article dedicated to *L'aldilà* and *Black Cat*, Christophe Gans launched in a comparison that might not have pleased Fulci: "In the way *Inferno* prolonged and gave a new dimension to *Suspiria*, Fulci's latest is presented as the second part of a horrific saga which will comprise no less than seven, according to the number of the doors to hell scattered over the surface of Earth and in the director's imagination." Gans hypothesized that the upcoming *Quella villa accanto al cimitero* would stand as the third entry in the series and concluded that "given Fulci's rate of filming, his cycle will no doubt be finished long before Dario Argento's revelation of Mater Lacrymarum."[21]

After praising the director's work on the visuals, Gans analyzed Fulci's approach to Grand-Guignol, pointing out how he didn't hesitate in

systematizing his methods as a horror filmmaker to the point of conferring his new film the appearance of an eloquent catalog of monstrous deaths—prodigiously bloody outbursts that not even the Americans would dare to consider today under a censorship all too generous in libelous "X ratings. And while the U.S. filmmakers overcome this problem by stretching the hide-and-seek parts (*The Burning*) and the supernatural paraphernalia (*Fear No Evil*), Fulci purifies the fantastic manifestations and all the other slownesses to the point of bypassing them abruptly. What is, then, that danger glimpsed by the widow in the morgue? We will never know, for what matters is only the result, in this case a face slowly gnawed by acid, which goes through all the colors of decom-

position before twitching under the pressure of boiling blood.[22]

Gans had his share of reservations on the result, however, noting that "this complete rejection of explanations, although likeable, prevents a renewal of the much-overused zombie theme…. This gratuitousness is also not relieved by the swiftness of the narrative, which is less paced and structured than *Paura nella città dei morti viventi* and doesn't always hold its bad inclinations toward ghost train-like staging…. In short, excess is preferred to that minimum of cohesion which was the true quality of *Paura*…." Gans ultimately judged the director's new effort a far less convincing effort than *Paura nella città dei morti viventi* (which he called "a remarkable film teeming with many aesthetic ideas very subtly linked"), and concluded: "Fulci tries to keep its theme by sticking blindly to the recipes and ingredients of his earlier films and forgets to explain them."[23]

Released in Italy with a V.M.18 rating under the somewhat pompous title *…E tu vivrai nel terrore! L'aldilà* (without suspension points in the screening certificate), the film opened on April 29, 1981. It did OK business, grossing about 750 million *lire*, considerably less than Fulci's previous zombie films, but it was well-distributed all over the world, including Hong Kong, Mexico and the principal European countries, performing notably well at the Spanish box-office.[24] It was released in the U.S. in 1983 through Aquarius Releasing, under the title *7 Doors of Death*, with heavy cuts to tone down the murder scenes and a new score by Walter E. Sear. The film received a limited theatrical release in its uncut form in the States only after Fulci's death, by Grindhouse Releasing. In the U.K. it was originally passed by the BBFC with an X rating and with several cuts for cinema release; it was included in the DPP list of "Video Nasties" made public in 1983, in Section 2, among non-prosecuted films. After a 1987 video release (with approximately 2 minutes cut) it was finally released uncut to home video in 2001.

Over the years, news of a sequel to *L'aldilà* came to the surface. In 1993, issue #4 of the British fanzine *Book of the Dead* even included the title *Beyond II*, a.k.a. *Beyond the Beyond* ("announced but never released") in an Italian zombie filmography. But neither Sacchetti nor Fulci ever worked on such a project. In 2011, however, the scriptwriter penned a reboot of

Italian lobby card for *...E tu vivrai nel terrore! L'aldilà* **featuring Cinzia Monreale (left) and Maria Pia Marsala.**

sorts set in Scotland, *Beyond Evolution*, which remains unfilmed to this date.[25]

NOTES

1. October 6, according to Rome's Public Cinematographic Register. Albiero and Cacciatore report October 20 as starting date.

2. Giuseppe Salza, "Le retour de Lucio Fulci," *L'Écran fantastique* #44, April 1984.

3. Schlockoff, "Entretien avec Lucio Fulci" (1981), 21.

4. Sacchetti declared he wrote the script in 10 days, at De Angelis' request, with the help of "three or four packets of cigarettes a day, and one or two bottles of vodka. I worked overnight, and often two or three days in a row, without stopping." Albiero and Cacciatore, *Il terrorista dei generi*, 277. On another occasion, however, Sacchetti contradicted himself, claiming that he had written the script in 1979, long before watching *The Shining* (which came out in the U.S. in May 1980, and in Italy in late December of that year, when shooting for *L'aldilà* had already begun). Dardano Sacchetti interviewed, in www.davinotti.com (http://www.davinotti.com/index.php?option=com_content&task=view&id=57&Itemid=79).

5. Albiero and Cacciatore, *Il terrorista dei generi*, 276.

6. Schlockoff, "Entretien avec Lucio Fulci," (1982), 12.

7. Robin Wood, *Hollywood From Vietnam to Reagan ... and Beyond* (New York: Columbia University Press, 2003), 14.

8. The prologue, black-and white and sepia-tinted in the Italian prints, was retained in color for the German release.

9. A script of *L'aldilà* (both in Italian and English language, as *The Beyond*) is deposited at SIAE and registered on July 14, 1980.

10. Interestingly, the original summary (first distributed by De Angelis at Milan's MIFED in order to gain financings) turned up again in promotional flyers concocted by the English distribution company. Apparently, nobody realized that the synopsis didn't correspond to the movie.

11. Romagnoli, *L'occhio del testimone*, 17

12. Gomarasca and Pulici, "La paura dell'aldilà," 69.

13. Schlockoff, "Entretien avec Lucio Fulci" (1981), 20.

14. Dardano Sacchetti interviewed.

15. *Ibid.*

16. Manlio Gomarasca, "Intervista a Catrona MacColl," November 17, 2017, www.nocturno.it (http://www.nocturno.it/intervista-a-catriona-maccoll/).

17. "I think it was near the end of Winter 1981. I saw *L'aldilà* in a theater in Milan, at the midnight show. There were few people in the audience, the right climate to appreciate the indiscreet charm of fear. And in fact, that's what happened: and so, I fell in love with that movie ... and with Lucio Fulci, master craftsman of Cinecittà, with a long and varied career." Claudio Carabba, "Memorial Fulci," in *Mystfest '84. 5° festival internazionale del giallo e del mistero* (Cattolica: Edizioni del Mystfest, 1984).

18. Kezich, *Il nuovissimo Millefilm*, 148.

19. Reported in *Il Patalogo Quattro. Annuario 1982 dello spettacolo cinema e televisione* (Milan: Ubulibri, 1982), 20.

20. Philippe Ross, "L'au-dela," *La Revue du cinéma* #367, December 1981, 48.

21. Gans, "Les deux nouveaux films de Lucio Fulci," 56.

22. *Ibid.*

23. *Ibid.*, 57.

24. According to the official ministerial data, it was seen by 329,513 spectators and grossed an amount corresponding to 342,406 Euro. (http://infoicaa.mecd.es/CatalogoICAA/Peliculas/Detalle?Pelicula=622451).

25. Manlio Gomarasca and Davide Pulici, "Al di là dell'aldilà," *Nocturno* #115, March 2012, 70.

Fantasma d'amore (Ghost of Love)

D: Dino Risi. *S*: based on the novel *Fantasma d'amore* by Mino Milani; *SC*: Dino Risi, Bernardino Zapponi; *DOP*: Tonino Delli Colli (Technicolor); *M*: Riz Ortolani (Ed. C.A.M.); *E*: Alberto Gallitti; *PD*, *SD*: Giuseppe Mangano; *ArtD*: Gianni Giovagnoni; *CO*: Annalisa Nasalli-Rocca; *MU*: Giulio Natalucci, Michel Deruelle; *Hair*: Corrado Cristofori; *AD*: Claudio Risi; *APD*: Gianni Giovagnoni; *C*: Carlo Tafani; *AC*: Sandro Battaglia; *KG*: Augusto Michisanti; *ChEl*: Giuliano Michisanti; *SP*: Paul Roland Pellet; *SO*: Vittorio Massi; *B*: Giulio Viggiani; *SOE*: Italo Cameracanna; *Mix*: Gianni d'Amico; *AE*: Lidia Pascolini; *SS*: Carla Giaré. *Cast*: Romy Schneider (Anna Brigatti Zighi), Marcello Mastroianni (Nino Monti), Eva Maria Meineke (Teresa Monti), Wolfgang Preiss (Count Zighi), Michael Kroecher (Don Gaspare), Paolo Baroni (Ressi), Victoria Zinny (Loredana), Giampiero Becherelli (Prof. Arnaldi), Ester Carloni (Count Zighi's Housekeeper), Riccardo Parisio Perrotti (The Magistrate), Raf Baldassarre (Luciano), Maria Simona Peruzzi, Liliana Pacinotti, Adriana Giuffré. *PROD*: Pio Angeletti, Adriano De Micheli [and Luggi Waldleitner, uncredited] for Dean Film, A.M.L.F. (Paris), Roxy-Film (Munich); *PM*: Mario D'Alessio; *PS*: Alberto Passone, Rossella Angeletti; *ADM*: Roberto Mezzaroma, Marcello Nusca. *Country*: Italy/West Germany/France. Filmed on location in Pavia and at Cine International Studios (Rome). *Running time*: 96 minutes (m. 2614). Visa n. 76387 (3.13.1981); *Rating*: all audiences. *Release dates*: 4.3.1981 (Italy), 4.29.1981 (France), 12.2.1981 (Spain), 5.21.1982 (West Germany), 10.1982 (USA; Chicago International Film Festival); *Distribution*: Ceiad. *Domestic gross*: 412,000,000 lire. *Also known as*: *Fantôme d'amour* (France), *Fantasma de amor* (Spain), *Die zwei Gesichter einer Frau* (West Germany), *Fantasma de Amor* (Portugal).

Note: In the Italian version Romy Schneider is dubbed by Vittoria Febbi.

Pavia. Nino Monti, a well-to-do accountant, meets on the bus a woman he loved in his youth, Anna Brigatti, now aging and ugly. The meeting takes place in conjunction with a heinous crime, as a concierge is murdered near the place where Anna appeared. Nino learns from a doctor friend that the woman died of cancer three years ago, after marrying Count Zighi and moving to Sondrio. Nino goes to Sondrio to meet the count and comes across Anna, now looking still attractive as she was in her prime. They settle for an appointment on the banks of the Ticino River, in the places of their youthful love, but Anna falls from the boat and drowns. Sometime later Nino meets Anna again, old and ugly, in Pavia, but she disappears in the river once more. Nino becomes convinced that he has met a ghost and gets hospitalized in a nursing home where Anna reappears in the guise of a young nurse...

Four years after *Anima persa* (1977), Dino Risi returned to the Gothic genre with *Fantasma d'amore*, a crepuscular ghost story set in Northern Italy, amid the shadows and fogs of the Lombard town of Pavia, based on the novel published in 1977 by Mino Milani and adapted by Risi and Bernardino Zapponi.

As in *Anima persa*, the story focuses on the mid-life crisis of its protagonist, Nino, played by Marcello Mastroianni. Again, then, Risi investigates the dread of growing old: whereas in *Anima persa* the Dorian Gray syndrome resulted in the Engineer's (Vittorio Gassman) crazy alter ego sporting a childish behavior, in an obsessive and desperate infantile regression, here the apparent acceptance of fleeting time is eroded by the tide of memories which submerge Nino when he finds himself in front of Anna, the woman he loved years earlier. She now appears first as an old faded lady, and later in her past splendor, bringing back in him the burning awareness of happiness gone forever, and of a quiet but loveless marriage.

Compared with the eerie Venetian setting of *Anima persa*, Risi and Zapponi immerse their Gothic tale in an everyday, almost trivial reality, amid bus rides, bourgeois parties and reunions between old friends. Hence, the moments that openly deal with the Fantastic—and, as with the sequence of the murder of the concierge, with horror—stand out even more. In addition to the stylized and evocative flashbacks (see, for instance, Nino and Anna's bike trip), the director often finds a convincing balance between romanticism and dread: the kiss between Nino and his beloved, now reduced to an old woman with rotten teeth and (presumably) a putrid breath, with the man immediately cleaning his mouth in disgust afterwards, looks like a nod to the Tolstoy story which Mario Bava adapted for *I Wurdalak*.

Although with a sometimes-finicky approach, bedraggled by product placements and narrative hesitations, and denoting a modesty that borders on shyness in its approach to the supernatural (see the rather botched subplot about the defrocked occultist priest, played by Michael Kroecher), *Fantasma d'amore* reaches the same conclusions as so many Italian Gothic horror films of the past. The dead return for revenge, but especially for love, and time and its effects are mostly an illusion that the living have built as a barrier ("You really believe time exists … time which makes us age, which consumes us, that indeed exists. But inside of me, I'm not aged at all," Anna says), and the boundaries between life and death are fragile and pervious. "You see, my dear sir, what they say about the beyond, about this life, those are all nonsense … because we are still ourselves, we are dead, and we are alive at the same time…" says Nino in the end.

Fantasma d'amore was shot on location in the Lombard town of Pavia, in Fall 1980: according to Rome's Public Cinematographic Register, filming started on October 26. A strikingly cinematic town, Pavia had been used several times over the years by filmmakers, most notably by Alberto Lattuada (*Il cappotto*, 1952), Renato Castellani (*I sogni nel cassetto*, 1957), Dario Argento (*Le cinque giornate*), and Eriprando Visconti (*La orca*, 1976, and its sequel *Oedipus Orca*). As Milani recalled, "Pavia was, and had always been, a city of long autumns and thick fogs, and that kind of rain that moistens without wetting…. In the film, then, some scenes were patently grey and veiled; but the weather did not cooperate, and Risi had to resort to a fog machine. So, in the authentically old streets, and on the banks of the authentically poignant Ticino, Schneider and Mastroianni met amid floating, very costly artificial smokescreens."[1] In addition to a top-notch cast and crew, Risi managed to enroll another prestigious name: the then 72-year-old Benny Goodman, who played the solo clarinet in Riz Ortolani's moody orchestral score.[2]

Risi's film was released in several European

Hungarian lobby card for *Fantasma d'amore* (1981, Dino Risi), starring Romy Schneider and Marcello Mastroianni.

countries and was screened at the 1982 Chicago International Film Festival. Italian box-office results were disappointing given the two stars involved, and critics were perplexed too. *Fantasma d'amore* is indeed a disjointed work, which partly suffers from a subpar literary source. But it features an intense, poignant female character, beautifully played by Romy Schneider. Anna is not a vampire seductress but a victim of society and men alike, who can celebrate her victory only as a ghost, and yet is still radiantly superior to the male: her appearance to Nino, atop the villa stairs, strikingly recalls those of other Gothic heroines. Above all, Anna's love makes her able to live beyond death, like Elisabeth Blackwood in Antonio Margheriti's *Danza macabra*. "I am a woman, Nino, and women do not destroy anything, but they cultivate and preserve…" she says.

On the other hand, Nino—weak, submissive, petty, a "man without qualities"—suits himself to the situation. He soothes and suffers in silence, and when things go wrong he simply closes his eyes to the truth, dreaming that his beloved is still in his arms. In short, he clings to an illusion he calls happiness.

NOTES

1. Mino Milani, "Romy Schneider? Bellissima sotto il trucco da 'fantasma,'" *Corriere della Sera*, June 2, 2002.

2. Salvatore G. Biamonte, "'Re dello swing chiude col jazz': Torno alla musica classica," *Corriere della Sera*, February 20, 1981.

Murder Obsession (Follia omicida)

(*Murder Obsession*, a.k.a. *Fear*)

D: Riccardo Freda. S: Antonio Cesare Corti, Fabio Piccioni; SC: Antonio Cesare Corti, Fabio Piccioni, Riccardo Freda; *Dialogue adaptation*: Simon Mizrahi; DOP: Cristiano Pogany (Telecolor); M: Franco Mannino; E: Riccardo Freda [uncredited]; PD, CO: Giorgio Desideri; AD: Antonio Cesare Corti, Bernard Cohn [and Jacqueline Freda, uncredited]; C: Roberto Lombardi Dallamano, Guglielmo Vincioni; AC: Stefano Guidi; ACO: Alberto Tosto; AE: Anne Barrault; MU: Lamberto Marini, Sergio Angeloni; *Hair*: Agnese Panarotto; SO: Davide Magara; SE: Angelo Mattei, Sergio Stivaletti; SP: Debora Beer; KG: Gianni Savini; ChEl: Alberico Novelli; SS: Maria Luce Faccenna. *Cast*: Stefano Patrizi (Michael Stanford), Martine Brochard (Shirley Dawson), Henri Garcin (Hans Schwartz), Laura Gemser (Betty; English language: Beryl Fisher),

John Richardson (Oliver), Anita Strindberg (Glenda Stanford), Silvia Dionisio (Deborah Jordan); *uncredited*: Fabrizio Moroni (Michael as a child), Riccardo Freda (Elderly man on the set). PROD: Enzo Boetani, Giuseppe Collura, Simon Mizrahi for Dionysio Cinematografica (Rome), Societé Nouvelle Cinévog (Paris); PS: Antonio Boetani. PSe: Salvatore Carrara. *Country*: Italy/ France. Filmed at Palazzo Borghese, Artena (Rome) and at De Paolis In.Ci.R. Studios (Rome). *Running time*: 97 minutes (m. 2660). Visa n. 75784 (10.31.1980); *Rating*: V.M.18. *Release date*: 2.24.1981. *Distribution*: Regional. *Domestic gross*: n.a. *Also known as*: *The Wailing*; *Unconscious*; *Murder Syndrome* (USA—home video), *Angoisse* (France), *Obsessão Assassina* (Portugal), *Satan's Altar* (Greece), *Himomurhaaja* (Finland).

Note: On the poster for the foreign English language release titled *Unconscious*, Freda is credited as "Robert Hampton."

Following a violent raptus on the set that almost led him to strangle his co-star Beryl, actor Michael Stanford returns to the family home in Surrey after a fifteen-year absence, for a period of rest. He explains to his girlfriend Deborah, who accompanies him, that as a child he murdered his own father to protect his mother, and the event left him traumatized. His still young-looking mother, Glenda, takes a dislike to Deborah, whom Michael has introduced as his secretary. A few days later a director friend, Hans Schwartz, shows up with his assistant Shirley and Beryl. The three are poorly tolerated by Oliver, the enigmatic butler. Meanwhile, strange events occur: someone tries to drown Beryl in the bathtub, and Deborah experiences an upsetting nightmare in which she is subjected to a black magic ritual. The next day, during a walk in the woods, Michael and Beryl find an isolated spot and have sex: when Michael wakes up he finds Beryl's dead body next to him. Schwartz, who witnessed and photographed the murder, is brutally dispatched with an axe, and Shirley is decapitated with a chainsaw. All evidence points to Michael, to whom Glenda confesses that she was Oliver's lover: when Michael's father discovered them in the act of having sex, he killed the man and blamed the child for it. But Michael finds out that Oliver has committed suicide, leaving a taped confession where he reveals that it had actually been Glenda who murdered her husband, and she is also the one responsible for the gruesome killings. The woman, a practitioner of black magic, is morbidly jealous of her own son whom she believes is her husband rein-

carnated, and will stop at nothing to keep him with her...

Eight years after *Estratto dagli archivi segreti della polizia di una capitale europea* (1972), Riccardo Freda finally returned behind the camera to direct a low-budget horror film. Its genesis is as tortuous as it is emblematic of the subterranean threads that ran across Italian cinema of the period, connecting and tangling up people, ideas and stories like in a spider's web.

A former assistant director to Lucio Fulci, Edoardo Mulargia and Giuliano Carnimeo, in the early 1970s Fabio Piccioni had penned a short story titled *Il grido del Capricorno*, which he adapted into an adult comic book in the *Oltretomba* series (*Oltretomba Gigante* #9, February 1974, with drawings by José María Bellalta). Set in 1894, *Il grido del capricorno* was the story of a young musician, Ludwig von Mayer, who lives in the shadow of his late father, a composer and orchestra conductor, and is oppressed by a domineering mother who wants him to follow in his father's footsteps and become as famous as him. Meanwhile, a black-gloved killer starts dispatching the young man's lovers and friends in gruesome ways (and with ample display of nudity and sadism, as was customary with adults-only comics). The police and a criminologist start suspecting Ludwig, who is revealed to have killed his own father as a child but bears no memory of the event. Then, after Ludwig's wife-to-be Helga is horribly murdered too, a shocking truth is revealed.

Being in severe shortage of cash, Piccioni approached Salvatore Argento—with whom he was on good terms and whose office was just in front of his house in Rome—and sold him *Il grido del capricorno* for 500,000 *lire*. The deal had an ironic side which perhaps came unnoticed to both parts, given that a couple of scenes in the comic were blatantly stolen from *L'uccello dalle piume di cristallo* (1970), namely the killer terrorizing a woman in bed and ripping off her panties, and the maniac attempting to penetrate Helga's house, by jimmying the door with a knife, as the woman watches in terror.

Very little of *Il grido del capricorno* ultimately migrated into what became *Profondo rosso*, but it was vital to the film's plot: the relationship between Carlo (Gabriele Lavia) and his oppressive mother (Clara Calamai) derives from it, as does the brief opening flashback in which a child is seen picking up the knife that just killed his father, an image taken almost verbatim

from Piccioni's story (and the *Oltretomba* comic). The rest, of course, was all Dario Argento's invention. Still, it is no surprise that Argento chose not to follow the outrageous final twist, where the murderer is not only revealed to be Ludwig's mother, but the elderly woman turns out to be a man in disguise, his father's longtime lover.

Piccioni recycled several elements from *Il grido del Capricorno* once more, a few years later, for a story with a contemporary setting. The resulting script—concocted with the participation of Antonio Cesare Corti and Freda—was titled *Murder Obsession*.[1] It is the story of a young disturbed actor, Michael, who—after almost murdering an actress during the filming of a horror movie—returns to his secluded mother's house for a brief vacation, together with the film's director, the latter's assistant, the aforementioned actress, and his fiancée. Michael is obsessed by the memory of his late father, an orchestra director, and has a domineering, overly possessive mother. Unsettling, horrific events ensue: Michael's girlfriend experiences an eerie nightmare, supernatural forces seem to materialize, and most characters meet gruesome deaths. The horrible truth behind Michael's shady past is revealed: a flashback hints at the child apparently murdering his father, with the key image of the boy holding a bloody knife in his hand, as if hypnotized by the red stains on the blade. But the murderer turns out to be someone else...

Some sources list the script's original title as *L'ossessione che uccide*, whereas the script included in the Simon Mizrahi fund at the BiFi (Bibliothèque du film) in Paris is titled *Deliria*, signed by Corti (as "Tony Blond") and Piccioni, and dated 1976. The 4-page synopsis retained at Rome's CSC is already titled *Murder Obsession*. Marked January 18, 1980, it dates the project slightly after *Qualcosa penetra in noi (Le notti di Satana)*, a erotic horror film scripted by Piero Regnoli which Freda was supposed to direct in 1979 (taking over from Roberto Bianchi Montero, who was originally attached to it) but which never took off.[2] The CSC synopsis for *Murder Obsession* is basically identical to the finished film, save for the characters' different names: Michael's fiancée is named Frances, the director's name becomes Ken and Michael's deceased father was a Wilhelm von Holbach.

According to Jacqueline Freda, her father's aim when taking on the project was merely to resurface on the market in order to arouse the interest (and raise the money) for his biopic on

World War I ace aviator Francesco Baracca, which he had been trying to mount since the early 1970s.[3] A low-budget horror film seemed the easiest and fastest way. The director managed to involve producer Enzo Boetani, with his company Dionysio Cinematografica. Freda had become acquainted with Boetani since the late 1950s, when the latter collaborated as executive producer with Carlo Ludovico Bragaglia, but the two had never had the chance to work together, although they had tried to mount various projects. Such a one was a horror movie to be co-produced with a French company, whose title Boetani does not recall, whereas another was *Superhuman*, announced in the January 1979 issue of the *Foreign Sales Italian Movie Trade* magazine. According to the producer, it was in the vein of the superhero-cum-wrestler films that were all the rage in South America, and was aimed specifically at that market, with Freda attached to direct it, but it all came to nothing because of problems with the South American buyer.[4]

As Boetani recalls "It was Riccardo who came to me with the script for *Murder Obsession* and suggested an Italian/French co-production. The relationship between me and Freda was of mutual esteem, and honestly I must say I agreed to make the film for Riccardo—to make him and the crew work, since it was a difficult period for many of us—rather than because of the script's inner qualities." The film would be an Italian/French coproduction, and the French financer would be Freda's longtime friend, film critic Simon Mizrahi. "It was a low-budget movie, I think around 120 or 130 million *lire*, and we had to follow a tight shooting schedule," Boetani explained. "However, with Simon the situation was not so idyllic in the end, as there were problems with the French financiers."[5]

Filming went on for three weeks, in April 1980, mostly in Borghese Palace in Artena—one of the staple locations of Italian Gothic since Renato Polselli's *L'amante del vampiro*—and at Parco della Mola, in Oriolo Romano, where Laura Gemser's murder was filmed. Jacqueline Freda worked on the film as her father's uncredited assistant. Boetani cast three actors who had just finished working in a film he produced, Franco Molè's *Prima della lunga notte (L'ebreo fascista)* (1980): Ray Lovelock, Silvia Dionisio and Molè's wife Martine Brochard. Dionisio was cast as the fiancée, now called Deborah, a part originally to be played by Janet Agren, whereas

Lovelock (who even recalled having been prepared for the role and having made a screen-test) was replaced at the last minute by Stefano Patrizi for the role of Michael.

Born in Milan in 1950, the blond and handsome Patrizi had arrived in Rome in 1971, and took his first steps in the movie business thanks to his fiancée Barbara Mastroianni (Marcello's daughter), first as assistant editor (for Ruggero Mastroianni, on Visconti's *Ludwig* and Francesco Rosi's *Lucky Luciano*), and then as an actor, on Visconti's *Gruppo di famiglia in un interno* (a.k.a. *Conversation Piece*, 1974), followed by a number of often prestigious titles, including George Pan Cosmatos' *The Cassandra Crossing* (1976), the grim crime film *Liberi, armati, pericolosi* (a.k.a. *Young, Violent, Dangerous*, 1976, directed by Romolo Guerrieri and written by Fernando di Leo)

The Italian poster for *Murder Obsession* (1981), Riccardo Freda's final film.

and the controversial *Lion of the Desert* (1980, Moustapha Akkad), starring Anthony Quinn and Oliver Reed.

Michael's mother, Glenda, was played by Anita Strindberg, an oft-seen presence in 1970s *gialli*, such as Fulci's *Una lucertola con la pelle di donna* and *La coda dello scorpione* (a.k.a. *The Case of the Scorpion's Tail*, 1971, Sergio Martino); John Richardson (*La maschera del demonio*) was cast as the enigmatic butler, Oliver. The bare-bones cast also featured Laura Gemser (the star of the *Black Emanuelle* series) as Beryl and Henri Garcin as the director, Hans Schwartz.

Filming was not a pleasant experience for most of the people involved. "*Mamma mia* what a nightmare!" Laura Gemser recalled. "I remember that I had to shoot a scene with Anita Strindberg who had to grab a real knife and pretend to stab me. I shouted at Freda: 'You're crazy? What if she really hits me?!' He said: 'What are ya gonna do?' They would have done anything to save money on these sets. On top of that, I was naked, just for a change, and I was lying on the bank of a lake and it was freezing!"[6]

Martine Brochard's recollections were not happy either: "I remember I did not have much fun doing it, especially a scene where there was a glass which had been cut expressly so that I could put my head over it, and the camera was over a chainsaw that came closer and closer, and there I must confess I was really scared."[7] Brochard was not kind about Freda too: "He was a very tough type, of a wickedness I did not expect and which upset me, so much so that on the very first day I answered him back, but then I took him aside, talked to him and he softened a bit. There were two French actors in the film and he treated them so badly that there was this actor, who worked on stage and was an important name in France [Author's note: Henri Garcin], who was desperate, and I used to translate everything to him because on that set nobody translated anything."[8] Silvia Dionisio had recently separated from her husband Ruggero Deodato, and according to Brochard she just looked forward to finishing the movie; it was her last film role, followed in 1982 by Daniele D'Anza's TV mini-series *La sconosciuta*, before her early retirement.

Stefano Patrizi was on the verge of retirement as well: *Murder Obsession* was his last film, and then he moved to Milan to work in an advertising agency: "I did not like being an actor and was bored to death by such a job: the endless waits and the estrangement from the working reality on set were undermining. I had decided to quit that job, and sincerely I really did not consider myself up to it ... after six months in Africa shooting *Lion of the Desert* I was spent, and had decided to move away from Rome, with the aim of settling in Milan and starting over with something that would give me a more solid future and a full involvement...." Patrizi candidly admitted to this writer that he has no recollection whatsoever of *Murder Obsession*: "I vaguely recall Freda as a harsh man, of a few words and not very affable."[9]

Boetani—who maintains that Freda always behaved deliciously with him, and even introduced the producer to his future wife, script girl Maria Luce Faccenna, the daughter of producer Angelo Faccenna—adds a significant anecdote. "Once I came on the set and watched him direct a scene. He set up the camera, yelled 'Action' ... and turned his back on the actors! (laughs) 'But Riccardo, why are you doing that?' 'Well, you know, I can't make them act to save their life! Even if I don't watch them, that's the same—if it's good for the camera, then it's good for me too!' (laughs) You know, he was joking, but I think he really meant that...."[10] Overall, the feeling between the director and the cast was mutual: "He hated them," Jacqueline maintains. "He thought they were just terrible."[11]

The film opens with a quote allegedly from a 17th century philosopher named Hieronimus A. Steinback. "For centuries, theologians, philosophers, and poets have delved into the universe in search of proof of the existence of the devil. It would have sufficed to look into the depths of their own souls." In the glorious tradition of Italian Gothic, the line is totally made up, and the name "Hieronimus A. Steinback" is a fabrication on the part of the scriptwriters. Still, besides functioning as a commentary on what we will witness in the following 97 minutes, it ideally reconnects to a line uttered by a parish priest (Umberto Raho) in *Lo spettro* (1963): "The Devil is more real a person than our modern world would have it."

Murder Obsession begins with a little bit of self-referential, film-within-a-film oddity. A beautiful girl (Gemser) returns to her flat, engulfed in darkness. She goes to the window to open it, and, revealed by a sudden lighting in a quasi-Expressionist shot, a male silhouette appears behind the curtain. The man (Patrizi) grabs the girl by the neck, rips off her clothes and starts choking her. His face is splashed with a bright, unexplained red light, almost like in a Bava film—or rather, in Freda's earlier Gothics, such as *L'orribile segreto del Dr. Hichcock* or *Lo spettro*. But it all turns out to be part of a low-budget horror movie. As the camera recoils with an exquisitely fluid tracking movement, revealing the tiny set on which the film is being made, we can glimpse an elderly man on the right corner, leaning on an armchair and wearing a plaid cap. It is Riccardo Freda. As the scene continues, his unmistakable voice is heard in the background, commenting: "It was not quite a brilliant idea…." One wonders whether this bit reflected the director's own reservations about the uneasy pairing of stylish *mise-en-scène* and cheap material, old-style lighting and sound effects and gratuitous nudity.

Even though *Murder Obsession* falls in the realm of the splatter film, Freda despised such practices, and his attitude is patent in the way he deals with the gory murder scenes, namely an axe to the head and a decapitation via chainsaw, courtesy of Angelo Mattei's workshop, with a very young and still inexperienced Sergio Stivaletti in his debut.[12] The results are as crude and unpleasant as the killings in *L'iguana dalla lingua di fuoco* (1971) and the central massacre in *Estratto dagli archivi segreti della polizia di una capitale europea*. According to Boetani, Martine Brochard's decapitation scene was concocted by the director himself: "He shot it right in my office," the producer recalled. "He employed a trick with mirrors. It was amazing, one of the brilliant things I saw him do. He was a genius in this respect! And he shot it all with just a cameraman, the actress, and three mirrors…."[13] Nevertheless, *Murder Obsession* contains at least one remarkable gory scene, when Michael wakes up next to the naked Beryl, and slowly starts caressing her leg, contemplating her nudity—as the audience does—until the camera pans on the woman's torso, revealing a gruesome gash on it. Only then he realizes (as we do) that she is dead. Desire becomes disgust, the perspective is reversed. Despite a somewhat imperfect framing that gives away the macabre twist a bit too early, it is a remarkable reflection over the forms of horror and desire in cinema, and one that exudes an almost pornographic visual power.

Murder Obsession is usually labeled as a *giallo*, and indeed it features a black-gloved killer who employs such gruesome tools as an axe and a chainsaw. But the *giallo* elements—Beryl's at-tempted drowning in the bathtub, the close-ups of the murderer's gloved hands, Schwartz and Shirley's killings, a negative film capturing the murderer's identity as in *Blow-up* (1966)—feel tacked on to a Gothic-oriented storyline, and not the other way around. Take the central role played by the mansion where the characters move, eat, sleep, make love, dream and die: with its tight stairs, eerie basements and old-style half-lighted rooms, it acts as a character of its own, and seems to control the protagonists' feelings and actions with its intermittent lights that go out every now and then, forcing them in the dark. This haunted house feeds on old memories and secrets and does not let anyone come out alive: when the massacre is seemingly over, its doors close by themselves, arbitrarily shutting the survivors inside. Such a *huis clos* seems to belong to an indefinite era, and the odd contemporary details—such as Oliver's blue jeans and tennis shoes—are as disruptive as the sudden bursts of gore, adding to the film's overall sense of unease. The theme of the double, a Gothic trope, here becomes a further instrument to disrupt the difference between past and present, which, as in Bava's *Lisa e il diavolo*, ultimately get confused and indistinguishable: not only does Michael look exactly like his father (Freda did not even try and have Patrizi made up in a different way, but simply relied on different clothes for the flashbacks), but in the end he becomes one and the same with him in the eyes of his crazed mother.

The distance from the *giallo* can also be detected in the pacing and plot construction. It takes almost an hour before the first killing occurs (and offscreen, too: we get to see only the aftermath of Beryl's demise), and the following murder sequences are carried out in a rather idiosyncratic way, with the director avoiding the use of POV shots of the killer—the *giallo*'s trademark—and relying on abrupt bursts of violence. The resolution is also tortuous, and the final revelation of the murderer's identity and its motives comes off as rather disregarding of the surprise in itself: Oliver's taped confession, which Michael listens to, unrolls as one of those digressions that were typical of the director's beloved popular novels.

Freda places mood over pacing. He lingers on the interiors of Borghese Palace and sets up slow and elegant camera movements, leaving aside the direction of his clueless cast. He also avoids the *gialli*'s visual frenzy, and often comes up with stylized frame compositions that even recall the silent era, as in Michael's flashback of his father's alleged death. Despite not being satisfied with the actors, the director got along very well with the young d.o.p. Cristiano Pogany, the son of the great Gábor, Freda's longtime collaborator[14]: "My father adored him," Jacqueline Freda recalls. "Cristiano was one of the few people he really cared about and treated well on the set—and believe me, on the set my father was a wild beast! In his private life he was extremely good-natured, but when it came to his job he was frightful—with me as well! Whereas with Cristiano he was incredibly sweet…."[15]

Indeed, the cinematography is quite good despite the painful budgetary shortcomings. Freda claimed that he thought of Bava while making the film,[16] and some photographic tricks (such as the jellies in the "astral body" scene) recall the work of the Sanremese director. The use of miniatures and *maquettes*, on the other hand, is typical of both filmmakers, but several moments hark back unmistakably to Freda's past, for better or worse. The crude night views of Michael's house—incidentally, the same camera angle as that of Hitchcock's mansion in *L'orribile segreto del Dr. Hichcock*—were obtained via a photo of the palace placed before the camera: they recall *I vampiri* (1957) and *Caltiki il mostro immortale*, but also the awkward "exterior" shots in the spy story *Coplan ouvre le feu à Mexico* (1967). What is more, the nightmarish bit when Silvia Dionisio's character is running across a wood of malevolent branches echoes Barbara Steele's mad run in the villa's garden in *L'orribile segreto del Dr. Hichcock*; later, in the scene of Deborah fleeing from the haunted house at night during a thunderstorm, the obvious blueprint is the extraordinary opening sequence in *Beatrice Cenci* (1956). Freda was likely drawing from his cinematic memory and career to reshape a half-baked script into something as close as he could to his own cinematic vision.

Murder Obsession shows an in-depth involvement with the supernatural and the occult which was always part of Freda's character. Rather surprisingly for such a disenchanted and rationalistic figure, the director repeatedly professed his interest for superstitious beliefs and magical practices. "I have always been fascinated with esoteric and magic problems, and instead of *Little Red Riding Hood* I used to read Eliphas Lévi's manuals. My adolescence was dotted with Seals of Solomon and elderberry twigs plucked

in nights with no moon."[17] Magic had been a recurring presence throughout his career, too. In 1946, when Freda could not find anyone interested in financing his next film, his elderly maid performed a ritual to chase away the "evil eye" from him: that very day he got in touch with producer Nino Angioletti, who would finance his first box-office hit, the swashbuckler *Aquila Nera*; in 1948 he and Gianna Maria Canale witnessed a macumba ritual in Brazil which resulted in the actress falling ill; in 1950 he directed the short *Magia a prezzi modici* (Low-price Magic), which played with the clichés of superstition and the occult in a tongue-in-cheek manner.

The story and dialogue are literally packed with esoteric references, and each character seems to have a connection with magical practices, which manifests itself through a physical object (often a jewel) they have on them. Beryl mentions the voodoo rites she witnessed and took part in, in her home country of Martinique; Shirley owns a bracelet depicting an *ouroboros*, the serpent eating its own tail (in the dialogue, though, it is referred to as a "winged serpent"), a symbol of eternal return and an alchemical seal; Glenda is revealed to wear a necklace with occult symbols, including a vampire bat, whereas Deborah is spared because she is wearing the Seal of Solomon. But there is more: "The camera is my third eye," Hans Schwartz quips, and later Oliver covers his face so as not to be photographed by him (displaying the same annoyance as the natives in *Caltiki* when their dance ritual was disturbed by the explorers). Beryl hypothesizes that this is because he is scared that the camera might capture his soul.

As in Paul Muller's final monologue in *Estratto dagli archivi segreti della polizia di una capitale europea*, there is much talk of an "astral body." We even find out that Oliver can detach himself from his physical body and wander through the house at night, in a scene rendered in a rather crude yet endearing manner through subjective shots distorted by a jelly and the stop-motion appearance of muddy footprints on the staircase, in a perhaps fortuitous homage to Bava's *La frusta e il corpo*. Of all the characters summoned at Michael's house, Hans Schwartz—not just a film director but one resembling Freda: notice the glasses and cap he wears and the cigar he smokes—seems to be the most aware of the role of magic in the universe. "It's the only way to solve the mystery of life …

magic," he observes, and when we see him leafing through an occult book in plain sight in the lounge, one senses that he is not simply trying to waste time during an insomniac bout.

Hans Schwartz's monologue on the astral body and on the necessity to analyze the moment when the soul separates from the body ("But to do this, we must be capable of killing with our own hands so that no breath of life escapes us") strangely predates the theme of *Martyrs* (2008, Pascal Laugier) and its obsession with the afterlife. Schwartz also points out that he believes in reincarnation as "the only way to explain the moral and material unhappiness of mankind because of its bestial, degrading past life"—a line that is 100 percent Freda. His dialogue with Glenda, carried out like a subterranean seduction scene, is a fascinating and often overlooked moment that provides *Murder Obsession* its core. It is also one of several scenes absent in the version originally released to home video in the United States as *The Wailing*, which also attempted to make the film pass off as a standard *giallo* by way of adding a trivial synth score to flesh out (and replace in parts) Franco Mannino's haunting piano rendering of classical music by Bach and Liszt, itself another element that pronounced Freda's distance from the contemporary ways of horror cinema. On the other hand, at least one cut is welcomed, as the English language version did not feature one of the film's most awkward lines: in the scene following Shirley's chainsaw murder, Oliver is serving dinner, when out of the blue he passingly mentions to Glenda that the chainsaw is missing.

Another interesting example of the film's emphasis on the occult is Deborah's nightmare—one of *Murder Obsession*'s most derided sequences, and understandably so, given the ridiculous appearance of patently fake bats flapping about on wires and a giant rubber spider which the girl runs across at one point. Deborah is chased in the mansion's crypt by a pair of hooded, monstrous-looking figures, finds a way out into the garden, experiences horrid visions (such as skulls hanging from a tree like ripe fruits and dripping blood from their empty eye sockets), is tied to a St. Andrew's cross and subjected to an incomprehensible ritual. At first glance, the scene seems pointless, a shock segment whose only function is to provide cheap thrills to an undemanding audience. And yet, despite its sloppy effects work, which elicits comparison with a similarly awkward moment

in Luigi Batzella's *Nuda per Satana* (a.k.a. *Nude for Satan*, 1974)—or, again, an adults-only comic book like Ediperiodici's *Lucifera*, which in one issue featured a panel depicting a woman being raped by a giant spider—the sequence is not devoid of interest. On the technical side, it is characterized by fluid long takes, whereas thematically it carries out several of the plot's key themes and further underlines the director's fascination with the subject matter.

Scattered with magic symbols, Deborah's dream becomes the key to penetrate the true nature of the mystery. Note, for instance, the presence of the spider. In *Estratto dagli archivi segreti della polizia di una capitale europea*, a stone spider figure could be glimpsed on the fireplace during the occult ceremony at the Alexander mansion, and since Freda sometimes took care of sculpting props for his films, that could have been the case as well (after all, he even bothered to write the words for the bad song heard throughout the movie). Here the arachnid figure returns, with an overly symbolic significance. First Deborah runs into its web; then, during the rite, the spider reappears and takes a semi-human form, its paws eerily turning into furry, vaguely human hands which lusciously caress the girl's legs. The spider is an ancient symbol of mystery, power and growth: in India it is associated with the term "Maya," meaning the illusory nature of appearances, whereas in Egypt it is paired with the process of creation and recreation, and other civilizations saw it as a spinner of fate. Christian cultures have linked it with duplicitous meanings, but mostly as an evil force that sucks blood. As we will find out in the end, Michael himself has been trapped into a web of deception, and his own mother is revealed to be the spider-like spinner of the events that—in typical Freda fashion—lead to a circular ending, an eternal return that mirrors the ineluctability of fate.

On *Murder Obsession* the director returned to the primordial core of his conception of Gothic: a family melodrama, excessive and morbid, soaked with psychoanalytic undertones, in which the horror blossoms and feeds on the dynamics of parental relationships. As portrayed by the ravishing 43-year-old Anita Strindberg, Glenda is Freda's last and perhaps ultimate monster, the true point of no return after the incestuous father of *Beatrice Cenci*, the beauty-obsessed nubile old lady of *I vampiri*, the necrophile husband of *L'orribile segreto del Dr.*

Italian lobby card for *Murder Obsession*, featuring Silvia Dionisio (left) and Anita Strindberg. The tagline promises "*100 minuti di terrore*" (100 minutes of terror).

Hichcock, and the scheming wife of *Lo spettro*. She is a young-looking, sexy, desirable mother, who meets her son in bed while dressed in a transparent nightgown, and whose feelings for her offspring leave no room for doubt. She is also a vampire of sorts, feeding off other men's lust for her, and using them like puppets.

"The story nevertheless interested me. What can happen in our tragic childhood? What are the consequences when guilt and murder mingle?"[18] the director observed, while offering a psychoanalytic reading to his film. The weight of the past is connected to a horrific primary scene that is repeated twice—half-*Rashomon*, half-*Marnie*—to bring to the surface, and to human form, the torments of the unconscious which previously took the shape of grotesque nightmarish creatures. Freda's ultimate mockery is to load his unhappy Oedipus with a burden of guilt that is not his own; here the sins of the mother are literally passed on to the son, who must cope for the better part of his existence with the fabricated notion of having murdered his father. The process of discovering the truth— that is, his own innocence—leads him to ruin all the same. To Freda, as it has ever been, evil

is a vital part of human nature, and as such it will always win.

The director's reversal of the ancient Greek myth is sneering: not only is it Jocasta who lusts after her son, but she ends up killing the object of her desire in order to forever keep him with her. Freda ends the film with a final and blasphemous act of annihilation, with one of the most powerful—perhaps at least in part because unexpected—endings in his *oeuvre*, one that openly recalls those of *Il conte Ugolino* (1949) and *Lo spettro* and which truly lives up to Jacques Lourcelles' definition of the director as "one of the great aesthetes in cinema history."[19] The scene recreates one of the most awe-inspiring icons of classical art, Michelangelo's *Pietà* (Pity), in a way that is as elegant as it is cruelly mocking. The image of the Virgin Mary cuddling Jesus on her womb after crucifixion becomes the sight of a murderous mother who cries over the dying son whom she has just killed; a "hellish composition" in which "through the harmony of Renaissance art, dear as always to Freda as a painter and sculptor, and within the most reassuring image, the mother with her son ... earthly monstrosities thrive."[20]

As Jacqueline Freda recalls, "we spent one day on that scene. It was the only one in the movie which took a whole day to shoot—and one day, to my father, was like a whole week on a normal set! But he really cared about it. I think it was probably the only thing he really cared about in the movie...."[21]

Once again, as in *Lo spettro*, the camera's eye takes on a moral function. But the film's memorable final image can be read in many ways. Perhaps, to Freda, it was an ideal way to connect to his own past, to his early days as a sculptor in Adolfo Wildt's shop, where he tried his hand at reproducing the *Pietà*; in a way, it was yet another circular ending, like the ones he loved most. Moreover, it even works as a biting metaphor on the state of the Italian film industry, murdered by the maternal hands of the State by way of absurd and useless laws, its remains exposed for us to mourn. Therefore, the door that closes by itself, peremptorily, subtracting the mother, the son and the heroine to the world and to our view, and delivering them to oblivion, acquires a further, powerful symbolic meaning. It is Freda's hand that closes that door, sealing—with this premature yet late burial—his own film career, and a whole season of Italian cinema.

Murder Obsession was submitted to the rating board on October 15, 1980, and given a screening certificate on October 31; yet it took several months before it came out to theaters. Even though it was initially announced to have been selected in competition at the 1980 Sitges Film Festival,[22] eventually it was replaced by another Italian film, Antonio Margheriti's *Apocalypse domani*. Released in Italy in June 1981, after being screened at that year's Mystfest, it did mediocre business: Boetani blames the distributor, who also failed to pay back the expected sum. Reviewers were also rather tepid, praising the cinematography and the narrative tension but blaming the poor script and bad acting.[23] Nevertheless, the film was met with enthusiasm by a small group of fierce supporters, including the eminent film critic and historian Goffredo Fofi (who helped Freda put together his memoir, *Divoratori di celluloide*, released in 1981 as well, and mostly derived from the interviews the director had given during the previous decades in France) and critic/scriptwriter Patrizia Pistagnesi.

Over the years, Freda's swan song underwent a peculiar fate. On the one hand it was harshly dismissed by its author, who once went so far as labeling it "shit." When the interviewer asked him why such a severe judgment, Freda curtly answered, "It's not a good film. The actors were poor and so was the budget. I'd rather not talk about it."[24] He was less trenchant, but equally critical toward *Murder Obsession*, when discussing it with fellow film director Giuseppe Tornatore:

> Unfortunately it didn't turn out as I had wanted, also because there just weren't the necessary means, because it's strange how people are convinced that horror films are easy to make, even though they're some of the most difficult because you're always trying to balance, like a tightrope walker, right? It just takes one wrong footing and you fall, you can't save yourself by doing another sequence like in other films.... Here, there's nothing you can do, either you fall into the ridiculous, or it gets boring, or you achieve the desired effect.[25]

On the other hand, over the years the film has been overrated and championed by some as the director's testament and a culmination of his whole body of work, with a blind eye to its many flaws, both in style and substance, starting with the blatant budgetary limits and the compromises on the part of Freda in order to adapt to a market that demanded conspicuous bouts of nudity and violence. Most reviewers would rather focus on the overall mood which conveyed the feeling of the end of an era—the same that exuded from the pages of Freda's own autobiography.

Far from being a summation of his own work, *Murder Obsession* was supposed to be a shortcut for the director to return to the limelight. Immediately after finishing it, in fact, Freda was attempting to put together new and more ambitious projects. Such a one was an adaptation of Alexandre Dumas' *Ascanio*, on which the director worked in late 1980, whereas the other, co-written with the French critic Jacques Lourcelles, was *La Dernière momie d'Egypte* (The Last Mummy of Egypt), a story of love and reincarnation that should have been produced by Tarak Ben Ammar. Neither ever materialized.

Several months after the making of *Murder Obsession*, Boetani and Freda traveled to New York to discuss the possibility of making more low-budget horror movies with American producers. The director was trying to cash in on his by-now established fame as the father of the Italian horror film, but the timing and circumstances proved unfavorable. "Since Riccardo was not in good economic conditions in that period, I agreed to go with him and help him find a deal," the producer recalls. "We went and stayed there for a couple of weeks, but without really coming up to anything concrete, because we realized that those potential financiers were not so brilliant and, so to speak, reliable."[26]

In the 1980s and 1990s, Freda's work met a renewed interest on the part of critics, film festivals and young cinephiles. His status of "master of horror" was also celebrated in a three-part TV program called *Il cinema della paura*, directed by his former assistant Marcello Avallone and Patrizia Pistagnesi, and broadcast in November 1986 on Rai Tre. The elderly director appeared in the first installment: sitting on an armchair by a fireplace, in a studio set made to look like a castle hall, complete with thunder and lightning, he played with gusto the part of the world-weary lord of the castle, explaining for the umpteenth time his conception of fear and of the horror film in general with his usual eloquence and property of language. Despite his age, he was as sharp and intellectually brilliant as ever, but the many sincere homages only served to underline his belonging to a past age that would never come back.

Freda would never make another movie before his death in 1999. *La Fille de d'Artagnan* (1994), a project concocted with the help of his friend Bertrand Tavernier, turned up a bitter disappointment. Freda walked off the set and was replaced by Tavernier himself. It was one last, definitive sign that cinema—now a very different creature from the one he had learned to know and master since his early years in Egypt—did not need Riccardo Freda anymore.

NOTES

1. "It is a basic scheme, in which, from time to time, you can put everything," Piccioni commented. *See* Davide Pulici, "Il grido del capricorno," *Nocturno Cinema* #147, January 2015, 95.
2. For more details on the project, see Curti, *Italian Gothic Horror Films, 1970–1979*, 68.
3. Jacqueline Freda, interview with the author, May 2015.
4. Enzo Boetani, interview with the author, August 2016. As of this writing, *Superhuman* is still listed as completed in Freda's filmography on the IMDb.
5. *Ibid.*
6. Manlio Gomarasca and Davide Pulici, *Io Emanuelle. Le passioni, gli amori e il cinema di Laura Gemser* (Milan: Media Word Publications 1997).
7. Ippoliti and Norcini, "Una favola chiamata cinema. Intervista a Martine Brochard," 36.

8. *Ibid.*
9. Stefano Patrizi, phone interview with the author, February 2016. Patrizi did one more acting appearance in 2006, in the movie *Quale amore*, whereas he denies having worked on 2008's *Chi nasce tondo* … which nevertheless is listed in his IMDb filmography.
10. Boetani, interview with the author.
11. J. Freda, interview with the author.
12. "'Is it true that your first film was *Murder Obsession* (1981) by Riccardo Freda?' 'Yes, I have been attributed this paternity [*sic*], but it is not a film that I can say I signed. I collaborated with Angelo Mattei who did the effects, I was in his workshop, but I only did a few things, working on some tricks. Nothing special.'" Pierpaolo De Sanctis, "Intervista a Sergio Stivaletti," www.nocturno.it, May 13, 2015.
13. Boetani, interview with the author.
14. Cristiano Pogany was married to actress Pamela Villoresi, whom he had met in 1978, and they had three children. He died of cancer in February 1999, at only 51.
15. J. Freda, interview with the author.
16. Riccardo Freda, *Divoratori di celluloide* (Milan: Edizioni del Mystfest, Il Formichiere, 1981), 80. In Poindron's interview book, however, he claimed differently: "I never thought of Bava. It is a gory and perverse story like those he loved, but when I made it, I did not think of anyone. I tried to put myself in the criminal's skin…." Éric Poindron, *Riccardo Freda. Un pirate à la camera* (Lyon-Arles: Institute Lumière/Actes Sud, 1994), 350.
17. *Ibid.*, 88.
18. Poindron, *Riccardo Freda*, 349.
19. Jacques Lourcelles, *Dictionnaire du cinéma. Les films* (Paris: Robert Laffont, 1992), 1440.
20. Patrizia Pistagnesi, "Omaggio a Riccardo Freda," in Freda, *Divoratori di celluloide*, xiv.
21. J. Freda, interview with the author.
22. "Un festival del terrore in Spagna," *La Stampa*, June 19, 1980.
23. See a.v. [Aldo Viganò], "Il regista Freda è tornato con l'horror di un delitto," *La Stampa*, July 3, 1981.
24. Gian Luca Castoldi, "Riccardo Freda o del decadentismo dell'orrore," *Amarcord* #8–9, May–August 1997, 109.
25. Giuseppe Tornatore, *Il quarto moschettiere. Quattro chiacchiere con Riccardo Freda* (Taormina: TaorminaFilm-Fest, 2007), 24–25.
26. Boetani, interview with the author.

Quella villa accanto al cimitero (*The House by the Cemetery*)

D: Lucio Fulci. *S*: Elisa Livia Briganti; *SC*: Lucio Fulci, Giorgio Mariuzzo, Dardano Sacchetti; *DOP*: Sergio Salvati (Kodak, LV-Luciano Vittori); *M*: Walter Rizzati [and Alessandro Blonksteiner]; *M*: Vincenzo Tomassi; *PD, CO*: Massimo Lentini; *MU*: Maurizio Trani; *SE*: Gino De Rossi; *AMU*: Antonio Maltempo; *Hair*: Maria Pia Crapanzano; *AD*: Roberto Giandalia; *C*: Franco Bruni; *AC*: Maurizio Lucchini; *AE*: Pietro Tomassi; *SD*: Mariangela Capuano; *PrM*: Rodolfo Ruzza; *SO*: Ugo Celani; *B*: Eros Giustini; *Mix*: Gianni D'Amico; *STC*: Nazzareno Cardinali; *SP*: Antonio Benetti; *ChEl*: Alfredo Fedeli; *KG*: Giacomo Tomaselli; *ACO*: Claudia D'Obici;

W: Bertilla Silvestrini; SS: Daniela Puccini, Daniela Tonti; *DubD*: Pino Colizzi. *Cast*: Katherine [Catriona] MacColl (Lucy Boyle), Paolo Malco (Dr. Norman Boyle), Ania Pieroni (Ann), Giovanni Frezza (Bob Boyle), Silvia Collatina (Mae Freudstein), Dagmar Lassander (Laura Gittleson), Giovanni De Nava (Dr. Freudstein), Daniela Doria [Daniela Cormio] (First Female Victim), Giampaolo Saccarola (Daniel Douglas), Carlo De Mejo (Mr. Wheatley), John Olson [Kenneth A. Olsen] (Harold), Elmer Johnsson (Cemetery Caretaker), Ranieri Ferrara (Victim), Teresa Rossi Passante (Mary Freudstein); *uncredited*: Lucio Fulci (Prof. Muller). *PROD*: Fabrizio De Angelis for Fulvia Film (Rome); *UM*: Paolo Gargano, Fabrizio De Martino; *PSe*: Guglielmo Smeraldi; *ADM*: Otello Tomassini. *Country*: Italy. Filmed on location in New York, Boston and Concord, Mass. And at De Paolis In.Ci.R. Studios (Rome). *Running time*: 86 minutes (m. 2362). Visa n. 76953 (8.14.1981); *Rating*: V.M.18. *Release dates*: 8.14.1981 (Italy), 1.13.1982 (Spain), 3.24.1982 (France), 8.23.1982 (Denmark), 10.15.1982 (UK), 11.26.1982 (West Germany), 1.6.1983 (Netherlands), 3.1.1984 (USA; New York); *Distribution*: Medusa (Italy); Almi Pictures; Levy Films (USA). *Domestic gross*: 1,407,981,297 *lire*. *Also known as*: La maison près du cimetière (France), Aquella casa al lado del cementerio (Spain); Slagtehuset ved kirkegården (Denmark), Das Haus an der Friedhofsmauer (West Germany).

Professor Norman Boyle, a New York historian, is entrusted with the work of a dead colleague, Prof. Eric Petersen, who has murdered his fiancée and hanged himself. Boyle leaves with his wife Lucy and his little son Bob for the small New England town of New Whitby, where Petersen was conducting his research. Bob is warned of an upcoming danger by a strange girl, Mae, whom only he can see. In New Whitby, the Boyles settle in Oak Mansion, the gloomy house where Petersen lived. Soon they experience strange phenomena, and an unknown presence lurks in the basement. The real estate agent is horribly murdered, and so is Ann, a local girl hired as babysitter. Through Petersen's recorded diary, Boyle finds out that in the 18th century Oak Mansion was inhabited by a Dr. Freudstein, a mad doctor who conducted gruesome experiments centered on regenerating his own flesh. But the undead Freudstein is still hiding in Oak Mansion, thirsty for new victims. Boyle's family is in grave danger...

During post-production for *L'aldilà*, Fulci

was already at work on a new film. The title, *Quella villa accanto al cimitero*, echoed the Italian one for Tobe Hooper's *Eaten Alive* (1976)—released in 1977 as *Quel motel vicino alla palude* (That Motel Near the Swamp)—and did a wonderful job at summarizing the story's Gothic and pulp elements. Shooting lasted eight weeks, from March 16 to May 1981,[1] on a budget of about 600 million *lire* and with two weeks' exteriors on location in Concord (near Boston) and New York before the crew moved back to Rome for the interior shoots at the De Paolis studios.

Compared with the director's previous horror films, the story had a more traditional Gothic feel. Fulci claimed that once again he had paid homage to Lovecraft, adding that "after *L'aldilà* and *Black Cat*, I wanted to make a film

The Italian poster for *Quella villa accanto al cimitero* (art by Enzo Sciotti). The menacing, knife-wielding figure turned up again in other posters by Sciotti, namely *Assassinio al cimitero etrusco* (1982, Sergio Martino).

that would embrace all the ravings of the Providence writer, without necessarily being based on one of his stories."[2] Scriptwriter Dardano Sacchetti claimed that the inspiration came from Henry James' 1898 ghost novella *The Turn of the Screw*, from which the film reprises the central role of two kids and the setting in a villa which retains a malevolent presence. But Sacchetti spiced the tale with some autobiographical elements:

> The theme of the claustrophobic house in *Quella villa accanto al cimitero* is linked to my childhood. I was born in a big country house, with a huge dark basement, full of ambushes.... There was no running water, no electricity, no toilets. It was the other side of life, a true adventure.... At the age of 9, in that tiny village in Molise, I had to prove my courage by crossing the cemetery at night ... much of what I have written comes from these experiences, but indirectly.[3]

In his 1992 biography *L'occhio del testimone* the director was harsh toward Sacchetti (see entry for *L'aldilà*), and when discussing *Quella villa accanto al cimitero* he claimed that the script was "spiced in this case as well with sequences stolen from other films, particularly *La residencia* by Juan [Author's note: the name is actually Narciso] Ibáñez Serrador."[4] The nods to Serrador's 1970 film—known also as *The House That Screamed* and *The Finishing School*, and starring Lilli Palmer and John Moulder Brown—are basically those regarding Dr. Freudstein's habit of collecting the body parts of his victim to regenerate his own body, whereas in *La residencia*, Brown's character kills and mutilates the girls at the finishing school led by his overprotective mother (Palmer), in order to build an "ideal woman" with assorted body parts.

But the main sources of inspiration were recent American horror films, namely *The Amityville Horror* and, once again, *The Shining*. The references to Kubrick's adaptation of Stephen King's novel are multiple: Norman Boyle traveling by car with his wife and kid to the place of his new job; Bob's "invisible friend" warning him not to go; the looming shadow of Boyle's predecessor who committed a massacre; Boyle becoming increasingly detached from his family and obsessed with his colleague's death; the image of a pool of blood emerging from Freudstein's gravestone; Bob playing with his toy car around the house; and, last but not least, the sequence where Freudstein pushes Bob against the basement door while on the other side his father tries to break through the door with an axe, which replays one of *The Shining*'s most famous moments while also reprising the "premature burial" scene in *Paura nella città dei morti viventi*, with a savior who could actually harm the defenseless person he is trying to rescue.

For all its derivativeness, *Quella villa accanto al cimitero* is surprisingly effective, and full of intriguing themes and nuances. In James' novella the story is told by an unnamed female narrator, a governess who takes care of two children, Flora and Miles, and who begins to suspect that her predecessor Miss Jessel and another employee named Peter Quint had an affair. Both Jessel and Quint are dead, but the governess becomes convinced that their ghosts have a bad influence on the children. However, in the end the governess turns out to be an unreliable and possibly crazed narrator, and most likely she causes Miles' death. That the reader is never sure whether the ghosts are real or a product of a woman's imagination, is a testament to James' extraordinary book. Fulci's film apparently does away with such ambiguity right from the opening sequence, in which a couple of young lovers are slaughtered by the evil inhabitant of the "house by the cemetery," but then it reintroduces several ambiguous elements which baffle the viewer and give the story a disturbing nightmarish quality.

For instance, who is really Ann (Ania Pieroni), the elusive green-eyed babysitter who says she was hired by the local real estate agency to care for Bob? She appears to be a menacing character, especially for the family's unity: see the game of looks she and Norman exchange, hinting at a possible affair, in a scene which recalls the one between Joe the plumber and Martha in *L'aldilà*. But, in fact, she is doomed to death, as Bob (and we) have already seen a decapitated mannequin with her features in a shop window, in a scene where Fulci plays with the dichotomy between animate and inanimate that was at the core of Bava's vision of the *fantastique*. And what about Norman Boyle, whom other characters keep saying has already been there at Oak Mansion, even though he claims the contrary? Is he a liar, a man with a double life which he keeps concealed to his family, or is he experiencing something that has already happened in the past? In a way, like Jack Torrance, who has always been the caretaker at the Overlook Hotel, Boyle has always been at Oak Mansion, and therefore he is destined to die again and again, like his predecessors.

Then, there is Mae, the little girl who becomes friends with Bob. We first see her behind a window which turns out to be part of an enlarged picture of Oak Mansion: like a Bava character (or like Bob and Liza in *L'aldilà*) she is forever trapped in another dimension, which here takes the form of a photograph (echoes of *Blow-up*) that seemingly changes from time to time, a modern-day version of the paintings in Gothic tradition, and possibly a nod to a renowned M.R. James story, *The Mezzotint* (as well as to the celebrated ending of Kubrick's masterpiece). But Freudstein himself is an elusive presence whose very nature is ambiguous. His voice is that of a newborn baby who keeps crying all the time—a chilling contrast with his monstrous appearance, and in the scenes where we only see his arms and hands, the right one is rotting but the left one is obviously a woman's (actually, a girl's: Silvia Collatina explained that she was the stand-in for Freudstein in the murder scenes as well as in the door/axe scene).

The multiple Gothic elements of *Quella villa accanto al cimitero* concur to form an original and faceted take on the genre. As with *Paura nella città dei morti viventi* and *L'aldilà*, Fulci draws from elements of American folklore. The setting is an imaginary New England town called New Whitby, and Oak Mansion is a typical New England abode, aesthetically and architecturally integrated with the American tradition.[5] To quote Robin Wood's famous definition, it can well be labeled as a "terrible house," that is, "one of the most important and enduring schemata of American culture, whose line of descent can be traced from Poe (*The Fall of the House of Usher*) to Hooper (*The Texas Chainsaw Massacre*)."[6] The "terrible house," even more than the haunted houses in the classical English Gothic novels, represents "an extension or objectification of the personalities of the inhabitants" and signifies "the dead weight of the past crushing the life of the younger generation."[7] A disturbing concept in American culture, where it goes against the celebration of the past (the Founding Fathers, the revolution against the British, the manifest destiny and the frontier myth), in the hands of an Italian filmmaker it acquires unexpected nuances. Moreover, Freudstein's appearance, wearing a costume that looks very much like a Confederate uniform, hints at a dark historical past which is literally locked and forgotten underneath the surface, where it lurks and awaits.

Freudstein keeps himself "alive" (as a maggot-infested body driven by a ruthless survival instinct) by regenerating his own self with the bodies of the living, and especially children. In this sense he is a literal, putrefied version of such ogres as the predatory preacher Harry Powell in *The Night of the Hunter* (1955, Charles Laughton) and as such it embodies all kinds of symbolic references. The name itself, Freudstein, is a blatant crasis of two modern Prometheuses, a real-life and a literary one: Sigmund Freud and Victor Frankenstein. The former explored the dark corners of the mind and the latter tested the limits of the body. Both saw themselves as creators, even Gods; here, they are *the* monster. As Sacchetti explained, the name was invented by Fulci "on the basis of some assonance which at the moment I don't recall, but which back then was supposed to bring good luck, because it recalled something good."[8] It elicited irony on the part of the reviewers of the period, whereas Fulci scholars tend to overestimate its significance, without taking into account the director's irony and disdain toward psychoanalysis in general, and Freud in particular. However, through a psychoanalytic reading, *Quella villa accanto al cimitero* can also be seen as a horrific depiction of the disintegration of a family, and of human relations as a whole.

Is Freudstein—Fulci's most explicit version of the boogeyman so far—just an embodiment of a much earthlier monster, the product of a young boy's fantasy as a way of turning real horror into something more acceptable to his mind—a dark fairytale where the rules and the roles of good and evil are always to be followed? Freudstein is a baby in a decrepit man's body: his is a baby's voice, as the monster retains the characters of the victims that have become part of him, and even Freudstein's own procedure of sawing together body parts of the ones he has killed is more akin to a child putting together parts of his favorite toys like a puzzle, rather than to Frankenstein's dream of creating life through death.

The utter monstrosity of Oak Mansion and its evil inhabitant is juxtaposed with the ordinary, grey humanity that populates the film. Just as in *L'aldilà* we were treated to the banal chatter of Bob and Liza at the bar, here most dialogue scenes revolve around superficial topics, and characters appear disinterested, elusive, almost worried to end the conversation as soon as possible in order to return to their train of thoughts.

See, for instance, the opening dialogue between Boyle and Prof. Muller (an uncredited Fulci, with his inseparable pipe), with the latter trying to cut the discussion short and take a taxi; or the scenes between the Boyle family and Laura's assistant at the real estate agency, and between Norman and the clumsy library assistant (Giampaolo Saccarola). It's a world of uninteresting, superficial, insecure people (such as the fragile and neurotic Lucy Boyle) who seem to be vegetating while waiting for their hour to come. As Kazanian said in *Inferno*, "The only true mystery is that our very lives are governed by dead people," and the tombstone in the living room in Oak Mansion (Fulci's version of the "elephant in the room," that is, death) is a memento of that. Not by chance, in the film's third act the characters are repeatedly attracted to the underground lair where they will all lose their life, and they keep descending that set of stairs which leads only to horror and death.

The story's central character is the kid, Bob. Throughout the film, he oscillates between this world and another dimension, in the scenes where he sees or plays with Mae, who cannot be seen by any other person. At the end he completes the transition, emerging from Freudstein's gravestone into another dimension, where he and his little friend will remain forever, in a perpetual but—judging from the stern look of the woman who will look after them—unhappy childhood. The ending, as in *L'aldilà*, is a clever *coup de théâtre* which Robert Schlockoff, while interviewing the director in *L'Écran fantastique*, suggested being a reference to the ending of Hitchcock's *North by Northwest* (1959). Fulci amiably conceded it, just as in the same interview he had claimed to have met Antonin Artaud ("He looked at me with those crazy eyes, 30 years ago"). The epilogue plays with the limits of time and space and soothes the terrible notion at the heart of the story, that is Freudstein's unstoppable need of fresher and younger bodies. In Fulci's cinema, children often die in terrible ways, but not in *Quella villa accanto al cimitero*, and this is yet another indication of the film's

French lobby card for *Quella villa accanto al cimitero*, featuring the titular house—Oak Mansion in the film—which hides a horrible secret...

core, which despite its overall gruesomeness is filled with a gripping melancholy, underlined by the closing line that appears on screen: "No one will ever know whether the children are monsters, or the monsters are children." In a move typical of the glorious tradition of Italian Gothic horror cinema, the quote—attributed to Henry James—was in fact made up by Fulci and/or Sacchetti.

One of the main differences between *Quella villa accanto al cimitero* and Fulci's previous Gothic films is that it is centered on a couple of kids, marking at the same time a return to the themes of *Non si sevizia un paperino* as well as anticipation of some of his future works in the genre, focused on horror as seen through the eyes of children, namely *Manhattan Baby* (1982), *La dolce casa degli orrori* (1989) and *Voci dal profondo* (1990). With her red hair and pale complexion, Silvia Collatina somewhat recalls Nicoletta Elmi, and is quite convincing as Freudstein's ghastly child, who acts as a link between the world of the living and the afterlife; she would appear again, uncredited, in *Murderock—Uccide a passo di danza* (1984). On the other hand, the blond Giovanni Frezza would turn up again in next year's *Manhattan Baby*. Reportedly, the director maintained a detached attitude toward the kids, "like a schoolteacher who demanded things from us and wanted them exactly as he said,"[9] as Collatina recalled.

The rest of the cast comprised familiar faces in Fulci's cinema, such as Catriona MacColl, Carlo De Mejo, Dagmar Lassander and renowned voice actor Giampaolo Saccarola. The lead, Paolo Malco, was a capable stage and TV actor who had starred in such diverse works as Antonio Bido's *giallo*, *Il gatto dagli occhi di giada* (1977) and Franco Brogi Taviani's *Masoch* (1980), a biography of Leopold von Sacher-Masoch; he would turn up again in *Lo squartatore di New York* (1982). As for Ania Pieroni, her stunning looks were not enough to make up for her limited acting (something she was not asked to do in *Inferno*), and reportedly the director was very harsh toward her.

But the main star of *Quella villa accanto al cimitero* is Fulci's direction, which is more controlled and subdued than in the past. With the help of Massimo Lentini's inventive set pieces (most notably the narrow metal staircase which leads to the bottom of Freudstein's gravestone, like a theatrical stage trap), the director enhances the spatial qualities of the titular house—and its contrast between the ground and top floor on the one hand and the basement on the other—through dollies and tracking shots, and builds an unnerving mood through a crescendo which confines most of the gore to the last part, unlike *Paura nella città dei morti viventi* and *L'aldilà*. Some of the gory sequences are played for their nerve-wracking value, like the one where Boyle is attacked by a bloodthirsty bat (a nod to *Suspiria*'s bat scene but done better). Others are an exercise in the macabre, like the one where Boyle listens to a tape with Petersen's comments about Freudstein's experiments, with Fulci's prowling camera wandering in the basement amid severed body parts and disemboweled bodies, thus hinting at the doctor's macabre experiments.

Despite the credits indicating the special make-up effects as the work of Giannetto De Rossi and Maurizio Trani, only the latter did in fact work on the film, creating Freudstein's decomposed face as well as the other effects. Gino De Rossi took care of the special effects. Fulci liked to work with the same team of collaborators, as in the old days of genre cinema, but *Quella villa accanto al cimitero* marked at least one important difference from the previous films, with the music score being composed by Walter Rizzati: the result differs notably from the director's other films of the period, and has a remarkable melancholic quality, starting with its impressive Bach-inspired main theme.

As with *L'aldilà*, *Quella villa accanto al cimitero* underwent remarkable changes from Elisa Briganti's original story and Dardano Sacchetti's script—originally titled *La notte dell'inferno* (The Night of Hell), which became *La casa di Freudstein*, then *Quella casa accanto al cimitero*—to the screen. Sacchetti's script—written as usual on a tight schedule—was then revised by Fulci and Giorgio Mariuzzo. As for his contribution, without going into detail, Mariuzzo claimed to have acted as script doctor, changing here and there to make the screenplays work: Sacchetti's scripts, he said, were often too short, in accordance with Fulci's claims, and even Fulci's script supervisor Rita Agostini agreed with this. Sacchetti's version is as follows: "Mariuzzo always intervened afterwards, either because I had to leave to work on another film or refused to make those changes that Lucio demanded. That was the reason for our arguments. I accused Fulci of looking for shortcuts, and trivializing things. He wanted simpler, more traditional stories. He hadn't identified himself yet with the role of master of horror."[10]

A look at the script deposited at the CSC—titled *Quella casa accanto al cimitero*, with the original *La casa di Freudstein* erased in pen, and credited to Elisa Briganti (story) and Dardano Sacchetti (screenplay)—can help get an idea on who wrote what. It is dated February 10, 1981, one month before shooting began, and it is likely the last version before the rewritings. At 223 pages, it looks considerably long, but many pages consist of extremely brief scenes of a couple of lines, often describing just one shot (i.e., the exterior of the house) and making it seem much longer than it really is. The script displays interesting differences with the finished film, revealing the extent of Fulci and Mariuzzo's contribution, which is considerable.

The CSC script opens with a lengthy introductory sequence (33 pages long) which differs sensibly from the one in the film. Two lovers are exploring Freudstein's house (not called Oak Mansion here), when suddenly the man stabs the girl in the head (the knife protruding from her mouth is the only detail kept in the film) and drags the body in the basement—apparently, he brought her to the villa to get rid of her. But he remains locked downstairs in the dark too and meets a grisly end in turn. "By the light of the flame the most terrifying image that the human mind can conceive appears before his eyes, an image originated from infernal darkness": the fleshless, rotten face of a living cadaver. Leaving aside the grotesque build-up (the man gives the girl a ring box which turns out to contain a maggot instead of a ring), this rather senseless murder scene gives away Freudstein's appearance immediately, and the horrible doctor will turn up repeatedly during the course of the story, a choice that Fulci wisely discarded.

Speaking of Freudstein, the script describes it as follows: "Then the incredible monstrous being gets up and shows itself: an unequal body, with two right arms, an enormous head, disproportionate, on a very thin torso" (p. 106); "He is very tall, very skinny, completely bald, the face reduced almost to a grinning skull, covered with horrible putrefied flesh ... he looks like he is composed of body parts from several men" (p. 209). Trani had indeed devised an alternate make-up for Freudstein similar to the one described in the script, as a skinned man with flesh and tendons in sight, predating the sight of the dead Frank (Oliver Smith) in *Hellraiser* (1987),

but Fulci was not satisfied and eventually dropped it in favor of the make-up we get to see at the film's climax. Another key detail missing from the CSC script is Freudstein emitting baby cries, while on the other hand, in an inane dialogue exchange, Boyle describes Freudstein as "a Barnard before its time," referring to the noted heart surgeon Christiaan Barnard, to which Lucy replies: "Or a Baron Frankenstein, if you prefer." Fulci could indeed turn hollow dialogue into an asset, as with the scene of McCabe and Liza flirting in the bar in *L'aldilà*; but he was well aware of the border between the disposable and the ridiculous.

The CSC script is totally devoid of the ambiguous, ghost story elements that we find in the film. There is no Mae Freudstein, but an 8-year-old kid, Mark Hauser, who is very much alive, and whom we first meet listening to the grisly stories on Freudstein told by his grandmother. Mark becomes Bob's friend and turns up in the final scene as the savant. Missing are also the backstory of Boyle's predecessor, the scene between Boyle and Muller in New York, the meeting with the real estate agent Laura (a character absent from Sacchetti's script), and the references to Boyle having been there in the past. Ann the babysitter is just a normal girl (no sign of the ominous shop window sequence), the Boyles are a happy couple, and most of the elements borrowed from *The Shining* are absent. The only connection might be seen in the fact that Norman Boyle here is a historian, who moves to Freudstein's house for a couple of months to complete his book on the Civil war. Incidentally, the references to the American Civil War are much more relevant than in the film: Freudstein's backstory deals with him performing transplants on the unfortunate soldiers he operates—and in one of the final scenes he is explicitly described as wearing "an old and dirty army uniform" (p. 209)—until the doctor was lynched by an angry mob (an idea recycled from the prologue of *L'aldilà*) when they found out he was also using children for his experiments. The mob killed Freudstein's wife Mary and buried her outside the villa—hence the gravestone in the garden that features prominently in the script.

Boyle's research is more conventionally developed in Sacchetti's story. He finds out that pages from a history journal regarding the mysterious Freudstein are missing. The CSC script introduces a character absent in the film, a librarian named Howard Grimm, who turns up at Boyle's house in his absence to hand him the missing pages and becomes one of Freudstein's victims, as would happen to Dagmar Lassander's character in the film. Other horror scenes, such as the bat attack and Ann's murder, are almost identical on paper, but in the movie Freudstein kills by way of ordinary weapons, such as a knife and a poker, while in the script he uses his bare hands, gouging victims' eyes out and so on (something too similar to what the zombies did in *L'aldilà*, evidently).

The CSC script features some odd details that Fulci discarded. For instance, Lucy Boyle discovers dozens of human teeth in a drawer, in a nod to Edgar Allan Poe's story *Berenice*. Another sequence has Lucy discover a hole in the closet wall, from which a swarm of moths— "black, horrible, disgusting"—come out, covering her face in a moment obviously patterned on the infamous maggot rain in *Paura nella città dei morti viventi*. In the hole, Boyle will find a box with documents on Freudstein's dismissal from the army because of his experiments (a much less suggestive idea than the tape recording from his predecessor that he listens to in the film). The marble gravestone in Freudstein's house (which in the script is placed in the kitchen) doesn't lead to the basement, but, once Boyle opens it, it reveals a grave "four feet deep, a rottenness in which maggots, limbs, bones, skulls and feet teem."

If Fulci decided to tone down Sacchetti's fondness for all things putrefied, it was not only to limit the similarities with his previous zombie films, but also to enhance the ghost story side of the tale. This is all too evident in the script's climax, which is disappointingly conventional compared to what we see in the film. Here Fulci and Mariuzzo added a self-reference to enhance the tension (Freudstein pushing Bob against the door while Boyle is breaking the door with an axe), and completely revised the ending. In the CSC script, Freudstein kills Norman and Lucy (whom we see disappear in the dark of the basement, dragged away by the monster), but Mark shows up at the last minute with a bucket full of petrol, which he throws against Freudstein before setting him on fire with a match. The end. No wonder Fulci disliked such a banal and simplistic ending, more suited to some Hollywood PG scary flick.

Overall, the noticeable improvements from Sacchetti's earlier script bring out the measure of Fulci's attempt to go beyond genre conven-

tions. Moreover, the Henry James connection, which is very feeble on paper, comes to the fore in the film thanks to the addition of the character of Mae Freudstein and her mother as well as of the final literary epigraph (a recurring element in the director's later work, as shown by the quotes from Balzac and Hawthorne that open his diptych in the TV series "*Le case maledette*").

Despite Sacchetti's remarks about Fulci's indecisiveness toward his status as "master of horror," *Quella villa accanto al cimitero* comes off as one of the director's strongest films. It may lack *L'aldilà*'s visionary qualities, but it is taut and scary as few other Italian horror films and stands up to repeated viewings. Fulci considered it one of his best works, going so far as claiming it as an influence on subsequent and far more celebrated titles—a retribution of sorts for a film born as a patchwork of other, more famous works. In a 1990 interview he raised the suspicion that Spielberg might have taken inspiration from his film for *Poltergeist* (impossible, as filming for *Poltergeist* took place from May to August 1981)[11]; in one of his last interviews he even accused Paul Verhoeven of having ripped off the scene where MacColl is dragged down a set of stairs in *Robocop* (but with the titular robot in the woman's place).[12] An attitude which recalls that of some Fulci scholars who obtusely—and without even checking whether it might actually be *possible*—try to pinpoint influences of Fulci's work in that of American filmmakers, as if this would make it more valuable.[13]

Quella villa accanto al cimitero had some marginal issues with the rating board, who requested a brief cut (3.20 meters, about 6 seconds) in the sequence of the killing of Dagmar Lassander's character Laura Gittleson before granting a screening certificate with the expected V.M.18 rating. This can be noticed in the shots showing the aftermath of the killing, as Laura appears to have had her left eye gouged out (most likely with the poker used to puncture her chest and throat). It opened in Turin on August 14, 1981, while the director was leaving to the U.S. to shoot his next horror film with Fulvia Film, a hyperviolent *giallo* with erotic undertones titled *Lo squartatore di New York*. With over 1.4 billion *lire* grossed at the Italian box-office, *Quella villa accanto al cimitero* did better than Fulci's previous horror films of the decade, despite negative reviews. The *Corriere della Sera* called it mockingly "the Italian *Shining*" and the reviewer summed it up as "a condensation of rip-offs, commonplaces and badly repeated horror conventions."[14] *La Stampa* complained about the presence of kids: "to see children involved in such a gruesome and oppressive horror story will perhaps cause disconcert and discomfort, rather than pity, in many spectators."[15]

The film was also released theatrically overseas (as *The House by the Cemetery*) and in the major European countries such as West Germany, Spain (where it was a notable box-office success[16]) and France (as *La Maison près du cimetière*). Panning the movie in *La Revue du cinéma* with a ferociousness even harsher than his Italian colleagues, Philippe Ross concluded: "It is high time, however, that this Stakhanov of horror cinema, who must benefit from advantageous prices on hemoglobin, finally learns how to handle a camera and shows us something other than these endless scenes of butchery who truly become more and more painful and soporific."[17]

Prior to its official French theatrical release, the film was screened at the 11th "Festival international du film fantastique et de science-fiction" in Paris together with *Black Cat*, and it was accompanied by a retrospective screening of *Una lucertola con la pelle di donna*. The public's response wasn't enthusiastic, though, and *Quella villa accanto al cimitero* ended up at the seventh place in the audience ranking (*Black Cat* ended up ninth).

The January 1982 issue of *L'Écran fantastique* dedicated *Quella villa accanto al cimitero* a two-page review penned by Christophe Gans, followed by another lengthy interview with Fulci conducted by Robert Schlockoff. The latter was nothing short of celebrating: "Lucio Fulci realizes that there exists an audience for his films, *his* audience: ready to enter full foot in worlds of nightmares, to be fascinated by visions so terrible that they become surrealist, to applaud the artistic brilliance of each of his movies, to appreciate his language which refuses to refer to the usual codes of horror cinema."[18]

On the other hand, Gans' review was once again less than favorable. "Aware of having reduced his latest film to an inventory of atrocities, Lucio Fulci wanted to win back some of the audience, disappointed or frankly shocked by *L'aldilà*," he noted. But he pointed out: "Shaken up by gore, the theme of the haunted house loses its Anglo-saxon pedantry while maintaining its most conclusive flaw. Playing with the audience's frustration as a way to be subtle is fundamentally

irreconcilable with the Italian director's marked points of view," Gans added. "Except for two or three welcome details … the suspense "for laughter," so appreciated by American filmmakers, here becomes particularly tedious." The reviewer blamed the paper-thin characterizations, pointing out: "The failure of the film's first part relies on this systematic sabotage of any psychological credibility. With ample use of intempestive zooms, Fulci tries in vain to dramatize the insufficiently played sequences. He doesn't succeed better in filling the gaps of the script with caricatural sophistication…. In this film, Fulci hasn't resolved to give up to his pseudo-Lovecraftian cycle, but the failure of *L'aldilà*, a shaky copy of *Paura…*, obliged him to sidestep the issue."[19]

Gans' praise of the film's visual virtues, namely its "melancholic, wintery photography" and its final vision of the beyond as a "benevolent afterlife," didn't cancel his reservations:

> Major innovation: would there be place for a possible paradise in Fulci's cinema? The distinction and the undoubted success of the scenes with the ghosts … only emphasize the director's lack of distance with respect to the gore effects…. Fulci henceforth comes and goes between the defused outbidding (*L'aldilà*) and the risky slowness…. This indecision goes hand in hand with a progressive destruction of the characters' importance, as they move around only to serve the horror despite good sense…. But in this repertoire of gimmicks repeated or borrowed from Argento, our greatest regret is the absence of madness in the explanation of the monster, yelled amid the din of a stretched suspense.[20]

Quella villa accanto al cimitero faced lots of censorship issues in the United Kingdom. The cinema version, distributed by Eagle Films, was passed with cuts by the BBFC on December 29, 1981: the sequences of Ann and Laura's murders were heavily trimmed, for a total of about one minutes and a half, and the copy ran 84 minutes and 49 seconds. The same print was released on video. Nevertheless, it ended up in the video nasties list after the 1984 Video Recordings Act. It resurfaced to home video only in 1988, in a print pre-edited by 34 seconds (removing the cinema cuts) and then with additional cuts amounting to 4 minutes and 11 seconds, which meant the hacking of all the violent sequences, including the bat attack and the infamous subjective shot in the basement amid body parts. It was re-released in 2001 with 33 seconds cut and finally in its uncut form in 2009.

NOTES

1. According to Rome's Public Cinematographic Register.

2. Romagnoli, *L'occhio del testimone*, 18.

3. Albiero and Cacciatore, *Il terrorista dei generi*, 296.

4. Romagnoli, *L'occhio del testimone*, 18.

5. According to Fulci, the titular house was a school for disabled kids owned by a hippie couple. See Schlockoff, "Entretien avec Lucio Fulci," (1982), 12.

6. Wood, *Hollywood from Vietnam to Reagan ... and Beyond*, 14.

7. *Ibid.*, 82.

8. Albiero and Cacciatore, *Il terrorista dei generi*, 298.

9. *Ibid.*

10. *Ibid.*, 296.

11. Bruno Maccaron and Patrick Nadjar, "Lucio Fulci: 'Je suis un monstre!' Le grand retour du maître Italien de l'horreur" *L'Écran fantastique* #116, October 1990.

12. Garofalo and De Lillo, "Il cinema del dubbio. Intervista a Lucio Fulci," 19.

13. Example? Albiero and Cacciatore hypothesize that the sequence of Boyle listening to Peterson's tape, with the camera showing the horrors of Freudstein's basement, influenced Sam Raimi's *The Evil Dead* ... without considering that Raimi's film was shot between November 1979 and January 1980. Albiero and Cacciatore, *Il terrorista dei generi*, 304.

14. G. Gs. [Giovanna Grassi], "'Shining' italiano," *Corriere della Sera*, September 18, 1981.

15. a.v. [Aldo Viganò], "Nella horror story anche i bambini," *La Stampa*, August 18, 1981.

16. According to the official Spanish ministerial data, it was seen by 535,523 spectators and grossed an amount corresponding to 584,617 Euro. (http://infoicaa.mecd.es/CatalogoICAA/Peliculas/Detalle?Pelicula=652251)

17. Philippe Ross, "La maison près du cimetière," *La Revue du cinema* #368, January 1982, 53.

18. Schlockoff, "entretien avec Lucio Fulci" (1982), 10.

19. Christophe Gans, "La maison pres du cimetière," *L'Écran fantastique* #22, January 1982, 8.

20. *Ibid.*, 9.

1982

Amityville II: The Possession

D: Damiano Damiani. *S*: based on the novel *Murder in Amityville* by Hans Holzer; *SC*: Tommy Lee Wallace [and Dardano Sacchetti, uncredited]; *DOP*: Franco Di Giacomo (Technicolor); *M*: Lalo Schifrin; *E*: Sam O'Steen; *PD*: Pier Luigi Basile; *AD*: David Ticotin, Aaron Basky; *C*: Daniele Nannuzzi; *AC*: Stefano Coletta; *2ndAC*: Crescenzo G.P. Notarile, Francesco Damiani; *ArtD*: Ray Recht; *SD*: George DeTitta Jr.; *SPFX*: John Caglione, Jr.; *AsstSPFX*: Stephen Dupuis, Ed French, Joe Cuervo; *SE*: Glen Robinson; *AsstSE*: Gari Zeller; *AE*: Nicholas Smith, Lori Bloustein; *CO*: William Kellard; *STC*: Vic Magnotta; *PrM*: Richard Adee, Wally Adee; *KG*: Dennis Gamiello; *Dolly grip*: John Mazzoni; *Construction grip*: Arne Olsen; *Scenic chargeman*: Richard Hughes; *ChEl*: Michael Burke; *SE*: Glen Robinson; *Transportation*: Mike Houriman; *Hair*: Warner Sherer; *W*: Rose Triamarco; *SO*: Neil Fallon; *B*: Kevin Meehan; *SOE*: Stan Bochner; *Mix*: Kim Ornitz; *Casting*: Navarro Bertoni; *SS*: Sheila Page. *Italian version*: Cesare Noia; *Dial*: Francesca Marciano; *DubD*: Mario Maldesi; *AsstDub*: Maura Vespini. *Cast*: James Olson (Father Adamsky), Burt Young (Anthony Montelli), Rutanya Alda (Dolores Montelli), Jack Magner (Sonny Montelli), Diane Franklin (Patricia Montelli), Andrew Prine (Father Tom), Moses Gunn (Detective Turner), Ted Ross (Mr. Booth), Brent Katz (Mark Montelli), Erica Katz (Jan Montelli), Leonardo Cimino (Chancellor), Danny Aiello III (Removal Man 1), Gilbert Stafford (Removal Man 2), Petra Lea (Mrs. Greer), Alan Dellay (Judge), Martin Donegan (Detective Cortez), John Ring (Police Chief), Peter Radon (Assistant Chancellor), Lawrence Bolen (Funeral Director), Tony Boschetti (Elderly Man in Church), John Clohessey (Police Officer 1), Hollis Granville (Police Officer 2), Frank Patton (Police Officer 3), Kim Ornitz (Police Officer 4), Lindsay Hill (Police Officer 5), Rudy Jones (Gardener), Todd Jamie (Guest at Birthday Party), Ken Smith (Prison Doctor). *PROD*: Ira N. Smith and Stephen R. Greenwald for Dino De Laurentiis Corporation—Giada International (USA); *EP*: Bernard Williams; *PS*: Michael Dryhust; *AP*: José López Rodero for Media Technology (Mexico); *PM*: G. MacBrown; *GM*: Martha Schumacher [Martha De Laurentiis], Wendy G. Glickstein, Sherri Taffel Brown; *PM*: G. MacBrown; *Location manager*: Jeffrey Silver. *Country*: USA/Mexico. Filmed in Mexico City. *Running time*: 102 minutes (m. 2791). Italian visa n. 78655 (3.30.1983); *Rating*: V.M.18. *Release dates*: 9.24.1982 (USA), 1.5.1983 (France), 4.8.1983 (Italy), 5.12.1983 (Australia), 2.10.1984 (West Germany); *Distribution*: Orion Pictures (USA), Gaumont (Italy). *Domestic gross*: $ 12,534,817 (USA); *Also known as*: *Amityville Possession* (Italy), *Amityville II—Der Besessene* (West Germany), *Amityville II: le possédé* (France).

Note: Ed & Lorraine Warren are credited as "demonology advisors." Father Thomas Bermingham is "religious consultant."

The Montelli family—father, mother and four sons—moves to a house in Amityville, in the state of New York. The place turns out to be haunted by demonic entities, and soon eerie things start happening, such as blasphemous writings on the wall of the children's bedroom which prompt them to kill their parents. Through the Walkman's headphones, the devil talks to the elder son, Sonny. A priest, Father Adamsky, suspects the truth, but can't do anything to save the family. Incited by Satan, Sonny seduces his sister Patricia and then slaughters the whole family. After his arrest, Father Adamsky persuades detective Turner to allow him to take Sonny back to the house and perform an exorcism on the young man. The demon leaves Sonny's body and takes possession of the priest. The house is up for sale again...

Amityville II: The Possession came as a surprise to those who were familiar with Damiano Damiani's oeuvre, as the director's body of work consisted mainly of socially and politically committed films which dealt with such themes as Mafia, terrorism and corruption, often developed within crime plots which nevertheless were far removed from the typical genre trappings of the *poliziottesco*. Still, in the early 1980s Damiani was finding it harder and harder to make the films he wanted: after the harsh *L'avvertimento* (1980), starring Giuliano Gemma and Martin Balsam, he made a 2-part TV movie on terrorism, *Parole e sangue*, but had to give up to a project on the hardcore porn film industry, to be shot in the States and produced by Dino De Laurentiis. "It was the story of a porn actress, even though I didn't want to shoot any hardcore scene, because I'd ruin the film completely," Damiani recalled. "I met many porn actresses.... I even paid a visit to the one who did *Deep Throat*, Linda Lovelace, and when I was introduced to the director, Gerard Damiano, they told me, 'Mr. Damiano' and I said, 'But I'm Damiano, too!' and we had a laugh."[1]

Even though it is an American production, *Amityville II: The Possession* has an Italian core to it, and not just because it was financed by an Ital-

ian producer, Dino De Laurentiis, who had relocated to the States in the previous decade. In the past, De Laurentiis had tried to involve Italian directors in his productions, most notably Mario Bava, whom he wanted to direct his 1976 remake of *King Kong*: Bava notoriously refused, not least because of his previous unhappy experience with the producer on *Diabolik* (1968).

The script by Tommy Lee Wallace was an evolution from a pre-existing story by Dardano Sacchetti, *L'orco*, which Sacchetti had developed into a script co-written with Colin Wilson, *The Ogre*, for De Laurentiis. Damiani's name was attached to it as early as 1980. "One morning Dino told me that the director would be Damiano," Sacchetti recalled.[2] A couple of years earlier the scriptwriter and Damiani had worked on a story called *Il re della mafia* which was left in the drawer, and they were in good terms. When Damiani showed up in New York for *The Ogre*,

Belgian poster for *Amityville II: The Possession* (1982, Damiano Damiani).

he was adamant with Sacchetti that his heart wasn't in it. The two spent lots of time in New York doing research for Damiani's film on the porn industry instead, hoping to convince De Laurentiis, but eventually the project was shelved, and the director came back to Italy. He returned to the States in 1982 to shoot *The Ogre*, which in the meantime, after several more drafts, had turned into *Amityville II: The Possession*, sold as a prequel to Stuart Rosenberg's 1979 film, *The Amityville Horror* (the Montelli family of Damiani's film standing for the De Feos in the previous one). The result, if superficially akin to possession films and closer to American Gothic, nevertheless has a personality of its own.

Damiani's only out-and-out horror film, *Amityville II: The Possession* dealt with themes the director had already touched during his career. He had already made a very interesting Gothic in the 1960s, *La strega in amore*, and had dealt with the Devil in his 1974 film, *Il sorriso del grande tentatore*, a thought-provoking allegory set in a convent and starring Glenda Jackson and Claudio Cassinelli. Still, Damiani—never a self-eulogic filmmaker—hastily dismissed *Amityville II: The Possession* in interviews. "I followed a script that already existed. It's a movie that doesn't say anything, it just wants to scare people. You might say it's a silly movie, and certainly I had no urgency to make it, but it's not badly made.... Exorcism, appearances, diabolical things, it's stuff I was never much interested in. When man cannot explain the world by himself, then he invents these stupefying things, which become almost a consolation."[3]

However, the director retouched the script here and there, adding some interesting elements. Firstly, the family which falls under the curse of the Amityville house and its evil entities is not very happy to start with. As we learn from the very opening sequence, the father of the family Anthony Montelli (played by the ever-slimy Burt Young, of *Rocky* fame) is a violent, domineering type who makes life a living hell for his wife and four sons. Montelli is the kind of patriarchal monster to be found in many retrograde families, the kind Damiani had depicted in his grim Sicilian Mafia drama *La moglie più bella* (1970): he beats his children with his trouser belt, harasses his 18-year-old first-born son Sonny (Jack Magner) as if he were a disobedient kid whenever he has the chance to, keeps his poor spouse submitted like a slave, forcing her to have sex with him whenever he likes, and

beats her too if she raises her voice to protect their offspring. Such an unhealthy family environment nurtures monsters, and their moving to the house in Amityville only brings to the surface long-buried issues and awareness.

Damiani depicts the crescendo that leads to the slaughter with enviable lucidity. One could say that, even if there weren't any demons speaking to Sonny from his headphones, it would be only a matter of time before he'd pick up a gun—that is to say, the tissue of family itself is the foundation for evil. In this sense, Damiani's film recalls such predecessors as Bava's *I Wurdalak* and Giorgio Ferroni's *La notte dei diavoli* (1972), both portrayals of hidebound patriarchal families where repression and violence spawned tragedy. Here the unresolved issues take the form of sibling incest before murder ensues, which gives the result a halo of morbidity akin to Italian Gothic. Religion is powerless against it, because Father Adamsky (James Olson) represents that very system of Catholic values which must prosper to spawn more monsters in its recesses. It is indeed quite a different environment than the problematic, but ultimately healthy one of Rosenberg's film.

The third act is much more conventional and predictable, and the script even throws in an image which combines *The Sentinel* and *The Shining*—the deformed damned souls emerging from the extradimensional threshold inside the house, announced by a river of blood on the floor. As the *Monthly Film Bulletin* reviewer maliciously put it, "unable to decide how to finish, Damiani and Wallace leave all four possible endings intact: the uplifting (Sonny, freed, rises up in a blaze of light), the "it isn't over: the creature walks among us" (Father Adamsky with undulating rubber arms and throat), the ironic (a final pull back to the "For Sale" sign), and the apocalyptic (a ball of fire engulfs the house). The fact that they are mutually exclusive doesn't appear to have bothered anyone."[4]

However, despite the script's many shortcomings, the direction is never banal, and sometimes refreshingly inventive. Damiani got to work with a mainly American crew and cast, but some of his key collaborators were Italian, most notably d.o.p. Franco Di Giacomo. "I see this film in continuous movement," Damiani told him. "You know, I'm not familiar with these American actors. The moving camera helps me a lot to tell the story."[5] The film does not feature the Steadicam, but the director and Di Giacomo employed mainly hand-held camera and dolly shots, preferring to capture the disturbing atmosphere in long takes and with special effects performed on camera (such as in the chilling sequence shot of an unseen presence that wanders at night through the haunted house, or a candle that won't extinguish in Sonny's birthday scene). They devised some remarkable shots, such as the one where the camera follows Sonny from behind, climbs over him and frames him from ahead, upside-down, before making a 180-degree rotation on its axis and ending on a frontal close-up of the actor—an amazing visual stunt achieved through a complex combination of a dolly and a revolving device designed by Damiani himself. Di Giacomo recalled that the scene was very difficult to shoot, and it took at least three takes to achieve the desired effect. It is a testament to a period where bravura shots were the result of an attempt to overcome the limitations of technique: nowadays such a scene would be very easy to accomplish, thanks to light video cameras and post-production digital effects, but it wouldn't have the same significance. Here, Damiani manages to wonderfully evoke the physical weight and consistence of evil. It's a moment worthy of Bava, in an otherwise underrated film.

Shot mainly in Mexico City for economic reasons, starting in February 1982,[6] *Amityville II: The Possession* was released theatrically in September of that year in the U.S., and reached Italy only the following year: it was given a V.M.18 rating "due to the particularly gruesome scenes and the theme which might influence negatively adolescent viewers." Released as *Amityville Possession*, it gathered moderately positive reviews, despite the critics' bias toward the genre. The *Corriere della Sera* wrote: "Retracing themes from *The Exorcist*, but also *The Shining* (the cascade of blood), *Poltergeist* (the house was illicitly built on an Indian cemetery) and *Entity*, without losing dignity compared with his American colleagues, and cunningly mixing sex and blood…. Damiani manages to accomplish a spectacular result, even with a stale subject matter."[7] *La Stampa*, even though pointing out that "one could expect something more from Damiani, a filmmaker of strong civic commitment," judged the director's "American vacation" favorable, and concluded that the film was "shot skillfully, well-served by the special effects, well set … played by physically fit actors, it does not fail to grip, although it doesn't display any other am-

bition than to traumatize particularly impressionable viewers."[8]

In the meantime, Damiani had returned to his favorite themes, and by this time he understood the small screen would be the only way he could develop them the way he wanted. His TV mini-series on the Mafia, *La piovra* (1984), was a commercial triumph, with an audience of over 15 million viewers. It would mark the history of Italian television indelibly, as well as the collective imagination and everyday language.

NOTES

1. Alberto Pezzotta, *Regia Damiano Damiani* (Udine: Centro Espressioni Cinematografiche—Cinemazero, 2004), 102.
2. *Ibid.*, 310.
3. *Ibid.*, 104.
4. Nick Roddick, "Amityville II: The Possession," *Monthly Film Bulletin* #586, November 1982.
5. Pezzotta, *Regia Damiano Damiani*, 308.
6. Ernesto Baldo, "Ma quel bugiardo di Fellini in America non c'è mai stato," *La Stampa*, January 28, 1982.
7. M. Po. [Maurizio Porro], "È il Diavolo stereo che rovina le famiglie," *Corriere della Sera*, April 9, 1983. The *Poltergeist* connection can be ruled out, however, since *Amityville II: The Possession* was shot before Hooper's film came out.
8. a.v. [Aldo Viganò], "Il posseduto da Satana duella con l'esorcista," *La Stampa*, May 24, 1983.

Assassinio al cimitero etrusco (*The Scorpion with Two Tails*)

D: Christian Plummer [Sergio Martino]. *S*: Ernesto Gastaldi, Dardano Sacchetti; *SC*: Ernesto Gastaldi, Maria Chianetta, Jacques Leitienne; *DOP*: Giancarlo Ferrando (Eastmancolor, LV-Luciano Vittori); *M*: Fabio Frizzi (Ed. Clitumno); *E*: Eugenio Alabiso, Daniele Alabiso; *PD, CO*: Antonello Geleng; *AD*: Massimo Manasse, Alain Sens Cazenave; *SS*: Donatella Botti; *C*: Fabio Conversi; *AC*: Bruno Cascio; *SO*: Roberto Petrozzi; *B*: Raffaele De Luca; *ACO*: Rossana Romanini; *W*: Stella Battista; *SP*: Giorgio Garibaldi Schwarze; *MU*: Franco Rufini, Giovanni Rufini; *Hair*: Sergio Gennari; *PrM*: Adriano Tiberi; *SE*: Paolo Ricci; *SPFX*: Sergio Stivaletti; *ChEl*: Armando Moreschini; *KG*: Matteo Giordano; *Generator Operator*: Egidio Stiffi; *AE*: Teresa Negozio; *2nAE*: Monica Sabatini, Silvana Di Legge; *Mix*: Bruno Moreal. *Cast*: Elvire Audray (Joan Barnard), Paolo Malco (Mike Grant), Claudio Cassinelli (Paolo Dameli), Marilù Tolo (Countess Maria Volumna), Wandisa Guida (Heather Hull), Gianfranco Barra (Police Commissioner), John Saxon (Arthur Barnard), Van Johnson (Mulligan), Mario Cecchi, Franco

Garofalo (Gianni Andrucci), Maurizio Mattioli (Masaccio), Carlo Monni (Giorgio Senaldi), Anita Sagnotti Laurenzi (Prof. Sorensen), Jacques Stany (Nick Forte), Luigi Rossi (Old flute player), Nazzareno Cardinali (Maria's Bodyguard), Angela Doria (Hilda), Antonio Maimone (Boss in New York), Fulvio Mingozzi (Customs Officer), Lucia Monaco (Julie), Mario Novelli (Maria's Bodyguard), Bruno Rosa; *uncredited*: Bruno Alias (Townsman), Giuseppe Marrocco (Airplane Passenger), Ettore Martini (Archeology Worker), Gennarino Pappagalli (Archaeologist), Anna Maria Perego (Elder Woman). *PROD*: Luciano Martino for Dania Film (Rome), Medusa Distribuzione (Rome), Imp.Ex.Ci.Sa. (Niece), Les Films Jacques Leitienne (Paris). *PM*: Sergio Borelli, Maurizio Pastrovich; *PS*: Francesco Fantacci; *PSe*: Antonio Saragò, Alberto Paluzzi, Colette Guedon; *ADM*: Danilo Martelli, Anna De Pedis. *Country*: Italy/France. Filmed on location at Volterra, Cerveteri, Formello, New York and at R.P.A.-Elios Studios (Rome). *Running time*: 98 minutes (m. 2663); 180 minutes (TV version). Visa n. 78090 (9.10.1982); *Rating*: all audiences. *Release dates*: 9.17.1982 (Italy), 11.24.1982 (Spain), 8.19.1983 (Portugal), 8.24.1983 (France); *Distribution*: Medusa. *Domestic gross*: n.a. *Also known as*: *Crime au cimetière étrusque* (France), *El asesino del cementerio etrusco* (Spain), *O Escorpião de duas caudas* (Portugal), *O Mistério etrusco* (Brazil), *El asesino etrusco* (Mexico).

Joan Barnard, a young American woman with parapsychological powers, has recurring dreams of herself as an Etruscan priestess. Meanwhile, her estranged husband, archaeologist Arthur Barnard, discovers an Etruscan tomb in Tuscany, but soon after he is murdered in the same way as the Etruscans killed their sacrificial victims, with his neck broken and his head twisted backwards. Joan flies to Italy to find out what happened, accompanied by her friend Mike Grant. But the killings continue, and two more victims are found with their necks broken. Joan and Mike are joined by her father, Mr. Mulligan, who finances Barnard's research but is running a drug smuggling ring under the cover of his archaeology business. Joan locates a secret tomb where Arthur had hidden a crate full of heroin destined to Joan's father, but the drug has disappeared. A shootout between two rival gangs in the tombs ends with most drug traffickers dead, including Mulligan. More killings ensue, and Mike is later found dead in the necropolis. Joan investigates

with the help of archaeologist Paolo Dameli, and realizes that the murderer is trying to locate a legendary Etruscan treasure...

Sergio Martino's return to the thriller genre took form as an 8-part TV series, originally titled *Il mistero degli Etruschi* (or *Lo scorpione a due code*[1]) written by Ernesto Gastaldi from a story concocted with Dardano Sacchetti, to be produced for Turin's Quartarete TV. It would be Martino's first work for the small screen, co-produced by his brother Luciano's Dania Film and Medusa, who secured also the distribution rights for a theatrical version, put together by drastically abridging the 8 parts, each 50 minute-long.

Such a project shows how television was gradually taking center stage in the market. As Martino himself recalled in his memoirs,

> until a few years earlier cinema, especially commercial one, didn't have any outlet on TV, and the few movies that were broadcast on State television were either great masterpieces or works of cultural interest. After their theatrical run, movies became like yesterday's newspaper, that is, wastepaper: nobody thought they would have a future life, nor did anyone foresee the future of commercial cinema on television. Only a few forward-looking individuals had imagined a possibility in this sense.[2]

One of these individuals was Silvio Berlusconi, who with his company Fininvest had quickly become the leader of the commercial network market. Berlusconi had secured the TV rights to hundreds of films, thus marking a dramatic change of perspective: from the late 1970s onward, people were becoming more and more addicted to television, not the least because they could comfortably watch all kinds of movies in their own living room, instead of having to take the car, go to a theater, pay a ticket and sit in uncomfortable, smelly venues. This meant the beginning of the end for second and third-run theaters.

Martino assembled a good cast which featured Paolo Malco, Claudio Cassinelli, the still ravishing Marilù Tolo, Luciano Martino's ex-wife and former *peplum* starlet Wandisa Guida (in her last film role), plus a couple of American has-beens (John Saxon, Van Johnson) in quick "special participations" and a supporting cast which included the sleazy-looking Franco Garofalo as well as Tuscan comedian Carlo Monni (who had started as Roberto Benigni's straight man in their early appearances as a double act). The presence of a French co-producer, Jacques

Leitienne (who also got a credit, purely for bureaucratic reasons, as co-scriptwriter[3]) led to Martino casting a French protagonist, the blonde Elvire Audray, in her first starring role. Audray, who bore a passing resemblance to Edwige Fenech, would star in several Italian films over the next few years, including the hit comedy *Vado a vivere da solo* (1982, Marco Risi). Shooting went on for four months, on 16mm (later blown up to 35mm for the theatrical release), on location in Tuscany and partly in the U.S. The director decided to sign the film as "Christian Plummer" (the first time he used an English pseudonym) in order to make the result more commercially viable: the name "Sergio Martino" was by then associated with comedy after the series of amusing farces he had directed since the mid–1970s.

The fate of *Assassinio al cimitero etrusco* was quite different from the one Martino had envisioned while making it. Quartarete TV was attempting to enter the private television market as a competitor to Fininvest, but eventually its owners gave up, and the TV series, although ready for broadcast, was shelved. The theatrical version was distributed earlier than expected, to modest box-office (incidentally, the poster by Enzo Sciotti recycled the same menacing long-haired, knife-wielding figure from *Quella villa accanto al cimitero*). In the late 1980s the series was purchased by Reteitalia and reduced to a 180-minute, two-part version, *Lo scorpione a due code*, to be broadcast on Canale 5. This abridged version, reedited by Claudio Lattanzi, was never aired on Berlusconi's network and turned up on local networks over the years. The original negatives, according to Martino, were damaged.

If the idea of a mystery related to Etruscan tombs recalls Armando Crispino's *giallo*, *L'etrusco uccide ancora* (1972), Sacchetti and Gastaldi's story blends *giallo* and supernatural elements in a way that echoes the Gothic made-for-TV mini-series of the 1970s, such as *Il segno del comando* and *Ritratto di donna velata* (the latter also shot in Volterra).[4] The victims are killed with their neck snapped and head twisted according to an ancient Etruscan curse, but, as one of the characters underlines at one point, nobody remotely believes in the supernatural explanation, and a subplot about heroin smuggling keeps the story on a mundane level.

On the other hand, Joan Barnard has much in common with Gothic's heroines in peril, who end up in danger because of their overt sensi-

tivity and their capability to see beyond everyday reality. She is immediately introduced as a psychic, and her dreams and visions (starting with the opening credit sequence, which depicts a sacrificial rite in an Etruscan tomb) reveal her as the reincarnation of an Etruscan queen and high priestess (a so-called *luchmon*). In one of Gothic cinema's favorite twists, she has the same features as a woman portrayed in an Etruscan mural painting, who also wears the same necklace (depicting a scorpion with two tails, hence the title) which has miraculously saved her life in a shootout. Far from being simply a red herring, the supernatural becomes an integral part of the story, also by way of a mysterious old man (Luigi Rossi, best known as the amiable lawyer who addresses the audience and tell anecdotes about the main characters in Fellini's *Amarcord*) who plays the "*aulos*" (the typical ancient wind instrument similar to the flute) and acts as the link between the past and the present.

Gastaldi's script has a field day milking the supernatural angle for all it's worth, and the scenes set in the Etruscan necropolis, recreated by Antonello Geleng at R.P.A.-Elios studios, have an endearing fantasy-like quality that evokes the *Conan the Barbarian* rip-offs made around the same time (as well as Duccio Tessari's *Tex e il signore degli abissi*, 1985) but they also highlight one of the film's main issues, the attempt of covering too many disparate bases in an effort to please the mass audience.

Despite some good camerawork, the direction is mostly uninspired, and the story drags along confusingly, with a continuing series of plot twists and new characters introduced, in a manner not unlike old-time serials. The fact that the theatrical version is severely abridged doesn't help. At 98 minutes, it drops some subplots completely, such as Joan's little brother being kidnapped by an American drug kingpin, who blackmails Joan into recovering the drugs for him, or Joan and Mike taking a trip to the Niagara Falls. The theatrical cut also discards several atmospheric sequences, such as photographer/graverobber Gianni Andrucci (Garofalo) penetrating a tomb and experiencing aural and visual hallucinations in front of the mural paintings, and Joan discovering the body of another graverobber, Senaldi (Monni). On top of that, some actors, such as Bruno Di Luia, appear only in the TV version. In addition to the many cuts, the theatrical version featured some differences in the dubbing as well: for instance, in the TV

French lobby card for *Assassinio al cimitero etrusco*, featuring Claudio Cassinelli (center) and Elvire Audray (right).

version Claudio Cassinelli dubs himself, whereas in the film he is dubbed by Pino Colizzi.

Despite the convoluted plot, the mystery angle is by-the-numbers, with the villain introduced one hour into the film, and turning out to be (in one of Gastaldi's favorite plot twists: see *La morte accarezza a mezzanotte*, 1972) a potential love interest for the heroine. On top of that, the climactic revelation is disastrously staged, with the worst case of a dead-man-apparently-returning-from-the-grave-to-unmask-the-murderer ever committed in a *giallo*. The final explanatory monologue includes yet another photographic blow-up that reveals the murderer's identity (a detail which adds nothing to the mystery) and a ludicrous clarification about the true nature of one key character (a covert agent who studied Etruscan archaeology to infiltrate a gang of smugglers!).

Martino eschews explicit gore, but the few make-up effects (by a young Sergio Stivaletti, uncredited) leave a lot to be desired, while the odd macabre touches (such as Joan seeing maggots pop up from the photograph of an Etruscan site) fail to inject much-needed frissons. Even the reliable Fabio Frizzi's score seems on autopilot, to the point that it recycles themes from *Paura nella città dei morti viventi*. No wonder Martino himself regretted having had anything to do with it, since "it didn't add anything to my career, not even from an economic standpoint."[5]

NOTES

1. There are two original stories signed by Sacchetti and Gastaldi and deposited at the SIAE archives, *Il mistero degli Etruschi* (dated January 5, 1982) and *Lo scorpione a due code* (dated April 23, 1982)
2. Sergio Martino, *Mille peccati ... nessuna virtù?* (Milan: Bloodbuster, 2017), 178.
3. The credits also list Gastaldi's wife Maria Chianetta as co-scriptwriter, presumably for similar reasons.
4. For an analysis of *Ritratto di donna velata*, see Curti, *Italian Gothic Horror Films, 1970–1979*, 222.
5. Martino, *Mille peccati ... nessuna virtù?*, 179.

La casa stregata (The Haunted House)
D: Bruno Corbucci. S: Mario Amendola, Bruno Corbucci, Mario Cecchi Gori; SC: Mario

Amendola, Bruno Corbucci, Enrico Oldoini; *DOP*: Ennio Guarnieri (Technospes); *M*: Detto Mariano (Ed. Slalom); *E*: Daniele Alabiso; *PD*: Giantito Burchiellaro; *ArtD*: Bruno Amalfitano; *CO*: Giulia Mafai; *AD*: Roberto Tatti; *SS*: Cinzia Alchimede; *C*: Renato Ranieri; *AC*: Maurizio Fiorentini; *2ndAC*: Francesco Damiani; *SO*: Benito Alchimede; *SP*: Giuseppe Botteghi; *MA*: Rocco Lerro; *MU*: Alfredo Tiberi, Pierantonio Mecacci, Gianfranco Mecacci; *APD*: Antonia Mirella Rubeo; *AE*: Brigida Mastrolillo, Marcello Cannone; *PROP*: Vittorio Troiani; *KG*: Ennio Picconi; *ChEl*: Amilcare Cuccoli; *Mix*: Romano Pampaloni; *SE*: Antonio Corridori; *W*: Clara Fratarcangeli; *Publicist*: Francesca De Guida Canori. *Cast*: Renato Pozzetto (Giorgio Allegri), Gloria Guida (Candida Melengo), Lia Zoppelli (Anastasia), Yorgo Voyagis (Oscar), Marilda Donà (Lucia), Angelo Pellegrino (Elpidio Tommasini), Rita Forzano (Allegri's colleague), Leo Gavero (Bank manager), Angelo Nicotra (Allegri's colleague), Aldo Ralli (Allegri's colleague), Giulia Valli, Fernando Cerulli (Real estate agent), Vittorio Ripamonti (Don Alvino), Nicola Morelli (Albani), Franco Diogene (Dilapidated house owner), Tony Scarf [Antonio Scarfone] (Robber); *uncredited*: Bruno Corbucci (Veterinarian), Antonio Conte (Bus driver), Mario Donatone (Hotel Concierge), Mimmo Poli (Client at the bank). *PROD*: Mario Cecchi Gori, Vittorio Cecchi Gori for Intercapital Films. *AP*: Achille Manzotti; *GM*: Mino Barbera; *PM*: Giandomenico Stellitano; *PS*: Mino Barbera; *PSe*: Tommaso Pantano; ADM: Mario Lupi, Danilo Martelli. *Country*: Italy. Filmed on location in Milan, Rome, at Villa Giovanelli-Fogaccia (Rome) and at De Paolis In.Ci.R. Studios (Rome). *Running time*: 95 minutes (m. 2630). Visa n. 77630 (3.4.1982); *Rating*: all audiences. *Release date*: 3.4.1982; *Distribution*: Cineriz. Domestic gross: 1,483,589,000 *lire. Also known as*: *Das verhexte Haus* (East Germany).

Giorgio Allegri, a bank accountant in Milan, moves to Rome. There, he starts looking for a house where to move along with his beautiful fiancée Candida (with whom he has not made love yet), her mother Anastasia, and his Great Dane dog Gaetano. He eventually settles in a beautiful huge villa outside the city, on the Via Appia, for a ridiculous sum. As Giorgio soon finds out, the house is haunted: a thousand years earlier, an Arab warrior and his lover were caught by the woman's mother, who cast a spell on them, turning them into pillars of salt. To break the spell, Candida must remain a virgin until the first night

of the full moon. Therefore, Giorgio and Candida's attempts to make love are systematically frustrated, often by the intervention of the mysterious Omar, who is actually the ghost of the two lovers' servant. This results in poor Giorgio suffering many absurdist accidents. To make matters worse, Giorgio's colleagues are suspicious about the luxurious house he lives in, and believe he is in cahoots with the criminals who often rob the bank...

Renato Pozzetto's second Gothic spoof after *Mia moglie è una strega* is a ghost story that dealt with the theme of reincarnation and a secular curse, declined in an amiably funny way: "Metempsychosis? Isn't it some sort of a pneumonia?" asks Giorgio (Pozzetto), the unaware reincarnation of a Saracen warrior turned by his witch mother-in-law into a pillar of salt together with his beloved and cursed by a thousand-year-old spell. The bulk of the movie centers on Giorgio's vain attempts to have sex with his virgin fiancée Candida, while the ghost of the warrior's servant prevents him with all sort of magic tricks, as the spell will be broken only if she loses her virginity on the exact expiration of the thousand years' span, on a night of full moon, finally releasing the two unfortunate spirits.

Pozzetto teams up with the gorgeous Gloria Guida, in one of her last film appearances before retiring from the movie business (that same year she starred alongside her husband Johnny Dorelli in Dino Risi's *Sesso e volentieri*), whereas Yorgo Voyagis plays a similar guest star role as Helmut Berger in *Mia moglie è una strega*. Corbucci (who concocted the script with his usual collaborator Mario Amendola, and with future film director Enrico Oldoini) crams the thin plot with all the required elements, revisited in a farcical way: a Middle-age prologue (set in the eerie 16th century park of Bomarzo, seen in *Il castello dei morti vivi*), assorted poltergeist manifestations, flying objects galore, and even a talking Great Dane (who speaks in a Neapolitan accent). All this is merged with Pozzetto's surreal one-liners as well as with satirical stabs at contemporary Italy. A recurring gag has Giorgio and his colleagues quietly discussing their personal affairs while lying on the floor with criminals pointing gun at them, in the middle of some bank robbery to which they are now totally accustomed, hinting at the crime wave of the period. On the other hand, Giorgio's misadventures in search of an apartment where to move in Rome, where all houses seem to be either impossibly expensive and/or dilapidated (a funny scene has the landlord showing him a half-destroyed flat while magnifying its virtues as if it was a royal palace), recall the basic plot of an old Totò classic comedy, *Totò cerca casa* (1949, Mario Monicelli and Steno).[1]

The gags range from the old-hat banana peel to absurdist segments: during a bank robbery, Giorgio gets angry and turns into the Incredible Hulk, in a nod to the TV series starring Lou Ferrigno, then very popular in Italy: the transformation and Giorgio/Hulk's feats (such as eradicating a security door from the wall) are filmed in slow-motion, and exactly mimic the series. However, the funniest bit has Giorgio and Candida recreate a typical stag movie situation to fool the ghost and finally have sex: he dresses up as a rude plumber (complete with a Ron Jeremy mustache and phony Roman accent) and she plays the nympho housewife. Too bad the trick doesn't work…

Critics pointed out the similarities between *La casa stregata* and Giorgio Capitani's *Bollenti spiriti*, released the previous year, and criticized Corbucci's listless direction.[2] However, compared with *Mia moglie è una strega*, Corbucci at least knows how to handle the genre's visual elements: an example is the scene where Candida's severe mother Anastasia (Lia Zoppelli) is mysteriously awakened from her sleep and follows a ball of wool which eerily rolls across her flat (shown by Corbucci through Anastasia's POV) … only to discover her daughter and her fiancé about to make love. Not only the Gothic elements, unchanged, are systematically turned to parody, but even the uncanny combination of time and space lends itself to be reinvented into a gag. In a scene, Giorgio and Candida flee the title's haunted mansion and take refuge in a hotel on the coast; but upon entering their room they find themselves again inside the villa, in a spatial short circuit that recalls those to which the main characters of *Operazione paura* and *Danza macabra* fall victim.

The movie underwent minor tampering in order to receive an "all audiences" rating: producer Vittorio Cecchi Gori agreed to eliminate a few lines of dialogue featuring four-letter words, for an amount of six seconds—further evidence of the ongoing taming of comedies in order for them to be accessible to younger audiences and be more commercially viable to the general public. Nevertheless, some critics complained about Pozzetto's foul language, "repetitive to the point of boredom."[3] *La casa stregata*

grossed almost 900 million *lire*, ending up at the twentieth spot among the top-grossing films of the season. That year, two more Pozzetto films, *Culo e camicia* (1981, Pasquale Festa Campanile, co-starring Enrico Montesano) and *Nessuno è perfetto* (1981, Pasquale Festa Campanile, co-starring Ornella Muti) ended up respectively at the fourth and sixth spot, making him Italy's most popular comedian after Adriano Celentano.

NOTES

1. In turn, *Totò cerca casa* (partly inspired by the comic strip *La famiglia Sfollatini*) featured a side-splittingly funny segment in which Totò and his family move to a new house next to a cemetery where he must be the caretaker, which resulted in an amusing spoof of horror clichés.
2. A.V. [Aldo Viganò], "La coppia Pozzetto-Guida perseguitata da un fantasma," *La Stampa*, 13 March 1982.
3. L.A. [Leonardo Autera], "Pozzetto e Gloria Guida con il cane parlante," *Corriere della Sera*, 8 March 1982.

Manhattan Baby (*Manhattan Baby*, a.k.a. *Eye of the Evil Dead*)

D: Lucio Fulci. *S and SC*: Elisa Livia Briganti, Dardano Sacchetti; *DOP*: Guglielmo Mancori (Eastmancolor, Telecolor); *M*: Fabio Frizzi (Ed. Deaf); *E*: Vincenzo Tomassi; *PD, CO*: Massimo Lentini; *SPFX*: Giannetto De Rossi; *SPFX*: Maurizio Trani; *MU*: Antonio Maltempo; *Hair*: Luciano Vito; *AD*: Roberto Giandalia; *C*: Franco Bruni; *AC*: Aldo Marchiori, Adriano Mancori; *APD*: Mariangela Capuano; *PrM*: Rodolfo Ruzza; *AE*: Pietro Tomassi, Rita Antonelli; *SP*: Franco Bellomo; *ChEl*: Franco Brescini; *KG*: Ennio Brizzolari; *W*: Maria Spigarelli; *Set Technicians*: Fabio Traversari, Roberto Pace; *SO*: Eros Giustini; *B*: Guglielmo Smeraldi; *Mix*: Bruno Moreal; *SS*: Rita Agostini; *DubD*: Pino Colizzi. *Cast*: Christopher Connelly (Prof. George Hacker), Martha Taylor [Laura Lenzi] (Emily Hacker), Brigitta Boccoli (Susie Hacker), Giovanni Frezza (Tommy Hacker), Cinzia de Ponti (Jamie Lee), Laurence Welles [Cosimo Cinieri] (Adrian Marcato), Andrea Bosic (Eye doctor), Carlo De Mejo (Luke), Enzo Marino Bellanich (Wiler), Mario Moretti (Tennant), Lucio Fulci (Dr. Forrester), Tonino Pulci (Orderly); uncredited: Martin Sorrentino (Caretaker). *PROD*: Fabrizio De Angelis for Fulvia Film (Rome). *PM*: Palmira De Negri; *PS*: Paolo Gargano; *PSe*: Luca Santolini; *ADM*: Otello Tomassini. *Country*: Italy. Filmed on location in Egypt, New York and at De Paolis In.Ci.R. Studios (Rome). *Running time*: 89 minutes (m. 2441). Visa n. 78081 (8.10.1982); *Rating*: V.M.14. *Release dates*: 8.12.1982 (Italy),

11.11.1982 (Spain), 7.12.1983 (Australia), 7.27.1984 (USA); *Distribution*: Fulvia Films (Italy), 21st Century Corporation (USA). *Domestic gross*: 409,424,657 *lire*. *Also known as*: *The Possessed* (UK), *La malédiction du pharaon* (France), *Amulett des Bösen* (West Germany), *L'ensorcelée* (Canada).

Cairo, Egypt. The young Susie Hacker, daughter of archaeologist George Hacker, is given a mysterious medallion by a blind old woman. Meanwhile George explores a tomb of an Egyptian evil deity called Abnubenor, which results in the death of his assistant and in him being blinded by a ray of blue light. Back in New York, while George slowly recovers his sight, Susie and her younger brother Tommy experience strange phenomena and a series of gruesome deaths ensue, which involve their building's caretaker, a journalist friend named Luke, the kids' babysitter Jamie Lee, and Hacker's colleague Wiler. George and his wife Emily ask for the help of antique dealer/occultist Adrian Marcato, who tells them that Susie's medallion is a powerful talisman which unleashes the forces of evil. Marcato exorcises Emily, but in turn he falls victim to the curse of Abnubenor. At the end, the blind old woman passes on the medallion to another girl...

The last movie Fulci shot for Fabrizio De Angelis' Fulvia Film marked a departure from the ultra-gory style of his previous works and was an attempt at a more subdued and ambitious Gothic horror story. *Manhattan Baby* was initially conceived as the most expensive film of the lot, with many special electronic effects: in a way, it was an effort on the part of De Angelis to win a more mainstream audience. But the project underwent drastic budget cuts (from 800 million *lire* to about 400, according to Dardano Sacchetti), and the downsizing weighed heavily on the result. Shooting took place between March 8 and the end of April 1982,[1] partly on location in and around Cairo, then in New York and finally at the familiar De Paolis studios, for the interior scenes. During the New York shooting, De Angelis had also another crew filming second unit work for Enzo Castellari's *1990—I guerrieri del Bronx*, a project the producer likely cared more about, and whose success would pave the way for another successful *filone*.

The cast comprised a few recurring Fulci actors, such as Carlo De Mejo and Cosimo Cinieri: the latter, already seen in *Lo squartatore di New York*, would turn up again in *I guerrieri dell'anno 2072* and, as Lieutenant Borges, in *Murderock—Uccide a passo di danza* (both

1984). But this time the director had a new "blonde in peril," Laura Lenzi (billed as "Martha Taylor") replacing Catriona MacColl. As with *Quella villa accanto al cimitero*, the story featured a couple of kids, played by Giovanni Frezza, in his second and last Fulci film, and Brigitta Boccoli (who became a noted showgirl together with her sister Benedicta) in a role originally devised for Silvia Collatina. Fulci never got along with Brigitta and her domineering mother, who followed her on the set, and with his usual mordacity he nicknamed the girl "*la nana*" (the midget).

The script retained at Rome's CSC, titled *L'occhio del male* and dated February 15, 1982, is very similar to the finished film but with several interesting differences, most notably the absence of the blind sorceress who gives Susie the medallion (we see Emily losing sight of her daughter in the crowded Cairo market, then finding her again with the girl already donning the pendant), and a different ending: in the script, George returns to the pyramid to defeat the millennial evil entity.

The Egyptian framework, however, was not in Elisa Briganti and Dardano Sacchetti's original story, about a girl who has the gift of ubiquity and is able to travel into different dimensions during her sleep, pushing her astral body into the beyond; her travels become more and more physical, as the girl brings back objects from the otherworld; in doing so, she turns into an instrument for obscure entities to reach our own reality. In a way, Sacchetti was referencing *L'aldilà*, while at the same time exploring the Henry James–like quality of *Quella villa accanto al cimitero* (something which the finished film somehow retains, starting with the two children at its core). It was De Angelis who insisted on adding the Egyptian framework, and the theme of the ancient curse (by way of the evil god Abnubenor) because, according to the scriptwriter, "he didn't know what an astral body was, and was afraid that the audience wouldn't understand it either."[2] After the producer's intervention, the starting point (an archaeologist's daughter possessed by an Egyptian spirit) recalls Mike Newell's *The Awakening* (1980), based on Bram Stoker's story *Jewel of the Seven Stars*, released in Italy in February 1981, which had been a modest success in the country thanks to the presence of Charlton Heston (Fulci even cast a Heston lookalike of sorts, Christopher Connelly, for the role of the archaeologist).

Manhattan Baby opens with a quote attributed to H.P. Lovecraft, "*Il mistero non è attorno alle cose, ma dentro le cose stesse.*" (Mystery is not around things, but within things themselves.) That said, there is little of the world of the Providence writer in *Manhattan Baby* besides the notion of a powerful evil harking from centuries back and ready to be unleashed in today's world. The opening sequences set in Egypt sweep away the Lovecraftian and Christian references of the previous films and replace them with nods to Oriental religions, including the use of the "Eye of Horus" (a symbol of protection, royal power and good health) as the catalyst of evil through the medallion which is the starting point for a series of horrific events.

On the other hand, Kim Newman points out a couple of additional interesting literary references, as the film "retreats into childhood fantasies derived from C.S. Lewis and Ray Bradbury (*The Veldt*) as the nursery becomes a children-only limbo into which adults venture at the risk of their lives."[3] Whether Sacchetti was aware of this or not, the Bradbury reference provides a stronger nod to literary Gothic. His 1950 story *The Veldt*—adapted for the screen as part of *The Illustrated Man* (1969) and inspiring the *Mr. Tiger* episode in the 1973 Amicus horror anthology *Tales that Witness Madness*—is an example of Bradbury's employment of Gothic tropes within a sci-fi setting, to unsettling results. In addition, Newman acutely underlines one of *Manhattan Baby*'s central motifs, the insistence on the horrors of childhood and their detachment from the world of the adults. In one of the most unnerving scenes (and a key one in order to grasp the story), Hacker and his wife are at their little girl's bedside while Susie is apparently experiencing some terrible nightmare, screaming and trembling; in the next bed her brother Tommy—indifferent to the situation and calmly reading a comic book version of *Jaws* (1975), in one of Fulci's typical ironic touches—says there's nothing to worry about, as "Susie always screams when she goes on a voyage" and adds, "it's part of the rules. The game she invented."

In addition to this, the film assembles the usual array of references to other movies, in an even more complex and cannibalistic layering than Fulci's previous works. Take, for instance, the nod to *The Exorcist*, which climaxes in the medical examination scenes, or the elevator sequence modeled upon an infamous "creative death" in *Damien: Omen II* (1978, Don Taylor), to the point of making the victim a black man. The opening in the Egyptian tomb with its dangerous devices and traps vaguely recalls *Raiders of the Lost Ark* (and Connelly would later star as an Indiana Jones–type in a couple Italian rip-offs of Spielberg's film, namely Ruggero Deodato's *I predatori di Atlantide* and Antonio Margheriti's *La leggenda del rubino malese*, released respectively in 1983 and 1985), but the death of the archaeologist's guide evokes also the director's own *Black Cat*. On the other hand, Fulci's film does not, as some have surmised,[4] draw from *Poltergeist*, as the latter was only released in the U.S. the following November.

As in *L'aldilà*, the film makes ample use of animals (scorpions, snakes, birds) as agents of horror. The scene where sorcerer Adrian Marcato—a name which nods to Polanski's *Rosemary's Baby*, also referenced by the Italian title and vaguely hinted at through the medallion given to the protagonist, which recalls the tannis root necklace Minnie Castevet gives Rosemary—is attacked and killed by his stuffed birds was a last-minute addition to the script (originally, Marcato had his skull transfixed against an iron bar, while escaping from a wolf that had materialized in the room).

The most obvious antecedent to the scene is *The Birds*, but Fulci dismissed the reference ("It's not Hitchcock, the birds here are stuffed") and claimed that he liked the idea that the character would be "killed by the animals that he forced to stay around him."[5] The use of editing and suspense also draws from *L'aldilà* (the spider scene), but another less-explored, surprising analogy, quite possibly unbeknownst to the director himself, can be found in a similar sequence in Jess Franco's *Count Dracula* (1970), where the stuffed animals in the house rented by Dracula near the clinic come to life and attack Harker and Quincey Morris (a scene conceived by Franco during shooting). Fulci claimed that Marcato's death was his favorite bit in the movie, and "among the best sequences I have ever filmed,"[6] despite the all-too-obvious sight of wires guiding the birds in some shots (the special effects crew used fishing rods and nets to make the birds "fly").

Even though *Manhattan Baby* has its share of gruesome effects, the gore is not nearly as copious as in Fulci's previous horror films. The director prefers to create a constantly unnerving mood, and his obsession with eyes here reaches

EYE OF THE EVIL DEAD

 Starring **CHRISTOPHER CONNELLY**
and **MARTHA TAYLOR**

American lobby card for Lucio Fulci's *Manhattan Baby* (1982), released in the U.S. as *Eye of the Evil Dead*, featuring a moment of the climactic bird attack on occultist Adrian Marcato (Cosimo Cinieri).

a peak: a good part of the story is characterized by extreme close-ups on corneas and pupils (sometimes opaque and blind, like those of Emily in *L'aldilà*), and the "Eye of Horus" also acts as a red thread throughout the film. Even circular elements that recall the eyes take center stage, as the pulsating lights in the elevator sequence. The Scope format is thus compressed and saturated to the point of imploding with such details, and the camera almost becomes a speculum, trying to zoom into the impenetrable. Formally, Fulci masters his use of space, jumping from long shots to extreme close-ups with suggestive results, especially in the Egyptian sequences; moreover, the use of fade-to-whites creates an intriguing atmosphere of dread, related to dazzling light (which illuminates things but can also make one blind).

Still, the result just doesn't quite gel. Overall, *Manhattan Baby* is a somewhat undecipherable film, with a story that often eludes the viewer's comprehension like the sand escaping between

Susie's fingers in one of the opening scenes, in the film's most iconic image. Quite often, the viewer is lost among unexplained events and gropes in the dark just like Christopher Connelly's character. How can it be, for instance, that no one asks what happened to the character played by Carlo De Mejo, who disappears with no trace from the children's bedroom and turns up dead among the sands of a desert which recalls the desolate lands of *L'aldilà*? The potential of Sacchetti's elliptical ideas is evident, but at the same time one has the feeling of a botched script that, possibly due to the last-minute rewrites and patch-ups, ultimately goes nowhere. Fabio Frizzi's score (again featuring Goblin members Agostino Marangolo, Fabio Pignatelli and Maurizio Guarini) recycles themes from *Paura nella città dei morti viventi* and *L'aldilà*, enhancing the feeling of sloppiness. As the composer explained, the director rejected one of the tracks (*Baby sequenza 1*, which can be found in the original soundtrack) as he thought it was too "flirtatious," "and so, in order not to make me waste more time, we used the best from *L'aldilà*'s score."[7] Fulci, who was always dismissive toward the film, claimed he liked the melancholic saxophone theme which accompanies the scenes of New York at dawn: "The sax solo music is more or less the one you can really listen to day and night through the streets of New York, played by wanderers and bums."[8]

Despite his care for atmosphere, Fulci failed to give the film an incisive pacing. Even though it is mainly focused on visual analogies and symbols, and would-be iconic images nicely rendered by Guglielmo Mancori's photography, *Manhattan Baby* drags along to a less-then-satisfying circular ending, a sign that this time the director didn't care enough for the material. Fulci claimed that he shot *Manhattan Baby* to "get him [De Angelis] out of my balls,"[9] but he was paid 40 million for the film, the highest salary that De Angelis ever gave him: Sacchetti recalled that during filming the director took a trip to Cannes, where producer Giovanni Di Clemente—who behaved like a tycoon, unlike the thrifty De Angelis—hired him to make *Conquest*, offering him 90 million *lire*, and upon his return Fulci's mind was somewhere else.[10]

Manhattan Baby came out on August 12, 1982, in a venue in Rivabella, on the Romagna coast, marking the seventh Fulci film released theatrically in Italy in two years (*Luca il contrabbandiere* being released on August 8, 1980). Italian critics pointed out the similarities with *The Exorcist* and called the story "unconvincing and rather predictable," although some noted the director's "usual—and even more refined—technical skills."[11] But most reviewers still dismissed Fulci as a hack. In the *Corriere della Sera*, Leonardo Autera launched a scathing comparison: "They say that Lucio Fulci, the director, is the most gifted heir in the "Italian horror" genre, of the late Mario Bava. But there is a substantial difference: Bava knew how to follow Poe's lesson that even the absurd must have an inner logic; Fulci, instead, navigates in the most absolute arbitrariness, the kind not even the old-time "Grand-guignol" would have dared."[12]

The film was distributed by Fulvia Film itself, which possibly influenced its negative commercial impact in Italy. With a little more than 400 million *lire* grossed, it was a box-office disappointment, and marked the end of the director's stint with De Angelis. The attempt at establishing Fulci as the box-office rival of Dario Argento had failed, and the producer was moving on to new territories and trends, like a surfer looking for the following wave to catch: the *First Blood* rip-offs would be next, and De Angelis himself made his debut behind the camera with *Thunder* (1983). As for Fulci, his association with Di Clemente resulted in *Conquest* (1983), an ambitious *Conan the Barbarian*-inspired fantasy yarn with plenty of horrific elements which was an embarrassing box-office bomb, grossing less than 100 million *lire*. The decline had started, and the director's following films of the early to mid–Eighties would be as many efforts to get on the bandwagon of such diverse genres as the post-apocalyptic (*I guerrieri dell'anno 2072*), the *giallo*, spiced with references to the dance movie thread spawned by *Flashdance* (*Murderock—Uccide a passo di danza*), and the morbid erotic drama (*Il miele del diavolo*, 1986).

Manhattan Baby was picked up for distribution overseas in 1984 by 21st Century Distribution, as *Eye of the Evil Dead*, but it was released theatrically only in 1986 to little success. In the U.K. it was released directly on video in 1983, as *Possessed*.

NOTES

1. Reported in Albiero and Cacciatore, *Il terrorista dei generi*, 314. Thrower reports March 22 as starting date (Thrower, *Beyond Terror*, 201).
2. Davide Pulici, "Manhattan Baby," www.nocturno.it (http://www.nocturno.it/manhattan-baby/).
3. Newman, *Nightmare Movies*, 259.
4. Albiero and Cacciatore, *Il terrorista dei generi*, 315.
5. Garofalo and De Lillo, "Il cinema del dubbio. Intervista a Lucio Fulci," 19.
6. Salza, "Le retour de Lucio Fulci."
7. Palmerini and Mistretta, *Spaghetti Nightmares*, 257.
8. Romagnoli, *L'occhio del testimone*, 49.
9. Garofalo and De Lillo, "Il cinema del dubbio. Intervista a Lucio Fulci," 19.
10. Pulici, "Manhattan Baby."
11. A.V. [Aldo Viganò], "Terrore in casa dell'archeologo," *La Stampa*, August 26, 1982.
12. L.A. [Leonardo Autera], "Quella pietra blu combina disastri," *Corriere della Sera*, August 23, 1982.

Notturno con grida (Nocturne with Screams)

D: Vittorio Salerno, Ernesto Gastaldi. *S and SC*: Ernesto Gastaldi, Vittorio Salerno; *DOP*: Benito Frattari, Marco Frattari (Eastmancolor, Telecolor); *M*: Severino Gazzelloni, conducted by Luciano Michelini (Ed. Eter); *E*: Dario Spaccapeli; *ArtD, CO*: Amarilli Gastaldi; *SO*: Luciano Muratori; *Mix*: Adriano Taloni; *El*: Mario Loris Zamariola; *SS*: Giuseppina Gastaldi; *PA*: Nino Vendetti. *Cast*: Mara Maryl [Maria Chianetta]

(Brigitte Benoit), Gerardo Amato (Gerard), Alan Collins [Luciano Pigozzi] (Paul Benoit), Gioia Maria Scola [Gioia Maria Tibiletti] (Sheena), Franco Molè (Christian Coreau), Martine Brochard (Eileen). *PROD*: Welcome Films and Television Coop. (Rome). *PM*: Armando Govoni. *Country*: Italy. Filmed on location in and around Soriano nel Cimino (Viterbo). *Running time*: 94 minutes (m. 2580). Visa n. 78119 (9.29.1982); *Rating*: V.M.14. *Release date*: 10.12.1982; *Distribution*: Samanda Film. *Domestic gross*: approx. 200,000 *lire*. Also known as: *La fuerza del demonio* (Spain).

A medium, Brigitte, her husband Paul and their friends Gerard, his fiancée Eileen and their young acquaintance Sheena organize a séance. They evoke the spirit of Christian—who was killed ten years earlier in the same room and whose body disappeared—to find out who is the murderer. In a couple of days Christian will be declared officially dead and all his fortune will be inherited by his ex-wife Eileen. The next morning the party of five takes a trip in the nearby beechwood, which Eileen and Gerard plan to cut down to build an exclusive residential center. Soon, however, they fall prey to strange events. Meanwhile, we learn the characters' secrets: Sheena and Gerard are lovers and plan to kill Eileen after the wedding to gain her wealth, while Paul (an ex-seminarian) and Brigitte also have unspeakable skeletons in their past. One by one they fall victim to supernatural forces, and Gerard becomes convinced that Brigitte is a witch…

"It was 1980 and I hadn't shot a single foot of film in five years. I went hunting woodcocks on the Cimini mountains near Viterbo," Vittorio Salerno recalled about the genesis of *Notturno con grida*. "At about noon I came back to my car … and took a walk in the beechwood with my dog."[1] The ninety-feet tall, imposing beeches had been there for centuries, and covered an area of over 56 hectares. Salerno strolled around the woods and came upon the so-called "trembling stone." It is an enormous millenarian oval stone of volcanic origin, of 90 cubic meters, 8 meters long, 7 meters wide and 3 meters thick, weighing 250 tons and balanced on a very narrow base. It can be made to vibrate by prying under it with stick used as a lever. Because of this peculiarity, Pliny the Old defined it "*naturae miraculum*" (natural wonder) in his book *Naturalis historia*.

Salerno was dumbfounded. The sight of that imposing and sinister rock, whose upper part looked like the scaly back of a prehistoric beast, set his imagination on fire. "What if that gigantic stone coming from a distant past had some form of mysterious life, I thought, some magic, occult power?"[2] That night Salerno stood up thinking about that "petrified beast" and came up with a story about five characters who hate each other and get lost in the woods. They are attracted by the mysterious rock, which becomes "the amplifier of their bad desires, their projects of mutual duplicity … and mysteriously, no one will get out of the woods alive."[3]

Salerno discussed the idea with his friend Ernesto Gastaldi, who suggested they provide the protagonists with a background; hence the idea of reusing the same characters from their debut *giallo*, *Libido* (1965), and turn the project into a sequel of sorts to that film. To gather the necessary financing, they resorted to article 28 of the 1965 "Corona law" (Law 1213, 4 November 1965), which allowed the State to finance up to 30 percent of the budget of films with cultural or artistic aspirations in which the cast and crew participated in the cost of the production. Article 28 had been scarcely used in the 1960s and 1970s, but after the economic crisis became more severe with the new decade, more and more filmmakers started using it as a shortcut to put together their films, and it became a staple in Italian film production in the Eighties. It was originally intended as a loan, but very rarely did any of the films financed with it turn a profit. Over the years, article 28 lost its initial purpose (that is, being a special resource for debuting filmmakers who were developing artistic innovative work) and became the main source of finance for Italian cinema, along with television.

In order to have access to the 60 million *lire* granted by the Ministry of Spectacle, Gastaldi and Salerno came up with an ingenious trick: they submitted the project to the Ministry under the title *La coscienza*, pretending it to be some sort of avant-garde psychological drama. After obtaining the financing, they founded a cooperative together with the actors, and established their fees as quotas on the distribution grosses. The cast included Gastaldi's wife Maria Chianetta under her a.k.a. Mara Maryl, their friend Luciano Pigozzi, who had already starred in *Libido*, plus only three more actors: the French Martine Brochard, Michele Placido's brother Gerardo Amato (with whom Salerno had worked the previous summer on a stage adaptation of Giovanni Verga's novelette *La lupa* directed by his

brother, Enrico Maria), and the young and rav-
ishingly beautiful Gioia Maria Scola.

Notturno con grida was shot in three weeks
and a half in April 1982, on 16mm and with
direct sound, under the working title *La forza
del male* (The Force of Evil). The two directors
worked with a bare-bones crew, comprising only
the five actors and four technicians: d.o.p. and
cameraman Benito Frattari (who had shot Ja-
copetti's *Africa addio* and Gastaldi's own *La
lunga spiaggia fredda*), his nephew Marco as assistant cameraman, a sound technician and a
boom man, plus a handyman (provided for free
by the mayor of Soriano nel Cimino) who
helped the 60-year-old d.o.p. carry the heavy
crate with the camera and the accessories. To
cut costs, Gastaldi and Salerno took care of all
the other technical duties. As for lighting, the
filmmakers used mostly natural lights, taking
advantage of the peculiar illumination of the
area. Only a flash was used for close-ups. The
experience of working with two directors at once
was not particularly satisfying for Brochard,
who complained: "One day you shoot with one
director and he tells you one thing, the next day
the other tells you the opposite...."[4]

Given the tiny budget, it's no wonder that
Notturno con grida relies so heavily on dialogue
that it almost looks like a play of sorts, recalling
in this some of Gastaldi's earlier works as a
scriptwriter. His trademark snappy dialogue
here is filled with grim jokes and one-liners,
which in the case of Maryl's typical airhead performance often sound grating, such as when she
quips, "But what was Pliny the Old's name when
he was young?" The overall mood conveys a
pessimistic vision of humanity, with five despi-
cable characters doomed to self-destruction,
who are deservedly punished for their sins.
Brigitte herself, a psychic whom the others
believe to be a witch, is a typical character in
Gastaldi's scripts, a mixture of naiveté and nastiness, childishness and greed, while Paul and
Gerard are weak male figures who end up defeated by their own schemes and fears. "Do you
believe in life after death?" someone asks, and
the reply is: "The darkness before is the same as
the darkness that follows. Before we are born
and after we die, it's the same." Yet someone
returns from the afterlife: Christian (a special
participation by playwright Franco Molè,
Brochard's husband, in the role played by Giancarlo Giannini in *Libido*), a supernatural avenger
from the grave who may or may not be an em-

bodiment of the protagonists' dirty conscience
(Salerno's interpretation is that in the end he is
possessed by the Devil[5]).

The supernatural element, which is pre-
dominant in the film from the very opening
séance sequence, makes *Notturno con grida* a
late addition to the Gothic thread, presented in
a minimalistic way and with very sparse special
effects. Some reviewers have noticed similarities
with *The Blair Witch Project* (1999, Daniel Myrick,
Eduardo Sánchez) and not just because of the
eerie subjective shots in the woods (surprisingly
akin to those in Sam Raimi's *The Evil Dead*, which
however was released in Italy only in 1984). Like
in the 1999 film, the characters get lost in the
woods and cannot find their way out, and space
and time coordinates seem to lose significance—
a recurrent theme in Italian Gothic. Paul's watch
stops, a wound in his hand reopens, the protagonist's car disappears from its parking place, an
apple appears out of nowhere next to Brigitte as
if thrown by an invisible hand, a book of Latin ex-
orcisms is found.

Gastaldi and Salerno incorporate sepia-
toned footage from *Libido* in the story, liberally
altering the previous film's plot: for instance, the
characters of Paul and Eileen, who were murdered in the first film, here are revived via
clumsy expository dialogue. Paul, who in *Libido*
fell from a cliff to his death, here explains that
the apparently deadly fall resulted only in his
legs being broken, a decidedly hard-to-swallow
plot contrivance. Some scenes from the 1965
film were interpolated with footage shot in 1982
and toned sepia, featuring Maryl and Pigozzi,
the former carefully lit to conceal the age difference. Gastaldi and Salerno also added simili-
tudes with the first film: in the climax, Maryl is
tied spread-eagle to a rock just as in *Libido* she
was tied to a bed.

For a film whose literal title (Nocturne with
Screams) hints at Chopin's solo piano pieces
(*Nocturnes*), it was no wonder the directors decided to invest the 3 million *lire* they had been
left with after post-production in the music
score. The choice fell on Severino Gazzelloni,
the world's best-known flautist: in Salerno's
idea, a flute-driven score would suggest the god
Pan and enhance the film's peculiar eerie mood.
Gazzelloni accepted: he composed the main
theme and improvised the rest on the spot, while
watching the film. He completed his work in six
hours, coming up with about one hour of improvised, dodecaphonic music. The soundtrack

includes also a couple of themes taken from Luciano Michelini's score for *Morte sospetta di una minorenne* (1975).

The profits Salerno and Gastaldi hoped to see never materialized. *Notturno con grida* was barely distributed, at a time most second and third run theaters were being replaced by red light cinemas, and was screened virtually only in Soriano nel Cimino, the village near its main filming location, with a total gross of only 200,000 *lire*. It soon found its way to home video, on the General Video label, but it was sold in Spain as well, where it came out on VHS as *La fuerza del demonio*.

NOTES

1. Davide Comotti and Vittorio Salerno, *Professione regista e scrittore* (Salerno: Booksprint, 2012), 58.
2. *Ibid.*
3. *Ibid.*
4. Ippoliti and Norcini, "Una favola chiamata cinema. Intervista a Martine Brochard," 37.
5. Comotti and Salerno, *Professione regista e scrittore*, 62.

La villa delle anime maledette—The Damned (*House of the Damned*, a.k.a. *Don't Look in the Attic*)

D: Carlo Ausino. *S and SC*: Carlo Ausino; *DOP*: Carlo Ausino (Staco Film); *M*: Stelvio Cipriani (Ed. CAM); *E*: Giuliano Mattioli; *C*: Giuseppe Lino; *MU*: Lucia La Porta; *Hair*: Giusy-Pietro Pennisi; *SS*: Vera Marchivi; *W*: Claudia Amione; *KG*: Salvatore Schiavo: *PM*: Gregorio Cardone, Corrado Colecchia; *ChEl*: Lello Roppolo; *SO*: Claudio Chiossi; *Mix*: Romano Checcacci. *Cast*: Beba Loncar [Desanka Lončar] (Martha), Jean-Pierre Aumont (Ugo Ressia), Annarita Grapputo (Elisa Bruino/Elisa's mother), Giorgio Ardisson (Casati), Paul Theisheid [Teitcheid] (Caretaker), Tony [Tonino] Campa (Tony Ferraro), Fausto Lombardi (Bruno Ferraro), Ileana Fraia (Sonia), Remo Vercellin, Benedetto Mocellin, Victor Bally, Mimmo Morleo, Attilio Cagnoni, Sandro Zambito, Mario De Gregorio, Michele Malla, Amelia Vercellino, Enrico Slataper, Renzo Gobello, Enzo Zamunner. *PROD*: Michele Peyretti and Carlo Ausino for Antonelliana Cinematografica (Turin); *PM*: Nunzia Ausino. *Country*: Italy. Filmed on location in Turin and at Icet-De Paolis (Milan). *Running time*: 84 minutes (m. 2243). Visa n. 77660 (4.15.1982); *Rating*: V.M.14. *Release date*: 5.14.1982; *Distribution*: Cinevinci (regional). *Domestic gross*: n.a.

Turin, 1955. On a stormy night, in a hillside villa, two men and a woman kill each other in an unexplained murderous frenzy. 22 years later, attorney Ugo Ressia and his associate Casati summon the heirs for the reading of the will. The three heirs are affiliated with each other but are located outside Turin. Elisa is in Paris, her cousin Bruno lives in Rome with his wife Sonia and Bruno's brother Tony resides in Istanbul. Upon reading the will, Elisa, Bruno and Tony find out that they have inherited the huge family villa located in the hills, but on one condition: they must live together in the property and are not allowed to sell it. As soon as they move to their new home, a series of chilling events begin to overwhelm the family: the two brothers have arguments, Elisa receives warning messages from her dead mother, Sonia is killed in a car accident, and Bruno sets his eyes on Elisa. Ressia's secretary Martha, a student of black magic, suspects that Casati might be involved in the events. She alerts Ressia, but the man is mysteriously killed. Eventually it turns out that the sinister elderly caretaker is the key to the mystery…

Born in Messina in 1938, Carlo Ausino left Sicily in 1960 and moved to Turin with a projectionist license in his pocket and the dream of making movies in his head. "Take the story of *Cinema Paradiso*, set it in Turin and here's the story of my life. For me, cinema was everything. Even nowadays, if I don't watch at least two films a week, I'm not well," he explained. "As a kid I used to sell the milk bottles which I'd stolen from my mother to get the money to go to the movies. I collected the frames that projectionists threw in the trash, turned them into slides and projected them to my five sisters, my very first audience. According to what I had found I invented the story, of which I was of course the main character."[1]

In Turin Ausino saw his dream come true. He was an uncredited assistant on the set of Mario Monicelli's masterpiece *I compagni* (1963) and eventually he became a director himself. In 1969 he made his feature film debut, the black-and-white World War II drama *L'ora della pietà*, shot in 16mm and starring Emanuel Cannarsa, who would be one of his recurring actors. As with his following works, Ausino was the director of photography as well. During that period, he also worked as a cameraman for RAI's newsreels and reportedly brought a more dynamic style to his reports.

Ausino's body of work is an example of regional cinema, conceived and produced far from

Italy's main production center, Rome: all his films were set and shot within the boundaries of the director's adoptive city. After failing to complete *Improvvisamente, un giorno*, a love story starring Vittorio De Sica and Marisa Solinas and set "in the last days of humanity, before an atomic conflagration ... to underline the individuals' solitude in a hostile society,"[2] Ausino helmed the similarly-themed *La città dell'ultima paura*, starring Cannarsa and Solinas, a sci-fi drama about a speleologist who survives a nuclear apocalypse that destroys human life in Turin, inspired by the *I Am Legend* adaptation *The Omega Man* (1971, Boris Sagal). The director claimed that the scenes in the deserted city (shot early in the morning without permits, blocking traffic temporarily) exuded a genuine sense of dread, but we have to rely on his word: shot over the course of two years, *La città dell'ultima paura* won the second prize at the 1975 Trieste Science Fiction Film Festival but was not distributed theatrically. The same fate occurred to the elusive *Prima che il sole tramonti* (1976), another sci-fi themed work about an alien invader, again starring Cannarsa and Solinas, which was never even submitted to the rating board. The director's following work, the crime flick *Torino violenta* (a.k.a. *Double Game*, 1977)—shot with a low budget of 60 million *lire* to cash in on the *poliziottesco* fever of the period and finally find a regular distribution—was an unexpected hit in Italy and was rumored to be head of Fiat Gianni Agnelli's favorite film.

Ausino's first horror movie, *La villa delle anime maledette*, was born almost by chance, as he struck a deal with a French distributor, Felix Film, which would allow him to use some moderately famous actors for a limited period, in the early Summer of 1980. The director cranked out the script in a couple of weeks[3] and the project took form: he could count on the French Jean-Pierre Aumont, the Yugoslav beauty Beba Loncar, and former Eurospy star Giorgio Ardisson. Despite being billed fourth in the credits, the true lead was ex-model Annarita Grapputo, who had debuted in Carlo Lizzani's *Storie di vita e malavita* (a.k.a. *The Teenage Prostitution Racket*, 1975) and had been the female lead in *Torino violenta*. For both Loncar and Grapputo, it would be the last movie role. Another recurrent presence in Ausino's films,

Paul Theicheid, was cast in the key role of the villa's elderly caretaker.

Shooting started on June 9, 1980, under the working title *La stirpe dei dannati (The Damned)*[4] and went on for four weeks, widely publicized in the Turin-based newspaper *La Stampa*. The film had its premiere screening in Turin only over one year later, on September 30, 1981, under the title *La villa delle anime dannate*[5] (in the meantime, another Ausino movie had come out, the ambitious *film noir Tony l'altra faccia della Torino violenta*, released in Turin in

Italian locandina for *La villa delle anime maledette* (1982, Carlo Ausino).

May 1981). However, proper distribution was postponed until May 1982.

Ausino's script draws from the standard Gothic tropes: the mysterious curse passed from generation to generation, the séance, the doomed family, the psychic heroine, plus the morbid element of incest, with the insane attraction of Bruno (Fausto Lombardi) for his cousin Elisa (Grapputo), as the man becomes convinced that she must give him a son to defeat the curse that plagues their dynasty. The theme of the double is employed not only by having Grapputo play a dual role (Elisa and her mother), but it also has a vital part in the rather incoherent final twist, when it turns out that one key character has the capacity of mutating his appearance at will. The ending is virtually lifted from *The Sentinel*, as the heroine secludes herself in the villa, and thus, by remaining the last of her bloodline, she puts an end to the curse.

Despite the impressive cast and the setting in a villa just outside Turin, *La villa delle anime maledette* leaves a lot to be desired overall. The prologue tries hard to set an ominous tone, with two men fighting to the death during a thunderstorm, driven by a mysterious homicidal frenzy, while a woman (also played by Grapputo) desperately tries to separate them. One of the men stabs the other, and the woman in turn stabs him. She then runs away in the villa's garden, which conveniently hosts a private cemetery, only to be dragged underground by a hand protruding from the ground. The use of lighting draws back to classical Gothic, with plenty of silhouettes and light/shadow games, but one cannot help noticing the performers' poor acting, the cheap special effects (with the demonic entity portrayed via a pulsating red flashing light and a chair being dragged forward by an invisible force) and the recycled Stelvio Cipriani score.

Still, the pre-credit sequence is easily the film's most exciting moment. The story drags along interminably, with no tension or detectable suspense, and looks more like a warped family drama than a horror movie. Moreover, the low budget shows at every turn: for instance, the Paris scenes are introduced via a cheap b&w still of the Eiffel Tower. Aumont and Loncar are wasted in thankless secondary roles, and the special effects are poor throughout: in a scene, while Grapputo is taking a shower in the hotel, a supernatural entity appears in the form of some dry ice entering the bathroom … and leaves a message written on the mirror's surface. The dialogue must be heard

to be believed, with such exchanges as: "Why do you always have to turn up so silently?" "I kept the light step of when I dedicated myself to hunting." The score, compiled from Cipriani's back catalogue, reprises themes from Pier Carpi's occultist devil movie *Un'ombra nell'ombra* (1979). Overall, the best thing about the film may well be Ausino's photography, which retains an old-style elegance and gives it a watchable look.

Rather surprisingly, *La villa delle anime maledette* got a V.M.14 rating "for the distressing atmosphere that pervades the whole film and the murders committed in a particularly gruesome way," which makes one wonder whether the board members actually watched it, as graphic violence is virtually non-existent. Distribution in Italy was scarce, and reviews were predictably scathing: the *Corriere della Sera* called the story "extremely deranged, developing despite any logic," and labeled script, direction and photography as slapdash, giving moderate praise only to Grapputo's performance, which in the reviewer's opinion made the result "a step forward from *Torino violenta*, one of the most disgraceful products in this spectator's memory."[6]

After quickly disappearing into oblivion, the movie found a second life in the home video market, both in Italy (released by the popular GVR label) and abroad, in its English language export version *House of the Damned* (misspelled *House of the Danned* in the titles). It surfaced overseas on tape as *Don't Look in the Attic*, and it even earned some perplexing good reviews in specialized magazines and studies of the horror film. The illustrious *Aurum Film Encyclopedia* praised it as follows: "Ausino makes ample and effective use of dolly shots to create and sustain his parapsychological spells, and at times manages to evoke the flamboyantly funereal romanticism of the Italian master Mario Bava."[7] Again, one wonders whether the reviewer actually saw it, as there are less than a handful of dolly shots in the whole movie.

Overall, *La villa delle anime maledette* stands as a testifier that re-proposing a by-now fallen archetype, the standard Gothic yarn, was a lost cause. Even more so, it proves the impossibility of survival for that type of low-budget genre cinema that could cut itself a small slice of market in the second and third-run circuit via regional distribution. In fact, Ausino's following work was mostly destined to oblivion. *Senza scrupoli 2* (1990) a sequel of sorts to Tonino Valerii's *Senza scrupoli* (1986), was his last film with a proper theatrical and home video distribution, and the director himself asked for it to be seized because of the arbitrary inclusion of hardcore sequences on the part of the producers. *Nebuneff*, an occultist horror set in Turin, London and Cairo, shot over a period of years between 1988 and 1995,[8] remained unreleased due to legal issues. Ausino's last film to date is 2006's *Killer's Playlist*, a thriller starring George Hilton, which was briefly screened in Turin and then disappeared from sight.

NOTES

1. Fulvio Montano, "Carlo Ausino e l'esperienza di Torino violenta," www.effettonotteonline.com (http://www. effettonotteonline.com/enol/archivi/articoli/interviste/2002 10/200210in00.htm).

2. "Marisa farà perdere le testa a De Sica," *L'Unità*, April 27, 1972.

3. a. per., "Horror sulla collina," *Stampa Sera*, June 9, 1980

4. a. vald., "Ardisson ritorna al cinema e ruba confidenze a Brazzi," *Stampa Sera*, June 9, 1980.

5. [not signed], "Ecco la villa delle anime dannate," *Stampa Sera*, September 30, 1981.

6. L.A. [Leonardo Autera], "Quella villa maledetta," *Corriere della Sera*, June 9, 1982.

7. Phil Hardy (ed.), *The Aurum Film Encyclopedia. Horror* (London: Aurum Press, 1996), 390.

8. Stefano Della Casa, "Torino set," *La Stampa*, June 16, 1995.

1983

La bimba di Satana (*Satan's Baby Doll*, a.k.a. *A Girl for Satan*)

D: Alan W. Cools [Mario Bianchi]. S: Gabriele Crisanti; SC: Piero Regnoli; DOP: uncredited [Franco Villa and Angelo Iannutti] (Telecolor); M: Nino Catanese (Ed. Overplay); E: Cesare Bianchini; PD: Salvatore Siciliano; AD: Spartaco Antonucci; C: Franco Campanile; AC: Maurizio Fiorentini; SO: Silvio Spingi; SS: Paola Villa; CO: Itala Giardina; MU: Rosario Prestopino; AE: Gabriella Marsetti. Cast: Jacqueline Doupré (Miria), Mariangela Giordano (Sol), Marina Hedman (Maria), Aldo Sambrell [Aldo Sanchez Brell] (Antonio Aguilar), Alfonso Gaita (Ignazio Aguilar), Joe Davers [Giuseppe Carbone] (Isidro), Giancarlo Del Duca (Dr. Juan Suarez). PROD: Gabriele Cristanti for Filmarte; PM: Gabriele Crisanti; PS: Marcello Spingi; PSe: Gianfranco Fornari, Giancarlo Straniero, Mirella Cavalloro. *Country*: Italy. Filmed on location at the Castle Piccolomini, Balsorano, Palazzo Braschi (Rome) and at Icet-De Paolis Studios (Milan). *Running time*: 74 minutes (m. 2024; softcore version); 88 minutes (hardcore version). Visa n. 77904 (6.11.1982); *Rating*: V.M.18. *Release dates*: 2.25.1983 (Spain, softcore version), 7.29.1983 (Italy); *Distribution*: Film 2. *Domestic gross*: n.a. *Also known as*: Orgasmo di Satana (Italy; hardcore version); *La hija de Satanás* (Spain), *Dr. Porno und sein Satanszombie* (Germany; hardcore version); *Sexorgien im Satanschloß* (Germany; softcore version).

In a remote Spanish castle, the Aguilar family is mourning the passing of Countess Maria, whose body lies in the crypt, waiting to be embalmed. Despite the family doctor, Suarez, ruling Maria's death as a heart attack, her husband Antonio had a hand in it. Maria was the lover of Antonio's brother Ignazio, now bound to a wheelchair after a stroke, but she also seduced Suarez, and was carrying on a lesbian affair with Sol, the novice nun who takes care of Ignazio. The family butler, Isidro, evokes otherworldly forces, and the Countess' spirit possesses her teenage daughter Miria, who becomes the instrument of her revenge. One by one, the members of the Aguilar family are dispatched by the vengeful spirit…

"Remaking *Malabimba* was a stupid move. I didn't want to do the sex scenes. I felt used, abused and exploited,"[1] Mariangela Giordano commented about her last film with her then-partner, producer Gabriele Crisanti, which marked not only the end of their artistic collaboration, but of their personal relationship as well. Between 1979 and 1981, Crisanti had involved the actress in a handful of flicks that stand out among the most extreme products of the era, because of their sheer amount of sex and violence: Mario Landi's *Giallo a Venezia* and *Patrick vive ancora*, and Andrea Bianchi's *Malabimba* and *Le notti del terrore*.

In a shameless recycling move, Crisanti and screenwriter Piero Regnoli opted for a retelling of *Malabimba* with minimal changes, even recasting Giordano in the same role as the unfortunate nun who becomes the spirit's last victim. The malevolent spirit who possesses the teenage girl is that of the mysteriously deceased Countess Maria (we will later find out that she has been murdered). She proceeds to kill her heroin-addicted widower, his wheelchair-bound brother-in-law, the family doctor, a novice named Sol—all of them her previous lovers—and a scary-looking butler who is also an expert on the supernatural, and who concocted an arcane ritual to bring her back to life. In the end, the infamous lesbian seduction-cum-fisting scene of the 1979 film is replaced by a Sapphic interlude atop a tomb between Maria and Sol which ends, as in *Venus d'Ille*, with the novice being crushed to death between her lover's arms, possibly evidence of Regnoli's literary erudition rather than an unlikely homage to the late Mario Bava.

Unlike most of Crisanti's earlier sex-horror hybrids, the target for *La bimba di Satana* was the hardcore porn market, which by then was in full bloom. The casting of Marina Hedman Bellis, then Italy's most famous porn star (better known to the public as Marina Frajese, or Marina Lothar), was telling, as was the presence of Alfonso Gaita, a regular of early Italian hardcore. Director Mario Bianchi (Roberto Montero's son, and only a namesake of *Malabimba*'s director Andrea Bianchi) cast his friend Aldo Sambrell, a recurring presence in the director's early Westerns, as the repugnant, drug-addicted Antonio Aguilar: "When there was need of this kind of father figure, or a king like in *Biancaneve & co.*, I called him, and he came over, for two farthings, and sometimes he did not even get to have those!"[2]

Bianchi was probably relying on Sambrell to sell the product in the latter's home country (hence the Spanish setting). The actor was even involved in one of the non-simulated sex scenes with Marina Hedman, which he later recalled as follows: "We had to shoot a love scene, Marina and I… Well, I was lying on the bed, waiting for her, and when she showed up we started making out; after a while I realized that she was doing it for real and I had to stop her and call Crisanti, the producer, because I could not work that way."[3] Sambrell was replaced by Gaita for the explicit close-ups. As for the weird-looking character actor Giuseppe "Pino" Carbone (credited as "Joe Davers"), he was a self-appointed clairvoyant: a couple of years earlier the press reported that Carbone was about to direct a feature-length film titled *La fattura*, starring people with para-

normal powers who would be in a trance in several scenes.[4] The project never took off.

Apart from the sex scenes, Hedman's acting consists mostly in lying still over a grave in the nude, pretending to be dead. Giordano, for her part, takes off her clothes with admirable abnegation, and a scene where her character washes Ignazio's pubic area with a damp cloth testifies to the actress' willingness to do anything for Crisanti. As for the elusive Jacqueline Doupré, who reprises Katell Laennec's role in *Malabimba* and, despite amply showing her body, does not perform any explicit sex scene, she mustn't be confused with the French porn actress Catherine Doupré. Bianchi recalled: "Jacqueline Doupré was a stage name, because she was a gal

The Italian poster for *La bimba di Satana* (1983), inspired by Boris Vallejo's 1979 painting *Vampire's Kiss*.

who lived in Ostia, but I can't remember the real name, and however I think the poor girl only did this movie."[5] One can understand why, since Doupré pales in front of her model, and in fact she is actually given little to do in the film.

Compared with the already threadbare narrative of *Malabimba*, *La bimba di Satana* gives new meaning to the word "minimalistic." The cast comprises only seven people (plus a rotten-looking zombie mummy that pops up just in time to dispatch the butler), who for most of the running time wander in the empty castle,[6] its crypts and dilapidated surrounding, in long, dialogue-less sequences accompanied by Nino Catanese's score, which combines Goblin-esque, keyboard-driven parts, eerie chants and distorted guitars. The ghost story elements are barely sketched too: in a lengthy sequence Isidro the butler falls into an epileptic trance in the crypt while evoking the spirits of the dead, with the camera following his grimaces and convulsions in close-up, and a subjective POV shot traverses the empty halls and corridors, accompanied by heavy breathing on the soundtrack, to Miria's bedroom. It climaxes with Isidro biting the neck off a rooster like a sideshow geek.

When the actors open their mouth, it gets worse. Isidro's monologues are a hodgepodge of lowbrow mysticism, and when Sambrell's character becomes verbally abusive toward Sol, he comes up with such laughable lines as "Even though you're not a nun yet, desecrating a temple has always been my dream!"

Admittedly, Bianchi tries to inject some style in the proceeding. He makes use of tracking shots, and even films a scene in a long take, when Antonio takes his wheelchair-bound brother Ignazio to the crypt to let him die of starvation (Ignazio will meet another grisly fate, not before being orally pleasured by Maria's ghost). The camera, placed on the wheelchair between Gaita's feet, accompanies the two actors in a low-angle shot across the rooms of the castle, as Sambrell hams it up, exposing his deadly plan while pushing the wheelchair and Gaita impassively listening to him (the character is supposed to be a vegetable after a stroke) while using only his eyes to simulate concern— a moment which at least shows an attempt at *mise-en-scène*, in a movie which otherwise lacks any semblance of rhythm, suspense, and narrative progression.

Shot in the Summer of 1981 (according to the Public Cinematographic Register filming started on August 17[7]), *La bimba di Satana* was submitted to the rating board in June 1982, in a softcore version which ran slightly over 73 minutes and got away with a V.M.18 certificate after a cut (for about 25 seconds) in the sex scene between Hedman and Sambrell, in "the part where the woman's mouth slides over her husband's lower belly." The board justified the rating not only because of the abundant sex and nudity, but also because of the rooster sequence as well as the bit in which Sambrell's character shoots heroin, which "lingers on the technique to inject drugs." It was released only the following year, in late July 1983.

Crisanti likely attempted to have it both ways, with an erotic horror movie that could be safely distributed in regular theaters as well as an out-and-out porn version. However, the latter, titled *Orgasmo di Satana*, likely fell into oblivion, and over the years Bianchi and Crisanti repeatedly denied its existence, despite the scant running time of the existing prints would suggest otherwise.[8] It finally resurfaced in 2007 on German DVD.[9]

The hardcore version credits Bianchi with his own name and includes five sequences not included in the softcore prints (where the director is credited as "Alan W. Cools"). First is the two-minute pre-credit (simulated) lesbian sequence between Mariangela Giordano and Marina Hedman. It is shot from below and has the hand-camera slowly circling around the two women: Marina is kneeling as in adoration before the other woman, who is standing atop a table like a living statue and wears only white stockings, and the shots of the two lovers are interspersed with images of the frescoes on the place's walls and ceiling. The other four sequences are Giordano's lengthy masturbation scene, which features next-to-hardcore details; a hardcore scene (about six minutes long) involving the Swedish actress and Gaita, which restages the infamous fellatio scene of *Malabimba*, for what can well be the movie's *pièce de resistance*; the aforementioned four-minute hardcore sequence between Hedman and Sambrell, with the latter replaced by Gaita in the hardcore close-ups; and, finally, a brief Sapphic scene between Giordano and Doupré.

Despite the director's assurance that the film "performed very well worldwide,"[10] *La bimba di Satana* was released theatrically only in Spain, in 1983, several months earlier than in its home country, in a softcore version titled *La hija de Satanás*.[11]

NOTES

1. Alan Jones and Mark Ashworth, "Diva Divina. The Mariangela Giordano Story," in Stefan Jaworzyn (ed.), *Shock Xpress* #2 (London: Titan Books, 1994), 72.
2. Stefano Ippoliti and Matteo Norcini, "Mario Bianchi. Il mio cinema pizza e fichi," in *Cine 70 e dintorni* #5, Summer 2004, 28.
3. Gian Luca Castoldi, "Aldo Sambrell. L'uomo che morì 1000 volte," *Amarcord* #16, January/February 1999, 84.
4. Reported in *Cinema d'oggi*, September 25, 1979.
5. Ippoliti and Norcini, "Mario Bianchi. Il mio cinema pizza e fichi," 28.
6. The castle seen in exterior shots is Castle Piccolomini in Balsorano, whereas the indoor scenes were filmed at Palazzo Braschi, in Rome.
7. Filming was also reported in *Cinema d'oggi*, September 22, 1981. The script deposited at Rome's CSC is dated July 1981.
8. The Italian softcore version released to VHS on the Video Arcadia label ran only 64 minutes.
9. The U.S. DVD release, on the Severin label (as *Satan's Baby Doll*), includes the softcore cut, whereas the German one, on the X-Rated label and with the title *Dr. Porno und sein Satanszombie*, is the hardcore version.
10. Ippoliti and Norcini, "Mario Bianchi. Il mio cinema pizza e fichi," 28.
11. According to the official ministerial data, it was seen by 20,230 spectators and grossed an amount corresponding to about 30,200 euro. (http://infoicaa.mecd.es/CatalogoICAA/Peliculas/Detalle?Pelicula=716551).

Zeder (*Revenge of the Dead*)

D: Pupi Avati. S: Pupi Avati; SC: Pupi Avati, Maurizio Costanzo, Antonio Avati; DOP: Franco Delli Colli (Technovision-Telecolor, Kodak); M: Riz Ortolani (Ed. New Point); E: Amedeo Salfa; PD: Giancarlo Basili, Leonardo Scarpa; CO: Steno Tonelli; MU: Alfonso Cioffi; AD: Cesare Bastelli; APD: Laura Casalini; C: Antonio Schiavo Lena; AC: Andrea Barbieri; AE: Piera Gabutti; 2ndAE: Loretta Mattioli; SO: Raffaele De Luca; B: Paolo Cottignola; Mix: Romano Checcacci; SOE: Luciano Anzellotti, Massimo Anzellotti; SP: Piermaria Formento; SS: Fiorella Lugli; W: Luisa Cavazza, Clara Masina Berti; PrM: Faliero Reggiani. Cast: Gabriele Lavia (Stefano), Anne Canovas (Alessandra), Paola Tanziani (Gabriella Goodman), Cesare Barbetti (Dr. Meyer), Bob Tonelli (Mr. Big), Ferdinando Orlandi (Giovine), Enea Ferrario (Mirko), John Stacy (Prof. Chiesi), Alessandro Partexano (Lt. Guido Silvestri), Marcello Tusco (Dr. Melis), Aldo Sassi (Don Mario), Veronica Moriconi (Young Gabriella), Enrico Ardizzone (Benni), Maria Teresa Toffano (Anna), Andrea Montuschi (Inspector Bouffet), Adolfo Belletti (Don Emidio), Paolo Bacchi (Mr. Big's Secretary), Giuseppina Borione (Helena, First Victim), Imelde Marani (Nurse), Gianluigi Gaspari, Carlo Schincaglia (Don Luigi Costa), Luciano Bianchi, Pino Tosca, Giovanni Bussadori, Sergio Lama, Giuseppe Lentini, Giancarlo Bandini; *uncredited*: Ghilka Muzzi Matteuzzi (Ms. Hubert). PROD: Gianni Minervini and Antonio Avati for A.M.A. Film (Rome), with the collaboration of Enea Ferrario for RAI-Radio Televisione Italiana; PM: Francesco Guerrieri; PS: Luca Bitterlin; PSe: Rosa Mercurio; ADM: Raffaello Forti; Cash: Francesca Moneta. *Country*: Italy. Filmed on location in Bologna, Milano Marittima and Cesenatico, Chartres (France) and at R.P.A. Elios Studios (Rome). *Running time*: 100 minutes (m. 2751). Visa n. 78586 (2.19.1983); *Rating*: V.M.14. *Release dates*: 8.10.1983 (Italy), 5.8.1984 (USA); *Distribution*: Gaumont (Italy), Motion Picture Marketing (USA). *Domestic gross*: 334,000,000 *lire*. *Also known as*: Revenge of the Dead (USA), Zeder—Denn Tote kehren wieder (West Germany)

Chartres, France, 1956. In an isolated villa, Dr. Meyer conducts an experiment with the assistance of a young girl with psychic powers, Gabriella Goodman, to find the grave of the mysterious Paolo Zeder. Gabriella is attacked and mutilated by a monstrous being, and human remains are found in the villa's basement, which Meyer identifies as Zeder. Bologna, 1982. A young novelist, Stefano, is given by his wife Alessandra an old typewriter as a present. Stefano notices on the old ribbon a mysterious message about the so-called "K-Zones," areas where death ceases to exist and bodies can return from the afterlife, which had been researched in the early 1900 by a scientist named Paolo Zeder. Intrigued, Stefano starts investigating, and becomes increasingly obsessed with the mystery around Zeder and the K-Zones. His investigation leads him to a secluded area near Rimini, where a team of scientists from the Vatican, led by Dr. Meyer and Ms. Goodman, are conducting secret experiments with surveillance cameras and monitors. The property is sited on a K-Zone, and the object of the experiments is a dead defrocked priest, Don Luigi Costa. Stefano, who has rented a room in a nearby motel, witnesses Costa's return from the dead as a flesh-eating zombie, which results in the massacre of Meyer and his men. But Stefano finds out that his wife has been kidnapped and murdered by the conspirators. Desperate, he buries Alessandra in the abandoned property, so that she will come back to life…

In the Summer of 1982, three years after the release of *Le strelle nel fosso*, Pupi Avati started shooting another fantastic-themed film, his second out-and-out horror after *La casa dalle finestre che ridono* (1976). During those three years Avati had established himself as a critically-respected *auteur* thanks to his successful TV mini-series *Cinema!!!* (broadcast in November 1979 and starring Lino Capolicchio, Gianni Cavina and Carlo Delle Piane) and *Dancing Paradise* (broadcast in June 1982 and starring Cavina and Delle Piane). *Dancing Paradise* showed that Avati hadn't abandoned his predilection for the *fantastique* and the unusual: it was a musical fairy tale about the son (Cavina) of a legendary drummer who goes in search of his father and is helped in his quest by a benevolent ghost (Delle Piane). Avati's only theatrical feature film after *Le strelle nel fosso* had been *Aiutami a sognare* (1981), starring Anthony Franciosa and Mariangela Melato, a romantic love story between a widow and an American pilot during World War II: although a box-office flop, it had been a success on TV where—as was customary in that period—it was broadcast in a longer, three-part version. To many, then, the news that Avati was working on a new project about "a stateless person who conducted bizarre research on the afterlife,"[1] as the upcoming movie was briefly described in the press, came as unexpected as it was puzzling. As the director later explained, "I returned to the Fantastic for strategic and commercial needs ... going back to the big screen with a genre film seemed the easiest choice."[2]

Moreover, the horror genre gave Avati the chance to explore some of his longtime passions, namely esotericism and occultism, and draw from his own readings and research. Some years earlier, the director had been studying the life and works of French alchemist Fulcanelli, the author of *Le Mystère des Cathédrales* (The Mystery of the Cathedrals, 1926) and *Les Demeures Philosophales* (Dwellings of the Philosophers, 1929), for a "serious" project which he described as "a very ambitious story on the origins of the Gothic and the Templar Knights and on their research under the ruins of the Temple of Solomon during their eight years' stay in Jerusalem."[3] The film would delve also into the legendary Ark of the Covenant, which the Templars had allegedly brought back with them on their return to Europe.

The release of *Raiders of the Lost Ark* (1981, Steven Spielberg) marked the early end of the project, but Avati managed to reprise some notions about Fulcanelli in his script. The eponymous character of Paolo Zeder is a mysterious stateless person—that is, someone not considered as a national by any state under the operation of its law—whose condition makes him a symbolic modern-day variation on the Wandering Jew, condemned to wander over the Earth as punishment, without the hope of rest in death till the second coming of Christ. Zeder never appears in the film, if not in the form of a pile of bones found inside a coffin, but his shadow looms over the story, and his studies about the "K-Zones" are the object of an enduring obsession in the film. He was modeled upon the fascinating and elusive alchemist and esoteric writer, who had inspired Argento for *Inferno*, and whose real identity was never found. The director told *L'Écran fantastique*:

> It seems that the first thing American secret services did, just after entering Paris during the liberation [in August 1944], was to try and locate Fulcanelli. But they couldn't find him. He had disappeared, and even today we don't know whether he is alive or dead. When I decided to make a new genre film, I used this character. Later, in order to be freer, I changed his name to Zeder and I also had him make investigations on the afterlife, the world of the dead, the K-Zones, the oracles and the sanctuaries.[4]

Avati drew also from the works of Peter Kolosimo (real name Pietro Domenico Colosimo, 1922–1984), an Italian journalist and a pioneer researcher of fringe archaeology akin to Robert Charroux and Erich von Däniken; in the early 1970s Kolosimo launched the magazine "Pi Kappa" (the name comes from his initials) devoted to his favorite themes, and there is a chance the term "K-Zone" (spelled in Italian as "*terreni kappa*") was a subtle reference to Kolosimo.

The idea for the story gradually took form from assorted suggestions, from the chilling idea of a camera inside a coffin which monitors a dead body uninterruptedly to the notion of the "K-Zones," burial areas where the dead will resurrect. The latter concept was linked to a tale Avati had heard of a dog buried in a swamp area and later sighted in the countryside, proving that the director's stories were always rooted in popular folklore (as with the story of the exhumed priest that had provided the inspiration for the shocking twist ending in *La casa dalle finestre che ridono*). Avati linked the concept of "K-Zones" to the ancient Etruscan rites and cemeterial sites—a recurring theme in Italian Gothic and *giallo* from *L'etrusco uccide ancora* (1972) to *Ritratto di donna velata* and *Assassinio al cimitero etrusco*—thus drawing a red thread from Italy's ancient pre–Christian times to the modern age, not unlike he would do in the extraordinary TV mini-series *Voci notturne* (1995). All this, transported to the typical regional background of Avati's cinema, the Emilia Romagna area.

But the spark that ignited the film was related to the act of narrating itself. The director had bought an electric typewriter from composer Amedeo Tommasi, and after a while he had to replace the ribbon: while changing it, he noticed that the words written by the previous owner could still be read on the used ribbon. The discovery had a morbid voyeuristic feel to it: it was like spying on someone else's life and becoming aware of its most intimate secrets. It was just what Avati needed: the protagonist of his film would be a down-on-his luck novelist who cannot find an idea for his next book. He would be involved in the story by reading the mysterious words impressed on a typewriter's ribbon—a modern day version of the manuscript found in a bottle, or the ancient gravestone with a cryptic message engraved on it—and would become obsessed with it. The thirst for knowledge and creativity would ultimately lead him to perdition.

Backed by his company A.M.A., with participation from Rai Due (who had the right to broadcast the film 18 months after its theatrical release), and a budget of about 500 million *lire*, Avati assembled a varied cast. Some of his regular players (Ferdinando Orlandi, Bob Tonelli) were joined by renowned dubbing artists Marcello Fusco and Cesare Barbetti (the Italian voice of Robert Redford, and soon to become another member of Avati's "repertoire company"), plus some odd presences. One such was the Australian-born John Stacy, who had relocated to Italy at a young age and was an oft-seen face in Italian cinema since the early 1950s, in such varied works as Antonio Margheriti's *Il pianeta degli uomini spenti* (1961), Mario Bava's *La ragazza che sapeva troppo* (1963), Fellini's *8½* (1963) and Carlo Lizzani's *Mussolini ultimo atto* (1974). This was his penultimate film.

For the role of Stefano, Avati cast Gabriele Lavia. Already one of Italy's most noted stage actors, every now and then Lavia took a break from his theatrical commitments to act in a movie (his latest turn had been in *Inferno*), but

Pupi Avati (center) on the set of **Zeder** (1983) with actors Paolo Bacchi (left) and Bob Tonelli (courtesy Luca Servini).

this would be his first film as protagonist; he and Avati knew and liked each other, and Lavia was a profitable name to attach to a horror movie, given his previous works with Argento as well as his participation in *Chi sei?* (a.k.a. *Beyond the Door*, 1974). Alongside him, Avati cast the French Anne Canovas, whom he had seen in Giacomo Battiato's TV movie *Colomba* (1982), based on Prosper Mérimée's story, even though his initial choice was Lavia's partner Monica Guerritore.

Filming lasted ten weeks, from July to early September 1982, and took place in Chartres (for a few exteriors) and mostly in Emilia-Romagna, between Bologna and the coastal towns of Rimini and Milano Marittima. There, Avati found the perfect setting for the film's most horrific scenes, set in the abandoned children's colony where a team of researchers conduct experiments on the dead: the Provincia Varese colony in Milano Marittima. As was customary, the director used almost exclusively real locations and left some room for improvisation. But the atmosphere on the set was tense, and at a certain point near the end of the shoot there was an argument between the director and the crew, which resulted in a number of technicians leaving the set and going back to Rome.[5]

In interviews of the period, Avati talked about the movie in a detached way, underlining that the choice of making a horror film was mainly a commercial move ("The average TV viewer is above 40 years old, whereas moviegoers are around 20"). He even stated that *Zeder* was "in some sense, only half-mine, a proof of good will that I wanted to offer to the producers," concluding that "without television, an Italian filmmaker like me would have no work space at all."[6] But the result is among his very best works, and as a horror movie it is just as scary as *La casa dalle finestre che ridono*, if not as original.

Even though his film was about people returning from the dead and feeding on the living, Avati only superficially related to the zombie movie thread of the early 1980s. *Zeder* rejects the traditional living dead iconography and the subgenre's narrative mechanisms and focuses on a conspiracy movie-like paranoia—everyone near Stefano, including his closest friends, turns out to be a conspirator—eschewing graphic gore in favor of suspense and dread, with the same sense of an implacable destiny closing in on the hero. "I don't like the cruelty and the gruesome effects typical of some *auteurs* who have been

lauded and rediscovered in France,"[7] the director claimed upon the film's release, possibly referring to Fulci.

In Avati's cinema, horror is closely linked to religious and superstitious beliefs, which often become blurred. The exhumation of Zeder's physical remains looks like the discovery of the relics of a saint or a prophet, met with jubilation by Dr. Meyer, and the Vatican hierarchy's secret inquiry on the mysterious resurrections recalls the Church investigating miraculous events such as weeping statues or inexplicable healings, which spread false beliefs among the masses. Here, the dead returning from the afterlife—a recurrent theme in Avati's vision of the *fantastique*: see also *Le strelle nel fosso*, *Voci notturne*, and *L'arcano incantatore* (a.k.a. *The Arcane Enchanter*, 1996)— are perverse variations of Lazarus' story in the Bible. Even though these zombies bite and tear chunks of flesh just like in Romero's films, the focus here is not as much on their violent behavior against the living but on the metaphysical horror of their experience. They grin, they whimper, and they laugh out loud, as if they had seen and learned something that is unknown to us, an exhilarating atrocious prank which we cannot understand. The joke is on us, and it's not funny. It's frightening.

Many key characters in Avati's cinema— the unlikely magician in *Balsamus l'uomo di Satana*, the actors in *Thomas ... gli indemoniati*, the "painter of agonies" and his sisters in *La casa dalle finestre che ridono*, the peasants in *Le strelle nel fosso*, the defrocked priest in *L'arcano incantatore*—are obsessed with communicating with the dead. Whereas Buono Legnani was attempting to fix on his canvas the moment of passing, here this obsession takes pseudo-scientific forms, by way of cameras and monitors poking into the motionless features of the recently deceased. Considering that the researchers in *Zeder* work on behalf of the Vatican, theirs is an act of *hybris*, as if dogmas and leaps of faith were no longer sufficient to soothe the anguish before the impending physical dissipation, and proof of the Biblical promise of immortality was needed. The director labeled the researchers' voyeuristic experiments as "a form of extreme violence. That's their "sin" ... there's nothing more indecent than spying on what happens after the burial, during death. It's the most vulgar thing there is, the most villainous."[8]

Avati's researchers are very much like some unfortunate predecessors, namely Dr. Barrett

(Clive Revill) and his aides, who are recruited to investigate "survival after death" at Belasco House in *The Legend of Hell House* (1973, John Hough) and the research team led by the petulant Peter Brock (Michael Bryant) in the made-for-TV *The Stone Tape* (1972, Peter Sasdy). Both films have in common with *Zeder* the attempt at reviving a typical Gothic tale in a contemporary setting, while replacing old-style clichés (séances, etc.) with state-of-the-art hi-tech. On the other hand, the remarkable similarities between *Zeder* and Stephen King's novel *Pet Sematary* seem to be the result of astonishing coincidences: the script for Avati's film was completed in March 1982, while King's book (published in November 1983 in the States) germinated as early as late 1978, and the American writer—who as well took inspiration from events linked with the death of a pet animal, his daughter's cat Smucky—completed the first draft in May 1979.[9] As for their literary antecedents, both Avati and King likely drew from H.P. Lovecraft's *Herbert West, Reanimator* and especially W.W. Jacobs' celebrated short story *The Monkey's Paw*, which inspired Bob Clark's *Dead of Night* (a.k.a. *Deathdream*, 1974) and was adapted in 1977 by Dan Curtis for the made-for-TV *Dead of Night*, in the episode *Bobby*. King most likely knew the two movies; the latter was broadcast in the U.S. in March 1977. There is a chance that Avati too was aware of them, as Clark's film was released in Italy in 1976 under the eerie title *La morte dietro la porta* (Death Behind the Door), while Curtis' film turned up on Italian private television stations as early as 1981, as *Notte di morte* (Death Night).

The story has also some vague (and most likely coincidental) similarities with Jacques Tourneur's unfilmed screenplay, *Whispering in Distant Chambers* (dating back to 1966), in which a millionaire tries to prove scientifically the existence of life beyond death by way of advanced recording technology. But Avati comes close to the French director's cinema for the method of building restlessness through lighting, inscribing the characters within sparse oases of light as opposed to areas of darkness that "are likely to reshape the contours of a familiar space or … thin down the usual boundaries between an imaginary space and the sphere of sensorial reception."[10] This similarity becomes an explicit homage in the swimming pool scene, which pays reference to a similar moment in *Cat People* (1942). In interviews Avati mentioned as

a main influence, for its "grammar of fear," Henri-Georges Clouzot's masterpiece *Les diaboliques* (1955).

The actual darkness which surrounds (and sometimes engulfs) the characters recalls the cognitive one that swallows them. This is partly due to their own physical impossibility of seeing, as in the case of Don Luigi Costa's blind, elderly sister—who recalls Robert Duval's character (played by Stanko Molnar) in Avati's co-scripted *Macabro*, for both are defenseless and cheated by those around them. But this perceptive darkness is also a consequence of their very human essence, the fact that we are destined to grope in the dark when considering the limits of our physical existence. Nevertheless, Avati's villains (and his heroes as well) just can't accept it, in an inexhaustible attempt to look (and know) *beyond* which characterizes the director's work in the Fantastic genre.

Avati's doomed hero, again named Stefano like the unfortunate painter in *La casa dalle finestre che ridono*, is yet another artist who moves from the big city to the countryside and becomes the victim of his own abnormal sensitivity toward the macabre and the mysterious. But his quest is first and foremost an introspective descent which goes far beyond the mere mystery angle of the story, and which leads him to an inescapable destiny. Like Prometheus, Stefano defies God (or *the gods*) by trying to learn things that shall remain unknown by mortals, and therefore he will be punished, as will all those who dare venture into the unknowable.

It's not the film's sole reference to myth and to ancient culture. Avati portrays two lovers attempting an illusory escape from the horrors that will swallow them, and in the story's chilling coda he evokes the myth of Orpheus who brings back his wife Eurydice from the underworld. The character of Alessandra conveys a natural, luminous sensuality (see the early scene where she awakes in bed) comparable to that of Francesca Marciano in the 1976 film, which once again makes her a more vulnerable victim. But the same sensuality becomes an element of horror in the ending, as the *revenante* displays the same inviting smile as when she was alive, before the final and supposedly lethal embrace with Stefano. She has become a carrier (and an incarnation) of Death, like other female characters in Avati's cinema, most notably Olimpia in *Le strelle nel fosso*, causing the hero's ultimate ruin.

As in *La casa dalle finestre che ridono*, Avati

turns the sunny and placid Emilia Romagna into an unlikely yet effective setting for a horror story. Except for the prologue set in 1956, which takes place in a typical haunted house with unseen presences lurking in the basement, *Zeder* is characterized by a matter-of-fact, very luminous photography. The hot summer Mediterranean sun pervades many scenes, characters sweat and pant, a blinding light accompanies Stefano's quest in the Riviera, so much so that Alessandra takes advantage of their trip to Rimini for a sunbathing session on the beach. Even a cemetery—the Gothic *milieu* par excellence—doesn't look so menacing in an August morning. But such a warmth and serenity are utterly deceptive. It takes just a few moments—such as when Stefano remains briefly trapped in the crypt where Don Luigi Costa's grave is located—for this mood to change completely and these places to reveal their sinister side.

In his previous horror film Avati had reinvented the Gothic haunted mansion, splitting it into two in the process: the isolated house where Stefano moves, which turns out to be the recipient of horrible secrets, and the titular "house with the laughing windows," a dilapidated hut near the river where the mad Buono Legnani worked on his paintings. A key role in *Zeder* is played by the imposing ruins of the Provincia Varese colony. Ruins have a central importance in the Gothic, as remnants of a forgotten or repressed past, and the choice of a Fascist building, although moved mainly by aesthetic reasons ("I think I've never had a more beautiful location" the director said[11]) is an interesting one on Avati's part, for it draws a red thread between Italy's past and the present.

Children's colonies were structures built in maritime locations which provided free summer holidays for kids, to preserve their health; the first one was created in Lucca in 1822, and their number grew steadily over the years. During the Fascist regime, children's colonies became an instrument of propaganda, a place to indoctrinate the younger generations on the values of Fascism, and many new structures were built, mostly on the Romagna coast, in the regime's typical Rationalist style. The huge, ghastly cement building in *Zeder* becomes a sort of relic, whose bare cement pylons stand out in the landscape like the carcass of a monstrous "white whale" stranded near the beach, a gigantic and looming memento of a wiped-out past. Note, for instance, how the image of the "*fascio littorio*"

(a bound bundle of wooden rods with an axe with its blade emerging), the main symbol of the Fascist regime, is featured prominently in the background wall behind Stefano during the film's horrific climax, the resurrection of Don Luigi Costa. There, the past literally comes alive again.

It's a felicitous choice for a film which revolves around the act of displacement and repression and its object *par excellence* in today's society—death. But the colony is also the remnant of a previous illusory wealth, which now has dissolved and turned into a mediocre, resigned routine, like that of the gas station owner who rents the rooms of his squalid motel on the opposite side of the street, for the few tourists who still show up every now and then. The irony in the film is that, to protect their private experiments and justify the renewed activity around the colony, the Vatican researchers have spread the rumor that the place is going to be reconverted into a luxury 5-star hotel, thus igniting the hope of a renewed well-being, an economic revitalization which echoes the physical one they are pursuing.

As in *La casa dalle finestre che ridono*—and in *L'arcano incantatore*, another film centered on someone's quest about the mysteries of the afterlife—the most horrific figure in the film is that of a priest. Those who have seen *Zeder* won't forget the toothless laughter of the defrocked priest Don Luigi Costa caught by the postmortem camera, as he awakens from death in the film's most unnerving sequence. Once again, Avati followed the example of Fellini and cast a non-professional actor for the role, a pork butcher from Bologna named Carlo Schincaglia. As Avati's a.d. Cesare Bastelli recalled, "With Pupi, for many years, it used to be like that: we arrived in a village without warning anyone and without going to the mayor's office for the shooting permits. We just placed the camera in the main square and waited. The first who approached us was regularly the fool of the village, and we cast him on the spot. We recruited many that way.... Schincaglia was one of them."[12]

The defrocked revenant is only one of several clergymen—not counting the Vatican's high hierarchies, represented by Bob Tonelli's character—whom the viewers meet in the film, the others being an ambiguous young priest (Aldo Sassi) who seems to know more than he claims to, and a (fake) parish priest who wears a gym suit and has brisk manners—a striking charac-

The dead rise from their grave and attack an unfortunate victim (Genoese dialectal actor Enrico Ardizzone) in a scary moment from *Zeder* (courtesy Luca Servini).

scientists record the effects but not the presence. The world is a dark and mysterious place, and nature itself turns out to be malevolent and menacing, like the earthquake that accompanies the resurrection of a dead man in the film's opening sequence. Despite centuries of enlightenment and the progress of science, we are ultimately revealed to be at the mercy of forces that we will never be able to control, let alone understand. All we can do is *believe*.

terization (by Avati's regular Ferdinando Orlandi) which perhaps hints at the director's diffidence toward heterodox clergymen.

Unlike the simple but coherent story behind *La casa dalle finestre che ridono*, *Zeder* has an intricate plot which ultimately doesn't add up. Its many unanswered questions and inconsistencies turn up from the very first sequences. If the K-Zones preserve the dead from rotting, why is Paolo Zeder exhumed as a skeleton? How did he manage to return in the coffin after attacking Gabriella, whose shoe is found *inside* Zeder's coffin? How can Stefano see Don Luigi Costa wandering around in the colony when his body is still locked in the zinc coffin? Is this a phenomenon of bilocation, a hallucination, a vision of the future? Who kills the parish priest Don Mario and old Benni? The viewer gropes in the dark just like the characters. But ultimately these loose ends enhance the overall sense of dread that the film conveys.

It is as if the director was contemplating the very concept of "miracle," that is, the unfathomable ways God works through nature with divine providence, or, in the words of St. Thomas Aquinas, "these works that are done by God outside the usual order assigned to things" and which leave us "astonished at a thing when we see an effect without knowing the cause." It is as if Avati is telling us that there are things in heaven and earth that it is better not to know: as the non-human POV shot that travels through the K-Zone at night, and of which the

Avati ends the film on an ambiguous and chilling note, the final embrace between two lovers who have finally found each other again, with Stefano's expression turning from tenderness to horrified awareness, as the man lets out a final scream of horror (and perhaps pain? Again, we can only guess) which lingers under the final image of the children's colony at night, before Riz Ortolani's synth-driven, dissonant score kicks off. The script included one more scene which Avati wisely chose not to shoot, an epilogue set at the deserted gas station, at night. Children are skating in the area. "Their shadows, their laughter, their screams. Silence," the script reads. On this final freeze-frame, a line appears: "…and what if even your garden was a K-Zone?" A tongue-in-cheek, laughable line worthy of some cheap B-movie (think of Tonino Ricci's *Bakterion*, 1982) which would have done no justice to the story. It is one of the few moments that differ from the finished film. Avati had also devised a slightly more elaborate version of the scene where Anna (Laura in the script) is killed. The director wanted to set it originally in the dancing room of the abandoned chalet near the lake at the Giardini Margherita park in Bologna (in the film it takes place underneath the wharf), and the murderer used a long Fascist stiletto (the weapon is hardly distinguishable in the film) with a silver eagle's head on its handle— another symbol relating the story to the country's Fascist past, hinting that perhaps at first Avati wanted to develop a discourse akin to that of the Nazis' fascination with the occult. Then, unlike in the film, Stefano finds himself face to face with Laura's body, as the dead girl appears before him and falls headfirst against the broken glass window, "pierced by hundreds of sharp glass splinters." Stefano tries to come to her aid, but it's too late. When he hears the police siren approaching, he flees.

Initially slated for a February release, *Zeder* was delayed until August 1983, and turned out a box-office disappointment despite favorable reviews. Moreover, in the meantime Avati had completed another feature film, the bittersweet period comedy *Una gita scolastica* (working title: *La passeggiata*), starring Delle Piane, which moved to a totally different direction, and was a critical and commercial success.

Filmed in English with an eye toward foreign sales, *Zeder* was distributed theatrically in the U.S. by Motion Picture Marketing the following year, in a heavily edited copy, as *Revenge of the Dead*. It was first broadcast in Italy on Rai Due on August 8, 1984. The TV version was a couple of minutes longer and featured an extended version of the introductory "anniversary sequence" in which Stefano and Alessandra exchange gifts. After putting on the bracelet Stefano has given her, she joins him on the sofa. He explains that he couldn't buy her a gift with his own money, as his publisher just rejected his latest novel, telling him that "it sucked," and so he borrowed some more money from Alessandra's father (whom we assume is very wealthy). The couple then start making out on the sofa but are interrupted by the concierge coming out of the kitchen: the elderly man has fixed the electrical cable of the typewriter Alessandra has purchased for her husband, a love gift which will ultimately turn out to be their ruin. In addition to fleshing out Stefano's characterization by hinting at his frustration as a novelist, the sequence shows the couple's passionate relationship, but it also hints at their class difference, with the man striving to come up with enough money to support the family without relying on his wife's rich father.

The commercial disappointment of *Zeder* resulted in Avati consigning his *fantastique*-related themes to an oblivion which would last over a decade. The director himself was never too fond of it, pointing out its "technological limits" and claiming that the movie "didn't give me great satisfaction, from any point of view,"[13] possibly because of its less than felicitous shoot. Over the following years, Avati's output consisted mostly of bittersweet comedies (*Noi tre*, 1984; *Festa di laurea*, 1985, *Storia di ragazzi e di ragazze*, 1989) or downbeat dramas (*Regalo di Natale*, 1986; *Ultimo minuto*, 1987; *Fratelli e sorelle*, 1991). Only in the early 1990s he decided to revive his interest in horror and the Fantastic, with the scripts for Maurizio Zaccaro's *Dove comincia la notte* (1991) and Fabrizio Laurenti's *La stanza accanto* (1994), in addition to the TV mini-series *Voci notturne*, before directing *L'arcano incantatore*. His next work in the genre would be sparse and limited to one horror movie per decade, namely *Il nascondiglio* (2007) and the upcoming *Il signor Diavolo*. The latter, based on Avati's own novel published in 2018, is a grim story set in 1952, about a young lawyer who is sent to Venice to follow a murder trial (a teenage boy has killed another one) which turns out to have chilling implications.

NOTES

1. Adele Gallotti, "Tutta Nizza si è messa a ballare nel "Dancing" di Avati," *La Stampa*, December 6, 1982.
2. Ruggero Adamovit, Claudio Bartolini and Luca Servini, *Nero Avati. Visioni dal set* (Genova: Le Mani, 2011), 146.
3. Lorenzo Codelli, "Entretien avec Pupi Avati. *Zeder*." *L'Écran fantastique* #36, July/August 1983, 92.
4. *Ibid.*, 91.
5. Adamovit, Bartolini and Servini, *Nero Avati*, 164.
6. si.ro., "Avati vuol far cassetta con l'horror e sceglie la faccia di Gabriele Lavia," *La Stampa*, January 14, 1983.
7. Giovanna Grassi, "Con *Zeder* brividi in Emilia," *Corriere della Sera*, August 24, 1983.
8. Codelli, "Entretien avec Pupi Avati. *Zeder*." 92.
9. Michael Gray Baughan, *Stephen King* (New York: Infobase Publishing, 2009), 59–60.
10. Frank Lafond, "Le cinéma de la peur selon Pupi Avati," in Frank Lafond (ed.), *Cauchemars Italiens. Volume 1: Le Cinéma fantastique* (Paris: L'Harmattan, 2011), 136.
11. Adamovit, Bartolini and Servini, *Nero Avati*, 152.
12. *Ibid.*, 150.
13. *Ibid.*, 167.

1985

Dèmoni (*Demons*)

D: Lamberto Bava. S: Dardano Sacchetti; SC: Dario Argento, Lamberto Bava, Dardano Sacchetti, Franco Ferrini; DOP: Gianlorenzo Battaglia (Eastmancolor Kodak, LV–Luciano Vittori); M: Claudio Simonetti (Universo Film);

E: Piero Bozza; *SupE*: Franco Fraticelli; *PD*: Davide Bassan; *CO*: Marina Malavasi, Patrizia Massaia; *AD*: Michele Soavi [and Fabrizio Bava, uncredited]; *SPFX*: Sergio Stivaletti; *AsstSPFX*: Barbara Morosetti, Sami Habib Ahmed; *SE*: Angelo Mattei (miniatures), Danilo Bollettini, Claudio Quaglietti, Ditta Corridori; *MU*: Rosario Prestopino; *AMU*: Giacinto Bretti; *Hair*: Teodora Bruno; *AE*: Roberto Priori; *2ndAE*: Sergio Fraticelli, Fabrizio Fraticelli; *AC*: Enzo Frattari, Claudio Nannuzzi, Daniele Cimini, Federico Martucci; *AsstSD*: Livia Pascucci; *SO*: Raffaele De Luca; *B*: Angelo Amattulli; *Mix*: Romano Pampaloni; *Dolby sound consultant*: Federico Savina; *SOE*: Massimo Anzelotti; *ChEl*: Cristo Verrillo; *KG*: Franco Serantoni; *PrM*: Maurizio Jacopelli; *W*: Carla Latini; *G*: Paolo Tiberti; *SP*: Franco Bellomo, Gianfranco Caira; *Stunts*: Ottaviano Dell'Acqua, Claudio Pacifico; *SS*: Daniela Tonti. *Cast*: Urbano Barberini (George), Natasha Hovey (Cheryl), Karl Zinny (Ken), Fiore Argento (Hannah), Paola Cozzo (Kathy), Fabiola Toledo (Carmen), Nicoletta Elmi (Ingrid), Stelio Candelli (Frank), Nicole Tessier (Ruth), Geretta Giancarlo [Geretta Geretta] (Rosemary), Bobby Rhodes (Tony), Guido Baldi (Tommy), Bettina Ciampolini (Nina), Giuseppe Mauro Cruciano (Hot Dog), Sally Day (Liz), Eliana Hoppe [Eliana Miglio] (Edith, woman in tent—Horror film), Jasmine Maimone (Nancy—Horror film), Marcello Modugno (Bob—Horror film), Peter Pitsch (Baby Pig), Pasqualino [Lino] Salemme (Ripper), Enrica Maria Scrivano (Blonde Victim), Alex Serra (Werner), Michele Soavi (Man in Black/Jerry—Horror film), Claudio Spadaro (Liz's Lover), Patrizia Lazzarini, Paolo Corazzi (Policeman), Emanuela Zicosky (June), Claudio Insegno (Policeman); *uncredited*: Sami Habib Ahmed (Kathy's Baby Demon), Lamberto Bava (1st Man Exiting Subway), Giovanni Frezza (Kirk), Sergio Stivaletti (Victim), Goffredo Unger (Jeep Driver). *PROD*: Dario Argento for DAC Film (Rome); *PS*: Guido De Laurentiis; *PSe*: Fabrizio Diaz, Rita Friggeri; *PAcc*: Ferdinando Caputo; *ADM*: Renato Rinaldo; *PrA*: Enrico Lucherini. *Country*: Italy. Filmed on location in Berlin and at De Paolis In.Ci.R. Studios (Rome). *Running time*: 88 minutes (m. 2403). Visa n. 80955 (10.4.1985); *Rating*: V.M.18. *Release dates*: 10.4.1985 (Italy), 4.26.1986 (Japan), 5.30.1986 (USA), 10.1.1986 (France), 10.14.1986 (Hong Kong), 8.12.1987 (Spain); *Distribution*: Titanus (Italy); Ascot (USA). *Domestic gross*: 1,225,490,000 *lire*. *Also known as*: Demonios (Spain), *Démons* (France), *Dämonen 2/Dance of the Demons* (West Germany).

Berlin, the present. A mysterious man in the subway gives a young music student named Cheryl two free tickets for a movie premierè at the gloomy Metropol cinema. A varied audience attends the screening: Cheryl and her friend Kathy; two clean-cut teenagers, George and Ken; a teenage couple; a black pimp named Tony and two prostitutes; a middle-age couple celebrating their anniversary; a blind man and his wife, the latter taking advantage of the opportunity to meet her lover. The film is a horror movie about four teenagers who violate the tomb of Nostradamus and unleash a series of gruesome events. Before the movie starts, one of the prostitutes, Rosemary, accidentally cuts her face with an iron mask exposed in the theater's hall. She soon undergoes a horrible transformation in the cinema restroom which turns her into a demon. One by one, the moviegoers are attacked and infected by the demons, while the survivors find themselves walled alive inside the venue. George, Ken, Cheryl and Kathy are among the few left alive. Meanwhile, a small group of punks break inside the theater, while the blind man, who has been infected, sneaks out and spreads the contagion…

After the low-budget *giallo*, *La casa con la scala nel buio*, Lamberto Bava had become stuck in B-movie territory with the violent action film *Blastfighter* (1983) and the sci-fi/horror hybrid *Shark-Rosso nell'oceano* (1984), both signed as "John M. Old Jr.," and was still looking for his big break. Bava was considering directing a three-part anthology written by Dardano Sacchetti, in the vein of his father's *I tre volti della paura*. One of the stories was set inside a movie theater where the spectators are attacked by monsters during the screening of a horror film. As Bava recalled, "Then, one day I started thinking that I didn't like the idea of a trilogy so much, and I didn't like the other two episodes that much, so I thought to myself: but this one episode, dilated into a full-length movie, would work perfectly."[1]

Bava and Sacchetti submitted a 25-page treatment to Fabrizio De Angelis, but they were disappointed to learn that the producer was planning to recycle footage from the Fulci films he'd produced as parts of the film-within-a-film to cut costs. So, around October 1984, they took the project to Luciano Martino, who suggested that Bava and Sacchetti produce it. The proposal was tempting as it would allow them total control, but the movie would cost almost 400 million *lire*, and it was to be a financial risk for the director and the scriptwriter, who would be paid with a 10 percent of the grosses and would recover the costs and see profits only after Martino had recovered his part.

In the meantime, after the box-office success of *Phenomena*, Dario Argento was toying with the idea of producing more horror movies, as he had done with *Dawn of the Dead*. Besides the economic motifs, in a way it was a move inspired by one of his masters, Sergio Leone, who in the Seventies had devoted himself to production with such diverse films as *Il mio nome è Nessuno* (1973, Tonino Valerii), *Un genio, due compari e un pollo* (1975, Damiano Damiani), *Il gatto* (1977, Luigi Comencini), and comedian Carlo Verdone's debut *Un sacco bello* (1980), while working on the project of *Once Upon a Time in America*. Argento's friend Luigi Cozzi had submitted to him a science fiction script the merit of which Dario was not fully convinced about, so he got in touch with Bava. "He told me: bring me an idea and we'll make the movie immediately." Lamberto seized the opportunity. "I told Dario the story [of *Dèmoni*] and on the tenth word he told me: 'That's an idea, we'll make it!' … At that point we worked on it as it should always be done in movies, that is, four people scripting for four or five months."[2]

Sacchetti's recollection of the scriptwriting sessions is not devoid of bitter remarks. "At that time, I was again cross with Dario. He esteemed me but didn't trust me. I have a completely different working method. First, he wanted to get Franco Ferrini on board, who didn't understand the film and only tried to please Dario. Then, since as everyone knows I have a bad temper, Dario paid me and got rid of me. He called me back a few months later for a final polish, but by then Sergio Stivaletti had become the film's *deus ex machina*, with his special effects."[3] Sacchetti claimed that the first part of his original story was virtually identical to the finished film, whereas the second half was set entirely in the cinema's basement, where the main characters "found all this stuff—movie posters, costumes, sets, etc.—and then there was this journey toward safety through what was left of an old theater's basement. Dario didn't want that, but he wanted a big demon coming out of the floor … he wanted something more in the style of a zombie film, with blood and gore, and Stivaletti's effects. I had thought of a more romantic twist,

more intellectual, perhaps better, but Dario surely went for something more effective."[4] On his part, Ferrini said that his main contribution to the script was postponing the appearance of the demons, which in an earlier draft came out of the movie screen almost at the beginning.

The title *Dèmoni* turned up later in the preproduction stage. Sacchetti maintains it was Argento who came up with it, while Bava recalls noticing Dostoyevsky's three-part novel *Demons* one day in his father's library—standing out because of its bright red binding—and being struck by it. It was as if Mario had provided one last piece of the puzzle. Lamberto immediately phoned Argento, who was enthusiastic about it too.[5]

Even more so than *Phenomena*, *Dèmoni* displays an explicit attempt at tagging along with the changes in taste and aesthetics of the decade. As a producer, Argento chose to lean on gory excess to create an economically viable project for the international markets on a par with the overseas products, while at the same time keeping it highly recognizable as Italian. With a substantial budget at his disposal (which Bava quantified as three or three-and-a-half billion *lire*), quite some time and effort was dedicated to Stivaletti's special make-up effects and creations.

Besides the nods to Romero, *Dèmoni* depicts perfectly the metamorphosis of the Gothic in a juvenile, postmodernist key. Both the film-within-a-film and the film itself revolve around teenage characters: Cheryl and her classmate have skipped school (possibly conservatory: Cheryl carries a book of Béla Bartók compositions) to go to the movies, while George and Ken don't miss the opportunity to sit close to the girls and court them—a blossoming blind date which goes horribly wrong. The city where the story takes place is never mentioned but it is obviously German—the film was shot in Berlin, and in the opening sequence Cheryl meets the masked man at the Heidelberger Platz station—and the makers pay homage to Expressionism by way of the movie theater's name (Metropol, hinting at Fritz Lang's *Metropolis*). But the setting refers also to one of the main centers of the Goth subculture, which included ample references to 19th century Gothic literature and Gothic horror films. As expected, however, youth culture is regarded with suspicion: in the opening scenes, Natasha Hovey's good girl character is travelling in a subway train filled with rather menacing-looking types lifted from *Christiane F.* (1981, Uli Edel), and halfway through the movie we are introduced to a quartet of obnoxious punk vandals who drive around the city listening to Go West and Billy Idol and sniffing cocaine. The soundtrack winks (rather confusedly, one might add) to the equation between hard rock and horror, as Argento had done in *Phenomena*, with a selection of hits and excerpts from songs by Scorpions, Mötley Crüe, Accept and Saxon. In turn, the main theme in Claudio Simonetti's score seems to have been inspired by Herbie Hancock's 1983 hit single *Rockit*—another sign of the evolution of taste from the days of the *Tubular Bells*-influenced theme from *Profondo rosso*.

Most significantly, the story takes place inside a cinema: the movie theater becomes the ideal replacement of the Gothic haunted houses, a cloistered container of horror and the natural setting of a story which has its strong point in the cinematic references. "This place is haunted," a character says, and the imposing Metropol theater seems to acquire a life of its own. Like in Buñuel's *El ángel exterminador* (1962) and in Giuseppe Bennati's 1974 Gothic *giallo*, *L'assassino ha riservato nove poltrone*, its doors are locked (even literally walled) by an invisible force and open only to let the contagion slip out; its walls sweat indefinable liquids; its interiors are a concoction of Escher-like secret passages, stairs and corridors that lead nowhere, and recall the impossible architectures of Mario Bava's films: at a certain point the survivors break through a wall that seemingly separates them from the outside world, only to find themselves inside a secluded chamber that *shouldn't be there*. And, finally, the Metropol's walls are filled with horror movie posters and memorabilia, the modern-day equivalent of the paintings and paraphernalia in classical Gothic.

It is cinema that acts as a thread between old-style Gothic—represented by the nameless film-within-a-film, which is set near a dilapidated church and cemetery, and deals with a mysterious prophecy and a curse from the past—and the present. The demons' curse possibly comes from a centuries-old prophecy by Nostradamus, but is transmitted through a horror movie, which acts as a contemporary variation on the old cursed manuscripts and written spells in classic Gothic. The screen itself becomes the source of horror, ripping open like an infected womb and giving birth to the menace, in a scene which in turn pays homage to Sara's

death in *Inferno*. Horror literally invades real life, and movies become a source of infection and perdition, as in the censors' worst nightmares.

One of *Dèmoni*'s cleverest touches is that, unbeknownst to all, the invasion has *already* happened when the film begins. The masked man played by Michele Soavi, who gives away free tickets for a movie premiere, is one of the characters from the movie that will be premiered that night, who has become a demon and walked away in the real world, to spread the infection. It's a paradox worthy of John Carpenter's *In the Mouth of Madness* (1994), and it's a pity that the script doesn't elaborate further on the idea, introducing the character again near the end only for a rather anticlimactic fight with the hero on the theater's roof.

Still, the film's central idea is striking. At the time, critics pointed out marginal similarities with Woody Allen's *The Purple Rose of Cairo* (1985), released earlier that year, but few recalled a much closer (and most likely casual) predecessor, Giuliano Montaldo's brilliant, made-for-TV *Circuito chiuso* (1978), a murder mystery set inside a movie venue where a killing takes place, and the culprit is eventually revealed as a gunslinger (none other than Giuliano Gemma) from the Spaghetti Western that was being screened.[6] But the setting also predates Joe Lansdale's 1988 horror novel *The Drive-In: A "B" Movie with Blood and Popcorn*, as does the way Bava piles on the absurd and the gruesome without need for much explanation, gleefully allowing the massacre to take center stage.

For a film centered on the notion of cinema as a source of horror, *Dèmoni* collects an impressive series of homages, nods, references, borrowings, and stealings. *Dawn of the Dead* is openly quoted in the image of Urbano Barberini's character riding a motorbike and decapitating monsters (with a Japanese sword instead of the machete Tom Savini employed in Romero's film), and in the sight gag of the helicopter inexplicably falling into the deserted theater, which results in yet another decapitation-by-helicopter-blade. But Argento himself is also evoked multiple times, from the opening scenes with Natasha Hovey walking in the deserted subway station to the poster of *4 mosche di velluto grigio* hanging in the foyer; a blind man has his eyes gouged out like the butler in *Inferno*, and the spectacular hanging of some characters in the middle of the theater recalls the opening

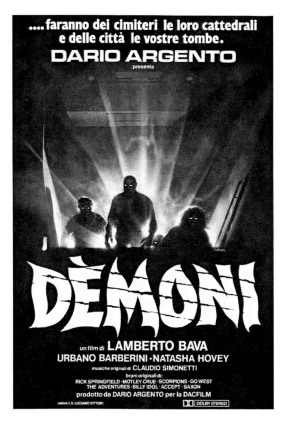

....faranno dei cimiteri le loro cattedrali
e delle città le vostre tombe.
DARIO ARGENTO
presenta

un film di **LAMBERTO BAVA**
URBANO BARBERINI · NATASHA HOVEY
musiche originali di CLAUDIO SIMONETTI
brani originali di:
RICK SPRINGFIELD · MOTLEY CRUE · SCORPIONS · GO WEST
THE ADVENTURES · BILLY IDOL · ACCEPT · SAXON
prodotto da DARIO ARGENTO per la DACFILM
colore L.V. LUCIANO VITTORI   DOLBY STEREO

Italian locandina for Lamberto Bava's *Dèmoni* (1985).

murder in *Suspiria*. Then, of course, Bava Jr. bows to the memory of his late father: the unnamed film-within-a-film develops like a modern-day remake of *La maschera del demonio* (and much more convincing, it must be added, than the one the director will helm for TV a few years later), and the contagion starts when a girl cuts herself while donning a "mask of the demon," vaguely hinting at Kruvajan reanimating Asa after accidentally cutting his hand in the 1960 film.

As for the demons, although openly inspired by Romero's zombies, they are in fact closer to the "crazies" in Umberto Lenzi's *Incubo sulla città contaminata*, and despite some overly naive make-up (such as the multicolored painted veins on their faces) they are impressive creations indeed. "The idea that the demons' eyes had to be fluorescent came to us on the set. It's not a visual effect, we didn't have CGI back then," Bava explained. "The demons are advancing straight to the camera, because the actors had pieces of refractive paper taped on their eyes. Behind the camera there was a huge flat lamp that made their eyes shine."[7]

Unlike the living dead, the demons are not cannibals, but they retain a mad urgency to attack, touch, bite and scratch their victims which is almost sexual, and in turn recalls David Cronenberg's early contagion films such as *Shivers* (1975) and *Rabid* (1977). It's unlikely Sacchetti and Bava had in mind a metaphor for AIDS, but nevertheless *Dèmoni* features an interesting sexual subtext, with its virginal teenagers and married women giving in to lust in the dark of a theater and, as a result, being menaced and infected by voracious ghouls. It's not the same situation as the one depicted in slasher films, however, specifically because the setting is very Italian: despite its alleged German setting, the Metropol looks very much like an old *seconda visione* Italian venue, with its uncomfortable wooden chairs, clandestine couples and unfriendly usherettes. The kind of movie theaters that were gradually disappearing, converted into bingo clubs or shopping malls. In this respect, the scenes in which the survivors destroy the projector and pull up the rows of seats are a grim prophecy of what would be the norm just a few years later.

In tune with *Dèmoni*'s postmodernist quality, the cast itself includes a parade of familiar faces of Italian horror and genre cinema, from Nicoletta Elmi (the eerie little girl from *Baron Blood*, *Il medaglione insanguinato*, *Profondo rosso* and other scary movies of the previous decade) to Giovanni Frezza (the kid from Lucio Fulci's films), not forgetting Stelio Candelli (*Nuda per Satana*) and Goffredo Unger. As the gigantic bald black pimp with sideburns, Bobby Rhodes looks as if he's just stepped out of a vintage Blaxploitation movie (despite being born in Livorno, in the Tuscan coast) and provides a temporary proletarian hero before his role is taken by the blond and noble Urbano Barberini, the descendant of one of the most ancient aristocratic families in Rome. But Bava's ace casting choice is that of the 18-year-old, blue-eyed Natasha Hovey, who had made a striking debut in Carlo Verdone's amiable romantic comedy *Acqua e sapone* (1983), and here proves a pitch-perfect teenage scream queen.

"*Dèmoni* expresses a great love for the genre. I shot it all with a small dolly, purpose-built, because I wanted the camera never to be still. Every shot had to make the viewer anxious, together with the use of noise and the soundtrack,"[8] Bava explained. Still, after a very tight first part, the movie suffers a bit from repetitiveness, so much so that the director and his co-scriptwriters isolate single characters to build some subplot of sorts, and then resort to fleshing out the ranks of the soon-to-be-victims by introducing the four punks from the outside, in a plot twist which also provides the narrative explanation for the apocalyptic climax. The second half drags quite a bit because of this, mainly because the story doesn't have the political and sociological foundations of Romero's film. But it provides some neat scares: in a scene perhaps inspired by *Alien*, an air conditioning duct becomes an illusory way of escape, and Bava plays with the source and direction of the menace with consummate skill and considerable irony.

Incidentally, *Dèmoni* is filled with pitch-black humor, targeted to the characters and the viewer as well. Some vignettes are absurd to the point of Surrealism, most notably the blind man who goes to the screening a horror film (the visual movie experience par excellence) and has his wife tell him what is happening on screen (the fact that she has a rendezvous with her lover next to him only makes the implausible situation even more amusing). But there are also punks sniffing cocaine from a Coca-Cola can (a decidedly irreverent sight gag), and a punkette girl stopping in the middle of the carnage to admire herself in front of a mirror and put on her lipstick, which results in a gruesome retribution (the scene somehow recalls Paola Senatore obliviously dancing in the nude in front of a mirror while the victims are piling up in *L'assassino ha riservato nove poltrone*). Bava even inserts a last-minute gag during the end credits, which start rolling and stop abruptly while the grim fate of a main character is revealed just when we think the perils are over. As the credits start rolling again, we are presented with a cynical punchline, in tune with the rest of the film.

For its Italian theatrical release, *Dèmoni* got a V.M.18 screening certificate (no minors allowed) from the rating board, something for which Argento and Bava were prepared.[9] "As a producer, Dario was undaunted by the prospect of substantial cuts. 'Who cares,' he said, 'let's keep the V.M.18.' And in fact, one of the reasons of *Dèmoni*'s commercial success was that it was hardcore gore stuff. Because if it had been softer, it probably wouldn't have had such an impact. And look, there's stuff we cut—I mean in the editing room—such as transformations, etc., which was a lot stronger."[10]

Stivaletti's pioneering effects, if inevitably dated nowadays, were unlike anything seen in an Italian horror film. The models were Rick Baker and Rob Bottin's prosthetic transformations in *The Howling* (1980, Joe Dante), *An American Werewolf in London* (1981, John Landis) and *The Thing* (1982, John Carpenter), as in the disturbing scene of the demon's monstrous fangs replacing human teeth in lingering close-ups. It was a neat departure from the old and often crude Carlo Rambaldi–style gore of the previous decade, and from the gruesome effects seen in Fulci and Massaccesi's films of the early 1980s. Many sequences display an almost playful will to repel and disgust: a case in point is the early scene where an abscess on a woman's face explodes in a triumph of pus, and the overreliance on the slimy colored foams and liquids which the demons are drooling. Bava gives the effects center stage, sometimes with even excessive enthusiasm, but some of the most over-the-top moments, such as the birth of a demon who emerges from a woman's back, albeit a bit too fake-looking for its own good, are show-stopping surreal moments which show how the makers were pulling all the stops. Stivaletti explained that the demon birth effect was much more complex than what can be seen in the finished film:

> Firstly, that wasn't the monster that had to come out, but it had been conceived for another scene, and then due to budgetary and time constraints we did a strange mixture between what had to be the demon's final transformation and the thing coming out from the back.... Whereas from the woman's back there had to emerge a creature similar to Menelik, which we created for the second *Dèmoni* film. And so, the fact that it came out of the body had people say, "That's like *Alien*!" but it wasn't! ... and then there was the aftermath, with the woman literally wilting on the floor: this was shot but not edited.[11]

Shot in nine weeks in June and July 1985, *Dèmoni* was released in its home country in October 1985 and benefited from a clever promotional campaign, with Dario Argento's name in evidence above the title (and three times as big as Bava's) and a tagline taken from the film-within-a-film, "*Faranno dei cimiteri le loro cattedrali, e delle città le vostre tombe*" ("They'll make cathedrals of their graveyards, and turn cities into your tombs") which in the grand tradition of Italian Gothic is attributed to a famed source (Nostradamus) whereas it was exclusively the fruit of Sacchetti's pen. With 1,225 million *lire*, it was the season's 39th top grossing film and the most popular horror movie of the year, outgrossing such titles as *Cat's Eye*, *Silver Bullet* and

A Nightmare on Elm Street and paving the way for a sequel.

The commercial potential of Bava's film resulted in it being distributed theatrically worldwide (although the U.K. release was apparently cancelled at the last minute, after some press screenings[12]). The reviews were often far from positive, though. The *New York Times'* Walter Goodman opened his scathing piece on the film with a sarcastic "Blame it on Nostradamus," and labeled it a "made-for-music-video blood gusher," long on gore and short on logic, concluding: "'This film contains scenes which are considered shocking,' says a line in the advertisements. 'No one under 17 will be admitted unless accompanied by a parent or guardian.' The kids have all the luck."[13]

Dèmoni proved very influential in the years to come: the apocalyptic outcome recalls Danny Boyle's *28 Days Later* (2002) and the French *La Horde* (2009, Yannick Dahan and Benjamin Rocher).

NOTES

1. Morsiani, "Conversazione con Lamberto Bava," 49. As for the other episodes, one was a story set in the Bermuda Triangle, while nothing is known of the third segment.

2. *Ibid.*

3. Dardano Sacchetti interviewed, in www.davinotti.com (http://www.davinotti.com/index.php?option=com_content&task=view&id=52&Itemid=79).

4. Dardano Sacchetti, "La verità" in *Genealogia del delitto. Il cinema di Mario e Lamberto Bava*, 57.

5. Maiello, *Dario Argento*, 300.

6. Even though the posters that can be seen outside the venue in Montaldo's film are those of *I giorni dell'ira* (1967), the clips used were from another Western starring Gemma, Giulio Petroni's *...e per tetto un cielo di stelle* (1968).

7. Gomarasca, "Intervista a Lamberto Bava," 41.

8. *Ibid.*

9. The appeal took place in July 1986, and the Appeal commission rejected the request of lowering the rating to a V.M.14.

10. Gomarasca, "Intervista a Lamberto Bava," 40.

11. Alberto Morsiani, "Intervista a Sergio Stivaletti," in *Rosso italiano (1977/1978)*, 93.

12. The film had been submitted to the BBFC by Avatar Communications Ltd. in January 1987, with the BBFC trimming 2 minutes and 4 seconds, resulting in a running time of 86 minutes and 16 seconds.

13. Walter Goodman, "Screen: *Demons*, by Bava," *New York Times*, May 31, 1986.

Fracchia contro Dracula (*Who Is Afraid of Dracula?*, a.k.a. *Fracchia Vs. Dracula*)

D: Neri Parenti. *S and SC*: Franco Marotta, Laura Toscano, Neri Parenti, Paolo Villaggio;

DOP: Luciano Tovoli (Telecolor); *M*: Bruno Zambrini (Ed. Alsa Maura); *E*: Sergio Montanari; *PD*: Giovanni Licheri; *CO*: Mario Carlini; *MU*: Maurizio Trani; *AMU*: Laura Borselli; *Hair*: Paolo Franceschi; *AD*: Marina Mattoli; *2ndAD*: Anna [Annalisa] De Simone; *C*: Giuseppe Tinelli; *AC*: Roberto Marsigli; *2ndAC*: Lorenzo Tovoli; *PM*: Massimo Cristofanelli; *PM*: Carlo Alberto Fantacci, Lionello Fantacci; *SP*: Vincenzo Savino; *SD*: Andrea Fantacci; *ACO*: Francesco Crivellini; *W*: Ruggero Peruzzi; *AE*: Carlo Bartolucci, Luca Montanari; *SS*: Mirella Roi; *SO*: Massimo Loffredi; *B*: Giulio Viggiani; *Mix*: Danilo Moroni; *Cast*: Paolo Villaggio (Giandomenico Fracchia), Edmund Purdom (Count Vlad Dracula), Gigi Reder (Rag. Filini), Ania Pieroni (Countess Oniria), Federica Brion (Stefania), Giuseppe Cederna (Boris), Susanna Martinková (Catarina), Andrea Gnecco (Kaspar), Filippo Degara [De Gara] (Butler), Paul Muller (Fracchia's Boss), Romano Puppo (Frankenstein), Isabella Ferrari (Luna); *uncredited*: Lars Bloch (Doctor), Giucas Casella (Himself), Plinio Fernando (Klema), Daniela Ferrari. *PROD*: Bruno Altissimi, Claudio Saraceni for Maura International Film (Rome), Faso Film (Rome); *GM*: Paolo Vandini; *PM*: Nereo Salustri, Francesco Benvenuti; *PSe*: Caterina De Angelis; *ADM*: Maria Lavinia Gualino; *AsstADM*: Gloria Del Gracco. *Press attache*: Lucherini-Vasile. *Country*: Italy. Filmed at Castle Fénis, in Valle D'Aosta, and at Cinecittà Studios (Rome). *Running time*: 94 minutes (m. 2597). Visa n. 81143 (12.19.1985); *Rating*: all audiences. *Release date*: 12.19.1985; *Distribution*: Titanus. *Domestic gross*: 818,235,000 lire. Also known as: *Zwei Vollidioten schlagen zu* (West Germany).

In an attempt to sell a property to the short-sighted accountant Filini, real estate salesman Giandomenico Fracchia accompanies him to visit a castle in Transylvania—which Fracchia has told Filini is just outside Rome. Upon their arrival by car, the two men find accommodation at an inn and learn that the villagers fear the mysterious Count Vlad. At the castle, they discover that it is still occupied by the mysterious Count and his sister Oniria, who sleep in coffins and turn out to be vampires. Oniria falls for Fracchia, who is still a virgin, and decides to marry him. However, the vampire girl is destined to marry the Frankenstein monster, who shows up at the castle. The Count has Fracchia and the monster challenge one another to a game of tennis and poker to decide who will marry Oniria, and Fracchia wins. At the ceremony, attended by a horde of monsters and zombies, *Fracchia and Filini are saved at the last moment by Luna, the sister of a deceased vampire hunter, and Fracchia accidentally kills the Count with his own umbrella. However, it all turns out to be a nightmare, as the fearful Fracchia had fallen asleep at the theater while watching a horror movie…*

Since the outstanding success of *Fantozzi* (1975, Luciano Salce), about a sad, awkward and unlucky accountant who is bullied by his bosses, colleagues and practically everyone he meets, Paolo Villaggio's consistent popularity at the box-office during the mid-to-late 1970s and the 1980s was guaranteed by the repetition of his trademark screen persona. In fact, in addition to the *Fantozzi* sequels, Villaggio brought to the screen other characters who, despite having a different name, were basically more of the same. Such was Giandomenico Fracchia, a meek accountant that the actor had first played on television in 1968, in the program *Quelli della domenica*. Pathologically shy, cowardly, slavish to the point of masochism, Fracchia is continually victimized by his superior ("*Com'è umano lei!,*" "How humane you are," is his catchphrase, which he utters after being insulted and humiliated by his boss). Villaggio reprised many of Fracchia's traits with Fantozzi, the protagonist of his 1971 novel and the subsequent films[1]; he revived the character in the 1975 TV miniseries *Giandomenico Fracchia— Sogni proibiti di uno di noi*, and eventually adapted it for the big screen with the slapstick comedy *Fracchia la belva umana* (1981, Neri Parenti).

However, the formula grew tired quickly, despite Villaggio's qualities as a comedian and the screenwriters' trick of "borrowing" from old movies for plot ideas: *Fracchia la belva umana* was inspired by John Ford's classic comedy *The Whole Town's Talking* (1935) and *Sogni mostruosamente proibiti* (1982, Neri Parenti) reworked the basic plot of the Danny Kaye classic *The Secret Life of Walter Mitty* (1947, Norman Z. McLeod). Villaggio's turns before the camera in the early 1970s had been characterized by a willingness to accept bold roles, with his participation in movies by important directors such as Nanni Loy (*Sistema l'America e torno*, 1973), Marco Ferreri (*Touchez pas à la*

femme blanche, 1974) and Pupi Avati (*La mazurka del barone, della santa e del fico fiorone*, 1975), but by the mid–Eighties the actor was merely treading water, offering his audience tired slapstick farces which repeated the same gags over and over, ad nauseam. This had to do in no small part with his family vicissitudes, namely his 23-year-old son Pierfrancesco's heroin addiction: in 1984, after many unsuccessful attempts at helping him, Villaggio had him hospitalized in the San Patrignano rehab community, where the young man would eventually detox from drugs.[2]

The second Fracchia movie, *Fracchia contro Dracula*, had the 53-year-old Villaggio and the co-scriptwriters Laura Toscano and Franco Marotta (a duo of comedy specialists who had worked among others with Giorgio Capitani on *Bollenti spiriti*) borrow again from a horror staple, after 1979's *Dottor Jekyll e gentile signora*, and marked the actor's eight teaming with Parenti, by then his regular director.

Italian poster for *Fracchia contro Dracula* (1985, Neri Parenti), a Dracula spoof starring Paolo Villaggio and Edmund Purdom (as Dracula).

The opening, with Fracchia watching a horror movie with his fiancée, recalls an episode of the anthology comedy *I motorizzati* (1961), where Ugo Tognazzi was scared to death by *La maschera del demonio*. Here, the film Fracchia cannot even bear to watch, to the point that he asks a little kid sitting next to him to tell him what is happening on screen, is *Return of the Living Dead* (1985, Dan O'Bannon), released in Italy by Titanus, the same distribution company as Villaggio's film. The punchline to the scene—the frightened Fracchia jumping back after a scare and causing a disastrous Rube Goldberg–like chain reaction, with all the rows behind him overturning and the rest of the audience ending up on the floor—is emblematic of Villaggio's comedy antics, which draw from the physicality of the silent movie era; yet it is so hastily rendered, cinematically speaking, that it gives away the slapdash nature of the *mise-en-scène*. Parenti is not a filmmaker on the level of Capitani, and it shows.

Still, the plot is more than just an excuse for the protagonist's antics, and despite some openly silly dialogue ("I'm Kaspar, vampire hunter" "Giandomenico Fracchia" "Exorcist?" "No, real estate agent") it is endearing and well-structured. Even though Toscano claimed that she liked the film very much, she pointed at budget constraints as the film's most blatant issue, its cheapness: "The effects were bad, the monsters were not as they should have been."[3] If *Fracchia contro Dracula* is at least one step up from the low level of many Italian comedies of the 1980s, characterized by careless filmmaking and poor production values, most of the credit goes to Luciano Tovoli's cinematography and Giovanni Licheri's production design. Tovoli tries hard to convey a Gothic feel with plenty of day-for-night scenes tinted in icy blue and splashes of bright red in the interiors, while the set pieces are atmospheric and subtly parodic, as is Bruno Zambrini's score.

Villaggio also reprises the Mr. Magoo-like character of Filini (played by his regular comedy aside Gigi Reder) from the Fantozzi series, and Reder provides some of the best gags, such as when the short-sighted Filini mistakes vampire bats for canaries, or says he smells a rotten goat whenever Dracula's stinking hunchback servant Boris (Giuseppe Cederna) is around. On the other hand, as Villaggio himself claimed, the imperturbable blind butler, played by veteran character actor Filippo Degara, was inspired by P.G. Wodehouse's character, Jeeves.

The film's use of Gothic stereotypes steals liberally from various sources, from the *Addams Family* TV series to Mel Brooks' *Young Frankenstein* (1974), not forgetting Roman Polanski's *The Fearless Vampire Killers* (1967). A fun macabre gag finds Boris having his hand chopped off by the butler (who is chopping meat for the soup), and later retrieving it from Fracchia's plate when dinner is served; in the same scene the butler keeps pouring wine outside Fracchia's glass just as the blind hermit played by Gene Hackman did with the hot soup in *Young Frankenstein*. A Frankenstein monster shows up too, played by stuntman Romano Puppo and addressed by Dracula as "advocate," and Villaggio and company exploit the monster's presence for comedy in the absurdist sequence of the tennis match, a rendition of a hilarious episode in the first Fantozzi film. The wedding ceremony, with the virginal Fracchia dressed in white like a bride ("Do I look good in this dress?" he asks Filini) and an attendance of various monsters—including another regular of the Fantozzi series, the freaky-looking Plinio Fernando in an uncredited bit role—is decidedly more amusing.

As Dracula, Edmund Purdom looks amused and suitably self-ironic, and seems more alive than in most of the roles he played over the years, in his special appearances in films ranging from mediocre to terrible. His best scene has him perform for his guest, playing the balalaika for Fracchia and Filini, and singing with different voices (including a woman's, which belongs to one of his previous victims: an interesting addition to the Dracula canon which goes lost in the story). As his "little sister" Oniria, the ravishing Ania Pieroni makes her last movie appearance. She would become one of the more influential personalities in Italian television. The cast also features two actors usually associated with committed *auteur* cinema: Cederna, seen in Marco Bellocchio's *Enrico IV* (1984) and later to become a renowned stage actor and writer, and Isabella Ferrari.

The reviews were rather positive: the *Corriere della Sera*'s critic Giovanni Grazzini praised the production values and wrote that "*Fracchia contro Dracula* displays a silliness that here and there touches the sublime."[4] Yet, despite a release during the Christmas holidays, the most commercially fruitful period of the year, the film was a disappointment at the box-office, with only 818 million *lire*, and ended up at the 60th spot among the top-grossers of the year. Despite the wave of horror and vampire comedies of the period, such as *Transylvania 6–5000* (1985, Rudy De Luca) and *I Married a Vampire* (1987, Jay Raskin), it didn't find much of an audience abroad: *Variety* labeled it "a hard sell."[5] It became marginally known as a curio, under the title *Who Is Afraid of Dracula?*, gaining some footnotes in reference books.

Villaggio's output for the remainder of the decade consisted mostly of hit-and-run, forgettable comedies, often teamed with other popular names such as Renato Pozzetto and Lino Banfi. By the end of the 1980s he decided to renew his image, and in the following years he alternated his more commercial work with several interesting projects, including Federico Fellini's last film, *La voce della luna* (1989), followed by *Io speriamo che me la cavo* (1992, Lina Wertmüller), *Il segreto del bosco vecchio* (1993, Ermanno Olmi), *Cari fottutissimi amici* (1994, Mario Monicelli) and *Denti* (2000, Gabriele Salvatores).

NOTES

1. *Fantozzi* (1975, Luciano Salce), *Il secondo tragico Fantozzi* (1976, Luciano Salce), *Fantozzi contro tutti* (1980, Neri Parenti and Paolo Villaggio), *Fantozzi subisce ancora* (1983, Neri Parenti), *Superfantozzi* (1985, Neri Parenti), *Fantozzi va in pensione* (1988, Neri Parenti), *Fantozzi alla riscossa* (1990, Neri Parenti), *Fantozzi in paradiso* (1993, Neri Parenti), *Fantozzi—Il ritorno* (1996, Neri Parenti) and *Fantozzi 2000—La clonazione* (1999, Domenico Saverni).

2. Natalia Aspesi, "Noi difendiamo Muccioli," *Repubblica*, May 12, 1984.

3. G. Gs. [Giovanna Grassi], "Fracchia e Dracula," *Corriere della Sera*, October 30. 1985.

4. G. Gr. [Giovanni Grazzini], "Fracchia alle prese col vampiro," *Corriere della Sera*, December 27, 1985.

5. *Variety*, February 19, 1986.

Monster Dog, a.k.a. *Leviatán* (*Monster Dog*)

D: Clyde Anderson [Claudio Fragasso]. *S and SC*: Clyde Anderson [Claudio Fragasso] [and Rossella Drudi, uncredited]; *DOP*: José García Galisteo (Technicolor); *M*: Grupo Dichotomy; *E*: Antonio José Ochoa; *Additional editing*: Gabrio Astori, Peter Teschner; *Additional editors*: Giorgio Conti, Mercedes G. Alted; *ArtD*: Andrés Gumersindo; *CO*: María Eugenia Escrivá; *SPFX, SE*: Carlo De Marchis; *AD*: Michael Gutierez; *C*: Julio Madurga; *AC*: Joe Villava, Michael A. Clavijo; *SO*: José Mendieta; *W*: Teresa García; *ChEl*: Vince Lozano; *G*: José Ferrándiz, Joe Garcia, Pedro Ramírez; *KG*: Alfonso Barambio; *SS*: Victoria Melian; *SOE*: Studio Anzellotti; *Dialogue editor*: Christopher Cruise;

Re-recording: Alberto Tinebra. *Cast*: Alice Cooper [Vincent Furnier] (Vince Raven), Victoria Vera (Sandra), Carlos Santurio (Frank), María José Sarsa (Marilou), Pepita James (Angela), Emilio Linder (Jordan), Charly Bravo (Lou), Barta Barri (Old man), Ricardo Palacios (Sheriff Morrison), Luis Maluenda (Deputy), Fernando Conde (Ed), Fernando Baeza (Jerome), Nino Bastida (Greg). *PROD*: Eduard Sarlui for Continental Motion Pictures, M&C Films, Royal Films; *EP*: Helen Sarlui [Szabo], Eduard Sarlui; *Line Producer*: Carlos Aured; *PM*: Roberto Bessi; *PA*: John Senovilla; *PAcc*: Jesse [Jesús García] Gárgoles; *PSe*: Vince Ortega. *Country*: Spain. Filmed in Torrelodones, Madrid. *Running time*: 84 minutes (U.S. version); 88 minutes (International version). Spanish Visa n. 963251 (8.16.1988); *Rating*: not recommended for those under 18 years old. *Release dates*: 7.15.1986 (USA—Home video); 9.11.1986 (U.K.—Home video); 8.16.1988 (Spain); *Distribution*: Trans World entertainment (U.S.—Home video); Union Films S.A. (Spain); Eureka Video (Italy; Home video). *Also known as*: *The Bite*; *Monster Dog—Il signore dei cani* (Italy); *Los perros de la muerte*; *Uma noite de Horror* (Brazil).

Note: The songs "Identity Crisises" and "See Me in the Mirror" are written by Alice Cooper, arranged and orchestrated by Terry Bautista.

Rock star Vince Raven, his girlfriend Sandra, and Vince's film crew drive to the singer's old childhood home to shoot a music video. Along the way they are warned by the local sheriff that there has been a wolf attack in the area. Soon the sheriff and his deputy are killed by a monster. After an encounter with a crazy old man who warns them of impending danger, Vince and his crew arrive at the house. A girl in the crew, Angela, has a nightmare about Vince being a werewolf, and he tells her that his father was affected by lycanthropy and was lynched by an angry mob. The video shoot is interrupted after the discovery of the dead caretaker's body, and some angry locals show up at the house to kill Vince, whom they believe is responsible for the murders. A shootout ensues, while a pack of wild dogs break into the house and cause havoc. Vince and Sandra try to get away but are attacked by the werewolf. The monster turns out to be the old man they first met, who in turn had been infected by Vince's father. Vince, who has been bitten, starts turning into a werewolf too, but Sandra shoots him.

"At first I thought I had to be like other Italian "high cinema" directors," Claudio Fragasso explained about his directorial debut, the little-seen *Passaggi* (1977, shot on Super8) and his sophomore effort, *Difendimi dalla notte* (1981), both "intellectual films" with ambitions. "In Italy, to be considered important, you must shoot something like that."[1] But Fragasso eventually followed his heart, which was deeply rooted in genre cinema. By the mid–1980s, at a little over 30, he was a veteran in the Italian genre film industry. He had been cranking out scripts since the mid–1970s, and in the early 1980s he had worked on several films with Bruno Mattei, ranging from sleazy women-in-prison flicks to gory horror movies, which he usually scripted and *de facto* co-directed (see entry for *L'altro Inferno*). However, for his third official venture behind the camera the Italian filmmaker moved to Spain.

The offer came from Dutch producer Eduard Sarlui, who contacted Fragasso upon watching his post-atomic extravaganza *Rats—Notte di terrore* (1984, signed as "Vincent Dawn" and co-directed with Mattei). "He told me he wanted me to make another movie with animals … after "Rats" now it was time for "Dogs," *Monster Dog* (laughs)."[2] Sarlui was looking for low-budget horror films to distribute on the home video market through his company Continental Motion Pictures, an umbrella organization registered in Panama but selling features in the U.S. through American Cinema Service and in Italy through Eureka Film International of Rome. For the script, Fragasso and his wife Rossella Drudi (who co-authored it uncredited) took inspiration from the new wave of American werewolf movies, such as *The Howling* and *An American Werewolf in London*, and added a mystery twist to the story, a bit in the vein of the Amicus werewolf whodunit *The Beast Must Die* (1974, Paul Annett).

Fragasso had an unlikely lead at his disposal: singer Alice Cooper, then undergoing a bad stretch after his peaks of popularity in the previous decade with such albums as *Billion Dollar Babies* and *Welcome to My Nightmare*. Cooper was detoxing from alcohol abuse and needed a project to focus on after the fiascos of his latest, new-wave spiced records. The singer had always liked to associate himself with a macabre and horror imagery, from the use of a fake guillotine on stage to such songs as "Ballad of Dwight Fry," whose title paid reference to the 1930s actor (Dwight *Frye*, not Fry, incidentally) who played Renfield in Tod Browning's *Dracula* (1931). It wasn't Cooper's first stint at acting, as he had appeared in several films, including a

memorable appearance (as himself) in Alan Rudolph's cult film *Roadie* (1980), starring Meat Loaf.

Working as line producer for Sarlui's company—and as his front for the Spanish red tape, for the film to be categorized as a Spanish production and benefit from the country's law facilitations—was also Carlos Aured, the helmer of several Paul Naschy films who gave up directing after his film *Atrapados en el miedo* but stayed in the movie business assuming production duties. *Monster Dog* was part of a two-picture deal that comprised also Deran Serafian's *Alien Predators* (a.k.a. *The Falling*). Both pictures were shot back-to-back, but Serafian's film went way over schedule and left Aured with a pile of unpaid debts, causing him to quit the movie business.[3]

Monster Dog was shot in five weeks[4] in Torrelodones, just outside of Madrid. The director was thrilled to work with Cooper and claimed they had become friends who used to watch horror movies together at night. Aured as well recalled the star's low profile and amiability. "I went to meet him at the airport and failed to recognize him! He was wearing white slacks and a jumper, looking like an Englishman dressed for cricket! He didn't give us any problems. He only made two 'demands'—to have a supply of cold Coca-Cola on set and a VCR in his room so he could watch old Western movies; he was crazy about Westerns. On weekends, he used to spend all his time playing golf."[5] Fragasso and Drudi even claimed that Cooper used to play golf in a miniature golf course in his Madrid apartment. The singer was known to all as "The American" during shooting, being the only foreign member in an all-Spanish cast which featured Victoria Vera (soon to become a prominent film and stage actress) and genre regulars such as Ricardo Palacios, Emilio Linder and Barta Barri.

Cooper's presence pushed *Monster Dog* in a direction akin to those horror films centered on rock bands such as *Terror on Tour* (1980, Don Edmonds), *Rocktober Blood* (1984, Ferd & Beverly Sebastian) and *Hard Rock Zombies* (1985, Krishna Shah). The film opens with a music video, in which Cooper's alter ego Vincent Raven sings the song "Identity Crisises" (spelled "Identity Chrises" in the end credits) and turns up as the various characters mentioned in the lyrics like a quick-change artist such as the famous Leopoldo Fregoli ("Sometimes I'm James

Bond/Sometimes I'm Billy the Kid/Sometimes I feel like Sherlock Holmes/Sometimes I feel like Jack the Ripper… "). The result is as naïve as some Italian music videos of the early 1980s, and curiously recalls the one Michelangelo Antonioni shot in 1984 for Gianna Nannini's song "Fotoromanza." Since the record company and the artist are (comprehensibly) unhappy with the result, the film has Raven and his crew move conveniently to an old dark house in the middle of nowhere to reshoot the video, an idea with some points in common with Luigi Cozzi's *Paganini Horror* (1989) and which provides the film with a suitable old-style Gothic mood.

Fragasso embraces the music video-inspired style of many early to mid–Eighties horror films to have the film look American and up-to-date, with dry ice aplenty and lots of silhouette shots in the exterior night scenes to make up for the scarce budget. He even inserts two more music videos in the film: "See Me in the Mirror" has Cooper reprising his typical vampire look (dressed in black, with heavy eye makeup and gloomy grin), while the ending features a reprise of the "Identity Crisises" video with excerpts from the story, presumably to pad out the running time. But Fragasso even throws in some Spaghetti Western-inspired scenes along the way, with an armed confrontation between Vince and some armed thugs, and during the third act the director seems possessed by the spirit of Sam Peckinpah, turning *Monster Dog* into a sort of remake of *Straw Dogs* (1971), with rednecks with bandoliers and guns moving around the house and shooting at the protagonists, and bullet-ridden bodies falling to the floor in slow-motion.

The result is less than earth-shattering, and some naivetés in the plot are annoying: for instance, when Vince Raven leafs through an old book called *Werewolves: Myths, Legends and Scientific Reality*, we get to see a full-page still of Lon Chaney, Jr., from *The Wolf Man* (1941), an unlikely choice for a presumably decades-old tome, and one that sabotages any attempt at old-style Gothic atmosphere. The film suffers from low-par special effects too: there is never a full graphic werewolf transformation, and in the climax we get to see some facial hair make-up plus a rubber, deformed dog-head mask.

According to Fragasso, the F/X caused many delays during the shooting and turned out a disappointment; namely, there were problems with the mechanical werewolf built by Carlo De Marchis, an Italian technician who lived in Spain. Originally the transformation would have to take place gradually, through various stages, and the monster was designed by Roman art director Antonello Geleng, following Fragasso's suggestion to make it look like a prehistoric animal or a panther, however more feline than a dog. But De Marchis' creature didn't look at all like Geleng's design. Moreover, the puppet (which could be maneuvered through wires and a cart) was ready only on the last week of filming, as the director explained. "In a scene (which was then cut) the monster breaks through a door and holds the head of one of the actors in its jaws. This was the first time that the puppet was used, but unfortunately it broke immediately, forcing us to move it manually in the following scenes."[6] This pushed Fragasso and Drudi to do some last-minute rewriting, while for the big climax they had to rely on facial make-up and rubber masks were used, to less than impressive results.

It wasn't the only issue that plagued the filming. The director and production manager Roberto Bessi—the third and last Italian in the crew, working with Sarlui for the second time after *Warrior of the Lost World* (1983)—had to deal with incompetent crew members and face many issues. Moreover, Fragasso (who is credited in the film with his Anglicized pseudonym Clyde Anderson) blamed Sarlui for having arbitrarily recut the movie:

> They did me wrong because about 20 minutes of film were cut. What is now circulating on VHS and DVD is not the film that I shot. It's a film that I do not disown, it didn't come out as I wanted but the fault is above all of the editing. When a director signs a deal with the Americans you never have the final cut, so your ideas for the editing need not necessarily be considered. In this case, in fact, the final edit was made by the producer. The deleted scenes are the best, all those of the transformation, all the splatter ones…. It's a pity but it is also true that in 1984/85 extreme splatter began to disappear.[7]

These cuts remain unconfirmed and there is no evidence of extra gory scenes left out of the film. However, in the featurette *Lord of the Dogs*, in the American Blu-ray release of the film, Fragasso and Drudi's recollection of the cuts was slightly different:

> When I did my cut, the director's cut, I came back to Italy and what happened later was a big mess in my opinion. When I saw the movie, I didn't recognize it. The movie was supposed to be longer, it had 20 minutes cut out and this kind of ruined the atmosphere that I wanted to create. I had counted on that. The

editing was a bit slower in my cut. They wanted to make it faster, but they made it more confusing. It was a pity anyway because I wanted to create a particular atmosphere, but I would need 15 or 20 more minutes of the footage I shot to give it that look. Then they did some clumsy things trying to fix the movie, but without the director you can't understand what is right to do. They only messed it up and it's a real shame [Fragasso].

It was completely different, there was different editing and many sequences were cut, they edited them in a way that makes the story confusing. The movie had a different meaning than before. We were very upset, both of us. Some very nice things that Claudio shot were cut [Drudi].[8]

The presence in the end credits of no less than four "additional editors" might as well suggest tampering on the part of Sarlui. By comparing the different versions of the film, it appears that the producer trimmed a handful of minutes for the American release, namely surrounding contextual footage consisting of dialogue exchanges—such as one between the sheriff (Ricardo Palacios) and his deputy (Luis Maluenda)—but leaving all the existing gore intact. A Japanese version, with a different audio mix and the extra bits, runs a full 88 minutes. In a typical practice in European productions, *Monster Dog* was shot without direct sound and the characters were redubbed later in post-production. Cooper's voice was provided by Ted Rusoff.

Despite reference books and IMDb claiming that it debuted in Italy in December 1984, *Monster Dog* wasn't even submitted to the rating board for a screen certificate and surfaced to home video some years later. The U.S. prints feature a 1985 copyright. Overseas it premiered on video in 1986, while in 1988 it was released theatrically in Spain. According to the official Spanish sources (which list it as a 1985 production titled *Leviatán*, 100 percent Spanish, and credit Carlos Aured as scriptwriter), it was seen by an audience of 53,438 spectators and grossed the equivalent of today's 128,737.53 euro.

Over the years, Alice Cooper often referred to his participation in *Monster Dog* in amused terms. In a February 1987 interview he explained:

I always wanted to do a really cheap splatter movie—one that would make me really big in somewhere like Pakistan. Then five years from now I'd like to be able to rent this movie for 79 cents. That's the level I wanted this to be on. They gave me a lot of money for it—it must have been half the budget—and we did it in Spain. A lot of the people who worked on it

were people who worked on the original *Alien*, and I was going, "Gee, I hope this isn't too good." But it ended up being just as bad as I thought. I get to kill like eight people in it, and I turn into a giant dog … so it's good.[9]

Fragasso went on to direct more horror films, some with Mattei, with whom he also filmed the additional scenes for Fulci's *Zombi 3*, and some by himself, such as the ultraviolent zombie yarn *After Death (Oltre la morte)* (1989). The latter was produced by Filmirage, who also financed Fragasso's *La casa 5* and the infamous *Troll 2* (both 1990). For *Troll 2*, the director came up with the a.k.a. "Drako Floyd"[10] so that Sarlui, who was involved in the financing and had had arguments with him on *Monster Dog*, wouldn't know that it was Fragasso directing the picture. As for Cooper, in 1987 he turned up for a special appearance, as one of the homeless people possessed by a devilish entity, in another horror film, John Carpenter's *Prince of Darkness*. Meanwhile his career as a singer and recording artist had gained momentum again, climaxing in the 1989 album *Trash*, his biggest hit in years.

Cooper's two songs were composed specifically for the film and were arranged by Spanish composer and arranger Teddy Bautista (who in the 1960s had been playing in the progressive rock band Los Canarios) and were played by the band Dichotomy. They remained unreleased until 1999, when they ended up in the 4-disc box-set *The Life and Crimes of Alice Cooper*. A numbered edition of 100 copies of a 7-inch single with the two songs from the film was released in 2012.

NOTES

1. Berger, "Claudio Fragasso's Gore Wars," 57.
2. Caddeo and Lopéré, "Passion devoreuse," 74.
3. Mike Hodges, "Aured Rises from the Tomb," Fangoria #189, January 2000, 71.
4. Palmerini and Mistretta, *Spaghetti Nightmares*, 76.
5. Hodges, "Aured Rises from the Tomb," 71.
6. Caddeo and Lopéré, "Passion devoreuse," 75.
7. *Ibid.*
8. Claudio Fragasso and Rossella Drudi interviewed, in Federico Caddeo, *Lord of the Dogs*, featurette included as extra in the U.S. Kino Lorber Blu-Ray release of *Monster Dog*.
9. Les Wiseman, "Coop Among Chickens," Vancouver, February 1987.
10. The pseudonym was conceived by Rossella Drudi, who took inspiration from the Dragon sign in the Chinese zodiac ("Drake") and from her love for Pink Floyd ("Floyd"). See Jacopo Coccia, "Conversazione con Rossella Drudi (Parte 1)," Bizzarrocinema.it (http://www.bizzarro cinema.it/interviste/altre-interviste/professione-scene ggiatore-intervista-esclusiva-a-rossella-drudi/).

1986

Anemia (Anemia)

D: Alberto Abruzzese and Achille Pisanti. S: based on Alberto Abruzzese's novel *Anemia. Storia di un vampiro comunista*; SC: Alberto Abruzzese, Achille Pisanti; DOP: Angelo Sciarra; M: Lorenzo Ferrero; E: Mirella Mencio; PD: Nicola Rubertelli; CO: Giovanna La Placa Wolmsley; AD: Gina Vitelli; *Collaboration to the direction*: Anna Albanese; SS: Marisa Vesuviano; C: Pietro Emozione; SD: Paolo Fabriani; AC: Enzo Leone, Antonio Maglione, Antonio Pascolini; SO: Rino Evangelista; B: Mario Di Iorio; MU: Enzo D'Anna; *Hair*: Alfonso Simonelli; ACO: Anna Morelli; ChEl: Mario Traditi; KG: Ciro De Pasquale; *Titles*: Giacomo Stabile; G: Domenico Milano, Mario Richiello; *Specializzati di ripresa*: Domenico Gervasio, Antonio Spampinato; AE: Danilo Fedeli, Renata Gengarelli; *Truka*: Claudio Soldati; *Luci di stampa*: Walter Abbondanza, Sergio Moscardi; *Negative cutter*: Rosa Iorizzo; *Dubbing director*: Elio Zamuto; *Dubbing asst*: Mirella Russo; SOE: Enzo Di Liberto; *Mix*: Marina Atzu. *Cast*: Hanns Zischler (Umberto U.), Gioia Maria Scola [Gioia Maria Tibiletti] (Marcella), Julian Jenkins (Shop assistant), Emily Marchi (Flower seller), Giuseppe Aprea (Alberto), Luigi Curcione (Barman), Roberto Pace (Young manager), Francesco Pettarin (Ice Cream Man), Linda Sini (Marta), Elio Polimeno (Man in Train), Helmut Plakolmer (Reporter), Enzo Salomone (Waiter in Train), Franco Gargia (Waiter in Restaurant), Lucio Beffi (Doctor), Nicola Esposito (Taxi Driver), Vera Matania (Innkeeper), Roberto Corcione (Tommaso), Gérard Landry (Grandfather), Margherita Rinaldi (Shop Assistant), Gabriella Rinaldi (Singer), Roberto De Francesco (Boy), Marina Ruffo (Hotel Owner), Nicola Vigilante (Hotel Owner's Son), Anna Calato (Waitress). PROD: Rai Tre, RAI Radiotelevisione Italiana; PM: Giorgio Scoppa; GM: Bruno Alongi; PS: Rolando Santorelli. *Country*: Italy. Filmed in Rome and on the Amalfi Coast. *Running time*: 90 minutes. *Release dates*: 9.9.1986 (Venice Film Festival); 10.27.1990 (First TV broadcast—Rai Tre); *Distribution*: not released theatrically.

Umberto, a leader of the Italian Communist Party, suffers from a severe form of anemia. He has to wear dark glasses in daylight and experi-ences hallucinations. Umberto's illness leads him to make a drastic decision: he'll retire for some time in his grandfather's secluded house by the lake. During the trip by train he recalls his love story with a TV reporter, Marcella, and his in-creasing detachment from the political life. At the house, he discovers a diary and learns from it that he is the last descendant of a vampire. Upon his return to the city, Umberto finally embraces his own destiny. He prepares to become the party's leader and leaves on a vacation with Marcella at an exclusive hotel where his real nature comes to the fore...

Born in Rome in 1942, Alberto Abruzzese is one of Italy's most highly reputed sociologists and semiologists. Between 1972 and 1992 he taught at the University of Naples and specialized in mass communication; he wrote several influential volumes on the matter, which often focused on literature, film and popular art, and gained the title of "theorist of the ephemeral." Among his works are *L'immagine filmica. Materiali di studio* (1974), *La grande scimmia. Mostri, vampiri, automi, mutanti. L'immaginario collettivo dalla letteratura al cinema e all'informazione* (1979) and *Pornograffiti. Trame e figure del fumetto italiano per adulti* (1980)—the latter a pioneering collection of essays on adults-only comics.

In December 1984 Abruzzese released *Anemia. Storia di un vampiro comunista*, a novelette published by a small Rome-based company, Theoria, who sought to give new life to the Fantastic genre by collecting works of contemporary Italian authors, such as Vincenzo Cerami (*Sua Maestà*), Aldo Rosselli (*A pranzo con Lukacs*), Antonio Caronia (*Il cyborg. Saggio sull'uomo artificiale*) and Giampiero Comolli (*Il banchetto nel bosco*). "We wanted Italian authors to confront the themes of fear and obsessions in today's Western society, that is, the ghosts, vampires, monsters of our everyday reality,"[1] claimed the company's head, Paolo Repetti.

In tune with Theoria's aim and with Abruzzese's interests, *Anemia* mixed references to film and literature within an openly political context. The story fleshed out the theme of vampirism as political metaphor: the protagonist Umberto U. is a member of the Italian Communist Party (PCI) who suffers from anemia, photophobia, and a growing attraction to blood. PCI was undergoing an identity crisis after the death of its historical secretary, Enrico Berlinguer, who suffered a major stroke during an electoral speech (broadcast live) in June 1984 and died a few days later. A much beloved political figure, even by people with different political ideas, Berlinguer left the party at its all-time maximum, with over 33-percent: during the European elections, PCI even surpassed its historic rival, Democrazia Cristiana, but soon its popularity started to fall, not least because of the events that marked European history throughout the decade, from the 1981 Polish golpe to the domestic reforms in Gorbachev's Russia, starting with 1986's *Perestroika*.

In late 1985, Abruzzese started working on a film version of his novel, in collaboration with the 34-year-old Achille Pisanti, who helped him adapt the material for the screen and shared the directorial duties with him. Shot in 16mm with a small budget, *Anemia* was produced by Rai Tre, the third and most experimental of RAI channels. The State television was intensifying its participation in production: that year's Venice Film Festival included no less than ten films produced in whole or in part by RAI and to be distributed by its consociate company Sacis, "an unequivocal sign of the vitality of Italian cinema," as the company proudly claimed.[2]

Abruzzese's approach to the modern-day Gothic tale shows immediately the author's agenda. The protagonist's transformation is a metaphor for the loss of political ideals. Umberto is described as "too young to have been a founding member of the party, too intellectual to have trained as a bureaucrat," and is said to have deluded himself into thinking he could change the PCI, whereas he was changed by it—starting with the use of cryptic but ultimately void language.

Abruzzese and Pisanti didactically depict the Roman PCI headquarters, located at the aptly named Via delle Botteghe Oscure (Street of Dark Workshops), as the modern-day version of a vampire castle—immersed in gloom and full of parasitic bloodsuckers (the party officials) who are busy exchanging favors, pulling the strings or concocting Machiavellian ways to keep their self-interest. *House of Cards* this ain't, however: the dialogue, heavy with political innuendo, is too blatant and self-referential in its depiction of aridness and political mischief, and the puns are telegraphed. "In future, you'll be

just like us, we've got the same blood," says the elderly party member to the protagonist.

The country's political malaise is heavily underlined by TV sets that broadcast news about the Brigate Rosse terrorist group (Abruzzese has a disinterested barman switch channels to a Fred Astaire musical to stress the average man's detachment from politics). Likewise, Umberto's gradual transformation into a vampire is shown with blatant symbolism: he wears shades even in badly-lit rooms, he feels attracted to crypts and cellars ("There's a good smell of earth here," he says to a flower girl after following her into the shop's basement), eats a raspberry ice-cream and gets his mouth all messed up in red.

The directors scatter many references to classic horror cinema and literature throughout the story, from *Nosferatu* and *Vampyr* to *The Castle of Otranto*, and deliver some nice evocative images. Umberto's night journey by train to his grandfather's house is patterned over Harker's trip to Dracula's castle; the long flashback which illustrates the memories of Umberto's vampiric ancestor (veteran French actor Gérard Landry, cast because of his work with Abel Gance) is set among cemeteries and fog-shrouded villas and aims at a silent movie-like intensity; in the final scene, Gioia Maria Scola's character moves forward sliding like the elderly lady in Bava's *La goccia d'acqua*. Abruzzese himself was adamant that the film be considered as a

> hypersensible journey among the literary and cinematic genres; a game of displacements, estrangements, misrepresentations amidst the ruins of TV and cinema; a nostalgic and musical game within the limits allowed by the "years of lead" ... a very hybrid game, indeed, aimed at rethinking the crisis of our cinema without the pretension of employing the Hollywood standard, but keeping in mind that ... the Italian spectator lives in a cinematic world which is heavily contaminated by models, emotions and myths coming from Hollywood movies as well as by styles inherited from Italian cinema, wavering between past and present imagery, widespread consumerism and cultural traditions. It is this type of viewer that we hope to please.[3]

As film critic Fabio Giovannini noted, "*Anemia* marks a moment of resurrection for the vampire figure [in Italian cinema] but also the exposition of the myth to dangers of contamination that might be fatal. The vampire, who uses contagion as a weapon, can die of contamination too."[4] That is, *Anemia* gradually succumbs to the very metaphors it deals with, and Abruzzese's ambition to sum up the crisis of Italy's major left-wing party and the end of ideologies as a Gothic tale turns out a cataleptic, cryptic and, indeed, anemic narrative. The movie is distinctly devoid of a strong cinematic style. Unlike its predecessors, such as Corrado Farina's *...hanno cambiato faccia* (1971), *Anemia* ultimately fails because it cannot find its own identity. The redundant, didactic dialogue in the first part is paired with an over-reliance on the voiceover during the flashback that forms the core of the tale, showing a direction which is not able to turn the literary background into a filmic vision.

The cast and production values don't help. Zischler (the protagonist of Wim Wenders' celebrated *Im Lauf der Zeit*, a.k.a. *Kings of the Road*, 1976) is far from being a convincing lead, while the gorgeous Scola—whose "close friendship" with Silvio Berlusconi's brother Paolo allowed her to gain some press exposure during the early-to-mid 1980s, even for such an obscure project as Abruzzese's film—is certainly an alluring presence but not the world's best actress. The music shifts uneasily between atmospheric moody synth pieces and Goblin-like, dance-oriented numbers, with horrible results; the only welcome interference is a brief excerpt from the music video for The Rolling Stones' "Neighbours," from the *Tattoo You* album.

Abruzzese claimed that he hoped the critics would "acknowledge the attempt at escaping the filmic tradition of these last ten years of Italian cinema,"[5] but this proved wishful thinking. *Anemia* was screened at the 1986 Venice Film Festival in a collateral retrospective (Spazio Aperto) and at the "Premio Italia" in Lucca, around the same time, to generally perplexed, if not downright bad, reviews.[6] "We have the feeling, confirmed by some, many, too many declarations on the part of Abruzzese, that the narrative core … is only a pretext," a critic wrote. "The narrative is intentionally a series of linear encounters with oneirism, eroticism, horror, sentimentalism, period-evoking flash-backs … all tied together by the extremely thin, yet logical, thread of the events lived by the protagonist. There are references to various genres, then, such as one can find at a stereotypical level in many countries' filmographies, especially American. As for the pleasantness of the result for the viewers … we have strong doubts."[7]

Any prospect of a theatrical release was quickly abandoned. *Anemia* was broadcast on television only a handful of times over the following years, late at night, in a copy with forced English subtitles.

NOTES

1. Nico Orengo, "Ecco il vampiro Made in Italy," *La Stampa—Tuttolibri*, January 5, 1985.
2. [not signed], "Dieci film Rai alla Biennale," *L'Unità*, August 5, 1986.
3. Alberto Abruzzese, "Ora vi racconto la mia sfida al cinema," *L'Unità*, August 24, 1986.
4. Fabio Giovannini, *Il libro dei vampiri: dal mito di Dracula alla presenza quotidiana* (Bari: Dedalo, [1985] 1997), 181.
5. Abruzzese, "Ora vi racconto la mia sfida al cinema."
6. L.t., "Nel mistero della vita anche i comunisti sono in crisi," *La Stampa*, September 9, 1986.
7. Piero Zanotto, "Dopo l'effimero viene l'Anemia," *Stampa Sera*, 9 September 1986.

La casa del buon ritorno (The House of Good Returns)

D: Beppe Cino. *S and SC*: Beppe Cino; *DOP*: Antonio Minutolo (Kodak; LV-Luciano Vittori); *M*: Carlo Siliotto (Ed. CAM); *E*: Emanuele Foglietti; *PD, CO*: Silvana Fantino; *AD*: Diego D'Innocenzo; *AsstD*: Paolo Scaffa, Stefano Gabrini; *MU*: Maurizio Fazzini; *SS*: Paola Di Giulio, *AsstSS*: Giovanna Lomagno; *AE*: Lucia Deidda; *C*: Giuseppe Venditti; *APD*: Pier Francesco Giordano; *SO*: Benedetto Santalucia; *B*: Fulgenzio Ceccon; *SP*: Elvira Castellano; *ChEl*: Giulio Bastoni; *El*: Alberto Rogante, Giovanni Angeletti, Roberto Stiffi; *KG*: Vincenzo Di Costanzo; *G*: Roberto Battistioli, Paolo Camera, Francesco Bastianoni; *Mix*: Franco Bassi. *Cast*: Amanda Sandrelli (Margit), Stefano Gabrini (Luca), Francesco Costa (Bruno), Fiammetta Carena (Ayesha), Lola Ledda (Lola), Stanis Ledda (Luca as a child), Fabrizio Capuani (Bruno as a child), Eloisa Cino (Girl playing piano), Eleonora Salvadori (Luca's mother), Elvira Castellano (Bruno's mother). *PROD*: Remo Angioli and Beppe Cino for Moviemachine S.r.l. (Rome); *PM*: Renata Crea; *EP*: Giuseppina Marotta; *PS*: Anda Fabrizi, Benedetto Atria; *PSe*: Patrizia Pierucci; *ADM*: Caterina Roverso. *Country*: Italy. Filmed in and around Rome. *Running time*: 91 minutes (m. 2492). Visa n. 82023 (11.29.1986); *Rating*: all audiences. *Release date*: 8.31.1986 (Venezia Film Festival); 2.13.1987 (Theatrical release); *Distribution*: C.R.C./Real Film. *Domestic gross*: n.a. Also known as: *Das Haus der blauen Schatten* (West Germany).

Luca returns to his parents' home after a 15-year absence with his fiancée Margit. There, as a kid, he pushed a little girl to her death from a terrace while playing hide-and-seek, and he is still haunted by the memory of the accident. Luca becomes obsessed with a mannequin that looks like the deceased girl and starts to see her everywhere. Meanwhile, strange things are going on in the house, and Luca's neighbors (and former child playmates) Ayesha and Bruno—who seem to be aware of his secret—keep spying on him. Luca slowly loses his mind. Suddenly a mysterious individual appears in the house, wearing a scary mask that once belonged to the dead girl. After an argument, Margit leaves the house and Luca finally succumbs to madness...

Coming three years after his debut *Il cavaliere, la morte e il diavolo* (1983), an uncredited adaptation of Arthur Schnitzler's novel *Traumnovelle* (a.k.a. *Dream Story*), *La casa del buon ritorno* marked Beppe Cino's second feature film. A CSC diplomat, and an ex-assistant of Roberto Rossellini from 1972 to 1975, Cino (born in Racalmuto, Sicily, in 1947) wrote and produced the movie on a small scale, shooting it in just twelve days, on 16mm and with a budget of 300 million *lire*,[1] with only one professional actor, Amanda Sandrelli. "It was a movie we decided to make quickly, like pulling out a tooth."[2]

The project had a curious genesis, as in Spring 1985 Cino had announced a film with the same title but a completely different plot, which revolved around the phenomenon of "repentant terrorists." "It is a story set in Rome in the arc of only one night, from dusk till dawn, during which the characters experience decisive happenings, which sow the seeds of doubt even in those who were irreducible."[3] The project eventually took form under the title *Rosso di sera*, released in 1989. Meanwhile the director recycled the title for a completely different story, which he described as "a Gothic-*fantastique* film, in which oneiric moments fit together with psychological, illusory and believable ones," even quoting Jorge Luis Borges as an influence.[4]

As was the case with his first film, *La casa del buon ritorno* was judged "of national cultural interest" according to article 28 of the 1965 Corona law, and therefore worthy of financial backup on the part of the State. The article was at the center of many controversies, since many of the movies that benefited from it had hardly any distribution or visibility, and often resulted in soporific or pretentious dramas which signaled a regression in the young generation of filmmakers, with a stoic refusal in dealing with genres, paired with wishful *auteur* ambitions. Unfortunately, Cino's film was no exception.

The story encompasses some typical genre elements, revised in a psychoanalytic way. The haunted house where Luca and his girlfriend move appears to be haunted not only by the protagonist's memory and his sense of guilt, but also by the mysterious Ayesha, a "timeless woman ... a keeper of a memory and a grudge"[5] who carries on a complex vengeance that is accomplished only in the film's last images. Is Ayesha, who does not seem to get older as years pass, a

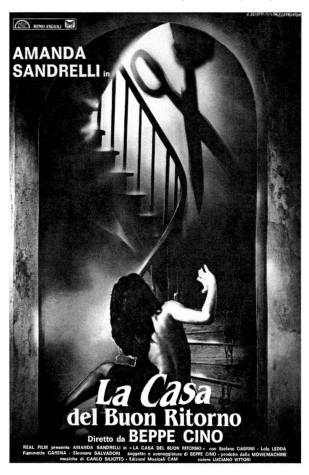

Atmospheric Italian *locandina* for *La casa del buon ritorno* (1986, Beppe Cino) (art by Enzo Sciotti, photograph by Angelo Frontoni).

real presence, or a supernatural one? Is she a witch who uses her magic powers to manipulate the other characters' will and actions? Cino keeps this ambiguousness throughout the whole story, "within that area of phenomena which are at the edge of pathology, but certainly cannot be labeled as 'paranormal.'"[6]

In developing the protagonist's descent into madness, *La casa del buon ritorno* sticks to the category of the "paranoid text" characterized, in David Punter's words, by "the shift towards the psychological, the increasing complexity of verification, the emphasis on the ambivalence of persecution."[7] Cino himself claimed it was necessary to reprise the themes of 18th and 19th century tradition with a renewed sensibility and awareness. "Nowadays, our contemporary world, the knowledge we have of the conscious and unconscious nature of our actions, are all elements to rethink our reality in a 'fantastic' way, without the need, as it was in Gothic literature, to plunder among the dumps of the supernatural."[8]

The "return of the repressed," linked with a grisly childhood trauma, brings the movie into a territory akin to Francesco Barilli's films, and the insistence on small unsettling details recalls Pupi Avati's Gothic works. The core of the tale revolves around Lola, the dead girl at the center of three individuals' obsession: Luca pushed her off a terrace and killed her, Bruno (who witnessed the act) is still in love with her memory, and Ayesha keeps a sort of pagan altar dedicated to her (an element that echoes Truffaut's *La chambre verte*). Another curious and intriguing reference is the Hannya mask (a typical mask in Noh theater, representing a female jealous demon) worn by Luca's persecutor, which recalls the one seen in Kaneto Shindo's *Onibaba* (1964).

But the psychoanalytic burden ends up drowning the film, which is also let down by the excessively slow pacing and bad acting. Stefano Gabrini, who played the lead and was Cino's assistant on the set and during post-production, was adamant about his inadequacy: "My turn as an actor had me suffer the schizophrenia of being on the wrong side of the camera, leading me to disown myself and the film as well."[9] Gabrini's character gradually transforms over the course of the story, in an overtly didactic explanation of his return to his past: first we see him with a long beard, which he shaves halfway through the film, keeping his mustache, and in the final scenes he is hairless as a child.

What is more, the style is unripe, with plenty of dull long takes and talky bits, and with the debatable addition of scenes where the camera, placed at ground level, frantically runs behind the main character across the street or a flight of stairs *à la The Evil Dead*—an ill-fated stylistic choice which plagued Cino's first film as well. The graininess and darkness of many scenes, the result of the low budget and haste, were highlighted when the 16mm negative was blown up to 35 for theatrical distribution.

La casa del buon ritorno premiered at the 1986 Venice Film Festival, in the collateral De Sica section, to scathing reviews. *La Stampa* dismissed it as "below an acceptable professional level.... Stefano Gabrini, awkward and awful, just cannot act. As for Amanda Sandrelli, her unfortunate line 'An asshole! That's what I am, an asshole!' was greeted by enthusiastic applause, which meant the audience agreed. But it wasn't the actress' fault."[10] The *Corriere della Sera* summed up effectively the film's main issues: "It is not clear whether *La casa del buon ritorno* is a thriller, a horror, a love story … or an analysis session: however, the unpleasant thing is that it seems something already seen, and it wishes to remain deliberately obscure."[11]

A clever distribution gave the film some minor notoriety: the title logo recalled the thread inaugurated by Raimi's *The Evil Dead*, distributed in Italy as *La casa* and leading to many spurious rip-offs and phony sequels. *La casa del buon ritorno* was also screened at Rome's Fantafestival, and even earned a prize. It was never dubbed in English, nor was it shown theatrically in the United States or the U.K.; it allegedly surfaced to home video in West Germany with the title *Der Haus der Blauen Schatten* (The House of the Blue Shadows). Nowadays it is only available in bad quality home video copies, which do not do justice to Cino's intentions, however flawed the movie might be. As for Gabrini, he debuted as director in 1991 with *Il gioco delle ombre*, another evocative ghost story financed via article 28.

NOTES

1. Giovanna Grassi, "Il regista che viene dalle nuvole," *Corriere della Sera*, August 14, 1986. The main locations were a couple of 1930s villas on the Nomentana road, and the rest of the film was shot in and around Rome (at the Testaccio market, and at the former slaughterhouse, plus a rail crossing along the Rome-Civitavecchia motorway). Thanks to Fabio Melelli and Beppe Cino for these bits of information.

2. Palmerini and Mistretta, *Spaghetti Nightmares*, 59.

3. [Ansa agency] "Ciak su terrorismo e pentitismo," May 23, 1985.

4. Grassi, "Il regista che viene dalle nuvole."

5. Palmerini and Mistretta, *Spaghetti Nightmares*, 59.

6. *Ibid.*

7. David Punter, *The Literature of Terror. Volume 1: The Gothic Tradition* (London: Routledge, [1996] 2014), 138.

8. Palmerini and Mistretta, *Spaghetti Nightmares*, 61.

9. Mario Bucci, "Buongiorno, Stefano Gabrini," www.effettonotteonline.com. (http://www.effettonotteonline.com/enol/archivi/articoli/interviste/200703/200703in00.html)

10. l.t. [Lietta Tornabuoni], "Una sola vita non basta, meglio due o tre," *La Stampa*, September 2, 1986.

11. M.Po. [Maurizio Porro], "Una "casa"-trappola per Amanda," *Corriere della Sera*, September 2, 1986.

Dèmoni 2 ... l'incubo ritorna (Demons 2)

D: Lamberto Bava. *S and SC*: Dario Argento, Lamberto Bava, Franco Ferrini, Dardano Sacchetti [and Sergio Stivaletti, uncredited]; *DOP*: Gianlorenzo Battaglia (Eastmancolor Kodak, LV-Luciano Vittori); *M*: Simon Boswell; *E*: Piero Bozza; *SupE*: Franco Fraticelli; *PD*: Davide Bassan; *CO*: Nicola Trussardi; *SPFX*: Sergio Stivaletti, Rosario Prestopino; *AsstSPFX*: Barbara Morosetti; *SE*: Antonio Corridori, Giovanni Corridori; *MU*: Rosario Prestopino, Giacinto Bretti; *AD*: Roberto Palmerini; *2ndAD*: Fabrizio Bava; *AE*: Alessandro Gabriele, Fabrizio Fraticelli; *C*: Guido Tosi; *AC*: Stefano Falivene, Federico Martucci; *SD*: Valeria Paoloni; *SO*: Raffaele De Luca; *SOE*: Studio Anzellotti; *Mix*: Romano Pampaloni; *B*: Angelo Amatulli; *Sound consultant*: Federico Savina; *ChEl*: Domenico Caiuli; *KG*: Franco Micheli; *G*: Paolo Tiberti; *PrM*: Maurizio Jacopelli; *SP*: Franco Bellomo; *Stunts*: Claudio Pacifico; *SS*: Francesca Ghiotto; *DubD*: Sergio Graziani. *Cast*: David Knight (George), Nancy Brilli (Hannah), Coralina Cataldi Tassoni (Sally Day), Bobby Rhodes (Hank), Asia Argento (Ingrid Haller), Virginia Bryant (Mary, the prostitute), Anita Bartolucci (Woman with dog), Antonio Cantafora (Ingrid's father), Luisa Passega (Helga Haller), Davide Marotta (Demon Tommy), Marco Vivio (Tommy), Michele Mirabella (Prostitute's client), Lorenzo Gioielli (Jake), Lino Salemme (Security guard), Maria Chiara Sasso (Ulla), Dario Casalini (Danny), Andrea Garinei (Partygoer waiting for Jacob), Luca De Nardo (Partygoer), Angela Frondaroli (Susan, bodybuilder), Caroline Christina Lund (Jennifer, bodybuilder), Karen Gennaro (Bodybuilder), Marina Loi (Kate), Silvia Rosa (Partygoer), Monica Umena (Partygoer), Lorenzo Flaherty (Partygoer), Fabio Poggiali (Muller, bodybuilder), Andrea Spera (Partygoer). Pascal Persiano (Joe—TV show), Robert Chilcott (Bob—TV show), Eliana Hoppe [Eliana Miglio] (Pam, girl with camera), Yvonne Fraschetti (Jacob's Girl), Bruno Bilotta (Jacob), Furio Bilotta (Man in the back of Jacob's car), Giovanna Pini (Girl in the back of Jacob's car/Woman in garage), Stefano Molinari (Demon on TV), Pasquale Valente (Tommy's Father), Kim Rhone (Tommy's Mother), Annalie Harrison (Sally's Mother); *uncredited*: Lamberto Bava (Sally's Father). *PROD*: Dario Argento for DAC Film (Rome); *PM*: Guido De Laurentiis; *EP*: Ferdinando Caputo; *PS*: Antonio Saragò, Fabrizio Diaz; *PSe*: Paola Rossi, Egle Friggeri, Andrea Caputo; *ADM*: Renato Rinaldo; *PrA*: Enrico Lucherini, Gianluca Pignatelli. *Country*: Italy. Filmed on location in Hamburg and at De Paolis In.Ci.R. Studios (Rome). *Running time*: 92 minutes (m. 2485). Visa n. 81851 (10.1.1986); *Rating*: V.M.14. *Release dates*: 10.9.1986 (Italy), 2.13.1987 (U.S.A), 3.25.1987 (France), 7.9.1987 (West Germany), 9.18.1987 (UK), 11.21.1988 (Spain); *Distribution*: Titanus (Italy); Artists Entertainment Group; Imperial Entertainment (USA). *Domestic gross*: 1,105,944,000 lire. *Also known as*: *Dance of the Demons 2/Dämonen* (West Germany).

A series of events take place in a high-rise in an unnamed city. During her birthday party, Sally locks herself into the room to watch a horror movie about a group of young people who find a tomb; in the film, the teenagers awaken a demon, and the monstrous being then turns toward Sally, comes out of the TV and attacks her. Sally turns into a demon under her friends' terrified eyes; she attacks the partygoers who turn into other demons. Because of the corrosive blood that comes out of Sally's body, a blackout ensues, and all the tenants remain locked in the building. Among them are George and his pregnant wife Hannah, gym instructor Hank, a little kid named Tommy who is home alone, and a teenage girl, Ingrid. Soon the demons invade the building, and the few survivors must fight for their life...

The box-office success of *Dèmoni* was a clear sign that the Italian public was experiencing a renewed interest in horror cinema. More precisely, teenagers were developing a strong appetite for the genre thanks to the expanding home video market. Besides the popular foreign titles, Dario Argento and Lucio Fulci films—albeit often released in pan-and-scan or even cut versions—were among the more frequently rented titles. Argento didn't waste time, and he and his collaborators immediately set to work on a sequel.

Shooting for *Dèmoni 2* started on May 19, 1986,[1] seven months after the release of the first chapter.

This time the budget was sensibly higher, and the script took several months to perfect. According to Bava, Sergio Stivaletti took part in some scriptwriting sessions[2] in order to better conceive the horrific moments and study the special creatures and effects in advance. Once again, the setting was a secluded one, a high-rise where the infection spreads—an idea which brings the movie closer to David Cronenberg's *Shivers* (and to the latter's uncredited inspiration, J.G. Ballard's novel *High-Rise*). Unlike *Dèmoni*, where tension rose from the forced cohabitation of various very different characters, here horror grows and develops within single familiar units, hinting at a sociological discourse that is rather disappointingly sketched. An obnoxious teenager is having a birthday party, a pregnant woman is left alone by her partner, a kid is home alone, a family is watching television, a prostitute is meeting a client, a group of bodybuilders are

Italian locandina for *Dèmoni 2 ... l'incubo ritorna* (1986, Lamberto Bava).

training in the gym. By having their monsters spread the contagion via TV screens, Argento and Bava unwillingly give their film a metaphoric significance which is much closer to Italian history: in September 1974, a small cable-TV, Telemilano, started broadcasting in the residential neighborhood of Milano 2, in Milan. In 1978, it was purchased by Silvio Berlusconi and became the founding stone of the mogul's TV empire, under the name Canale 5. It would change Italian history and culture forever.

As with the first chapter, the demons make the transition from a film to the real world, this time through a TV set. The nameless film-within-a-film is not the same as in *Dèmoni* but some sort of a replica, with different actors in similar roles and set in an abandoned industrial factory. Bava throws in a reference to his father's *La maschera del demonio*, as the demon's rebirth is caused by blood from a wound dripping over its face, as in the sequence of Asa's resurrection in the earlier film. Then, while Sally (Coralina Cataldi Tassoni) is watching the movie, a demon slowly advances to a close-up until it pushes the screen from behind and comes out of it. Bava renders effectively the transition by way of alternate point-of-view shots of Sally watching TV and a subjective shot of the demon from inside the television set, advancing toward her, an alternance which recalls *La maschera del demonio*'s celebrated opening. The effect looks very much like Rick Baker's famous "animated" television screen in *Videodrome*, but Bava maintained that he hadn't seen the movie[3]; he was very proud of the craftsman-like quality of the effect itself, worthy of his father. "Stivaletti and I had even thought of putting a TV set inside a bathtub with someone inside it ... then one night—because these ideas come at night—I came up with a Mario Bava–like trick: an empty TV set, a latex screen, a previously shot scene projected on it, and behind the screen somebody who, when the demon arrives in close-up, pushes it and comes out. That's my father's basic concept: the simpler the trick, the more effective the illusion."[4] The effect worked so well that what we see in the film is the first take. It was so good that Bava didn't have to shoot a second one.

As with the first episode, Argento didn't interfere in the shooting. "Dario, like few people, is one of those who persuades you to give your best ... and I must say that at the same time he fully respected my role as the director," Bava pointed out. "He showed up every once in a while, as were shooting, and watched the material like every producer does, but he never came over and said, 'Do this, do that.'"[5]

The director claimed that he liked *Dèmoni 2* even more than its predecessor, possibly also as a reaction to the critics, who were quite severe with the film. The makers stick to the repetition of a winning formula, and the script and direction go a long way to try and recreate the things that worked in the previous chapter, such as the shot of the demons advancing in slow-motion, their eyes glowing in the dark; but this time the plethora of ideas borrowed from other films become more tiresome, devoid of the wild boldness displayed by *Dèmoni*. For instance, the subplot about four types driving around town on their way to the birthday party is superfluous, and the use of pop and rock songs in the soundtrack—The Cult, Peter Murphy, Gene Loves Jezebel, Dead Can Dance—is debatable: The Smiths' "Panic" commenting a scene of people panicking is close to self-parody.

Even the direction leaves something to be desired. Besides some inexplicable out-of-focus scenes possibly shot by a second unit, the camera over-relies on close-ups of the drooling demons making faces and growling at the camera. With too many characters and too much buildup, the movie fails to reach the tension it aims for, and the most effective bits are isolated sight gags which are conceived and shot like showpieces in themselves, a bit in the way Argento does with his murder scenes. See, for instance, the opening sequence, where a menacingly-looking butcher's knife and a suspicious blood-red liquid turn out to be the tools of a pastry chef, and the birthday cake scene with Tassoni transforming after blowing on the candles. But the supposed centerpiece, with the pregnant Hannah (Nancy Brilli) pursued in her apartment by a grotesque-looking winged demon (which Bava and Stivaletti baptized "Menelik"[6]) erupted from a demonic child's chest, in a blatant rendition of the *Amelia* episode in Dan Curtis' *Trilogy of Terror* (1975), with the demon standing in for the Zuni doll, is let down by Stivaletti's unconvincing creature effects. The scene perhaps had an antecedent in Bava's unfilmed project *Gnomi*, which he had scripted in the early 1980s with Roberto Gandus and Alessandro Parenzo (see entry for *Macabro*).

The acting is worse too, with David Knight making for a very unimpressive hero. Two actors from the first film—Bobby Rhodes and Lino Salemme—turn up in different roles, and Rhodes (as a gym owner) once again plays the strong and charismatic leader of the survivors, while new cast members include Marina Loi (*Zombi 3*) and Michele Mirabella (*Tutti defunti … tranne i morti*, *L'aldilà*). Argento's daughter Asia turns up in a small role in her second film after the made-for-TV *Sogni e bisogni* (1985, Sergio Citti), and Antonio Cantafora (*Baron Blood*) plays her father.

Unlike the first film, this time Argento and Bava consciously toned down the gore to get a V.M.14 rating, not least because they were aware that a conspicuous part of the profits would come from television sales. Rather than to blood, they often resort to colored pus and slime (even corrosive, as in *Alien*), which gives the result a certain comic-book quality; even the lighting, with much of the movie taking place in partial darkness, was conceived in order not to show too much blood. Nevertheless, box-office grosses were slightly inferior to the original, with little over 1.1 billion *lire*. Like its predecessor, it was sold abroad and show theatrically in the major European countries (this time the BBFC passed it uncut) and overseas.

Dèmoni 2 was released theatrically less than a month after the debut of a new horror comic book, created by writer Tiziano Sclavi and centered on a self-styled "detective of the paranormal." The first issue of *Dylan Dog*, "L'alba dei morti viventi," came out in September 1986 and was a smash it. *Dylan Dog* comics were characterized by a postmodernist approach, for each story was filled to the brim with references and homages to (mostly) horror films and literature, and the mixture of splatter, humor, romanticism and philosophical antics proved to be irresistible. Within two years of its debut, sales sky-rocketed, with peaks of over 500,000 sales, and over the course of a few years it even outsold the classic Western comic *Tex*.

Significantly, Bava's original idea for the third part of the series was to shift the source of the contagion to paper. "It had to be a triptych: demons in movies, in television and on the printed page,"[7] namely a book whose pages, soaked with human blood, would give birth to the demons. But things took quite a different direction, and not by chance television had a big part in reshaping events. This time, however, no demons came out of a TV set, but rather a director—Bava himself—was sucked into it.

NOTES

1. According to Rome's Public Cinematographic Register. Alan Jones reports May 26 (Alan Jones, *Dario Argento. The Man, the Myths & the Magic* [Surrey: FAB Press, (2004/2012) 2016], 155).
2. Morsiani, "Conversazione con Lamberto Bava," 52.
3. *Ibid.*, 57.
4. Gomarasca, "Intervista a Lamberto Bava," 41.

5. *Ibid.*
6. Menelik was an infamous name for Italians. Menelik had been the first emperor of Ethiopia, and Menelik II (emperor of Ethiopia between 1889 and 1913) had declared war against Italy in late 1800, which led to the Italian army being defeated in the infamous battle of Adua, on March 1, 1896.
7. Gomarasca, "Intervista a Lamberto Bava."

1987

La croce dalle 7 pietre (Cross of the Seven Jewels)

D: Marco Antonio Andolfi. *S and SC*: Marco Antonio Andolfi; *DOP*: Carlo Poletti; *M*: Paolo Rustichelli (Ed. C.A.M.); *E*: Marco Antonio Andolfi; *PD, SD*: Massimo Corevi; *SE*: Eddy Endolf [Marco Antonio Andolfi]; *C*: Renato Doria; *AC*: Lucio Granelli, Andrea Doria; *SS*: Marisa Agostini; *MU*: Lamberto Marini, Angelo Mattei, Alfonso Cioffi; *Hair*: Claudia Bianchi; *CO*: Gilian; *W*: Liana Dentini, Anna Cirilli; *PM*: Amato Gabotti; *G*: Gualberto Franceschini, Michele Fedele; *El*: Aldo Mercenaro, Francesco Piccardi. *Cast*: Eddy Endolf [Marco Antonio Andolfi] (Marco Sartori), Annie Belle [Annie Brillard] (Maria), Gordon Mitchell (Black Mass Leader), Paolo Fiorino, Giorgio Ardisson (The Sicilian), Zaira Zoccheddu (Armisia, the Clairvoyant), Glauco Simonini, Giulio Massimini (Minister), Stefano Muré, Irmgard Konnertz, Marco Merlo, Giò Batta Merlo, Cristoforo Vetthen, Gino Lodero, Franco Altobelli, Mario Donatone, Piero Vivaldi (Totonno 'O Cafone), Umberto De Luca, Gino Serra, Antonietta Rinaldi. *PROD*: Compagnia di Prosa "Roma" G.C. Pictures; *PM*: Francesco Giorgi; *PS*: Tiziano Sarno; *Country*: Italy. Filmed in Rome, Zagarolo (Rome) and Naples. *Running time*: 83 minutes (m. 2270); re-edited version: 86 minutes. Visa n. 81656 (7.24.1986); *Rating*: V.M.14. *Release date*: 4.30.1987. *Distribution*: Compagnia Distribuzione Internazionale P.R. *Domestic gross*: n.a. *Also known as*: *Talisman* (1995 re-edit).

Bank employee Marco Sartori travels from Rome to Naples to meet his cousin Carmela, whom he hasn't seen in years. Soon after his arrival some thugs snatch a jeweled cross he carries on his neck. Marco and the police trace the thieves but find out they have already sold the jewel. The following day Marco discovers that the girl he met at the station was not Carmela, but her friend Elena. At a disco, Marco meets a girl called Maria, who falls for him. He goes to a fence, Totonno O' Cafone, in the hope of retrieving his cross, but finds out that the jewel has already been purchased by a Camorra boss, Don Raffaele Esposito. While Marco is questioning Totonno, midnight strikes: the young man undergoes a horrific transformation, turning into a werewolf, and kills the fence. It turns out Marco is the offspring of a member of a devilish cult impregnated by the demon Aborym, and that he is destined to turn into a werewolf every night at midnight; the cross is a talisman given to him by his mother, which can stop the transformation. Desperate, Marco continues his search and comes upon the presence of Don Raffaele Esposito, but the boss mistakenly believes him to be an undercover agent, investigating the Camorra traffics, and takes him prisoner. At midnight, the transformation takes place and Marco slaughters Don Raffaele and his men. He and Maria find out that the cross is in possession of a fortune teller, Armisia, who is also a prostitute: he turns into a monster again during intercourse with the woman and kills her. It is up to Maria to save Marco from his curse…

The Neapolitan-born Marco Antonio Andolfi had acting in his blood since the time he was a technician at the Singer sewing machines company: on Saturdays and Sundays he moonlighted as a thesp in a small theatrical company. After losing his job at Singer, Andolfi decided to take a leap and become an actor full-time, and founded the Roman-based Compagnia Roma, which then became Compagnia "Artisti Riuniti."

Andolfi's first steps in the movie industry proved more difficult. He claimed to have been just one step away from playing important roles in well-known films, such as Florestano Vancini's

Il delitto Matteotti (1973),[1] but this never happened, and he languished in obscurity, allegedly writing plays and photonovels for the *Lanciostory* magazine.

Eventually, Andolfi took the tiger by the tail and mounted his own feature film project. The inspiration for the story came from an autobiographical episode.

> One day I went to Naples wearing a pretty nice, valuable cross.... I was going to meet a girl, my fiancée.... And there was this snatch, which happened in a rather strange way. There were two bikes, you see, one passed near me and the passenger snatched the cross from my neck. I was about to react, but the young man passed the cross to the passenger of another bike. The second motorcycle fled. I pursued it ... I managed to reach the bike, hurl it to the ground and have those bastards arrested! From this theft the story of *La croce dalle 7 pietre* was born. I then soaked it with other imagery, drawn from my plays, comedies I wrote or comics.[2]

How Andolfi managed to get a 150 million *lire* financing from the State is still anyone's guess. However, *La croce dalle 7 pietre* benefited from the infamous article 28 of the 1965 cinema law (see entry for *Notturno con grida*) which guaranteed State loans for films with cultural or artistic aspirations. As a true Renaissance man, Andolfi undertook various tasks to carry his dream project home. In addition to writing the story and screenplay, he took care of the direction himself and played the starring role, hiding under the a.k.a. Eddy Endolf: "It was simply necessary so as not to show that I was the protagonist as well, otherwise the distributors would not even take me into consideration!"[3] He also did the editing, the special effects, and performed a couple of stunts which another actor was scared to attempt. Without any assistant director, he acted also as general manager and, for much of the shooting, as script supervisor. During post-production he was the dubbing director for both the Italian and English language versions, and even dubbed seven characters; he personally took care of the film's theatrical release (which apparently took place in Sicily, in the cities of Palermo and Trapani) and took the film to Milan's MIFED fair to sell it abroad. "Since it was my first movie and I came from the stage I was considered an incompetent, a fanatic able only to waste money. Everyone felt compelled to act like slackers, alluding, stealing and other pettiness ... they did not know that I had an iron fist, I was able to direct a thousand people like

a general. Many clashes occurred. Theater is a very harsh environment," the director recalled. "Then there was the Mafia of film distribution, dubbing, extras, and even the Mafia of development and printing labs. I had to do everything by myself, I was present everywhere ... there were also a few slaps and criminal complaints, it helped me that I had a powerful physique."[4]

Such a dedication to his work is truly remarkable, but worthy of a better cause. In addition to being Italy's first werewolf movie since *Lycanthropus* (1961, Paolo Heusch),[5] *La croce dalle 7 pietre* has a reputation of being one of the worst Italian movies ever made. It will take just a few minutes for the viewer to realize that such a title was no exaggeration. In the mind-bogglingly inept pre-credit sequence, set in what looks like a condo's basement, a cult leader (Gordon Mitchell) officiates some sort of Satanic ritual which consists mostly in several people in S/M outfits groping or whipping each other ("Your pain is my pleasure!"), and summons the demon Aborym, who looks like a man with a papier-mâché gorilla mask and fur like a Komondor dog. The rest of the film fares even worse, with atrocious acting and dialogue, goofy direction (with a perhaps unrivalled number of passers-by looking at the camera during exterior scenes), amateurish special effects and a plot which to call "demented" would be an understatement.

The script stems from an oft-employed Gothic cliché, a curse from the past which persecutes the hero. The theme is reminiscent of many other werewolf films, from *The Wolf Man* to the Waldemar Daninsky cycle, but Andolfi adds more to the recipe, as the supernatural element is bizarrely inserted into a sketchy crime story about the Neapolitan crime syndicate, the Camorra, which aims at exposing its ties with politicians. A subplot has a commissioner investigating the Camorra's involvement with a Senator, who maneuvers them for political assassinations and violent acts; "Tomorrow night Italy will tremble!" enthuses the commissioner's aide, after learning that many powerful names have been exposed. This climaxes in a dialogue confrontation between the commissioner and the politician, who rebukes the accusations by objecting that "there are so many congregations, or lodges, that nowadays like to put decent people into trouble," a reference to the 1981 "P2 Lodge" scandal that, if nothing else, underlines that Andolfi's story was several years old by the time it was filmed. Incidentally, the political-crime subplot is dropped at this point, and never mentioned again in the film. The happy ending features Andolfi (proudly wearing his cross on his chest) strolling with his girlfriend and their dog in St. Peter's Square, presumably on their way to a hearing with the Pope, under the accompaniment of a religious choir and with Jesus Christ's face (looking like it was taken from a holy picture) superimposed on the dome of St. Peter's Basilica—an image which gives an idea of Andolfi's delusions of depicting the eternal struggle between Good and Evil…

The special make-up effects consist primarily of a fur mask that covers the upper half of Andolfi's face: during his werewolf scenes he wears a pair of furry gloves and nothing else, except for a much welcome stretch of fur above his private parts. The central transformation scene brings the viewer back to the glorious days of Universal 1930s horror: for about 90 seconds, during a lingering close-up of Andolfi grinding his teeth, wolf-like fur appears progressively on his face via a series of cuts. The goriest bit has a man's face inexplicably melt down while the wolfman strangles him, while another scene shows a woman's face inflating and putrefying in real time under Aborym's demonic influence. Both effects were created by Lamberto Marini and Angelo Mattei, with decidedly poor results.

If Andolfi's acting leaves a lot to be desired, he is certainly not devoid of a good dose of narcissism. Despite his far from outstanding looks, all the girls fall for him in the blink of an eye ("Look at that hunk!" a couple of them comment as he sets foot in a disco). On top of that, he has a lengthy nude sex scene with a prostitute named Madame Armisia (Zaira Zoccheddu), which climaxes in Marco transforming into a monster and killing the woman *while* still humping her: Madame Armisia's moans of pleasure turn into horror and pain as the wolfman abundantly drools on her. Speaking of which, the author's view on the opposite sex is problematic to say the least: "I will forever have a negative memory of women. In *La croce dalle 7 pietre* there are many negative female characters and only a positive one…. 90% of the experiences I've had in Italy with women were negative. All of them sex-hungry, or duplicitous, or aiming at something, and so on. Treacherous. Evil."[6]

The Sardinian-born Zoccheddu—a hairdresser-turned-actress who became one of Italy's first porn starlets after her appearance in 1981's *Gocce d'amore*—is one of several familiar faces that turn up during the movie. The female lead, Annie Belle (then undergoing a bad period caused by alcohol abuse) did not remember anything about the film.[7] Gordon Mitchell and Giorgio Ardisson have minor roles, respectively as the cult leader, who in the end meets a grisly fate while Marco is freed from the curse (the melting effect achieved via drawing exposed parts of skull over his face), and as the "Sicilian," an Italian-American Mafia boss. "Mitchell and Ardisson were professionals," Andolfi recalled. "They knew better, and they soon realized that I could improve upon them. They were always punctual, obedient, professional, although their scenes could be shot in no more than two or three takes."[8]

The rating board gave *La croce dalle 7 pietre*.[9] a V.M.14 certificate after a minor cut (14 seconds) during the scene between Marco and

Italian poster for *La croce dalle 7 pietre* (1987, Marco Antonio Andolfi). The tagline promises "Mistero, intrigo, amore, orrore" (Mystery, intrigue, love, horror).

Armisia—quite surprisingly, given Andolfi's insistence on demented sex encounters between women and monsters, also in the flashback that graphically depicts Marco's mother mating with the grotesque demon Aborym. The movie disappeared almost immediately and turned up only several years later among collectors, where it acquired an underground cult fame under the phony title *L'uomo lupo contro la camorra* (The Wolf Man vs. the Camorra).

In 1995 Andolfi assembled a re-edited version, called *Talisman*, with money from foreign investors. The new edit partially reshaped the story, turning Marco Sartori's curse into a cosmic tale of evil. The prologue opens in the year 1962 with a line that reads as follows: "In the heart of Africa, a precious talisman was kept, which radiated well-being. One day it was stolen, and all over the world famines, war and disaster started." The new edit features shot-on-video scenes of African tribal dances taken from some newsreels and documentaries, plus footage from the 1990s Balkan wars, as well as excerpts from other films (a snake coming out of a skeleton's mouth comes from *The Serpent and the Rainbow*) mixed with the original black mass prologue. Accordingly, Andolfi could even use some outtakes given to him by the producers of *The NeverEnding Story*. An epilogue dated 1999 shows someone putting away the cross in its case, followed by more documentary footage (windy mountains and tropical fish swimming in the ocean) and African dances, hinting that (perhaps) the world is now at peace.

In the new opening credits, Mitchell is credited under his real name Charles Pendleton (misspelled as "Pendelthon"), while Annie Belle becomes "Annie Silvie"; the music is credited to "Jay Horus and Raphael Pike" thus confirming the rumors that have Horus as an a.k.a. of Paolo Rustichelli (who scored the original version); the direction is credited to "Allan Fleming." The film is listed as a "United Artists Company Production," with "Seven Stars Pictures" as co-producer.[10] *Talisman* was distributed abroad and apparently gained some cult following in Japan.

But Andolfi felt there was more to tell about his filmic alter ego. Twenty years later he wrote, directed, starred in, etcetera, the 30-minute featurette *Riecco Aborym*, which recycles footage from the previous film(s) and is, if possible, even more racist and misogynist—not to mention inept. Andolfi the actor gets all of three distinct mentions in the credits: as "Eddy Endolf

senior" he is his older self, whereas as "Eddy Endolf Junior" he appears in the footage from *La croce delle 7 pietre*. Finally, he is credited as "Marco Antonio Andolfi" for the role of Aborym. The author's ideas and delusions are well expressed in the following excerpt from a 2008 interview:

> *Riecco Aborym* can be seen as a short film, a TV movie, but also as a fiction documentary. It was born a bit like *La croce dalle 7 pietre*. I went to Kiev, looking for a job; I had to script and direct about 20 films, and I was in talks with the local State television. There was a woman involved and … I was kidnapped. All this happened to me in early 2007, and I wrote the script for the small fiction documentary some time later. I asked for a financing to IMAIE[11] and I built the movie around my misadventure—to be kidnapped and betrayed by the woman who went to bed with me and seemed mad with love, and who at the end even wanted to kill me. Instead of the Ukranians, I put Romanians in my film, also to give the story an actual feel, which is not so far removed from the facts you hear every day—of Romanians sneaking into houses and stealing everything, because they are like night wolves. And then, she, who looked so much in love, and is supposed to have undergone so many misfortunes with Eddy, because of the cross, the evil, the Romanians etc., at the end it is she who betrays me.[12]

NOTES

1. "My starring role in *Il delitto Matteotti* was 100% sure. Then Franco Nero fell in love with the role, and he played Matteotti. That was a film where I played the whole second part, and in the movie, everyone talked about me [as Matteotti]." Luca Ruocco, "Riassumendo Marco Antonio Andolfi," *Rapporto Confidenziale* #10, December 2008, 21.

2. *Ibid.*

3. Luca Ruocco, "Discutendo con Marco Antonio Andolfi [Eddy Endolf] dell'importanza di avere uno pseudonimo e delle molteplici forme del demonio," *Rapporto Confidenziale* #10, 23.

4. Marco Antonio Andolfi interviewed in CineWalk OfShame (https://cinewalkofshame.wordpress.com/tag/eddy-endolf-intervista/).

5. Not counting, of course, Claudio Fragasso's *Monster Dog*, a.k.a *Leviatán* produced with Spanish funds by Eduard Sarlui and filmed in Spain.

6. Ruocco, "Discutendo con Marco Antonio Andolfi [Eddy Endolf] dell'importanza di avere uno pseudonimo e delle molteplici forme del demonio," 24.

7. Manlio Gomarasca and Davide Pulici, *99 donne. Stelle e stelline del cinema italiano* (Milan: MediaWord Production, 1999), 73–74.

8. Marco Antonio Andolfi interviewed in CineWalk OfShame.

9. The official ministerial papers and the on-screen title list the film as *La croce dalle 7 pietre*, while the posters spelled it as *La croce dalle sette pietre*.

10. Here are the rest of the bogus credits (misspellings

included): The cast features Paul Travis, Jean Louis Serrault, Susan Shadix, Nicholas Muré, John Hicks, Elena Patnova; Casting by Wendy Zmann and Gerarda Monie; Executive producer: Mark Jess Medawar; Editor: Anthony Schwartz; Production designer: Jhon Charris, Jr.; Director of Photography Ed Charters; Written by Alan Fleming and Richard Garris; Produced by Alice Wess, Sam Reeves.

11. IMAIE (Istituto mutualistico per la tutela degli artisti interpreti ed esecutori) is an institution which protects the rights of artists and performers of musical, cinematographic and audiovisual works that are reused or broadcast on radio, television or any other user entity. IMAIE's activity is to collect, on behalf of the performers, the proceeds due to them following the reuse of their works, and, after identifying those entitled to compensation, distribute the proceeds collected.

12. Ruocco, "Riassumendo Marco Antonio Andolfi," 22.

Spettri (Specters)

D: Marcello Avallone. *S*: Marcello Avallone, Andrea Purgatori, Maurizio Tedesco; *SC*: Marcello Avallone, Andrea Purgatori, Dardano Sacchetti, Maurizio Tedesco; *DOP*: Silvano Ippoliti (Kodak); *M*: Lele Marchitelli, Danilo Rea (Ed. Gatta Ci Cova); *E*: Adriano Tagliavia; *ArtD*: Carmelo Agate; *CO*: Paola Collacciani Bonucci, Maurizio Marchitelli; *MU*: Dante Trani; *SPFX*: Sergio Stivaletti; *AD*: Vivalda Vigorelli; *SS*: Daniela Tonti; *C*: Enrico Sasso, Ettore Corso, Enrico Fontana; *AE*: Graziella Zita, Delia Apolloni; *SO*: Davide Magara; *B*: Stefano Rossi; *Hair*: Maria Fiocca, Claudia Reymond Shone; *SPFXAss*: Barbara Morosetti; *ChEl*: Sergio Spila; *El*: Marcello Cardarelli, Franco Cardarelli; *KG*: Mario Occhioni; *G*: Roberto Anzellotti, Roberto Rosati; *W*: Emanuela Curatolo; *Press*: Anna Rosa Morri; *SOE*: Cinesound; *SP*: Pennoni & Serto; *Mix*: Danilo Moroni. *Cast*: John Pepper (Marcus), Katrine Michelsen (Alex), Donald Pleasence (Prof. Lasky), Massimo De Rossi (Matteo), Riccardo De Torrebruna (Andrea), Lavinia Grizi (Barbara), Riccardo Parisio Perrotti (Gasparri), Giovanni Bilancia, Matteo Gazzolo (Mike), Laurentina Guidotti (Maria), Erna Schurer [Emma Costantino] (Catacomb Guide), Giovanni Tamberi (Gino). *PROD*: Maurizio Tedesco for Reteitalia S.p.A. (Milan), Trio Cinema e Televisione S.r.l. (Rome); *GM*: Eliseo Boschi; *PM*: Marco Donati; *UM*: Filippo Campus, Giovanni Ligato; *ADM*: Gabriella Nardi. *Country*: Italy. Filmed at R.P.A. Elios Studios (Rome). *Running time*: 92 minutes (m. 2523). Visa n. 82289 (2.12.1987); *Rating*: V.M. 14; *Release dates*: 5.7.1987 (Italy), 10.17.1989 (USA); *Distribution*: D.M.V.; *Domestic gross*: n.a. *Also known as*: *Espectros* (Spain), *Spectre* (France), *Specters—Mächte des Bösen* (West Germany), *Catacomb* (Sweden).

Note: the song "Never Change" (P.L. Germini—A. Cicco) is performed by Blue Visconti.

Rome. A team of archaeologists led by professor Lasky discover an ancient tomb, protected by an ominous inscription which alludes to an evil force being buried in it. Soon strange events follow, which affect not only the archaeologists, but also those who are close to them. Alex, a female singer and the fiancée of Lasky's assistant, Marcus, experiences frightening visions. Several people fall victim to the evil demon: a night club owner, a member of Lasky's team, a gay antiquarian and his right-hand man. Alex is abducted by the monster in her bed. After discovering that the bones buried in the tomb are not human, Marcus and Lasky descend underground, to finally face the monster...

Marcello Avallone's fourth feature film came a full decade after his third work, *Cugine mie* (1976), an erotic comedy which underwent lots of trouble with the censors.[1] The director explained that the idea of toying with the horror genre had come to him several years earlier, during a work trip to the United States:

> It was just 1980. I was there because Francis Ford Coppola's company Zoetrope was producing a documentary on new American cinema, together with Marina Cervi, who represented RAI. Doing this work, I immersed myself in the air that you breathed there, and I understood how much this kind of cinema—let's call it horror, even though I don't know if we can really call it horror—met the public's taste.... I realized how strong an impact it had in America. By then, almost all the horror movies that were made there were "B" pictures, but not in a derogatory sense.... So, I came back to Italy with the idea of making a horror movie.[2]

In the following years Avallone returned to the genre with a three-part TV program called *Il cinema della paura*, co-directed with Patrizia Pistagnesi and broadcast in November 1986 on Rai Tre. The show included excerpts from horror films and interviews with filmmakers, including Avallone's old mentor Riccardo Freda. In the meantime, Avallone's project was taking shape thanks to the help of Maurizio Tedesco, brother of actress Paola Tedesco, a former editor and assistant director, and an aspiring producer; ten years younger than Avallone, he shared the same vision as the director and was willing to take risks with a genre picture aimed at foreign markets. Avallone wrote the script with journalist Andrea Purgatori, a young reporter of the *Corriere della Sera* newspaper and the author of important reports on such themes as the Lebanon war and the Ustica plane crash (the latter became the subject of the 1991 movie *Il muro di gomma*, directed by Marco Risi). Luckily for Avallone and Tedesco, they joined forces with an important partner, Silvio Berlusconi's Reteitalia, which by then had entered steadily in the film production business.

Spettri was shot in nine weeks, directly in English. The male lead, John Randolph Pepper, the son of the noted *Newsweek* reporter Curtis Bill Pepper,[3] was an American in Rome: at just 5 he had played Caesarion in Mankiewicz's *Cleopatra* (1963), and he became a painter and a photographer. Over the years he had worked as assistant director on such works as *The World According to Garp* (1982, George Roy Hill), the TV mini-series *The Winds of War* (1983) and *Ghostbusters* (1984), and in 1986 he directed the English version of Eduardo De Filippo's stage play *Le voci dentro* (a.k.a. *Inner Voices*) at the Spoleto Festival in Charleston.

Obviously chosen more because of his fluent English than his acting skills in what would be his one and only leading role, Pepper was paired with the 21-year-old Katrine Michelsen, formerly Miss Denmark 1984; the Danish actress had become a starlet of Italian erotic cinema after Salvatore Samperi's *La bonne* (1986), where she played alongside Florence Guérin and amply displayed her stunning body, something she also does in Avallone's film. *Spettri* did not bring good fortune to the beautiful Michelsen. Around the same time, she starred in Sergio Bergonzelli's erotic thriller *Tentazione* (1987) and played a role in Lamberto Bava's sexy *giallo Le foto di Gioia* (1987) but her career would soon wane: one of the last roles in her scarce filmography would be in Lars von Trier's *Idioten* (1998). She died of bone cancer in 2009, at only 42.

Donald Pleasence, a recurring presence in Italian horror movies of the period, was the required "name" actor for export sales; as prof. Lasky (a tongue-in-cheek nod to the founder of Paramount Pictures?) he does very little besides looking worried and delivering insipid dialogue. Avallone even cast Erna Schurer, the star of his weird Gothic yarn *Un gioco per Eveline* (1971), in a small part. It would be the actress' last movie role.

Despite his name being featured in the credits, Dardano Sacchetti's participation to the screenplay was little more than nominal, as the screenwriter himself explained. In Sacchetti's words, Tedesco, Avallone and Purgatori were

three friends who had big motorbikes and went on trips together every Sunday. They had written the script together and believed in it a lot. Mediaset [Author's note: actually Reteitalia], who financed the enterprise, believed less in it, and Mediaset imposed me as film doctor ... the script didn't work well, but it had a fascinating idea: the mysterious subterranean Rome, the mithrea, the dovecotes, the sewers, the underground of the Colosseum, etc. We discussed, even in a spirited way, for more than a week, than one day they told me: "This is our film, we believe in it, and we want to make it this way." ... They said: "We're paying you all your fee but leave us our movie."[4]

Avallone's idea was to make a horror film deeply tied with Italy's ancient history. "I had two cities in mind to shoot something like that: Rome and Naples. Naples would have been perfect, because it has two faces. Above you have the serenades, pizza, the Vesuvio, and below there are strange and obscure realities. Rome was perfect as well: above there are the churches, the alleys, but then there are also the subterraneans, the long underground tunnels. There is the shadow of an ancient Rome which does not exist anymore, terrible and bloody."[5] The concept was not new: Rome's past as the subject for a Gothic story had been the core of the immensely successful TV mini-series *Il segno del comando* (1971), among others.

In interviews of the period, the director was nitpicking when labeling his project, perhaps as a way to win the critics' bias toward the genre: "*Spettri* is not a horror film. I'd rather define it a movie about fear, and the borderline, populated with shadows, between Good and Evil."[6] But, as the title suggests, Avallone & Co. looked at the success of the *Dèmoni* diptych, and tried to repeat the same mélange of old-style Gothic and new trends. In fact, the look of the film is heavily influenced by Lamberto Bava's work—notice the shots of people walking toward the camera lighted in silhouettes.

Moreover, Avallone liberally spiced the tale with references to classic and contemporary horror cinema. An elaborately deceptive sequence featuring Michelsen—wearing a stunning long red dress—falling prey to a monster emerging from a lake, which looks just like the Gillman in *The Creature from the Black Lagoon* (1954, Jack Arnold), turns out to be a horror-themed music video. Later on, Michelsen's character is menaced by an eerie-looking shadow whose features—pointed ears, long spiky fingernails—recall Max Schreck's vampire in Murnau's *Nosferatu* (1922). The hero's descent in the catacombs followed by his colleagues via a computer monitor, to an unexplored tomb whose walls look almost like organic, bone-like matter, recalls Ridley Scott's *Alien* rather than *L'etrusco uccide ancora* (1972). Finally, the bit with Michelsen's character hallucinating and seeing a snake instead of a microphone seems lifted out of the *A Nightmare on Elm Street* series—ditto for the scene where she is swallowed in her bed by the demon.

Avallone claimed he wanted to focus on "this mysterious city protected by darkness which lives beneath our feet and which maybe feels in its restless soul the echo of the urban degradation and of our malaise."[7] Indeed, the opening shots—the Colosseum, the Imperial Forum, a fountain with a monstrous stone head, menacingly lit by the water reflections—capture effectively the idea of an arcane, centuries-old Rome. The script ties it effectively with the scenes of men at work in the Rome underground—a nod, perhaps involuntary, to Fellini's *Roma* (1972)—and to archaeologists who study an ancient Roman burial site and find a portal with the ominous sign "*Hic vocatum atque non advocatum malum aderit*" ("Here, either summoned or not, evil will manifest itself"). "It is full of mystery, it's magic ... and it never stops fascinating me," says a character about the Eternal City.

But after such a promising beginning, things rapidly go downhill. Despite the many cinephile references, there is little tension in the movie. An early manifestation of evil, as a young couple are trapped in the catacombs amid rats and skeletons, is accompanied by naive lighting and wind effects that ape those seen in U.S. horror films of the period, but on the cheap. Not only is the plot so bare-bones that very little happens throughout, but the characters too are stereotyped if not laughable ciphers, such as the blind guy who, of all things, works as a guide in the catacombs ("One does not need eyes to find the way in these places dominated by darkness"). Blindness, in typical horror movie tradition (see *Manhattan Baby*) is the punishment for those, like professor Lasky, who dare look into the abyss.

When the evil forces finally manifest after a half-hour buildup, *Spettri* becomes a supernatural body count movie, in the vein of the current trends, although the creative deaths feature little blood and gore. The first one, the demise of the night club owner who ends up with his throat slashed by a glass door with a tiger drawn on it, borrows from the ending of Cornell Woolrich's novel *Night Has a Thousand Eyes*, while the murder of the gay antiquarian under the notes of Umberto Giordano's opera *Andrea Chenier* has a certain Argento-like quality to it, and features the film's goriest moment, but the other deaths are disappointingly lame, with elaborate build-ups to little ensuing effect. Sacchetti recalled Avallone's refusal to push the pedal on graphic violence: "He was in love with the scene where the specter embraces the girl and delicately pulls her underground, with no blood, no nothing. He liked it that way and would shoot it that way."[8] The prosthetic F/X created by Sergio Stivaletti are reduced to very little: a rubber-looking claw which rips apart a face, a head smashed and the long-awaited demon which finally manifests in the last ten minutes and rips somebody's heart out—too little, too late.

Given the decent budget (of one billion and a half *lire*)[9] and the use of such stunning natural locations as the Roman catacombs, a number of scenes have an atmospheric quality, heightened by the use of the Steadicam, and Avallone's direction is a step above the cheap Italian B-pictures of the period. Still, he does little to enhance the story. He makes ample use of close-ups and quick cuts, American-style, sometimes with goofy results: take the scene where the archaeologists prepare for an expedition, patterned over many similar moments in American cinema (*Rambo: First Blood Part II*, *Aliens*, etc.) with details of hands tying shoes, wearing jackets, closing belts or wearing earphones, which feels almost comically bombastic. Likewise, Silvano Ippoliti's photography sports a passably international look, but at the same time it feels banal and *déjà-vu*. In this sense, *Spettri* is indicative of the growing loss of personality of Italian cinema during the course of the decade.

The director was moderately happy with the film, albeit critical of himself: "When I see some scenes I feel ashamed, and if I were to reshoot them now I'd make them completely different, but this is normal. I find it absolutely decent and pleasant.... The special effects stand up well, considering that by then everything was done live on camera."[10]

Spettri was released on May 7, 1987, with a V.M.14 rating.[11] Despite being heavily publicized in the media, it did mediocre business in Italy and was panned by the critics. The *Corriere della Sera* reviewer blamed the "scarce internal logic" of the plot, "engulfed with unresolved ideas," and added: "All this could have had a sense, were it playfully treated. But Marcello Avallone's direction—undecided on which tone to adopt, uncertain between real or laughable scares, distressing in its attempt to dilate tensions that don't go off—has made a great mess of it."[12] Foreign sales were satisfying, though, and the film circulated worldwide in home video. A script for a sequel was deposited at Italy's SIAE on May 27, penned by Sacchetti, Purgatori, Tedesco and Avallone and bearing several titles: *Spettri 2*, *Il ritorno degli spettri*, *La vendetta degli spettri*, and *Spettri parte seconda*. But it never materialized.

On the same day, Purgatori, Tedesco and Avallone deposited the script for *Maya*, which would be Avallone's next film, again produced by Reteitalia. It was an even more ambitious project, a story set in Mexico which blended exotic adventure and the esoteric, with an opening quote by Carlos Castaneda and sparse Gothic elements (namely, references to the threshold between this world and the beyond, as in *L'aldilà*) to fortify a narrative structure very similar to *Spettri*. But the script was just as confused, with some "creative deaths" (a guy crashed by a car as in *Christine*; a woman having a bath who knocks her head against the faucets and the bathtub's edge; another ravaged by fish hooks, as in *Hellraiser*) and unlikely characters, including a hero

(played by the Australian Pete Phelps) as bland as the one in *Spettri*. *Maya* turned out a box-office flop upon its release in 1989.

NOTES

1. Originally titled *Noi siamo le vergini dai candidi manti…* (We Are the Virgins with the Candid Mantles…), it was rejected by the rating board as obscene. It was re-edited and resubmitted under the new title *Arrivan le vergini dai candidi manti* (Here Come the Virgins with the Candid Mantles) and approved with a V.M.18 rating. However, the distributor refused to release it and the producer was forced to change the title yet again.

2. Eugenio Ercolani, "Tra cinema e cavalli: Intervista a Marcello Avallone," *PaperBlog*, January 17, 2014 (http://it.paperblog.com/tra-cinema-e-cavalli-intervista-a-marcello-avallone-2144496/).

3. Lino Lombardi, "All'Olimpo la tribù delle tenebre," *Corriere della Sera*, October 4, 1986.

4. Dardano Sacchetti interviewed, in www.davinotti.com (http://www.davinotti.com/index.php?option=com_content&task=view&id=64&Itemid=79).

5. Ercolani, "Tra cinema e cavalli: Intervista a Marcello Avallone.."

6. Giovanna Grassi, "Paura nella Roma sotterranea," *Corriere della Sera*, November 8, 1986.

7. *Ibid.*

8. Dardano Sacchetti interviewed, in www.davinotti.com.

9. r.s., "L'incubo è "underground,"" *Corriere della Sera*, April 5, 1987.

10. Ercolani, "Tra cinema e cavalli: Intervista a Marcello Avallone."

11. It was subsequently re-examined by the board on April 9, 1992, in light of the Mammì law, and a new visa (n. 86950) was emitted, with the movie judged suitable for all audiences.

12. L.A. [Leonardo Autera], "Terrore tra le rovine della Città eterna," *Corriere della Sera*, May 9, 1987.

1988

Blood Delirium (Delirio di sangue)
(*Blood Delirium*)

D: Peter Storage [Sergio Bergonzelli]. *S and SC*: Sergio Bergonzelli; *DOP*: Raffaele Mertes (Telecolor); *M*: Nello Ciangherotti (Ed. Scogliera); *E*: Vincenzo Di Santo; *SE*: Raffaele Mertes, Delio Catini, Giovanni Corridori, Antonio Corridori; *AD*: Pierstefano Marangoni; *AC*: Stefano Pugini; *MU*: Guerrino Todero; *Hair*: Silvana Locatelli; *APD*: Massimo Cerquini; *ASD*: Giovanni Passanisi; *Mix, SOE*: Walter Polini; *W*: Giovanna Russu; *Color Technician*: Pasquale Cuzzupoli. *Cast*: John Phillip Law (Saint Simon), Gordon Mitchell (Hermann), Brigitte Christensen (Sybille Leclerc/Christine), Marco Di Stefano (Gérard Goupta), Olga [Olinka] Hardiman (Corinne),

Lucia Prato (Yvonne), Ezio Prosperi (Gallery Manager). *PROD*: Scino [Mushi] Glam for Cine Decima (Rome); *PM*: Filippo Campus; *PSe*: Antonio Mammolotti; *ADM*: Angela Melis. *Country*: Italy. Filmed at the Castle Piccolomini in Balsorano, and at Incir-De Paolis Studios (Rome). *Running time*: 90 minutes (m. 2464). Visa n. 83858 (8.8.1988); *Rating*: V.M.14. *Release date*: not released theatrically; *Distribution*: Azzurra (Home Video—Italy). *Also known as*: *Delírio Sangriento* (Brazil).

Note: Paintings by Maria Alborghetti, Marenza Azzopardi, Carlo Cirilli, Janos Gilevic, Livia Marcellini Gaddi, Giuseppina Laura Tarantola; Sculptures by Angelo Pizzicaroli.

Shocked by the death of his wife Christine,

a painter named Saint Simon loses not only his inspiration, but his mental balance as well. With the help of his wicked butler Hermann, Saint Simon even exhumes the skeleton of the deceased spouse. Then, at an exhibition of his works, he meets Sybille, a young pianist who is a dead ringer for Christine. Struck by the resemblance, Saint Simon invites her to his castle to try and revive his creative impulse, but to no avail. But the painter recovers his inspiration in an unexpected way: Hermann, attempting to rape a young girl, kills her, and Saint Simon finds out that human blood is just the right color he needed for his paintings. He sends Hermann to kidnap Sybille's friend Corinne, who is then drained of her blood and murdered. Sybille, now imprisoned in the castle by the two madmen, is likely to become Saint Simon's next target, but her fiancé Gérard arrives to save her just in time.

Blood Delirium, Sergio Bergonzelli's penultimate work, represented his first stab at the Gothic horror genre in a directorial career spawning three decades between Italy, Turkey, Greece, France and Spain, and within such diverse genres as adventure, pirate films, westerns, spy stories, *gialli*, erotic documentaries, sleazy comedies, and out-and-out hardcore. After dabbling with porn for the best part of the decade, the director had returned to mainstream filmmaking with the erotic thriller *Tentazione*, produced by Enzo Gallo and starring Katrine Michelsen, and *Blood Delirium* represented an attempt to hold on to genre filmmaking, by then waning and destined primarily to foreign consumption.

"I wrote that movie with Fabio De Agostini, a profound and very commercial author, aiming to make a shocking film,"[1] the director explained. De Agostini, whose name does not feature in the credits, had collaborated with Bergonzelli on several scripts, such as *Silvia e l'amore* (1968), *Le 10 meraviglie dell'amore* (1969) and *Nelle pieghe della carne* (1970). Besides his work as assistant director for the likes of Mario Bonnard, Joseph Losey, Sergio Grieco and Giacomo Gentilomo, De Agostini's main claim to fame had been the controversial erotic Nazi flick *Le lunghe notti della Gestapo* (1977).

Working on a low budget, Bergonzelli nevertheless managed to cast a rather prestigious has-been, John Phillip Law, for the role of the mad painter Saint Simon, who believes himself to be the reincarnation of Van Gogh. Law (who dubs himself in the film) accepted the role

mainly for the chance of working with his good friend Gordon Mitchell, who had helped him get started in Italian cinema. Mitchell had been in Bergonzelli's *Diamond Connection* (1982), and the director said of him: "He had a face that didn't have to be interpreted."

The rest of the cast was a mixed bunch. French porn actress Olinka Hardiman, who had turned up in *Tentazione* in one of her rare non-hardcore roles, had a small part which nevertheless allowed her to show her breathtaking body. The lead, Danish-born Brigitte Christensen, was a weird casting choice: born in 1957, Christensen was a stage actress who had established herself in Italy in 1983, when she founded the company Teatro della Luna with Marco Di Stefano and became the artistic director of a theater festival in Amandola, in the Marche region, based on the interaction between the audience, the townspeople and the artists.[2] Di Stefano also ended up in the movie, playing the heroine's pony-tailed fiancé, who earns his living rather improbably as a test pilot of fast cars and helicopters. Bergonzelli even managed to shoot in a pre-existing main location—the 13th century castle of Pereto, in the Abruzzo region—a typical production gimmick in tune with the common practices of 1960s horror films shot entirely in ancient manors.

The plot for *Blood Delirium* gathers characters and archetypes of the golden age of the Gothic and revolves around the themes of the double and reincarnation. The mad artist Saint Simon is obsessed with the woman he loved, Christine, who was also his muse, and whose death deprived him of his artistic inspiration. When he meets a young female pianist, who is the mirror image of his deceased wife, he jumps at the opportunity to keep her with him in his castle. The script plays on the idea that in every person there are two personalities, two halves who, even though separate, are linked by a spiritual bond: "This is what we are, two in one flame," Christine's spirit tells her other half, Sybille. In addition to that, Bergonzelli added an element that brought the story closer to H.G. Lewis' *Color Me Blood Red* (1965), as Saint Simon finds out that human blood gives "life" to his creations. "The most precious thing in the world is blood, and the painter of my story thinks that if he can paint with blood he can obtain a special communicativeness."[3]

Bergonzelli's take on the Gothic genre is filled with gratuitous nudity and gore, with an insistence on the grotesque and the excess that recalls extreme adults-only comics such as *Oltretomba* and *Terror*—all of this amply peppered with jaw-dropping dialogue. "I've sacrificed philosophy on the altar of entertainment, transferring my personal convictions in the movie,"[4] the director claimed. True to his philosophy studies, he threw in plenty of Pindaric flights, starting with Saint Simon's opening monologue, as the artist contemplates the sunset from the ramparts of his castle and is upset by the totality of the universe. "Emptiness. Overflowing emptiness. The presence of the infinite. Eyes without dimension. Wings of invisible light. The restless eye of the spirit dispels the arcane, glimpsing future fragments—always present, never seen." And this is just the beginning.

Sometimes one cannot decide whether Bergonzelli's tongue is in his cheek or not. Saint Simon's remark after he discovers that a soon-to-be-victim is about to pay him a visit ("Let her come.... I have just finished my color!") makes one suspect it is; and yet the hopelessly would-be-poetic tone of the dialogue suggests the opposite, with such lines as "The future is as real as the present—except that it exists in a dimension that eyes cannot see." In addition to that, the lack of means paves the way for the ridiculous: the French setting is phony, Saint Simon's paintings are obviously the work of different artists with very different styles, and in a scene, he listens to Sybille's piano concerto performance on a cheap, small boom box. The only redeeming quality of many scenes is Raffaele Mertes' cinematography. The talented d.o.p. would soon turn up in bigger productions, such as Michele Soavi's *La setta* (1991), Carlo Carlei's *La corsa dell'innocente* (1991) and Dario Argento's *Trauma* (1993). In the late 1990s he moved on to direction and worked exclusively for the small screen.

Though not a bad actress, the angular-jawed Christensen lacks the looks and physique of Gothic heroines, but she soldiers on admirably, given the material she must work with. John Phillip Law's hammy performance, all rolling eyes and frantic brushstrokes while creating his masterpieces, is a hoot, but Gordon Mitchell steals the show as Saint Simon's malevolent, sex-crazed butler-cum-factotum Hermann. "Son of the devil, but innocuous," the painter says of him, a debatable understatement indeed. In an early scene we see Hermann indulge in passionate lovemaking with the still warm body of the dead lady of the house—

"Sweet mistress, I loved you in silence..." he mourns—while his master is madly playing the organ, and later Hermann's sexual escapades provide the film's goriest bits, as he supplies Saint Simon with the blood of his victims and then gets rid of the bodies, which he either hacks to pieces or gives as food to his Doberman Pinscher dog (aptly named Satan), saving the best cuts for himself, cooked rare and with just a little bit of salt.

The climax must be seen to be believed. All hell breaks loose in the castle, as Christine's invisible spirit takes revenge on her husband: "You think you are Van Gogh? Now you are!," her voice announces, cutting off the man's ear. Then the castle crumbles down to pieces like the house of Usher in Poe's story, and Bergonzelli vainly attempts to overcome the shoestring budget with slow-motion shots of Saint Simon falling around, apparently slammed by invisible forces. The sight of Hermann submerged under Styrofoam columns and capitals incongruously raining down from the ceiling looks almost like a retribution for Mitchell's past as a *peplum* icon. The final image of servant and master holding hands in the moment of death plays like a homosexual riff on the closing shot of *Duel in the Sun* (1946).

Blood Delirium was released directly to home video in Italy, in a version devoid of the goriest bits, such as the sight of Hermann extracting the viscera from a victim's chest cavity. Over the years, it gained some sort of a cult status as an example of what Michael J. Weldon described as "psychotronic movies."[5] Those involved had a far less favorable opinion of it: "That one, yes, is extremely bad. When my Italian agent found out that I had starred in it, he practically exploded, 'John, you can't make movies like that! Don't you take yourself seriously?'" Law admitted.[6]

Bergonzelli directed only one more film, *Malizia oggi* (1990), featuring future porn actress Valentine Demy. He died in 2002.

NOTES

1. Massimo F. Lavagnini, "Sergio Bergonzelli. Una cinepresa in pugno al diavolo," *Nocturno Cinema* #2, December 1996, 77.
2. r.s., "Nelle case della gente il festival di Amandola," *Corriere della Sera*, August 23, 1989.
3. Lavagnini, "Sergio Bergonzelli. Una cinepresa in pugno al diavolo," 77.
4. *Ibid.*, 78.
5. Weldon described psychotronic movies as "the ones

traditionally ignored or ridiculed by mainstream critics at the time of their release: horror, exploitation, action, science fiction, and movies that used to play in drive-ins or inner-city grindhouses." *Psychotronic Video*, #1, 1989, 2.

6. Carlos Aguilar and Anita Haas, *John Phillip Law. Diabolik Angel* (Pontevedra/Bilbao: Scifiworld/Quatermass, 2008), 190.

Il bosco 1 (Evil Clutch)

D: Andrea Marfori. *S and SC*: Andrea Marfori; *DOP*: Marco Isoli; *M*: Adriano Maria Vitali (Ed. CAM); *E*: Andrea Marfori, Fabrizio Polverari; *PD*: Giovanni Albertini; *SPFX*: Studio Arte Fare [Bruno Biagi, Paolo Forti], Gianni Albertini; *AD*: Giulio Calcinari; *C*: Paolo Sanna; *AC*: Paolo Ferrari; *Steadicam*: Pippo Ciliberto, Vachi Mallaby; *ArtD*: Lisa Nisio; *SD*: Sebastiano De Caro, Simona Migliotti; *CO*: Giovanni Albertini, Lisa Nisio, Daniela C. Fava; *2ndUC*: Bruno Maltese; *AE*: Angelo Mignogna; *SP*: Stefano Carofei; *GA*: Stani Galasso; *BB*: Giovanni Galasso; *KG*: Sergio Fiori; *G*: Marco Due; *B*: Angelo Colone; *SO*: Sandro Aliscioni, Bruno Pupparo, Massimo Tucceri; *Soundtrack*: Luciano Anzellotti, Massimo Anzellotti, Dario Pasquale, Attilio Gizzi; *Music recording mix*: Marco Streccioni; *Mix*: Danilo Sterbini; *Dialogue coach*: Teresa Pase; *Screenplay dialogue*: Dinah Rogers; *SS*: Roberta Guastella, Silvia Nelvina. *2nd Unit*: *C*: Bruno Maltese; *AC*: Claudio Schiano; *GA*: Stefano Alessi; *BB*: Fabio Capozzi; *SS*: Susanna S. Rocchi; *Titles*: Fabio Testa. *Cast*: Coralina Cataldi Tassoni (Cindy), Diego Ribon (Tony), Luciano Crovato (Algernoon), Elena Cantarone (Arva), Stefano Molinari (Fango). *PROD*: Agnese Fontana for Fomar Film; *PSe*: Pietro Raschillà, Manuela Di Priamo; *Location manager*: Francesca De Filippi; *ADM*: Enrico Marfori. *Country*: Italy. Filmed in Giazza (Verona) and Rome. *Running time*: 85 minutes (m. 2338). Visa n. 85793 (6.26.1990); *Rating*: V.M.14. *Release dates*: 3.26.1988 (Brussels International Festival of Fantasy Films), 6.4.1992 (USA—Home video); *Distribution*: Eagle Home Video (Italy), Troma (International). *Domestic gross*: not released theatrically. *Also known as*: Horror Queen (U.S.A—Home video), *Evil Clutch—Die Rückkehr der Dämonen* (Germany)

Note: the song "Evil Clutch," by Vitali/Marfori, is performed by Elisabetta De Palo.

Two lovers, Cindy and Tony, take a trip to the Alps. On the road they help a girl, Arva (actually a witch whom we have seen castrating and killing her lover), who claims to have been attacked by something horrible at the cemetery. Tony goes to check and has the feeling of being spied on by something invisible. At a nearby village, the two meet Algernoon, a weird-looking horror writer whose sight makes Arva flee. Algernoon tells them that centuries earlier a local population, the Cimbri, practiced satanic rites in the woods. Cindy and Tony resume their journey and meet Arva again, who offers them to sleep in an isolated barn. There, the witch offers Tony some drugs, which he accidentally drops into a strange liquid that splashes on him. Soon Tony starts feeling ill and Cindy chases Arva away. The witch's victim pops up as a zombie and attacks them. Tony is possessed by an evil force and tries to rape Cindy, who runs away terrified. The boy is seduced by Arva, who transforms into her true self. Algernoon comes to their rescue but he is killed by Arva. Cindy and Tony (who has been badly injured) take refuge in the ruins near a spring, but the monster reaches them and beheads the young man. Cindy takes refuge in the barn where she slaughters Algernoon (who has returned as a zombie) and the other undead with a chainsaw. At dawn, Cindy runs away, but the horror is not over…

Born in Verona in 1958, Andrea Marfori had been a movie buff since an early age. It was fated that this passion would evolve into something more. Even though he got a degree in Philosophy in Bologna, Andrea wrote his thesis on F.W. Murnau, then he moved to Rome and got a master's degree in direction and editing at Rome's CSC in 1982. His first works were a documentary on the Verona Arena and some short films. Then, in April 1987, Marfori set out to make the short horror film *Gorysand—Sabbia insanguinata*: shot around Rome and at CSC's own studio with a handful of friends and CSC graduates, it was an experiment (or, in Marfori's words, a "pre-film") which paved the hand for the director's feature film debut. "There was the will to make a genre product, the passion for Gothic stories and the desire to create a product that was not auteurish, nor classic or ordinary. In fact, I wanted to make a commercial movie."[1]

Produced by Marfori with his CSC classmate Agnese Fontana on a budget of about 100 million *lire*, *Il bosco 1* was filmed over the course of three weeks, from late August to mid–September 1987. The director worked with a crew of about 20 and with a cast of five, led by Diego Ribon and the Italian-American Coralina Cataldi Tassoni, the latter a rather popular face at that time after her work with Dario Argento (*Dèmoni 2 … l'incubo continua*, *Opera* and the

TV program *Giallo*). On the first week, filming took place on location in the Venetian prealps, in the Lessinia plateau around Asiago before the crew moved to Filacciano, in the countryside near Rome, for two more weeks of filming in an estate owned by the family of Prince Del Drago.

Il bosco 1 (the number, in the director's own words, is an ironic nod to the plethora of horror movie sequels playing in theaters at that time) has a Gothic core to it. As Marfori stated, "I wanted to make a film about mountains and ghosts, in an openly Gothic key, by concocting a story with a mysterious atmosphere.... I wanted to create a style similar to the Hansel and Gretel tale, but in a Gothic version."[2] The story takes place in a handful of *milieux*—a small hamlet, a cemetery, a dilapidated farmhouse, a barn (but with a cuckoo clock incongruously placed on the wall)—and draws from the Gothic tradition, with the theme of the two lovers travelling in a foreign country (and getting lost in a remote and inhospitable region), and with the figure of the female witch.

The character of Arna is Marfori's version of the evil sorcerers who seduce and destroy the weak-minded males, a trope of Italian horror since its early days. (Let's put aside for a moment the fact that actress Elena Cantarone doesn't have an ounce of Barbara Steele's alluring power) Under her seductive façade, the witch conceals an ugly appearance, but not just that: in a mind-numbing riff on the theme of the "*vagina dentata*," a several feet long claw emerges from between her legs and grabs her unfortunate lovers in the crotch with gruesome effects, thus giving the film its English language title *Evil Clutch*. Such a depiction of sexuality as morbid and punitive recalls the past Gothic classics as well, albeit with a distinctly tongue-in-cheek attitude.

Another typical Gothic element are the ruins as containers of a past evil waiting to be unleashed. The character of Algernoon, the weird horror novelist who warns the protagonists about the dangers of the surroundings, is a bizarre sort of savant, who rides around in an outmoded motorbike and speaks through a voice device. Most notably, the film takes place in an Italian setting, the Venetian alps, an element which marks—at least ideally—a turning point from the many Italian horror movies set abroad, from Fulci's works to the *Dèmoni* diptych: the dialogue even mentions the Cimbri, a Germanic population who lived in the area and fought the Roman Republic in the 2nd century B.C. In the region, local people still speak a dialect, "*cimbro*," which retains German words.

Nevertheless, *Il bosco 1* tries hard not to *look* Italian. The form and directing style are blatantly influenced by *The Evil Dead* and *Evil Dead II* (1987) to the point of idolatry. The Steadicam prowls around the woods at ground level and fast speed as an evil entity is unleashed, and the violence is over-the-top and cartoonish. Besides the aforementioned "evil clutch," the film sports a fast-moving zombie who amputates a character's hands with a heavy stone and chases the heroine with a scythe (and later he hooks her like a fish by the cheek with a rod!), monstrous tree root tentacles coming out of the ground, a chainsaw-vs-axe showdown, zombies drooling multicolored pus and corpses melting like hot wax.

If this sounds amusing on paper, Marfori's direction turns out to be an ordeal for the viewer. *Il bosco 1* is conceived and shot with all the enthusiasm of a beginner who hasn't got a clue of what moviemaking is about. At less than 90 minutes, it looks and feels like an overinflated short film (the horror story Algernoon tells the protagonists, which has no other function than to pad the running time, consists of excerpts from *Gorysand*). The systematic use of long takes and POV shots is monotonous and pointless, with Marfori having his cameraman swirl around the actors like the invisible presence in Raimi's film (as in the cemetery scene) as if it were enough to create atmosphere: see, for instance, the expository scene where Cindy, Tony and Algernoon descend through a small hamlet and discuss the evil nature of the place.

Such an approach predates the film buff, fanboy mentality which will characterize many Italian indie filmmakers over the next decades, worried about wearing their influences on their sleeve and attempting bravura stunts in a misguided conception of what film technique is. Ditto for the scenes where the camera lingers on the gory aftermath to emphasize the make-up effects, not unlike the many independent U.S. horror films of the period. The F/X range from barely competent to overly clumsy, with the radio-controlled claw standing out, but the supposedly suspenseful bits are ruined by the amateurish *mise-en-scène*. Examples? Tony struggling with the tree root tentacles in a similar way as Bela Lugosi did with the rubber octopus in Ed Wood's *Bride of the Monster* (1955), the scythe-wielding zombie trying *not* to hit the heroine while chasing her, the final showdown between Cindy and the zombie.

The handful of characters that populate the story are the best indication of Marfori's approach, and perhaps the proof of *Il bosco 1*'s none too serious intentions. Tassoni is dressed like a Madonna lookalike and in the Italian version her character sports a hard-to-swallow American accent (which is on a par with the bad English spoken by the characters in the international version), while the surreal-looking Algernoon, in the director's words, looks like "a perfect cross between Snoopy and Lieutenant Columbo."[3] The script has them deliver stupid dialogue and behave in an incoherent way, with half of the film consisting of Cindy's character running away and screaming while the Steadicam is chasing her. Commenting on the atrocious, cartoonish acting, Marfori halfjokingly mentioned Werner Herzog's *Herz aus glas* (1976) as an influence of sorts: "They are not simply actors who act badly … they act weirdly."

The movie had its world premiere on March 26, 1988, at the 6th Brussels International Festival of Fantastic Films (BIFFF), and on June 7th it was screened at Rome's Fantafestival (on the same night as Fulci's *Zombi 3*). On both occasions it was presented with the international title *Evil Clutch*. However, it was submitted to the Italian rating board only in 1990 as *Il bosco 1*, earning a V.M.14 certificate, and was confined to home video in its country. Marfori claimed that for a young filmmaker like him to make a genre movie was an act so outside the box that the "official" film world ostracized his movie— a delusional view which simply doesn't consider the overall crisis of Italian cinema in the late 1980s. But Marfori managed to cut a deal with Troma, and *Il bosco 1* was picked up and released to home video by Lloyd Kaufman and Michael Herz's label in 1992 as *Evil Clutch*, with the director credited as *Andreas* Marfori. Reviews were scathing: "If you understand any of what's going on in this dubbed flick, you've probably been drinking what writer/director Andreas Marfori was," wrote *Fangoria*, adding "In all, this movie features a level of tedium and inanity to tax even the most diehard gorehound's patience."[4] As haphazard and trashy as it was, the movie found an international audience, which ultimately was just what Marfori wanted. "It has its own independent life, its soul," he commented about its enduring popularity among horror fans.

The director's next film was *Perduta* (1990),

based on the true story of the killing of a teenage girl, which was to be "a harsh recreation in the way of the 1970s Italian *poliziottesco*"[5] but was severely changed (and self-censored) in the making. He then made *Il ritmo del silenzio* (a.k.a. *Port of Crime/Mafia Docks*, 1993), an Italian/U.S. co-production featuring Rena Niehaus, Traci Lords and Randi Ingerman, and eventually landed on television, where he directed the soap opera *Un posto al sole*, as well as several documentaries. Marfori's name resurfaced in recent years, with the short film *The Unfortunate Life of Georgina Spelvin Chained to a Radiator* (2015) and the featurette *Soviet Zombie Invasion* (2016), co-financed with Russian festival organizer Viktor Bulankin and shot in HD cam in Moscow, which according to the director's intentions should be the pilot for a horror series.

In 2013 Marfori self-released a special 25th anniversary edition DVD of *Il bosco 1*. It included a celebrative feature-length documentary with the director evoking the genesis and the making of the film, commenting at length over the "most famous" scenes, acting as a tour guide for dozens of fans through the actual locations, signing autographs, and overall self-congratulating himself, savoring the cult status that his feature film debut has reached since its release and explaining it as follows: "It puts together unblendable things: cultured music, comics, trash, the absurd, the surreal … putting together all these elements was a heterodox gesture."

Notes

1. Brando Taccini, *Stracult Horror. Guida al meglio (e al peggio) del cinema horror italiano anni '80* (Rome: Quintilia Edizioni, 2012), 240.

2. *Ibid.*, 241.

3. This and Marfori's quotes, where not specified otherwise, come from the documentary *Il bosco 1–25th Anniversary Edition*, shot by Brando Taccini.

4. [not signed], "The Video Eye of Dr. Cyclops," *Fangoria* #118, November 1992, 35. Incidentally, the reviewer mistakenly believes the name of the zombie (Fango) to be "the ultimate ass-kiss" (*Fangoria* being usually called *Fango* by fans). But in this case, Marfori wasn't paying a tongue-in-cheek homage to the popular horror movie magazine: in Italian, Fango means "mud," and indeed in the film the zombie comes out of the mud.

5. Andrea Marfori interviewed, in www.jamovie.it (http://www.jamovie.it/intervista-ad-andrea-marfori-il-regista-del-mitico-il-bosco-1/).

La casa 3—Ghosthouse (*Ghosthouse*)

D: Umberto Lenzi. *S*: Umberto Lenzi; *Dial*: Sheila Goldberg; *SC*: Cinthia McGavin; *DOP*:

Franco Delli Colli (Telecolor, Eastman Kodak); *M*: Piero Montanari (Ed. Idra Music); *E*: Rosanna Landi; *PD, CO*: Massimo Lentini; *AD*: Alexander Colby [Massimo Antonello Geleng]; *SD*: Roberto Granieri; *MU*: Peter Moor [Pietro Tenoglio]; *Hair*: Paula White [Adriana Sforza]; *AD*: Clay Millicamp [Claudio Lattanzi]; *AsstArtD*: Rob Rockett; *SE*: Dan Maklansky, Robert Gould, Roland Park; *SO*: Larry Revene; *SOE*: Hubrecht Nijhuis; *AC*: Daniel Kalehoff [Daniele Massaccesi]; *G*: Brian Taitt [Elio Terribili], Mark Caruso, Sam Winston, Albert Ellis; *El*: Saul Barry, Jeff Herbert, Bob Siegel; *W*: Kou Ami; *SP*: Jeff Hest [Carlo Alberto Cocchi]; *AE*: Henry Robinson [Enrico Grassi]; *Generator Operator*: Silver Murray; *SS*: Olga Pehar; *DialD*: Sheila Goldberg. *Cast*: Lara Wendel [Daniela Barnes] (Martha), Greg Scott [Greg Rhodes] (Paul Rogers), Kristen Fougerosse (Henriette Baker), Mary Sellers (Susan), Kate Silver (Tina Dalen), Ron Houck (Mark Dalen), Martin Jay (Jim Dalen), Willy M. Moon (Pepe), Donald O'Brian [O'Brien] (Valkos), Susan Muller (Mrs. Baker), Alain Smith (Sam Baker), William J. Devany (Lieutenant), Ralph Morse (Coroner), Robert Champagne (Mortician), Hernest Mc. Kimnoro (Cemetery Custodian). *PROD*: Aristide Massaccesi for Filmirage Production Group (Rome); *PS*: Tony Hood; *PAss*: Mary Noolite, John Therrien; *ADM*: Charles Wallach. *Country*: Italy. Filmed in Boston and Cohasset, Massachusetts (USA). *Running time*: 95 minutes (m. 2632). Visa n. 83280 (1.23.1988); *Rating*: V.M.14. *Release dates*: 1.1988 (France—Avoriaz Fantastic Film Festival), 5.21.1988 (Japan), 6.1.1988 (France), 8.11.1988 (Italy); *Distribution*: Gruppo BEMA. *Domestic gross*: n.a. Also known as: *La maison du cauchemar* (France), *La casa fantasma* (Spain).

New England. When he finds out that his little daughter Henrietta has killed the family cat, Sam Baker punishes her severely, but soon he and his wife are horribly murdered. Boston, twenty years later: Paul and his girlfriend Martha receive a strange radio call which leads them to the deserted house where Henrietta's family once lived. There, they make acquaintance with a group of radio amateurs who are camping nearby. Weird things occur: the visitors are terrorized by the ghastly apparitions of Henrietta and her evil-looking clown doll, and one of them meets a horrible death. However, the police believe the killer is a crazed man named Valkos. While their friends stay at the house, Paul and Martha leave

to investigate and discover a trail of gruesome past events. It seems that the key to the mystery is the malevolent clown doll which Henrietta's father—a mortician—stole from a dead girl and gave her. Meanwhile, Valkos is still at large…

By the mid- to late-eighties, the Italian genre film industry was winding down. The home market would not welcome low-budget horror films if not in the summer season, where the lack of major releases would allow them a niche in the distribution circuit. Independent companies aimed mainly at the foreign markets, where their products would sell more easily, either to theatrical distribution or more likely to home video.

One of such companies was Aristide Massaccesi's Filmirage. Founded in 1980, it produced horror, sci-fi, and erotic films, with Massaccesi performing various duties, and operated with an eye firmly on foreign deals. For several years Filmirage churned out virtually only films directed by Massaccesi, usually under his alias Joe D'Amato (one exception was Mino Guerrini's comedy *Cuando calienta el sol … vamos alla playa*, where Massaccesi was the director of photography). By the mid–1980s Filmirage started producing low-budget horror films directed by other filmmakers, namely Deran Serafian's *Interzone* and Michele Soavi's *Deliria*, and it was Massaccesi's company who picked up the production of Umberto Lenzi's first horror film since *Incubo sulla città contaminata*.

Lenzi had written the story in January 1987, and immediately found Italian and American backing. Initially titled *Ghosthouse*, the project had to be financed by producer Roberto Di Girolamo, who backed out due to money issues. Then Massaccesi stepped in. As with many other Filmirage productions, shooting took place in the United States—as Massaccesi explained, filming abroad was far less expensive than in Italy—and on the cheap: Lenzi claimed the movie cost one billion *lire*. The crew was minimal: Lenzi's wife Olga Pehar acted as script girl, and Massaccesi took on as director of photography during the last three days of filming in Boston, after the titular d.o.p. Franco Delli Colli had returned to Italy. According to the director, "it was almost impossible to shoot under those conditions, the budget was too small."[1] The cast was an ensemble of unknown faces, except for Lara Wendel (who would soon appear in another Filmirage flick, *Killing Birds—Raptors*) and Donald O'Brien. Mary Sellers was a recur-

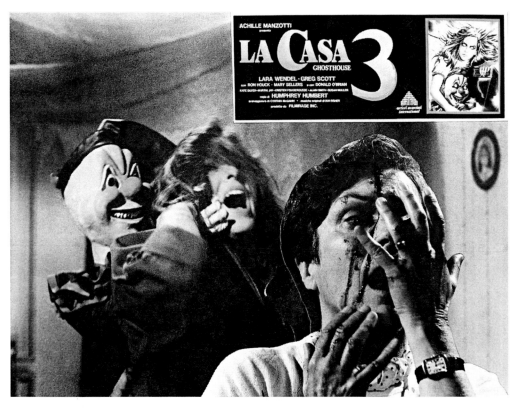

Italian fotobusta for Umberto Lenzi's *La casa 3—Ghosthouse* (1988).

ring presence in the company's productions, such as *Deliria* and *Eleven Days, Eleven Nights*.

The screenplay—credited to the elusive "Cinthia McGavin" but written solely by the director[2]—is a hodgepodge of ideas, filtered through Lenzi's own vision. "Terror, as far as I am concerned, stems exactly from the attachment to reality," he observed about his concept of the genre, while recalling the genesis of *Ghosthouse*. "The basic idea started from the documented existence of paranormal activities so that particularly sensitive people can have premonitions of gruesome events that perhaps are taking place in the opposite part of the world. The strength of my film is that the premonition was not made by a man, but by a radio. So you had a mechanical device which caught in the airwaves the cry for help of a person who was about to be killed."[3]

If the idea of a message intercepted through airwaves seems like an updating of a classic Richard Matheson story, *Long Distance Call*, the list of "homages" draws from varied filmic sources. The ghost of Henrietta, complete with a scary clown doll, comes from *Operazione paura*; the eerie lullaby which can be heard in the haunted house when the girl shows up (and which hides a message if played backwards) hints both at the typical *giallo* lullabies and at the "Satanic panic" around back-masking in the early 1980s; the mansion where the story takes place recalls both *The Amityville Horror* and *The Evil Dead* (see the scenes in the basement); the bit where a girl is cut in half by some sort of guillotine window (incongruously placed inside a room) comes from *Superstition* (1981, James W. Robertson); the final appearance of Death as a hooded, maggot-infested skeleton is a cheap recreation of the climax in *Inferno*. There are also nods to Fulci's *L'aldilà* and *Quella villa accanto al cimitero*, from the scene where an unfortunate guy falls into a pit of acid to the unsettling moment where Lara Wendel's character notices the evil doll in a shop's window; finally, the climax set in a cemetery's crypt, where the young hero exhumes the still-preserved body of Henrietta, buried with her doll by her side, and sets them on fire, is a poor man's riff on the ending of *Paura nella città dei morti viventi*. The few interesting ideas, such as a scene where a haunted room is filled with flying dolls and pillow feathers—Lenzi's horror reimagining of a famous moment in *Zéro de conduite* (1933, Jean Vigo), perhaps?—are ruined by bottom-of-the-barrel special effects.

The direction does not improve upon the scarce originality and minimal budget. Lenzi doesn't have Fulci's visionary talent, and for most of its running time he sticks to the movie's horror imagery-by-numbers—arms breaking through walls, dead bodies behind doors, faucets dripping blood—with a stolid lack of imagination. Overall, it is the prone sticking to 1980s U.S. body count horror that is most grating: once Italian Gothic was a matter of ladies in their nightgowns wandering through dark corridors; in Lenzi's film, it has become all about dumb teenagers with denim jackets and sneakers. It is not quite the same.

Eventually, though, *Ghosthouse* found its way to the home market as well. Distributor Achille Manzotti picked it up and retitled it *La Casa 3*, a title that artfully referred to *The Evil Dead* and *Evil Dead II*, released in Italy respectively as *La Casa* (House) and *La Casa 2*. The reference to a "house" in the title was common to many horror movies released over the course of the decade, starting with *Superstition*, which came out as *La casa di Mary*. Even Massaccesi's *Buio Omega* (1979) was re-released as *In quella casa Buio omega*, to jump on the bandwagon. This led to a series of sometimes bizarre retitlings: for instance, Steve Miner's *House* (1985) came out as *Chi è sepolto in quella casa?* (Who is Buried in That House?) and Harley Cokeliss' *Dream Demon* was retitled *La casa al n° 13 in Horror Street*.

Lenzi was initially credited as "Humphrey Humbert," an Anglicized pseudonym which echoed the name of the narrator (Humbert Humbert) in Vladimir Nabokov's novel *Lolita*. It seemed one of Filmirage's typical cheap marketing tricks (which even Fulci was not spared, when *Le porte del silenzio* was credited abroad to "Henry Simon Kittay"), and according to the director he sued the producers and had his name restored: in the Italian prints, the credits carry his real name. However, "Humphrey Humbert" was an a.k.a. Lenzi had used earlier in his career, for instance on *I tre sergenti del Bengala* (1964), so there is a chance he was aware of the stunt from the beginning.

Critics were severe: the *Corriere della Sera* praised only the photography and Piero Mon-

tanari's score, blaming the film's "great confusion and lack of accuracy."[4] But it reportedly proved a solid box-office success, and was sold well abroad, including France, Jana and Spain.[5] Massaccesi soon set to work on *La Casa 4*. On his part, Lenzi directed another movie for Filmirage, the thriller *Paura nel buio—Hitcher in the Dark* (1989).

NOTES

1. Manlio Gomarasca, *Umberto Lenzi* (Milan: Nocturno Libri, 2001), 256.
2. Palmerini and Mistretta, *Spaghetti Nightmares*, 98.
3. Gomarasca, *Umberto Lenzi*, 255.
4. G. Gs. [Giovanna Grassi], "Horror italiano," *Corriere della Sera*, August 20, 1988.
5. According to the official Spanish ministerial data, it was seen by 85,963 spectators and grossed an amount corresponding to 153,460 Euro. (http://infoicaa.mecd.es/CatalogoICAA/Peliculas/Detalle?Pelicula=966851)

La casa 4 (Witchcraft) *(Witchery)*

D: Martin Newlin [Fabrizio Laurenti]. *S and SC*: Daniele Stroppa; *DOP*: Gianlorenzo Battaglia (Eastmancolor Kodak, Telecolor); *M*: Carlo Maria Cordio (Ed. Idra Music); *E*: Rosanna Landi; *Casting*: Paul Werner [Werner Pochath]; *ArtD*: Alex Colby [Massimo Antonello Geleng]; *MU*: Maurizio Trani; *AD*: Allen Donner; *STC*: Brian Ricci; *C*: John Wynn; *AC*: Camillo Sabatini; *SO*: Keith Young; *SP*: Peter Bates; *AE*: David Shaw; *SS*: Laura Curreli; *G*: Paolo Tiberti, Franco Micheli; *El*: Marcello Montarsi, Ben Miller; *PrM*: Julie Duncan; *Stunts*: John Mason; *Mix*: Michael Barry. *Cast*: David Hasselhoff (Gary), Linda Blair (Jane Brooks), Catherine Hickland (Linda Sullivan), Annie Ross (Rose Brooks), Hildegarde Knef (Lady in Black), Leslie Cumming (Leslie), Bob [Robert] Champagne (Freddie Brooks), Rick Farnsworth (Jerry Giordano), Michael Manchester (Tommy Brooks), Frank Cammarata (Tony Giordano), Victoria Biggers (Secretary), Ely Coughlin (Satan), Kara Lynch (Cindy), James [Jamie] Hanes (Jon), Richard Ladenburg (Sheriff), George Stevens (Fisherman). *PROD*: Aristide Massaccesi for Filmirage Production Group (Rome); *PS*: Annie Jurgielewicz; *PSe*: Sophie Ali; *PAcc*: Walter Kelly. *Country*: Italy. Filmed in Scituate and Cohasset, Massachusetts. *Running time*: 95 minutes (m. 2510). Visa n. 84167 (11.26.1988); *Rating*: all audiences. *Release dates*: 12.1.1988 (West Germany), 7.1.1989 (Japan), 7.6.1989 (USA—Home video), 8.6.1989 (Italy); *Distribution*: Artisti Associati/Gruppo Berna. *Domestic gross*: 1,283,194,000 *lire*.

Also known as: Ghosthouse 2 (UK); *Encuentro con la maldad* (Spain); *Démoniaque présence* (France); *Hexenbrut* (West Germany).

A photographer, Gary, and his girlfriend Leslie arrive at an isolated house on an isle near the coast of Massachusetts to conduct research on a past legend. Supposedly, centuries earlier, a pregnant witch took refuge there from her persecutors and then committed suicide by throwing herself out of a window. In recent times the place was inhabited only by a retired actress. Other people arrive on the island: a pregnant young woman, Jane Brooks, who is looking to buy the house and convert it into a hotel, accompanied by her parents and her little brother Tommy; a real estate agent, Jerry, and an architect, Linda. Soon the group find themselves stranded on the island, after a mysterious lady in black has dispatched the boatman who brought them there. The guests start dying in horrible ways, and Leslie finds out that the witch is still out for vengeance...

The good commercial results of *La casa 3* convinced Aristide Massaccesi and distributor Achille Manzotti to follow along the same route, which resulted in Filmirage putting in the pipeline another sequel in name only to *La casa*. Umberto Lenzi had already submitted to the producers an idea for *La casa 4*, "a story in the vein of *Psycho*, about a woman who is released from jail and goes to live in a villa where years earlier bloody murders were committed, but they didn't even take it into consideration. They told me ... that these films made no money, and that they had no intention whatsoever of making a sequel. In fact, they not only made *La casa 4*, but also *La casa 5*!"[1]

Even though the only credited scriptwriter is Daniele Stroppa, Claudio Lattanzi claimed he had a part in concocting the scenario. "Daniele wrote all the screenplay, but I remember going to his place in the evening, to write the story together, because I had to direct it."[2] It was Lattanzi who suggested Massaccesi to aim high for the cast: "I kept telling Aristide: 'Come on, now that you have made a leap in quality and you are undergoing a felicitous period, why don't we cast Bette Davis for the role of the witch?' We talked again a few days later, and he told me: 'You know, maybe I really have a chance to have Bette Davis, because I know people who know her ... what a shot it would be!' and I: 'Well, if Bette Davis is in it, I'm making the movie for free!'"[3] Eventually the producer had to settle with Hildegarde Knef, possibly because of her role in Billy

Wilder's *Fedora*, which also featured a mysterious retired actress. The cast also included David Hasselhoff (still very popular in Italy after the TV series *Knight Rider*) and Linda Blair, who ends up again playing a possessed soul. For the main female role Massaccesi cast Leslie Cummins, on Lattanzi's suggestion: she had been in *Killing Birds* and had a brief liaison with the director. Massaccesi would regret the choice, given Cummins' utter lack of acting skills.

In the end, Lattanzi gave up directing the film—or Massaccesi decided he was unfit for the movie: Lattanzi's version on why he left the project is rather vague and unconvincing. The producer's old acquaintance Luigi Cozzi came aboard, only to resign after just two weeks of pre-production work: "The story didn't attract me, I found it too predictable and banal. Massaccesi wanted me to make a film which I didn't feel like mine, and without any special reason I decided to give up directing a horror movie aimed at the small screen."[4] Cozzi went on to make his own project, *Paganini Horror*, and Massaccesi replaced him at the eleventh hour with Fabrizio Laurenti, a debuting director who had made an impressive 30-minute vampire film shot in Super8, *The Immigrant* (1985), about a Transylvanian immigrant in New York who wakes up 80 years later in the East Side, thirsty for blood, which leads to a series of grotesque vicissitudes. *The Immigrant* had won the "Gabbiano d'oro" prize at the 1987 Bellaria Film Festival, and gathered favorable reviews in the press.[5]

La casa 4 tries hard to pose as an American horror movie. The vengeful witch and the references to the Massachusetts witch hunts recall among other things James W. Robertson's *Superstition*, the character of the "lady in black" is borrowed from Dan Curtis' *Burnt Offerings* (1976), the creative graphic deaths and mutilations take place in an extradimensional hell just like in *Hellraiser*, and the final bit of possession is the price to be paid to *The Exorcist*. But Stroppa's script adds even more fuel to the fire. The theme of the victims being symbolically punished for the deadly sins they represent recalls *La plus longue nuit du diable* (1971, Jean Brismée), the notion that the hotel is built on three doors of hell (respectively greed, luxury and ire) draws from *The Sentinel* and *L'aldilà*, and the witch's look was Lattanzi's homage to *Inferno*: "I liked the idea of showing the witch Argento-style ... with this long black cloak, while Daniele thought it was bullshit!."[6] Just like Argento did in *Opera*, incidentally, the leading man is dispatched in the epilogue.

The very insistence on Catholic guilt makes for a rather morbid subtext. "It is a childish superstition of the human spirit that virginity is a virtue and not the barrier that separates ignorance from knowledge," a line of dialogue states near the beginning, and Leslie's virginity—which turns her into the "final girl" as the rules of the American slasher film demand—leads to her being raped by Satan in an uncomfortable nightmare sequence which elicits further comparisons (Soavi's *La chiesa*) and allows for a telegraphed twist ending.

All this is assembled chaotically. For instance, only three victims are punished for their sins, respectively greed, luxury and ire, while other deaths are left unexplained, and some plot elements (such as the film-within-the-film starring the "lady in black") don't really make sense. On top of that, the series of events that keep the main characters stranded on the island demand a leap of faith rather than mere suspension of disbelief. The script also makes poor use of a child's Sesame Street tape recorder as a last-minute *Deus ex machina*.

The movie comes alive only now and then with the odd surreal moment, such as when Blair's character falls inside a bathtub and is transported into another dimension. Laurenti's depiction of hell looks like something that could have come out of a Goya painting, with witches dressed in rags and intent on munching on new-born children, and Satan is portrayed as a lecherous young man with his mouth sewn shut. The director stages the gory moments in a rather convincing way, and the film's *pièce de résistance* (Annie Ross' character having her mouth sewn shut with a huge pin in graphic details) has nothing to envy to a similar sequence seen in the "It's a Miserable Life" episode of the TV series *Freddy's Nightmares* (1988). Other gruesome showpieces include Hickland's body showing up with her throat transfixed by a swordfish's sword, her one-time lover being crucified upside down and burned alive, and Bob Champagne's neck veins inflating and eventually exploding, with make-up artist Maurizio Trani coming up with a passable imitation of Dick Smith's effects for *Scanners* (1981).

Overall, despite its many shortcomings and money-saving tricks—such as Carlo Maria Cordio's score lifted from *Killing Birds*: Massaccesi

would recycle it again for *La Casa 5* (1990)—*La casa 4* looks more polished than other Filmirage productions. Its appearance misled the film critic in the *Corriere della Sera*, who took it for a genuine U.S. production and (perhaps exactly because of this) reviewed it rather favorably, recommending it to genre fans "who will enjoy ... the usual American-style doggerel on family neuroses."[7] The film played theatrically in Italy almost a year after its release in other countries, to very good box-office: with over 1.2 billion *lire*, it ended up on the 60th place among the year's top grossers, right behind James Cameron's *The Abyss*, and outgrossing among others Brian De Palma's *Casualties of War* and Spike Lee's *Do the Right Thing*. It was sold abroad under various titles, such as *Witchery*, *Witchcraft* and even *Ghosthouse 2*, as if there were people who would pay to go and see a sequel to Lenzi's film.

Laurenti directed another horror picture for Filmirage, *Contamination .7* (a.k.a. *The Crawlers*, 1990), and then went on to make two films written by Pupi Avati, the intriguing but flawed *La stanza accanto* (1994), and the extraordinary TV mini-series *Voci notturne*, which unfortunately flopped badly. His subsequent career has been spotty, with a couple of documentaries which caused minor controversy: *Il segreto di Mussolini* (2005), about Benito Mussolini's secret son, which inspired Marco Bellocchio to make the powerful *Vincere* (2008), and *Il corpo del duce* (2011).

NOTES

1. Gomarasca, *Umberto Lenzi*, 256.
2. Manlio Gomarasca, "Claudio Lattanzi. La verità secondo Claude Milliken," in Davide Pulici (ed.), *Misteri d'Italia 3. Guida ai film rari e scomparsi. Nocturno Dossier #70*, May 2008, 56.
3. *Ibid.*
4. Luigi Cozzi interviewed, in www.davinotti.com (http://www.davinotti.com/index.php?option=com_content&task=view&id=49&Itemid=79).
5. Alberto Farassino, "Dalla Transilvania agli USA per svegliarsi dopo 80 anni con una gran sete," *Repubblica*, July 17, 1987.
6. Gomarasca, "Claudio Lattanzi. La verità secondo Claude Milliken," 56.
7. M.P. [Maurizio Porro], "Quei fantasmi maligni inclusi nel prezzo," *Corriere della Sera*, August 23, 1989.

Killing Birds—Raptors (*Zombie 5: Killing Birds*)

D: Claudio Lattanzi [and Aristide Massaccesi]. *S*: Claudio Lattanzi, Sheila Goldberg; *SC*: Daniele Stroppa; *Dial*: Sheila Goldberg; *DOP*: Fred Sloniscko, Jr. [Aristide Massaccesi] (Eastman Kodak, Telecolor); *M*: Carlo Maria Cordio (Ed. Idra Music); *E*: Rosanna Landi; *C*: Aristide Massaccesi [uncredited]; *MU*: Frank Moor; *Hair*: Paula Ross; *AD*: Antonio Bonifacio; *APD*: Rub Du Valier; *SO*: Larry Revene; *SE*: Harry Harris III, Robert Gould; *AC*: Dan Kalehoff [Daniele Massaccesi]; *SP*: Jeff Hest [Carlo Alberto Cocchi]; *G*: Brian Taitt [Elio Terribili], Sam La Falette; *El*: Marcello Montarsi, Rob Samuel; *W*: Angel Goodman; *AE*: Helen Robinson; *Locations*: David Ross McCarty; *SS*: Silvy Louis; *Bird consultant*: Buddy Valentine. *Cast*: Lara Wendel [Daniela Barnes] (Anne), Robert Vaughn (Dr. Fredrick Brown), Timothy W. Watts (Steve Porter), Leslie Cummins (Mary Brad), James Villemaire (Paul), Sal Maggiore, Jr (Brian), James Sutterfield (Rob), Lin Gathright (Jennifer), Brigitte Paillet (Steve's Mother), Nona Paillet (Steve's Grandmother), Ellis Paillet (Steve's Grandfather), John H. Green (Prof. Green). *PROD*: Aristide Massaccesi for Filmirage Production Group, Flora Film (Rome); *UM*: Roberto De Laurentiis; *PS*: Giorgio Bertuccelli; *ADM*: Charles Wallach. *Country*: Italy. Filmed in Thibodaux, Louisiana. *Running time*: 91 minutes (m. 2507). Visa n. 83457 (3.23.1988); *Rating*: all audiences. *Release dates*: 7.13.1988 (France), 8.19.1988 (Italy), 9.23.1989 (Japan); *Distribution*: D.M.V. Distribuzione. *Domestic gross*: n.a. Also known as: *Killing Birds—Uccelli assassini* (Italy—TV version), *Killing Birds—Zombi 5* (Italy—DVD), *Zombie Flesheaters 4* (UK), *L'attaque des morts-vivants* (France), *Los pájaros asesinos* (Spain).

Note: Lattanzi is credited in foreign prints as "Claude Milliken."

Louisiana. Upon returning from the Vietnam War, Fred Brown finds his wife in bed with her lover, and slaughters his whole family, sparing only his newborn son. After the massacre he is attacked and blinded by his falcon. Twenty years later, a group of ornithology students led by Steve go on the search for the almost extinct ivory-billed woodpecker. They are accompanied by a young reporter, Anne. Steve and Anne meet Brown, and camp at the man's former home, which is now empty and dilapidated. Soon grisly occurrences ensue, and during the night the boys are killed one by one by vengeful zombies. Steve and Anne are the only survivors. It is eventually revealed that Steve is none other than Brown's son. In the morning Anne and Steve leave the house while Brown is consumed by the angry ghosts…

Like many filmmakers of his generation,

Claudio Lattanzi (b. 1962) grew up dreaming of making movies. His first chance came in the mid–1980s, when he was chosen as one of the unpaid assistants for the filming of Bernardo Bertolucci's *The Last Emperor* (1987), but his family opposed, and it all came to nothing. Then, almost by chance, he managed to meet Dario Argento, who during that period was shooting *Phenomena*, and Michele Soavi. When the latter started working on a documentary on the director of *Suspiria*, tentatively titled *Katana* and later released as *Dario Argento's World of Horror*, Lattanzi gave him a hand; Soavi then asked Lattanzi to be his assistant on his feature film debut, *Deliria*, produced by Aristide Massaccesi's Filmirage. It was Massaccesi who gave Lattanzi the chance to become a director, when Soavi, who was supposed to direct *Killing Birds*, accepted Argento's offer to make *La chiesa* instead.

The genesis of the film was rather convoluted. According to Lattanzi, during the 1986 Christmas holidays he had written a story entitled *Il cancello obsoleto* (The Obsolete Gate) about a record producer who invites a rock band (who sent him a violent music video) to a gloomy deserted house where they would record a tune to accompany the video; unbeknownst to them, Nazi soldiers are buried in a cemetery near the house, and when one band member finds a sheet of music and plays it, the Nazi zombies resurrect. It turns out that the only way to have the zombies go back to their graves is to play the music in reverse. In the end, it turns out that everything has been tape-recorded in a secret room beneath an "obsolete gate," and the devilish record producer invites another rock band: the horrific events are about to start all over again.

Lattanzi's story mixed diverse influences, most notably *The Evil Dead* and Ken Wiederhorn's *Shock Waves* (1977), and it had weird analogies with *Paganini Horror*. Lattanzi maintains that Massaccesi asked him to reshape the story, keeping all the scenes with the zombies but discarding the rock band and the Nazis. The producer also suggested he introduce a new element—birds, and namely the search for the ivory-billed woodpecker—since he had in mind to shoot the film in Louisiana. "I rewrote the story completely, and titled this new version *Artigli* [Talons]," Lattanzi explained. "I thought it was a good title, but Aristide said: 'Nah, *Artigli* … seems like we're making a documentary on cats…"" [1] The screenplay was written by Daniele Stroppa, with the English language dialogue revised by Sheila Goldberg. However, Claudio Fragasso and Rossella Drudi maintained that *Killing Birds—Raptors* evolved from their own story, titled *Artigli*, but the Italian DVD of the film includes a pdf file of a 12-page treatment, *Artigli*, signed by Lattanzi and Bruna Antonucci and dated January 29, 1987, which is very similar to the finished film, thus dismissing Fragasso and Drudi's claims. Drudi's script for *Artigli* was recycled for another Filmirage production, *Contamination .7*, directed by Fabrizio Laurenti.

Killing Birds was filmed on location with a very small crew (8 or 9 persons, and only one camera) and a minimal budget, not to mention under harsh conditions (in the form of hot temperatures and heavy humidity). Most actors were locals recruited on the spot, with just a few exceptions. Leslie Carol Cummins, with whom Lattanzi had a brief affair during the filming, would also turn up in another Filmirage movie, *La casa 4*, and the director himself stood in for the unseen soldier in the opening scenes as well as for all the zombies that appear in the film. The only "name" actors were Lara Wendel (still a rather popular name after her role in Enrico Montesano's hit comedy *A me mi piace*, 1985) and Robert Vaughn, who turned up in a brief "special guest" appearance, for a couple of days: Lattanzi and Massaccesi wrote a couple of extra scenes for his character on the spot. Vaughn was supposed to wear blue contact lenses, and the eyes would be removed in post-production via chroma key; however, since the actor could not stand wearing the painful lenses, Massaccesi and Lattanzi opted for a crude prosthetic make-up, which the actor wore in one scene only; then the problem was solved by having Vaughn sport dark glasses.

Like other Filmirage productions included in this volume, *Killing Birds* is less a proper story than a jigsaw of ideas taken from other films. The gory opening sequence borrows heavily from *The Prowler* (1981, Joseph Zito), but climaxes with the raptors attacking the soldier who just slaughtered most of his family and gouging out his eye, and throws in a reference to Hitchcock's *The Birds*; the opening scenes look like a carbon copy of some 1980s slasher flick set in a campus; the sight of Lara Wendel's character crucified to a wall, her wrists pierced by huge nails, evokes *L'aldilà*[2]; the moment where a boy has his throat slashed by his own necklace which

got trapped into a generator recalls *Profondo rosso*; the zombies pay homage to Romero's films, and turn up in the middle of a thick fog like the specters of Botany Bay in John Carpenter's *The Fog* (1980); and so on. A scene where a zombie's hand breaks into the house from the roof and grabs a victim is a virtual restaging of a similar moment in Massaccesi's own *Antropophagus* (1980), but Lattanzi denied having taken inspiration from it.[3] The use of technology in the film borrows from American cinema, with involuntarily amusing effects: see the naive use of the personal computer in the film—at one point a character is putting data in it in order to find a way to escape!—which turns out as an instrument for the evil forces to manifest themselves and send messages to the unfortunate protagonists.

The result is confusing to say the least, as the script puts together different elements that never really gel. The narrative structure is that of a body count movie, while the scenes of the zombies preying on their victims provide the excuse for a few creative deaths. And yet the bulk of the tale is that of a standard ghost story. Most of the action takes place during one endless night in a haunted house, and the "return of the past" is embodied by the revenants that turn up to slaughter the innocent young ornithologists. (Bizarrely but incongruously, the ghostly persecutors are not after anyone, but just after those who show fear of them.) Moreover, the moment when Steve experiences a vision of the past massacre in the abandoned house where it occurred 20 years earlier features the same blending of past and present as in *Danza macabra* and other classical Gothics. Interestingly, the idea of the psychopomp birds that carry away dead people's souls to the beyond leads to a climax which is very similar to Stephen King's novel *The Dark Half*, published in 1989.

Even though terribly messy, the film benefits from decent cinematography (by Massaccesi himself, under one of his many aliases, Fred Sloniscko, Jr.) and features some suitably atmospheric moments. Lattanzi was quite happy with the scene where Steve, experiencing a nightmare, runs across several empty rooms, and we see the doors open one after another through his POV shots. On the other hand, the director regretted the cheap ending, with a flock of birds filmed in Rome and superimposed on the shot via a crude optic effect. The synth-heavy, percussive score by Carlo Maria Cordio was re-used in other Filmirage productions, namely *La casa 4* and *Paura nel buio*.[4]

As with other Filmirage releases, two versions of the film were prepared. The one for foreign markets was quite gory, with plenty of gruesome effects; the one released in Italian theaters[5] toned down the gore drastically, replacing most of the graphic bits with alternate footage, such as close-ups of birds or actors. Only the scene where Rob (James Sutterfield) is pulled into the generator, loses two fingers in the machine and has his neck cut by his necklace was considerably shortened in the TV edit. Lattanzi was credited with his own name in the Italian prints, and as "Claude Milliken" in the foreign ones.

The question on who directed *Killing Birds* is debated. Some sources state that Massaccesi took care of the direction, uncredited, because of Lattanzi's incompetence. On the other hand, according to Rossella Drudi,

> Claudio Lattanzi was a front for the direction, because Aristide could not be credited on too many films as producer and director, even though it was always him, a true underestimated genius.... I remember that in the last years he [Lattanzi] was always around in Aristide's office in viale delle Milizie, when even Michele Soavi left the factory to work with Dario Argento. Lattanzi was one of the last entries in the factory, the son of a pharmacist, and thus rebaptized "the pharmacist" by Aristide. He wanted to become a film director, but it seems he was not cut out for it.[6]

Lattanzi, while acknowledging the weight of Massaccesi's presence on the set and describing their work as "in symbiosis," also due to the very low budget, claims the paternity of the movie, and vindicates the choice of many shots and scenes. Massaccesi himself explained that he personally took care of the sequences featuring special effects, allowing Lattanzi to sign the film.[7]

Claudio Lattanzi never directed another movie. He worked (uncredited) on the story for *La casa 4*, which he claims he was slated to direct; he re-edited the TV version of Sergio Martino's *Assassinio al cimitero etrusco* (1982) into a 3-hour TV movie, with new music by Carlo Maria Cordio; and he developed a *giallo* script, *A un'ora dalla notte*, which ended up in the drawer after Massaccesi's death. In 2009, Lattanzi attempted to put together a sequel, *Killing Birds Return*, but the project never went beyond a 5-page synopsis written by Federico Monti.

NOTES

1. Gomarasca, "Claudio Lattanzi. La verità secondo Claude Milliken," 55.
2. Incidentally, the house where the story takes place is the same one as seen in Fulci's film.
3. *Uccelli rapaci*, extra in the Italian DVD of the film.
4. Lattanzi, a big Ken Russell fan, claimed he had edited the workprint using Thomas Dolby's score for *Gothic* (1986) as guide.
5. This version is the same one later released on DVD as *Killing Birds—Zombi 5*.
6. Samuele Zàccaro, "Intervista esclusiva a Rossella Drudi," www.darkveins.com, 21 March 2009.
7. Palmerini and Mistretta, *Spaghetti Nightmares*, 107.

Il nido del ragno (*The Spider Labyrinth*)

D: Gianfranco Giagni. *S*: Tonino Cervi; *SC*: Riccardo Aragno, Tonino Cervi, Cesare Frugoni, Gianfranco Manfredi; *DOP*: Nino Celeste (Kodak Eastmancolor, LV-Luciano Vittori); *M*: Franco Piersanti (Ed. S.B.K.); *E*: Sergio Montanari; *PD, ArtD*: Stefano Ortolani; *CO*: Nicoletta Ercole; *SVFX*: Sergio Stivaletti; *AsstSVFX*: Barbara Morosetti; *MU*: Renato Francola; *Hair*: Maria Angelini; *C*: Sandro Grossi; *AC*: Francesco Damiani; *2ndAC*: Cristiano Celeste; *AE*: Mario D'Ambrosio, Giovanni Pallotto; *AsstArtD*: Jo Chevalier; *SO*: Alberto Salvatori; *Mix*: Steve C. Aaron; *SOE*: Roberto Arcangeli Studio Sound; *DubD*: Gianni Bonagura; *MA*: Nazzareno Zamperla; *SP*: Enrico Appetito; *ACO*: Carlotta Polidori; *W*: Anna Inciocchi; *ChEl*: Agostino Gorga; *El*: Antonio Gasbarrini, Antonio Labarbera; *KG*: Tarcisio Diamanti; *G*: Claudio Brizzolari, Roberto Brizzolari; *Props*: Piero Riccini, Nazzareno Sgolacchia; *SS*: Margherita Reginato. *Cast*: Roland Wybenga (Prof. Alan Whitmore), Paola Rinaldi (Geneviève Weiss), Margareta von Krauss (Sylvia Roth), Claudia Muzii (Marta), William Berger (Mysterious Man), Stéphane Audran (Mrs. Kuhn), Valeriano Santinelli, Massimiliano Pavone, Arnaldo Dell'Acqua (Polgár Móricz), László Sipos (Inspector Blasco), Attila Lõte (Professor Roth), Bob Holton (Frank, Intextus Committee Member), Bill Bolender (Chancellor Hubbard), John Morrison (Reverend Bradley). *PROD*: Tonino Cervi for Splendida Film (Rome), Reteitalia; *PM*: Antonio Levesi-Cervi, Tamás Hámori; *EP*: Endre Flórián, Endre Sík; *PSe*: Carlo Gagliardi. *Country*: Italy. Filmed on location in Budapest and at Cinecittà (Rome). *Running time*: 86 minutes (m. 2363). Visa n. 83572 (4.27.1988); *Rating*: all audiences. *Release date*: 8.25.1988 (Italy), 10.31.1988 (West Germany—Home video), 4.22.1989 (Japan); *Distribution*: Medusa/Penta Film (Italy); *Domestic gross*: n.a. *Also known as*: *Spider Labyrinth—*

In den Fangen der Todestarantel (West Germany), *Noroi no meikyû: Rabirinsu in za dâku* (Japan).

Alan Whitmore, a young American professor of Eastern religions in Dallas, is sent to Budapest to meet Professor Roth, who is collaborating with him on the mysterious Intextus project. Upon arrival, the terrified Roth handles Alan a black booklet where, he says, his colleague will find the key to the enigma. The booklet contains notes about the discovery of a mysterious tablet. When Alan returns to Roth's house that night, he finds out that the professor is dead, and that the woman who lived with him and claimed to be his wife has disappeared. Alan does not give up, and continues his risky investigation, helped by Roth's assistant, Geneviève. Meanwhile, other deaths follow: a maid at the hotel where Alan is staying is brutally killed by a monstrous-looking woman, and the second victim is an antique dealer, Polgár Móricz. Alan finds out about the existence of a mysterious cult: its members—the Weavers—worship spider-like deities whose names are written in the tablet Roth had discovered. Alan recovers the tablet, but despite the help of a mysterious man he is captured, tortured and subjected to a horrible initiatory rite...

Born in 1952, Gianfranco Giagni had divided himself between radio and television since the mid–1970s, and worked sporadically in cinema as well, as assistant to Mauro Bolognini (*L'eredità Ferramonti*, 1976) and Alberto Negrin. Already an accomplished radio director, in 1981 he created the pioneering music program *Mister Fantasy*. Giagni directed some of Italy's first music videos for Vasco Rossi, Loredana Berté and Matia Bazar, but he also worked with foreign artists, such as Miguel Bosé and Madness. In May 1986 Giagni's short *Giallo e nero* won the "Gabbiano d'Argento" prize at the "Anteprima" Film Festival in Bellaria and was broadcast on television a couple of months later. Producer Tonino Cervi, who in turn had directed an interesting Gothic film, *Il delitto del diavolo*,[1] liked *Giallo e nero* very much, and got in touch with the director with an offer to make his feature film debut with a horror movie. "I accepted to direct it "for hire" in order to confront myself with the rules of genre filmmaking, as the masters of the American B-movie of the 1940s and 50s had done before."[2]

The original script for *Il nido del ragno*, by Cervi, Riccardo Aragno and Cesare Frugoni, dated from a few years earlier. As Giagni explained, "It seemed a bit dated to me, so I called

scriptwriter Gianfranco Manfredi and together we tried to give it a more modern framing story."[3] Manfredi was an eclectic figure in Italian popular culture, being a singer-songwriter, writer, scriptwriter, actor and soon-to-be comic book writer: in the 1990s he created the Western comic *Magico Vento* and wrote episodes for *Dylan Dog* and *Tex*. Firstly, Giagni and Manfredi changed the setting from Venice to Budapest, frequently visited by Italian cinema in those years (see also *La chiesa*, *Etoile*, and Carlo Verdone's 1987 hit comedy *Io e mia sorella*): "It is a city with many Gothic elements, with disquieting buildings in an apparently rational context … cities like Budapest, Prague or Sarajevo suggest a sense of anxiety: behind their 'normality' there lies in fact a hidden 'abnormality.'"[4]

Given the script and budget limits, the director also sought to balance the horrific and gruesome elements with more classic ones,

Italian locandina for Gianfranco Giagni's *Il nido del ragno* (1988).

with references to Hitchcock and Polanski. The latter's influence can be seen in the conspiracy angle of the story (see for instance the suspicious-looking guests of the hotel where the protagonist Alan Whitmore is staying), while the scene where Alan looks almost hypnotized at the opposite building, where the fascinating Geneviève takes off her clothes and then stares at him in the nude behind her window, silently luring him, nods to both *Rear Window* (1954) and *Le locataire*.

But Giagni's film has also several elements in common with past Italian horrors and thriller. The Eastern European setting brings to mind another classic conspiracy tale, Aldo Lado's political thriller *La corta notte delle bambole di vetro* (1971), while the idea of an evil cult spread all over the city and possibly worldwide recalls Francesco Barilli's *Il profumo della signora in nero*, in turn a grim Polanski variation; the bouncing black ball which erupts on the scene before each murder borrows from *Operazione paura*, while the murder scenes have Argento's name written all over them. In typical Argento fashion, the agents of evil employ very earthly weapons such as butcher's knives, and the killing of the maid openly draws from *Suspiria* and *Inferno*, with its eerie greens and the sheets around the poor victim acting like a white screen ready to be ripped open by knives or turning into artistic canvas to be sprayed with arterial blood. But Giagni maintained that the reference was subconscious: "I surely admire Argento very much, and I love his cinematic universality as well as the capacity of being essential at the same time: everyone can identify themselves in his movies, and while I shot *Il nido del ragno* I realized how difficult it was!"[5]

Il nido del ragno exudes an interesting and unusual Lovecraftian mood, with its reference to a submerged millennial cult that worships monstrous beings akin to the Providence writer's "Old Ones." In *The Complete H.P. Lovecraft Filmography*, one of the few English language books that analyzed the movie thoroughly, author Charles P. Mitchell went so far as calling it "one of the finest of all films inspired by Lovecraft,"[6] which seems a bit too much, given the variety of influences. Mitchell elaborates on the statement, claiming that except for its predictable denouement, Giagni's film "clearly demonstrates that Lovecraftian concepts can be adapted to the screen in a fresh, dramatic and interesting way if the material is treated with respect and devel-

oped thoughtfully," and adding that it "incorporates many ideas characteristic of HPL, from the shy, retiring scholar/hero to the forbidden historical text and the cabal of radical followers dedicated [to] the Old Ones."

It is likely that Cervi had in mind other sources for his original story, but the theme of the lone scholar who arrives in a strange town and confronts a mystery, only to find himself the designated victim to an obscure power, is truly Lovecraftian, as is the idea of monstrous ancient gods lurking in a world which reveals itself as nightmarish and absurd under a façade of apparent normality. The script riffs on the theme of the spider's web as a labyrinth with no way out, and Giagni depicts the transition between reality and nightmare in an eerie sequence where Alan is driving around Budapest in search of an antique shop, only to find the road blocked by a weird-looking barricade which vaguely recalls an oversized web. He soon gets lost in the labyrinthine streets of the old town, whose weird topography recalls those of Lovecraft villages. Later, Whitmore finds himself in another labyrinth, a surreal underworld filled with cadavers wrapped in web cocoons and car wrecks.

The film's *pièce de resistance* is the climactic appearance of the idol. Mitchell identifies the monster worshipped by the "weavers" in Atlach-Nacha, conceived by Clark Ashton Smith in his 1934 story *The Seven Geases* and described as "a darksome form, big as a crouching man but with long spider-like members…. There was a kind of face on the squat ebon body, low down amid the several-jointed legs."[7] Sergio Stivaletti's elaborate special effects combine the expected transformation with optical stop-motion. "I convinced the producer that I would do all the mechanical and optical effects in the film," Stivaletti explained some time before its release. "I was entrusted with the creative-technical part as well as the optical animation effects…. I can tell that there's a monster in the film, that this monster is not how you see it in the end but it turns like that through a transformation."[8] The scene is blatantly inspired by a famous moment in *The Thing*, with a suitably grotesque baby spider who undergoes a horrific metamorphosis, and the optical stop-motion effects *à la* Ray Harryhausen, albeit not impeccable, display Stivaletti's inventiveness and attempt to bring something new to Italian *fantastique* in terms of visual inventions. Back then, it looked like the 30-year-old Stivaletti was ready for the big step and make his directorial debut. However, not least because of the declining state of Italian cinema, it would take him nine years before finally making his first film as a director, *M.D.C.—Maschera di cera* (a.k.a. *Wax Mask*, 1997).

Compared with many other Italian horror movies of the decade, Giagni's direction is truly impressive, as it blends the visual elegance typical of the Italian masters of the genre and a polished style that is effectively international. The deliberate pacing is never boring, and each scene is carefully developed by way of camera angles and movements, lighting and frame composition. A particularly effective moment in this respect is Alan's dialogue with Mrs. Kuhn, played by Stéphane Audran: the woman is sitting in her room, rocking an empty cradle on the right side of the frame, while on the left, atop a piano, we see a big, weird doll highlighted by a source of light that falls right on it. What in other hands would have been a rather dull passage, aimed at providing some slight character development and a clue to the mystery, turns into a strikingly effectively atmospheric scene. Another outstanding moment is a passionate love scene between Alan and Geneviève which suddenly turns nasty, as the woman, while kissing her partner's body, secretes a thick foam that reveals her spider-like nature, unbeknownst to the oblivious Mark.

Giagni's accomplished direction overcomes the acting limitations of its leads. Paola Rinaldi is barely convincing as the femme fatale, despite her willingness to perform frontal nude scenes, while male fashion model Roland Wybenga, in his film debut, is the typical anonymous handsome hero seen in other horror movies of the period, such as *Dèmoni* and its sequel. Still, he is fit for the role, as the umpteenth weak detective hero who is deceived and defeated by his opponents, not unlike Lino Capolicchio's character in *La casa dalle finestre che ridono*, although the script does very little to characterize Whitmore, except for an opening childhood trauma scene in the vein of *La casa con la scala nel buio*. Wybenga, who turned up in a couple more films, including Enzo G. Castellari's *Sinbad of the Seven Seas* (1989), seemingly died of AIDS in 1995. Claude Chabrol's ex-wife and muse Stéphane Audran is quite effective as the mysterious hotel manager, and William Berger turns up in one of his rare good guy roles as the mysterious would-be savant, who is reserved one of the most inventive death scenes.

Commercial expectations were high, and Reteitalia managed to obtain some press exposure for the project. Giagni's name was mentioned together with those of Michele Soavi and two more debutants, Fulvio Wetzl (*Rorret*) and Andrea Marfori (*Il bosco 1*), and *Il nido del ragno* was compared to 1940s *film noirs* and to Kafka's *Metamorphosis* (an audacious but hazardous term of comparison, actually) in an article which spitefully dismissed Lucio Fulci "and other hacks" and welcomed the "new wave" of Italian horror.[9] But such expectations were doomed to be disappointed. Released with an "all audiences" rating despite its rather gory murder scenes and transformations, *Il nido del ragno* performed badly at the box-office and was barely noticed by critics.[10] On the other hand, the Catholic "Segnalazioni Cinematografiche" were harsh to the point of insult, stating: "The movie doesn't represent anything worth signaling, if not as a manic product, a mental test of a deranged, ranting mind."

When *Il nido del ragno* came out, Giagni was already at work on a more ambitious project, a TV series based on Guido Crepax's comic *Valentina*, starring U.S. model Demetra Hampton. Accompanied by a huge hype, the series' 13 episodes (25 to 30 minutes each) were broadcast between September 1989 and February 1990. Giagni, who penned the scripts with Manfredi, directed 9 episodes, while the remaining 4 were directed by Giandomenico Curi, himself a video maker and TV author and director. Despite being a moderate success, *Valentina* was not confirmed for a second season. Giagni made his second feature—the political thriller *Nella terra di nessuno*—only in 2001, which as of today remains his last fictional film; over the years he kept working in television, on several TV series and programs, and he also helmed several interesting documentaries on Italian cinema.

NOTES

1. See Curti, *Italian Gothic Horror Films*, 1970–1979,
2. Palmerini and Mistretta, *Spaghetti Nightmares*, 92.
3. *Ibid.*
4. *Ibid.*
5. *Ibid.*
6. Charles P. Williams, *The Complete H.P. Lovecraft Filmography* (Westport, CT: Greenwood, 2001), 187.
7. *Ibid.*, 191.
8. Morsiani, "Intervista a Sergio Stivaletti," 96.
9. Piero Perona, "Il nuovo regista ama l'horror," *Stampa Sera*, August 5, 1988.
10. One notable exception was the Turinese newspaper *La Stampa*, whose critic wrote a rather positive review of

the film, praising the makeup and special effects by Stivaletti ("a name who, as far as nightmares are concerned, is a guarantee"). Too bad the review was illustrated with a still from the very last scene, which gave away the ending. See a.pie. [Aldo Piersanti], "La ragnatela mortale del mostro di Budapest," *La Stampa*, August 31, 1988.

Nosferatu a Venezia (*Vampire in Venice*)

D: Augusto Caminito [and Klaus Kinski, uncredited]. *S*: Carlo Alberto Alfieri, Leandro Lucchetti; *SC*: Augusto Caminito; *DOP*: Antonio Nardi (Kodak, Telecolor); *M*: Luigi Ceccarelli (Artem Publishing); *E*: Claudio Cutry; *PD*: Joseph Teichner, Luca Antonucci; *CO*: Vera Cozzolino; *MU*: Sergio Angelponi Franco Corridoni, Luigi Rocchetti; *Hair*: Alberta Giuliani, Maurizio Lupi; *AD*: Andrea Prandstaller; *2nd UD*: Luigi Cozzi; *C*: Giovanni Ciarlo; *AC*: Luca Alfieri, Vincenzo Carpineta; *KG*: Tarcisio Diamanti; *G*: Vittorio Pescetelli; *SP*: Enzo Falessi; *W*: Palmira Tacconi; *AE*: Maria Elvira Castagnolo, Evandro Postorino; *PM*: Claudio D'Achille; *B*: Luciano Muratori; *SO*: Nick Alexander; *SOEd*: Fernando Caso, Claudio Gramigna, Edmondo Gintili; *Foley Artist*: Alvaro Gramigna, Claudio Gramigna; *Mix*: Primiano Muratori; *SE*: Franco Ragusa [and Luigi Cozzi]; *Stunts*: Ottaviano Dell'Acqua, Franco Pacifico; *SS*: Annamaria Liguori; *Adaptation/DubD*: Alberto Marras. *Cast*: Klaus Kinski (Nosferatu), Christopher Plummer (Prof. Paris Catalano), Donald Pleasence (Don Alvise), Barbara De Rossi (Helietta Canins), Yorgo Voyagis (Dr. Barneval), Anne Knecht (Maria Canins), Elvire Audray (Uta Barneval), Giuseppe Mannajuolo (Gianmarco Tosatti), Clara Colosimo (Medium), Maria Clementina Cumani Quasimodo (Princess), Micaela Flores Amaya "La Chunga" (Woman at Gypsy Camp); *uncredited*: Mickey Knox (Priest). *PROD*: Augusto Caminito for Scena Film Production (Rome), Reteitalia S.p.A.; *EP*: Carlo Alberto Alfieri; *PM*: Ennio Onorati, Angelo D'Antoni; *UM*: Giorgio Padoan, Silvano Zignani; *PSe*: Marco Alfieri, Marco De Rossi; *UP*: Luigi Biamonte; *PAcc*: Franco Maia. *Country*: Italy. Filmed on location in Venice and at De Paolis In.Ci.R. Studios (Rome). *Running time*: 98 minutes (m. 2700). Visa n. 83889 (8.20.1988); *Rating*: V.M.14. *Release dates*: 9.9.1988 (Italy–Venice Film Festival), 4.1.1989 (Japan); *Distribution*: Medusa. *Domestic gross*: n.a. Also known as: *Nosferatu in Venice*; *Prince of the Night* (USA); *Nosferatu in Venedig* (Germany); *Nosferatu à Venise* (France); *Nosferatu, el príncipe de las tinieblas* (Spain).

The Venetian noblewoman Helietta Canins invites to her home an English expert in vampirism, Paris Catalano. Helietta wants to end forever the gloomy atmosphere that still weighs in her palace, where she lives with her grandmother and her young sister Maria. Two centuries earlier, in fact, while in Venice raged the plague, one of her ancestors had been the victim of a vampire and vanished with him. In the basement of the palace there is still a mysterious iron-rimmed sarcophagus and Helietta, thinking that Nosferatu is right there, invites Catalano to destroy the undead. The vampire, evoked in a séance, arrives in Venice, while the body of the ancestor, Letizia, strangely resembling Helietta, is discovered in the tomb. But exorcising Nosferatu turns out to be an impossible undertaking. One after the other those around Helietta fall victim to the vampire's bite, and she dies too. Nosferatu knows he can be liberated and die on one condition: being loved by a virgin maiden. Helietta's half-sister Maria is the chosen one, but just when Nosferatu is about to achieve his goal—in a dilapidated villa on the Isle of Dogs, in the lagoon—Helietta's lover shows up and shoots the vampire, leaving the monster unharmed but mortally wounding Maria. After taking revenge on the man, Nosferatu vampirizes the girl and leaves Venice with her in his arms...

When in 1985 producer Augusto Caminito took over the project of *Nosferatu a Venezia* he did not imagine that it would become the worst nightmare in his career. In the mid–1980s, Caminito (born in Naples in 1940), a former scriptwriter turned producer, had decided to finance some thriller and horror films, which seemed a profitable investment for the Italian and foreign markets. With his company Scena Film, he had produced Lucio Fulci's *Murderock—Uccide a passo di danza*, and he would commission some more films to Fulci, which he would contract out to the Distribuzione Alpha company, owned by Antonio Lucidi and Luigi Nannerini, namely *Sodoma's Ghost* and *Quando Alice ruppe lo specchio*, plus the other titles distributed under the tagline "*Lucio Fulci presenta*."

Caminito came across the script for *Nosferatu a Venezia* through Carlo Alberto Alfieri, who had written the screenplay with Leandro Lucchetti, but couldn't manage to sell the idea to any distributor and hadn't enough money to produce the movie by himself; so, he offered it to other producers. The idea of a sequel to Werner Herzog's 1979 film *Nosferatu: Phantom der Nacht* seemed a brilliant commercial move to Caminito, especially since Alfieri was well-

Italian lobby card for *Nosferatu a Venezia* (1988), Augusto Caminito's ill-fated sequel to Werner Herzog's *Nosferatu: Phantom der Nacht* (1979), starring Klaus Kinski.

acquainted with Herzog's Nosferatu, Klaus Kinski, and had secured the actor's participation in the project. The Neapolitan producer and the Polish actor met, discussed some more film projects and found a satisfying agreement for both. On December 17, 1985, Caminito and Kinski signed a deal for two films, *Nosferatu a Venezia* and *Grandi cacciatori*, and Caminito promised that he would produce a third title, Kinski's pet project *Paganini*, which the actor had been dreaming for years, and which he had tried in vain to put together in 1980 with Alfredo Bini producing and Herzog directing.[1]

Caminito secured a distribution deal with Reteitalia, obtained a strong advance from the bank and hired Alfieri as executive producer. The film was to be directed by Maurizio Lucidi (who had already helmed a film set in Venice, the excellent 1971 thriller *La vittima designata*, starring Tomas Milian and Pierre Clementi), but Caminito decided that the Italian sequel to *Nosferatu* needed to be more ambitious. Luigi Cozzi, who worked on the film as a consultant on the set and during post-production at his friend Alfieri's request—the two had met when Cozzi di-

rected the erotic comedy *La portiera nuda* (1976)—explains: "Caminito realized that *Nosferatu in Venice* would probably be a hit if it had a bigger budget. He doubled the budget, but decided Lucidi was not the right director, and that he needed a "name" director for the film."[2] So, he fired Lucidi,[3] who only shot some footage of the February 1986 Venice Carnival with a small crew and without Kinski, and hired fellow Neapolitan Pasquale Squitieri, who had just helmed the crime drama *Il pentito* (1985) starring Franco Nero and Tony Musante. The producer also gathered an impressive supporting cast, which included such internationally renowned names as Christopher Plummer and Donald Pleasence, as well as Barbara De Rossi, Yorgo Voyagis, and Stefania Sandrelli's daughter, Amanda.

Squitieri rewrote the script, setting it in the near future, in 1996 Venice,[4] and had Alfredo Castelli and a number of comic book artists prepare a series of storyboards for the film's most spectacular scenes. Caminito found the result "too baroque"[5] and most of all too expensive for his economic possibilities. But Squitieri was not willing to resize the script according to the available budget; moreover, he and Kinski had already had a clash. Since he could not afford to lose his star, Caminito had no other choice but terminate the contract with Squitieri and pay him the agreed sum before the director filmed even a single shot. By then, he had already spent lots of money before the film even got started and was forced to reshape the project. He called Alfieri and told him the budget he was willing to spend on the film. As Cozzi recalls, "Alfieri told him that, since the project was rather ambitious, it would be very difficult not to go over budget, unless the movie was directed by a filmmaker they could trust—that is, one more concerned with respecting all the conditions laid down by the producer rather than dreaming of chimerical artistic peaks."[6]

The producer and Alfieri then hired Mario Caiano, another expert filmmaker who had already directed Kinski in the Seventies, in the Spaghetti Western/Kung Fu hybrid *Il mio nome è Shangai Joe* (a.k.a. *The Fighting Fists of Shanghai Joe*, 1973). Caminito and Caiano had worked together on a film shot in Africa by Mino Guerrini, *Le miniere del Kilimangiaro* (1986), which Caiano completed, finishing the action scenes in record time in Tor Caldara, near Rome. He seemed the ideal director to deal with Kinski and take care of the economical issues.

In Summer 1986 Caiano completed the casting and went location scouting, while Caminito frantically rewrote the script to make it more suitable for the by now drastically reduced budget. According to Cozzi, several scenes and characters were totally discarded with this last-minute rewriting.

Shooting started on August 25th,[7] but things went wrong from the beginning. Firstly, Kinski refused to shave his head and wear the prosthetic fangs as in Herzog's version, and insisted that he keep his hair long—or else he wouldn't do the movie. On the first day of shooting, Caiano shot the scene of the shipwrecked boat carrying the vampire's coffin, in Tor Caldara, then came the turn of shooting with Kinski. After filming a scene, he called cut. But, as Caiano recalled,

> Kinski didn't stop and kept doing his usual grimaces. I was incredulous. On that occasion, Caminito approached and told me that Klaus didn't want to be interrupted because—he said—he could come up with good facial expressions. Meanwhile, I heard Klaus ask who I was and what was the reason of my presence on the set. Despite my dismay, the next

morning I showed up regularly on the set. Without even saying hello, Kinski and Caminito locked themselves in the actor's trailer and stayed there the whole morning. Only then I understood the state of things: Caminito had promised Kinski, in addition to a Ferrari car, that he would let him direct the movie. Of course, the actor's "weight" was greater than mine. The only thing I could do was get in my car and go home.[8]

According to Caminito, Caiano's desertion came after a violent argument during filming the scene where Nosferatu arrives at the gypsy camp, shot in Tor Caldara. The producer ran to Kinski's trailer in a rage and the actor, still in his Nosferatu costume, told him, "Now you're directing the movie!" To which Caminito didn't object: "Truth is, I was terrified by the idea of directing the film myself, but at that time too many things in my life were not going right, and I was firmly convinced that I would finish the movie at any cost."[9] In interviews of the period, the producer diplomatically explained the change behind the camera as follows: "Mario Caiano's shyness clashed against the difficult roughness of Kinski's temper, and so Caiano left the set spontaneously. As you see, I decided to make the film myself."[10]

But working with Kinski turned out a nightmare for Caminito. The actor altered the script according to his whims and mood changes, and he made ample display of his erratic and offensive behavior with the crew: his favorite target was Alfieri, who, in Caminito's words, had become a true scapegoat for the actor's outbursts of anger. Cozzi recalled:

> When we were rehearsing a scene, Kinski moved in a certain way, and consequently the director of photography spent a couple of hours setting the lighting according to his movements on the set. But when we shot the scene … well, Kinski regularly behaved as the rehearsals hadn't even taken place and changed his acting and most of all his movements. Therefore, the d.o.p. had to design the lighting from scratch! This meant exhausting delays in the shooting schedule, and crew members were obviously exasperated, because they worked in vain and felt they were being made fun of. What's more, Kinski absolutely refused to reshoot the same scene twice … if the director asked to shoot another take … he just said no. Like Paganini, Kinski would not repeat![11]

Kinski's dominion over the film also manifested with an abrupt recasting. He demanded that Caminito fire Amanda Sandrelli, who played Helietta's (Barbara De Rossi) younger sister

Maria, whom he didn't consider sensual enough for the role of the virgin who offers herself to Nosferatu. Kinski replaced her with an inexperienced young girl—Yorgo Voyagis' girlfriend Anne Knecht, whom he noticed when she visited the set. The fact that the Dominican-born, dark-skinned Knecht didn't look Venetian (and Italian) at all, didn't seem to be a problem. It was just a matter of changing the script and turning Maria into Helietta's *adopted* sister.

Cozzi, who shot some scenes as second unit director—namely, Maria throwing herself from the San Marco steeple, Christopher Plummer and other characters on boat in the lagoon, as well as details of the duel scene between Plummer's character and the vampire—had to accompany Kinski around Venice at dawn to shoot additional scenes that weren't even in the script. "I think we ended up with about 10 hours of footage, which more or less consisted of the same thing: Kinski walking here and there."[12] Another such addition was the final scene of Nosferatu walking through the streets of Venice with a nude dead girl in his arms, filmed without permits: interminable and clumsy, with the actor struggling to carry the girl (who visibly clings to his shoulders so as not to fall), it is a testament to Kinski's delirious dreams of grandeur.

The actor's behavior with the other actresses was often downright offensive: for the scene in which Nosferatu vampirizes Helietta, the actor simply had to bend over the actress and pretend to bite her neck in close-up. But boom man Luciano Muratori, who was on the set, is adamant that on that occasion Kinski inserted his fingers in the woman's vagina. Muratori struggled with the impulse of grabbing the actor by the neck and flinging him away for that squalid act. After the scene, the actress left the set in tears.[13] Tension between Kinski and the crew rose day by day and at a certain point, according to Cozzi, the whole crew abandoned the set in protest against the actor, who had to apologize publicly for his behavior.

After six weeks' shooting on location in Venice, Caminito had completed only half of the scenes to be filmed there, and there was still a third of the script to be filmed. But he had no alternative than wrap the shoot and make do with the footage he had, no matter how incoherent. Born under a bad sign, and at the mercy of its undisputed master, *Nosferatu a Venezia* ended up an unlikely—and unfinished—concoction, which not even three editors managed to shape into a coherent whole. It was finally released theatrically in 1988, after premiering as the closing event at the midnight screenings of the 1988 Venice Film Festival—a choice that left critics perplexed.[14] Caminito and Kinski were about to leave for Africa, to film *Grandi cacciatori*, which turned out another ill-fated project for the producer.

In a short piece on *Nosferatu a Venezia* which appeared in the *Corriere della Sera* shortly before its Venetian screening, Caminito mentioned that the film was 1 hour and 46 minutes long,[15] whereas the copy submitted to the rating board was about 98 minutes, and the current version runs 89 minutes—a difference in length which speaks volumes about the mess that the movie had become. Its unfinished nature is evident from its haphazard, shaky narrative, barely tied together by a voice-over which explains various passages that were never filmed: according to Cozzi, for instance, the opening section was originally supposed to be in the middle of the story.[16]

The film opts for a different approach to the vampire myth than *Nosferatu*, and more akin to classical Gothic, and its visual style is miles away from Herzog's film. The vampire incarnates a "return of the past" which haunts a Venetian family for centuries, courtesy of a flashback set in 1786: "To him, this house is a door open in time," Helietta explains (or tries to). Nosferatu becomes an unlikely Byronic hero, his eyes perennially gazing toward the horizon, who crosses lagoons and quays as if they were centuries of immortality, and his only chance to end his torment on Earth is to make love to a virgin woman who loves him.

The script makes attempts at reshaping the vampire mythology. During a séance, Catalano (Plummer, giving the best performance in the film by far) explains that one can become a vampire "by being the illegitimate sons of illegitimate parents, the son of witches and warlocks, a man who takes his own life, those who died by hanging, those who died of the plague, those who died with blasphemy on their lips, murderers who die unpunished, and the descendants of vampires." Other details are sparsely mentioned in the dialogue: the vampire is said to sleep 24 hours every 24 days in a coffin leaning on cursed soil, he can walk around in the daylight, casts a reflection in the mirror, which in a scene he contemplates, and is not at all scared by crosses. The most interesting scene in this respect is Nosferatu's encounter with a group of gypsies on the beach, who are his worshippers, where an elderly woman offers him her daughter to be vampirized. The gypsy is Micaela Flores Amaya "La Chunga," a noted barefoot Flamenco dancer and painter who had been the muse of several writers and painters, including Rafael Alberti, Picasso and Dalí, and had appeared in a handful of films, such as *Tip on a Dead Jockey* (1957, Richard Thorpe).

The Venetian setting allows for a few arresting but repetitive images, such as Catalano arriving on boat at dawn, or Nosferatu on a gondola amid the fog of the lagoon, well-served by Luigi Ceccarelli's score (which covers a couple of movements from Vangelis' 1985 album *Mask*), but it betrays the filmmaker's simplistic approach: the city never becomes a living presence in the film (as it was in, say, *Don't Look Now*), but it serves merely as eye candy. In a way, *Nosferatu a Venezia* is telling of the Italian way of life in the 1980s, a country that lived above its means, and sported an abundance it couldn't really afford.

Despite the script's ambitions, the dialogue is often poor if not ridiculous: Nosferatu is pompously described as "adversary of life, dep-

ravation of humanity, great master of rottenness, champion of evil." Caminito injects some timid gore in the process, with a priest falling from a window and ending up transfixed by a spiked gate as in *Black Cat*, and gives room to the erotic aspect of vampirization, with some soft-focus nudity more in tune with 1980s soft porn. The lack of a firm directorial hand is dramatically evident in such scenes as the duel between the vampire and his hunters, which is filmed like some sort of Spaghetti Western showdown and comes off as utterly ridiculous. Apart from Plummer, the supporting players look mostly uninterested (Pleasence's wily and famelic priest is a case in point), or totally lost: poor Anne Knecht is embarrassing in her only screen role as Nosferatu's great love, a character so sketchily developed that it is almost ignored for much of the film.

However, it is Kinski who ultimately drowns the movie. His charismatic presence is vampirizing, and unlike in the actor's stints in 1970s Gothics—such as Sergio Garrone's *Le amanti del mostro* and *La mano che nutre la morte*—it becomes distracting and self-sabotaging. Rather than act, here Kinski simply is himself, histrionic

Nosferatu (Klaus Kinski) carrying his own coffin in a German lobby card for *Nosferatu a Venezia*.

and disturbed, spiteful of the story and the people surrounding him on the set, constantly moving as if to detach himself from the ordinary crowd, lost in his own train of thought and possibly dreaming of his life project, *Paganini*. But, like Nosferatu, leaving behind a trail of (cinematic) destruction.

Notes

1. Stefano Loparco, *Klaus Kinski. Del Paganini e dei capricci* (Piombino: Il Foglio, 2015), 54–58.
2. Luigi Cozzi, "Di Nosferatu e di altri mostri a Venezia," in Antonio Tentori and Luigi Cozzi, *Guida al cinema horror Made in Italy* (Rome: Profondo Rosso, 2007), 362.
3. However, Lucidi is still credited as the director in the 1986 Public Cinematographic Register, with the start of shooting date indicated as April 28, 1986.
4. Piero Zanotto, "Kinski assetato di sangue 'gira' per Venezia," *Stampa Sera*, October 6, 1986.
5. Loparco, *Klaus Kinski. Del Paganini e dei capricci*, 63.
6. Cozzi, "Di Nosferatu e di altri mostri a Venezia," 362.
7. Augusto Caminito, "Il vampiro Kinski," *Corriere della Sera*, August 28, 1988
8. Loparco, *Klaus Kinski. Del Paganini e dei capricci*, 64.
9. *Ibid.* The change in directing took place within the course of a few days, in late August or early September 1986. See Giuseppina Manin, "Miguel Littin: 'Ecco il mio Cile torturato,'" *Corriere della Sera*, September 7, 1986. On the other hand, an article on Kinski published a couple of days earlier still mentioned Caiano as the director. Lamberto Antonelli, "Klaus Kinski un vampiro sulla laguna per il secondo Nosferatu," *La Stampa*, September 5, 1986.
10. Zanotto, "Kinski assetato di sangue 'gira' per Venezia."
11. Cozzi, "Di Nosferatu e di altri mostri a Venezia," 367.
12. *Ibid.*, 368.
13. Loparco, *Klaus Kinski. Del Paganini e dei capricci*, 65–66.
14. Maurizio Porro, "Kinski, vampiro stanco che vuole andare in pensione," *Corriere della Sera*, September 11, 1988.
15. Caminito, "Il vampiro Kinski."
16. Cozzi, "Di Nosferatu e di altri mostri a Venezia," 371.

1989

La chiesa (*The Church*)

D: Michele Soavi. *S*: Dario Argento, Franco Ferrini [and Dardano Sacchetti, uncredited]; *SC*: Dario Argento, Franco Ferrini, Michele Soavi; *DOP*: Renato Tafuri (Eastmancolor); *M*: Keith Emerson, Philip Glass, Goblin [Fabio Pignatelli] (Ed. Bixio C.E.M.S.A.); *E*: Franco Fraticelli; *PD*: Massimo Antonello Geleng; *CO*: Maurizio Paiola; *MU*: Laura Borselli, Franco Casagni, Barbara Morosetti, Rosario Prestopino; *Hair*: Piero Cucchi, Assunta Emidi; *AD*: Filiberto Fiaschi; *C*: Alessandro Carlotto, Enrico Maggi; *Steadicam*: Nicola Pecorini; *AC*: Maurizio Cremisini, Alfonso Vicari; *1stAE*: Piero Bozza; *2ndAE*: Roberto Priori; *SD*: Caterina Napoleone; *AsstSD*: Daniela Giovannoni, Barbara Morosetti; *Set furnishing*: G.P. Postgione, E. Rancati; *SE/SPFX*: Sergio Stivaletti, Renato Agostini, Danilo Bollettini, Massimo Cristofanelli, Danilo Del Monte; *Props*: Fabio Altamura, Osvaldo Monaco; *Set construction chief*: Aldo Taloni; *Carpenter*: E. Tappezzeri; *W*: Carla Latini, Claudio Antonucci; *SOE*: Luca Anzellotti, Luciano Anzellotti, Massimo Anzellotti, Mauro Anzellotti; *B*: Claudio Paolucci; *Mix*: Giulio Viggiani; *Stunts*: Arnaldo Dell'Acqua; *SP*: Franco Vitale; *G*: Fernando Massaccesi; *KG*: Augusto Proietti; *SS*: Marisa Calia; *AsstD*: Claudio Lattanzi. *Cast*: Hugh Quarshie (Father Gus), Tomas Arana (Ewald), Feodor Chaliapin, Jr. (The Bishop), Barbara Cupisti (Lisa), Antonella Vitale (Bridal Model), Giovanni Lombardo Radice (Reverend), Asia Argento (Lotte), Roberto Caruso (Freddie), Roberto Corbiletto (Hermann, the Sacristan), Alina De Simone (Lotte's Mother), Olivia Cupisti (Mira), Gianfranco De Grassi (The Accuser), Claire Hardwick (Joanna), Lars Jorgenson (Bruno), John Karlsen (Heinrich), Katherine Bell Marjorie (Heinrich's Wife), Riccardo Minervini (Schoolboy), Enrico Osterman (The Torturer), Micaela Pignatelli (Fashion shoot photographer), Patrizia Punzo (Miss Brückner), John Richardson (Architect), Matteo Rocchietta (Younger Schoolboy), Isabella Rocchietta (School girl), Michele Soavi (1st Policeman at Lisa's house). *PROD*: Dario Argento for ADC, Mario Cecchi Gori, Vittorio Cecchi Gori for Cecchi Gori Group Tiger Cinematografica, in collaboration with Reteitalia; *EP*: Giuseppe Mangogna; *UM*: Saverio Mangogna; *PSe*: Ezio Orita, Daniela Rocco; *PAcc*: Carlo Du Bois; *Paymaster*: Carlo Cestari. *Unit publicist*: Enrico Lucherini, Gianluca Pignatelli. *Country*: Italy. Filmed in Budapest, Hamburg, and at R.P.A. Elios Studios and De Paolis In.Ci.R. studios (Rome). *Running time*: 100 minutes (m. 2728). Visa n. 84503 (3.10.1989; 4.12.1989); Rating: V.M.18/V.M.14. *Release dates*: 3.10.1989 (Italy), 8.18.1990 (Japan), 8.22.1990 (USA), 6.8.1992 (Spain); *Distribution*: Cecchi Gori (Italy), TriStar Pictures (USA) *Domestic gross*: 1,926,277,000 *lire. Also known as*: *Sanctuaire* (France), *El engendro del diablo* (Spain, Argentina), *Démonok temploma* (Hungary).

Germany, Middle Ages: an army of Teutonic knights discover a village of witches. They burn it, kill the inhabitants and bury them in a mass grave, on which a cathedral is built. The present: a librarian, Ewald, is hired to catalog the church's books and finds an ancient manuscript that reveals a secret about the cathedral. Assisted by a young restorer, Lisa, Ewald follows the indications on the manuscript and finds a heavy cross placed on the floor in the basement of the cathedral to seal the witches' grave. He removes the cross and releases the demons, who possess him. The following day lots of people gather in the church—a school class, a photographer doing a fashion photo shoot with some models, as well as many visitors and people in prayer. Ewald injures the sacristan, infecting him. In turn, the man infects other visitors, then commits suicide. His blood activates a mechanism which locks the church doors and traps all its visitors inside. A young priest, Father Gus, realizes that evil has been unleashed inside the cathedral, where the visitors are killing each other, and he finds out that the place has a secret self-destructing system. Ewald, who has turned into a demonic creature, mates with Lisa during an esoteric ritual. After saving little Lotte, the sacristan's daughter and the only one not yet infected, Father Gus activates the self-destruction mechanism....

In an interview with Lamberto Bava recorded on January 22, 1988, discussing the enormous success of *Dèmoni*, journalist Alberto Morsiani noted: "It is also quite rare that an Italian horror movie had a sequel, *Dèmoni* seems the first occurrence to me." To which Bava replied: "Yes, indeed it is the first, and I think it is even the first time that a third chapter is set into production. I think we'll make it, we're thinking about it, we're writing it."[1] Just a few days earlier, producer Dario Argento had confirmed the news, adding: "The next one in the series will not be called *Dèmoni 3*. I rather think it will have a title like *Ritorno alla casa dei dèmoni* [Author's note: Return to the House of the Demons]; people got tired of titles with

numbers. The film will be directed, as usual, by Lamberto Bava, who's very good."[2] Bava claimed that the third chapter was going to be rather different from the previous ones and pointed out: "We don't want to make a "Number 3," we want to make a film about demons, of course, but it's not going to be a sequel, let's say we'd like to reprise the "demons" subject from other points of view. A bit like when Spielberg and Lucas talked about the *Star Wars* movies: let's say it is a chapter of the *Dèmoni* saga."[3]

The original story, concocted with Franco Ferrini and Dardano Sacchetti, took place on a plane which, due to a perturbation, was forced to an emergency landing in a strange, extradimensional universe, near a volcano; there, the passengers had to face the demons' assaults. "The idea was that they ended up in some sort of a weird Hell," Sacchetti explained. "The plane was taken into consideration because we were looking for a closed, isolated place, in a totally adverse situation with danger inside as well as outside. Let's say something like *Alien*, with the plane instead of the spaceship and the demons replacing the nasty big bug."[4]

Argento and Bava even announced the news on television, during the TV show *Giallo*, where Argento was one of the hosts. But, even after several drafts, they could not come up with a fully satisfying script. According to Sacchetti, the story didn't work well because of the setting. "There is not much possibility of movement inside a plane: the characters couldn't run from one side to the other or act with freedom of movement in that secluded space. Moreover, we didn't have a clear idea of how many characters would be inside the plane, and if the demons could break through the cockpit and get in. On top of that: how would the ending be? ... Given such an amount of unanswered questions, we gave up."[5] Argento, initially enthusiastic about the idea, grew disillusioned with it, too.

So, the scriptwriters came up with a new story: the secluded place where to unleash the demons was to be a church, built on some sort of passage to hell. Not a novelty, considering Sacchetti's previous scripts for Lucio Fulci, but a theme that was closer to Argento's sensibility. During his work on *Suspiria* and *Inferno*, he had become familiar with Fulcanelli, the elusive early 20th century alchemist who had been the inspiration for the character of Varelli, and his book *Le Mystère des cathédrales*. This way, the new movie would ideally link to the previous diptych, especially for its reliance on alchemy and its mysteries.

However, the delay caused by the decision to start all over again with a new storyline had the effect of Lamberto Bava abandoning the project. The director had signed a deal with Fininvest and would start shooting another quartet of TV horror movies for the series "*Alta tensione*" in October 1988, and by July of that year it was clear that he would not be able to make the third *Dèmoni* film.[6] An argument with Sacchetti ensued, and the scriptwriter claims he was royally paid by Argento in order to keep quiet about his involvement in the film. Exit Bava, enter Michele Soavi, fresh from the success of *Deliria*.

With the new director on board, the project took quite a different direction. Now Argento had found a convincing title, *La chiesa*, which didn't connect the movie to the previous ones (except for the subtle reference of a stylized demon face on the letter "C" in the film's poster). Soavi suggested a new opening scene, set in the Middle Ages and inspired by John Milius' *Conan the Barbarian* (1982). Most importantly, in Sacchetti's own words, the directorial turnover affected the film drastically, resulting in a much more dynamic and engrossing visual style, different cinematography and color choices, and, most notably, a different approach to the narrative.

Despite the game of references and thefts that form a strong undercurrent in his work, Argento cannot be considered a postmodernist, focused on pillowing and reassembling old movies: his relationship with cinema of the past is an "occult metabolization"[7] rather than an open homage. Whereas Soavi, born in 1957 and the son of the noted poet Giorgio Soavi, is an out-and-out postmodernist filmmaker. *La chiesa* is an omnivorous and self-satisfied collection of a wide variety of explicit references, from Hieronymus Bosch' apocalyptic paintings to Boris Vallejo's comic book panels, from music videos to video games—and, of course, many films of the distant and close past, which turn up every now and then like pieces of a crazy jigsaw. The aforementioned prologue, for instance, takes place in a gloomy medieval setting influenced by the gruesome excesses of Paul Verhoeven's *Flesh+Blood* (1985), as well as by *Der Name der Rose* (a.k.a. *The Name of the Rose*, 1986, Jean-Jacques Annaud), although Soavi mentioned Eisenstein's *Aleksandr Nevskij* (a.k.a. *Alexander Nevsky*, 1938) for its depiction of the Teutonic Knights, which Eisenstein had totally made up.[8] *Der Name der Rose* also suggested the inclusion in the cast of the octogenarian Feodor Chaliapin, Jr., in a role vaguely similar as that of the "venerable Jorge" which he played in Annaud's film, as well as the idea of the riddles in Latin. On the other hand, another blatant influence is John Carpenter's *Prince of Darkness*, an (admittedly much more successful) blending of traditional Gothic motifs within a modern-day setting. The young director's cinephile taste also resulted in some surprising references for an Italian horror film, such as paying homage to Michael Mann's *The Keep* (1983).

Shooting took place from September to November 1988, on a budget of 3 and a half million dollars.[9] Many scenes were filmed at an imposing location, the astonishing Matthias Church in Budapest, in front of the Fisherman's Bastion, de-consecrated for the period of the shooting. Argento's 13-year-old daughter Asia was cast in one of the film's key roles. It was her third movie after *Dèmoni 2* and Cristina Comencini's *Zoo* (1988), where she was the protagonist. Around the same time, Asia was filming Nanni Moretti's political comedy *Palombella rossa*: it was an auspicious career start for the teenage actress, which would make her one of the most popular young thesps in 1990s Italian cinema.

Shooting was an exhausting experience for Soavi. "I was free, and I could do what I wanted … but I also suffered a lot because of the difficulties, the vicissitudes, the delays."[10] Lighting the church proved an ordeal due to the vast interior spaces, and the director had to give up the idea of shooting the scene of Barbara Cupisti's character coupling with a horned demon on location, due to the protests of the persons in charge of the cathedral. The scene had to be filmed at the De Paolis studios. But despite a rather weak and repetitive third act, *La chiesa* displayed Soavi's visionary technique, especially in the scene which starts in the Middle Age, in the church crypt, and ends in the present day, on the surface, with the camera travelling through space and time in what looks like a long take, even though there are a few cuts.

Even though Argento and his co-scriptwriters were drawing on Fulcanelli's work, with a dab of the esoteric and alchemic elements derived from *Suspiria* and *Inferno*, *La chiesa* looks like a paraphrase on film of Maurice Lévy's fascinating thesis on the Gothic novel, "*toute "his-*

toire gothique" se doit d'etre la mise en fable d'une demeure"[11] (every "Gothic story" should make a narrative out of a house). In *La chiesa*, the very title refers to the place where the story unfolds: it is the abode, the building, the enclosed area, the house—here, by definition, the "House of God"—which is the protagonist. It is the subject and the object, it affects the plot and acts as the (almost) unmoved mover of the characters' actions and tribulations. In turn, said characters are merely two-dimensional presences, barely sketched, and utterly expendable figures.

In his study of the Gothic genre, Lévy develops an analogy with architecture, and emphasizes the symbolic significance of the Gothic building and the concept of man's aspiration to the Divine it expresses. Such a concept is overturned in Soavi's film, where both the characters and the camera are attracted and driven downward, most notably in the impressive sequence in which a vast abyss opens under the gigantic cross that seals the crypt floor. As Edmund Burke wrote in his *A Philosophical Enquiry into the Sublime and Beautiful*, "I am apt to imagine likewise, that height is less grand than depth; and that we are more struck at looking down from a precipice, than at looking up at an object of equal height."[12]

Moreover, Lévy finds in the Gothic novel "an application, at the level of the dreamlike mechanisms, of the very structures of medieval art."[13] The same metaphor turns into images in *La chiesa*, and the film's dreamlike imagery literally take shapes which recall Medieval iconography. That is the case with the cross atop the mass grave of the victims of the plague, the monstrous tangle of bodies which emerge from the bowels of the Earth, the appearance of Satan in the shape of a goat, and the system of counterweights and gears which eventually causes the cathedral to collapse. The latter idea was reprised almost verbatim in Mariano Baino's film, *Dark Waters* (1993).

Writing about the Gothic romance, Lévy and his peers pointed out its incomplete and maze-like narrative structure, filled with enigmatic passages and aimed at peaks of suspense, lacking a real continuity between the various episodes and "more similar to a suite of fragments—we'd almost say a heap of romance "ruins"—than to an organic construction."[14] *Inferno* was an example of the same technique applied to film, and *La chiesa* is a further attempt at a potentially infinite container, in which the

episodes can multiply at will, and blossom from each other, from characters which are promoted within the space of a shot from mere extras or spectators of the story to makers and objects of horror, like the two young bikers, the arrogant fashion model, the elderly couple. They have a similar function as the figures in the bas-reliefs which decorate an apse, which at first get lost in the overall composition and only at second glance stand out in the small space allowed to them by the artist. It is the same method Argento and his collaborators experimented on *Dèmoni* and *Dèmoni 2*, and which only in *La chiesa*, thanks to the Gothic setting, finds a consistent point of arrival.

While preparing the film, Argento heard that Keith Emerson would be interested in writing the score. The idea of working again with the English keyboardist, nine years after *Inferno*, was tempting: it would not only be an attempt to top his previous works as a producer, but it would also bring back his own past (a trait which would characterize more and more Argento's following output as a director). Around the same time Alejandro Jodorowsky (who was making *Santa Sangre*, with Argento's brother Claudio producing) got in touch with Emerson too, having liked his work on *Inferno* very much. Unfortunately, things did not go as planned. When Argento received Emerson's twelve-track demo, he was in for a huge disappointment. "They were terrible. Not even a child would have written music like that. A sort of bombastic march, it sounded like the Carabinieri fanfare. I was aghast…. Naturally, Soavi and I looked for another musician. And some time later I found out that Jodorowsky had received a demo tape more or less like mine, and that he too had rejected Emerson's collaboration."[15] The incident left sore feelings on Emerson's part. What is left in the film of the English musician's work are three tracks: the organ-driven main title theme (in two versions), another titled *Possession*, and a rearranged version of Bach's *Prelude 24* which sounds like a blatant attempt to recreate the magic of Emerson's take on Verdi's *Va, pensiero*. For the rest, Soavi relied on Fabio Pignatelli (credited as Goblin, although his was in fact a solo work) and inserted two tracks by Philip Glass.

As with Argento's previous productions, his name appeared in evidence in newspapers, as if he was the director himself, a confirmation of his superstar status among Italian filmmakers and in the public eye.[16] However, the commercial expectations were destined to be partially un-fulfilled. At first, despite Argento's will to per-form some cuts, the rating board gave *La chiesa* a V.M.18 certificate "in consideration of the many, particularly violent and shocking scenes which are considered unsuitable for the sensi-tivity of the spectators in developmental age." The decision severely harmed the film's box-office potential: *La chiesa* ended up in 36th place among the year's top grossers, with a little less than 2 billion *lire*, only slightly more than Dario Piana's glossy erotic thriller *Sotto il vestito niente II*, and a trifle compared with the 17 billion and a half earned by the season's biggest Italian hit, Roberto Benigni's *Il piccolo diavolo*.

One year later, on appeal, the commission overturned its previous ruling and, considering that the "violent and shocking scenes … are not particularly and intensely underlined within the general context of the film," changed the rating into a V.M.14, a move which at least allowed the film a very favorable home video run in Italy and easier access to television broadcasting.

NOTES

1. Morsiani, "Conversazione con Lamberto Bava," 50.
2. Gianni Vitale, "Dario Argento, l'astratto immaginato. Conversazione con Dario Argento," in *Rosso Italiano (1977/1987)*, 31.
3. Morsiani, "Conversazione con Lamberto Bava," 60.
4. Dardano Sacchetti interviewed, in www.davinotti. com (http://www.davinotti.com/index.php?option=com_content&task=view&id=53).
5. Dardano Sacchetti quoted in Davide Pulici, "La terza volta dei demoni," *Nocturno* #182, February 2018, 56.
6. Giovanna Grassi, "Vi preparo quattro serate horror," *Corriere della Sera*, February 2, 1989.
7. Alberto Pezzotta, *La modernità imperfetta*, in Vito Zagarrio (ed.), *Argento vivo. Il cinema di Dario Argento tra genere e autorialità* (Venice: Marsilio, 2008), 84.
8. Maiello, *Dario Argento*, 309.
9. Jones, *Dario Argento*, 179.
10. *Ibid.*
11. Maurice Lévy, *Le Roman gothique anglais 1764–1824* (Paris: Albin-Michel, 2001 [1968]), VI.
12. Edmund Burke, *A Philosophical Enquiry into the Sublime and Beautiful* (London: Routledge, 2009), 72.
13. Lévy, *Le Roman gothique anglais 1764–1824*, 641.
14. Gian Mario Anselmi (ed.), *Mappe della letteratura europea e mediterranea: Dal Barocco all'Ottocento* (Milan: Paravia—Bruno Mondadori, 2000), 343.
15. Costantini and Dal Bosco, *Nuovo cinema inferno*, 85.
16. Giovanna Grassi, "Un incubo gotico color Argento," *Corriere della Sera*, February 28, 1989.

Etoile (Ballet Star)

D: Peter Del Monte. S: Peter Del Monte, Sandro Petraglia; SC: Peter Del Monte, Franco Ferrini, Sandro Petraglia; *DOP*: Acácio de Almeida (Kodak); *M*: Jürgen Knieper (Ed. BMG Ariola; Faso Edizioni Musicali); *E*: Anna Napoli; *Casting*: Michelle Guillermin, Francesco Cinieri; *ArtD*: Giantito Burchiellaro; *SD*: Bruno Cesari; *CO*: Giuseppe Crisolini Malatesta; *MU*: Massimo De Rossi, Andreina Ambrosini; *Hair*: Vincenzo Cardella, Giancarlo Lucchetti; *AD*: Roberto Palmerini; *2ndAD*: Pietro Sola; *C*: Antonio Scara-muzza; *AC*: Roberto De Nigris, Massimo Intoppa; *AsstArtD*: Mauro Borelli, Andrea Gaeta; *2ndAsstArtD*: Luca Tentellini; *ACO*: Mariella Dirindelli, Elena Carveni; *W*: Silvana Cocuccioni, Bertilla Silvestrin; *AE*: Ambra Giombolini, Fabio Maiuri; *PM*: Giancarlo Gabrielli; *Construction manager*: Luigi Sergianni; *Painter*: Claudio Tedesco; *G*: Delio Catini; *KG*: Sergio Serantoni; *G*: Paolo Tiberti; *SE*: F.lli Corridori; *SPFX*: Sergio Stivaletti; *SO*: Amelio Verona; *B*: Maurizio Merli; *Mix*: Danilo Sterbini; *Sound dubbing mixer*: Roberto Cappanelli; *Re-recording mixer*: Angelo Raguseo; *DubD*: Novella Marcucci; *SP*: Angelo Pennoni; *SS*: Daniela Tonti; *CHOR*: Zarko Prebil; *AsstCHOR*: Lia Calizza; *Ballet advisor*: Vittoria Ottolenghi. *Cast*: Jennifer Connelly (Claire Hamilton/Natalie Horvath), Gary Mc-Cleery (Jason Forrest), Laurent Terzieff (Marius Balakin), Olimpia Carlisi (Madam), Mario Marozzi (Balakin's servant/chauffeur), Donald Hodson (Dancer), Charles Durning (Uncle Joshua), Raffaella Renzi (Dancer: Odette/Odile); *uncredited*: Tom Felleghy (Concierge). *PROD*: Achille Manzotti for Gruppo Berna; Reteitalia (Rome); *EP*: Claudio Mancini; *PM*: Tullio Lullo; *Production Coordinator*: Massimo Iacobis; *PSe*: Cinzia Taffani; *PAss*: Stefano Mandini; *ADM*: Giancarlo Ciotti; *PAcc*: Archimede Orlando; *Cash*: Carlo Gagliardi, Angelo Frezza; *Press at-tache*: Lucherini-Fantoli. *Country*: Italy. Filmed on location in Budapest, and at Villa Parisi (Frascati, Rome), Spoleto and Cinecittà (Rome). *Running time*: 101 minutes (m. 2830). Visa n. 84344 (1.12.1989); *Rating*: all audiences. *Release dates*: 3.17.1989 (Italy), 10.14.1989 (Japan); *Dis-tribution*: Artisti Associati. *Domestic gross*: n.a. *Also known as*: Ballet, Os fantasmas de uma Es-trela (Portugal).

Note: P. Tchaikovsky's *Swan Lake* is played by the orchestra of the Unione Musicisti di Roma, directed by Franco Tamponi.

Ballet student Claire Hamilton arrives in Budapest to audition for a new production of Swan Lake. At the hotel she meets a young Amer-ican, Jason, who is immediately smitten with her.

When her moment comes, Claire is so overwhelmed that she ditches the audition. She then dances alone in the empty auditorium to find solace and is spotted by the enigmatic choreographer, Marius Balakin. One night a pair of mysterious ballet dancers, a woman and a man, sneak in Claire's hotel room and put a spell on her. Claire, now believing she is called Natalia Horvath, is led to an abandoned villa which belonged to the dancer, who died 100 years earlier. There she starts training for her leading role in Swan Lake, *under Marius' guidance. Jason, who followed them to the villa, starts researching on Balakin, whom he recognizes as the man in a 19th century portrait, and on Horvath. Jason's uncle, an antique dealer named Joshua, is hypnotized by the mysterious female dancer and attempts to take Jason back to the U.S., but the young man flees, and Joshua meets an accidental death. Jason discovers that Natalie Horvath played the prima ballerina in a performance of* Swan Lake *choreographed by Balakin, but she met a tragic fate on opening night. He returns to the villa to save Claire from Balakin's spell, and finds himself transported to the past, in the theater when* Swan Lake *is being performed in front of a 19th century audience, with Claire as the prima ballerina. He also discovers Balakin's unspeakable secret...*

Following *Giulia e Giulia* (1987), the first fiction film shot with Sony's HDVS high definition video system, Peter Del Monte continued in the exploration of the Fantastic genre, which he had already approached in an original and compelling way in the outstanding *Piccoli fuochi* (1985). Given *Giulia e Giulia*'s commercial success both in Italy and abroad, his new project was born with the aim of meeting an international audience. Producer Achille Manzotti provided the director with a small but impressive cast which included the ravishing Jennifer Connelly (Sergio Leone's *Once Upon a Time in America*, *Phenomena*), Gary McCleery (*Matewan*), Charles Durning (*The Front Page, Tootsie, To Be or Not to Be*) and Laurent Terzieff, a veteran of French and Italian *auteur* cinema. Filming took place in Budapest and Italy[1] in the Summer of 1988, under the working title *Ballerina.*[2]

The plot reprised one of the director's favorite themes, the search for one's own identity—already at the core of some of his previous films, namely *L'altra donna* (1980), *Invito al viaggio* (1983) and *Giulia e Giulia*—

in an unusual environment such as classical ballet, "the *milieu* par excellence which cancels any time dimension.... A mortuary ritual which repeats itself immutable."[3] The story, concocted with Sandro Petraglia, draws from a number of elements typical of the Gothic genre—the *Doppelgänger*, reincarnation, a revealing portrait, a mysterious villa which functions as a gateway between the past and the present, and an abandoned theater which travels in time like a ghost ship—albeit in a peculiar way, which eschews horror in favor of mystery and romanticism. Del Monte described it as "a black fairytale, an illusionistic game, a big firework show with terrifying moments, although without a single drop of blood."[4]

Co-opting screenwriter Franco Ferrini was possibly a move on the part of Del Monte (or Manzotti) to give the project a more commercial edge. A former film critic, Ferrini had worked with Dario Argento on *Phenomena* and *Opera*, as well as Lamberto Bava's two *Dèmoni* films, and had debuted as a director with a *giallo*, *Caramelle da uno sconosciuto* (1987). Ferrini's contribution is quite likely the reason behind

International poster for *Etoile* (1989, Peter Del Monte).

certain passages which look like they were borrowed verbatim from an Argento film, not just because of Connelly's presence and the protagonist being a ballet dancer. Not only is the opening, with Claire's arrival in Budapest, vaguely reminiscent of Susy Benner's arrival to the dance school in *Suspiria* (minus the storm, the witches and the murders, that is), but the ballet audition which she flees in a panic has a certain uneasiness to it, which recalls the way Argento depicted the petty, jealous dance students at the Tanzacademie.

The Argento connection returns in several scenes: Jason's visit to a library recalls *Inferno*, while the whole final part, with the young hero discovering access to Balakin's secret rooms, his climactic fight with the incarnation of evil and the stabbing by way of a mirror splinter—all this interspersed with the climactic ballet—all look like a much-toned down retelling of Susy's descent into the witch's lair. On top of that, Balakin's rendition of *Swan Lake*, albeit not quite as bizarre as Marco's (Ian Charleson) *mise-en-scène* of Verdi's *Macbeth* in *Opera*, is another nod to Argento's use of opera to convey suspense and dread. Some elements are lifted from *The Phantom of the Opera*, the source of inspiration for Argento's film as well: the tormented choreographer, who lives in the bowels of a theatre and can cross the boundaries of time, is part Phantom (minus the mask and the gruesome features) and part Svengali.

What *Etoile* has certainly in common with the scripts Ferrini delivered for Argento are the shaky logic and paper-thin characters. The backstory of Natalia Horvath is clumsily introduced via a quick expository scene in the library, and the final revelation—Marius' staging of *Swan Lake* is supposed to end with the triumph of the Black Swan and the unleashing of evil in the world—turns what looked like a case of *amour fou* through the ages into a hard-to-swallow mess about good and evil, clumsily explained via a brief diary excerpt. The hero's meeting and climactic fight with a giant black swan which symbolizes the forces of evil tries hard to be suspenseful but ends up an embarrassment (a much more interesting variation of the scene will be found in Soavi's *La setta*, 1991). The animatronic swan, courtesy of an uncredited Sergio Stivaletti, can be glimpsed in the film for a handful of seconds.

Ultimately, though, the major culprit is Del Monte, whose idea of cinema, self-conceited and riddled with psychological nuances, proves detrimental to a film which would have been much better had it been a simple, unpretentious genre tale. The opening scenes, set in the fascinating and arcane Mitteleuropean city, are suitably atmospheric, but the fantasy angle never comes alive, despite Acacio de Almeida's impressive cinematography and an interesting score by frequent Wim Wenders composer Jürgen Knieper, as the direction lacks the surreal quality such a project would have needed. Several scenes seemingly played for suspense (Claire menacing the sleeping Jason with a knife) turn out to be useless, throwaway diversions that show the director's uneasiness with the trappings of genre filmmaking, while the symbols— the juxtaposition of the White and Black Swan as the eternal ambiguity between good and evil, the references to the myth of Leda being seduced by Zeus in the form of a swan—are trite. The actors are poorly directed too and cannot breathe life into their characters: Durning is wasted in a thankless role, McCleery is a leading man as bland as Leigh McCloskey in *Inferno*, and Carlisi and Marozzi (of Rome's Teatro dell'Opera) fail to make an impression as the two mystery dancers.

Etoile was not the commercial success its makers had hoped for, and Italian critics ravaged it: "At first it looks like a remake of *Opera* with Tchaikovsky instead of Verdi, and, alas, without suspense.... Confused and not at all fascinating, persecuted by music, written ... in a semi-profound style, and riddled with clues as if something is going to happen which never does, *Etoile* is.... Del Monte's worst film."[5] It had marginal distribution abroad, although it was awarded the critics' award at the 1990 Fantasporto Film Festival, in Portugal. The director's subsequent project, an adaptation of Gary Devon's thought-provoking novel *Lost*, produced by Alberto Grimaldi and to be shot in the States, never materialized, and Del Monte returned to intimate psychological drama with the anthology *Tracce di vita amorosa* (1990).

In recent years, *Etoile* has regained some attention on the part of film buffs because of its many similarities with Darren Aronofsky's *Black Swan* (2010).

NOTES

1. The Italian locations (such as Villa Parisi in Frascati, whose unmistakable octagonal fountain can be glimpsed in the garden of the abandoned villa where Marius resides,

and the Teatro Nuovo Gian Carlo Menotti in Spoleto) blend seamlessly with the Hungarian ones (the Buda castle, Heroes' square, Városliget park).

2. Giovanna Grassi, "Jennifer Beals è della *Partita*," *Corriere della Sera*, July 15, 1988. The title refers to Jennifer Beals' starring role alongside Matthew Modine and Faye Dunaway in Carlo Vanzina's *La partita* (a.k.a. *The Gamble*, 1988), another production devised for the foreign markets.

3. Paolo Cervone, "Vi invito a una danza macabra," *Corriere della Sera*, January 4, 1989.

4. *Ibid.*

5. M. Po. [Maurizio Porro], "Quel 'mago' dei cigni," *Corriere della Sera*, March 22, 1989.

I frati rossi (*The Red Monks*)

D: John [Gianni] Martucci. *S*: Luciana Anna Spacca; *SC*: Pino Buricchi, Gianni Martucci; *DOP*: Sergio Rubini (Eastmancolor); *M*: Paolo Rustichelli (Ed. Nazional Music); *E*: Vanio Amici; *PD*: Joseph Teichner; *CO*: Silvio Laurenzi; *MU*: Rino Todero; *Hair*: Regina Usidda; *SO*: Antonino Pantano; *Mix*: Sandro Occhetti; *PrM*: Gianni Muzzi; *SP*: Franco Biciocchi; *KG*: Elio Bosi; *ChEl*: Antonio Leurini; *AC*: Mauro Masciocchi; *W*: Giovanna Russu; *AE*: Marco Buricchi, Carlo Pulera; *SS*: Annamaria Liguori; *Generator Operator*: Otello Simotti; *Driver*: Aldo Marcenaro. *Cast*: Gerardo Amato (Robert Gherghi), Lara Wendel [Daniela Barnes] (Ramona Icardi), Malisa Longo (Priscilla), Richard Brown [Chuck Valenti] (Ben), Claudio Pacifico (Mystery Man), Mary Maxwell (Lucille), Ronald [Gaetano] Russo (Riccardo Gherghi), Ludovico Dello Jojo (Notary Berti); *uncredited*: Bruno Di Luia (Lodorisio/Old Man), Luca Intoppa (Adept). *PROD*: Pino Buricchi for Natmas Productions (Rome); *PM*: Raniero Di Giovanbattista; *PSe*: Claudia Endrigo. *Country*: Italy. Filmed at Villa Giovanelli (Rome), Forte Portuense (Rome), Pratica di Mare (Pomezia, Rome), Monte Gelato Falls (Mazzano Romano) and at De Paolis In.Ci.R. Studios (Rome). *Running time*: 83 minutes (m. 2290); 85 minutes (Home video). Visa n. 84156 (11.18.1988); *Rating*: V.M.14. *Release date*: 8.24.1989 (Italy); *Distribution*: Chance Film. *Domestic gross*: n.a. Also known as: *Sexorgien der roten Mönche*; *The Red Monks—Der Todesfluch der roten Mönche* (Germany).

Note: Originally, in the opening credits Lucio Fulci was credited as "special effects supervisor"; a subsequent version, with newly designed credits, lists him as "Lucio Fulci presents."

The present. Riccardo Gherghi, the last of the Gherghi family, is visiting the old family villa he has inherited. He spots a mysterious veiled vi-olinist, and then a nude woman who wanders around the house. He follows her into the crypt, where the woman beheads him with a sword. 50 years earlier: Roberto Gherghi marries the young Ramona, whom he met casually in the park of his villa, much to the chagrin of his housekeeper Priscilla, who is also his mistress. On the wedding night Roberto is summoned in the crypt by a secret sect, the Red Monks, who warn him not to consummate the marriage, since Ramona will have to be sacrificed as a virgin four nights later. Roberto's refusal to perform his conjugal duties brings tension to the couple; what is more, Ramona is assaulted by a mysterious young man, and the French housemaid is decapitated by an unknown murderer. Ramona finds out that Roberto's family is plagued by a centuries-old curse which started in the Middle Ages, when the Grand Duke Lodorisio, the founder of the Red Monks, was killed by a hired assassin, Gherghi's ancestor, and his gypsy wife swore revenge…

With only five films directed between 1975 and 1988, Gianni Martucci was definitely not a prominent presence in national genre cinema of those two decades, and yet his scant filmography as director (with the addition of a few other works he scripted) is somewhat indicative of the various trends followed by the Italian film industry. Born in Rome in 1946, Martucci started scripting *gialli*, namely *Ragazza tutta nuda assassinata nel parco* (1972, Alfonso Brescia), co-authored with his friend, the elusive Peter Skerl, and *Il fiore dai petali d'acciaio* (1973, Gianfranco Piccioli); he moved on to erotic comedies (*La collegiale*, 1975; *La dottoressa sotto il lenzuolo*, 1976), crime films (*Milano … difendersi o morire*, 1978), slasher flicks (the obscure and absurdly titled *Trhauma*, 1980), Neapolitan melodramas (*Pover'ammore*, 1982, directed by Vincenzo Salviani and, uncredited, Fernando di Leo). His final movie, *I frati rossi*, marked the attempt at reviving yet another genre, the Gothic.

I frati rossi was produced by Pino Buricchi, who, together with his brother Marco, was also a distributor with the Marco Film Company. With such works as *L'ultimo treno della notte* (1975, Aldo Lado) and *La settima donna* (1978, Franco Prosperi), Buricchi's name was a warranty of sleaziness and exploitation; in the early 1980s he had jumped on such threads as the *Conan*-inspired sword-and-sandal as well as the glamorous period erotic in the vein of *La chiave*. The project was conceived for the foreign markets and was distributed with Lucio Fulci's name in evidence. In the official papers and in the opening credits, Fulci was credited as "special effects supervisor," but he never once showed up on set, nor did he take care of any special effect, as confirmed by the film's script girl, Annamaria Liguori, who believes his name was used without Fulci's knowledge.[1] But the most likely option is that he willingly accepted to "lend" his name for the credits of somebody else's film, not as much for personal pride and gratification but for mere economic reasons. Around that time Fulci got aboard the ill-fated series "*I maestri del thriller*" (a.k.a. "*Lucio Fulci presenta*") as well.

According to Martucci,

> Fulci did not participate in the making, he just agreed to "present" the movie, but this suited the distributors, who needed a "heavy" name for the sales abroad. By then Fulci had become a name, let's say, exportable. He was already very ill, and I met him to talk to him about the project. He agreed to lend his name to this as a "presenter" ... he never set foot on set, also because, as I said before, he was very ill. At that time, he was going through a particularly difficult stage of his illness. Then he managed to get well again, but at that time he couldn't even speak, devoured as he was by cirrhosis. He suffered a lot and had a very low level of concentration, a matter of minutes and then he needed to rest or take medicines, and I had to come back and talk the following day.[2]

The small cast comprised among others Lara Wendel, by then a veteran in the genre, Gerardo Amato, and Malisa Longo. As in the early days of Italian Gothic, shooting took place almost entirely in an existing location, Villa Giovanelli-Fogaccia, the palace of Prince Giovanelli in Rome, a luxurious villa usually rented for weddings, mundane events and parties, and seen in many Italian films since 1970, including Fernando di Leo's *Il boss* (1973), Umberto Lenzi's *Spasmo* (1974), Daniele D'Anza's TV mini-series *I racconti fantastici di Edgar Allan Poe*, and *La casa stregata*. Martucci recalled the pros and cons of such an accommodation: "If evenings were quiet, mornings were a disaster. Because at night he [Prince Giovanelli] went around to various mundane events, so he wanted to sleep late in the morning, and if you woke him up, he was pissed. Several times we had to wait for him to give us permission to shoot in a certain room. The villa is unique, it has the appearance of a fortress ... it looks very regal, princely, but in fact it is shabby, since he lives only in one wing. The rest is almost in a state of neglect, which

suited us."[3] Other locations were the Forte Portuense and the falls at Monte Gelato, one of the recurring sights in Italian genre cinema of the past decades.

Based on a story by Luciana Anna Spacca, Martucci's film looks back to an old-style Gothic mood. The tale revolves around such archetypal themes as a centuries' old family curse, a gloomy villa/castle replete with crypts, and, most interestingly, a central female character who turns out to be in tune with the idea of "devil as a female" which dominated the imagery of Italian Gothic.

The bulk of the story—count Roberto Gherghi (Amato) marrying the beautiful Ramona (Wendel) but being unable to consummate the marriage for his bride must be sacrificed as a virgin on a certain astrologically favorable night—allows for the same kind of sexual tension that could be found in such 1960s works as *L'orribile segreto del Dr. Hichcock*: the continually postponed "first night" between husband and wife leads to uneasiness, misunderstanding, detachment, and ultimately tragedy. The conjugal crisis is enhanced by Priscilla, the unfriendly housekeeper, Mrs. Danvers-style, who turns out to be Gherghi's mistress: unlike the characters played by Harriet White, though, here she has the gorgeous features of Malisa Longo, and is more than willing to display her body for the camera.

Despite the ample nudity, courtesy of Wendel and Longo, such a morbid and antiquated vision of marriage further enhances the movie's retro feel. *I frati rossi* even inherits the same narcoleptic pacing from its blueprints, with long and superfluous sequences featuring the nightgown-clad Wendel wandering in the crypts to the sound of Paolo Rustichelli's eerie lullaby score. However, if at first Ramona seems to be a designated victim, gradually she becomes aware of her own mission (and power): the revealing Medieval flashback explains her role as an avenging angel/devil of sorts, not unlike Barbara Steele's character in *I lunghi capelli della morte* (1964).

Spacca's story also drew from late 19th century/early 20th century *feuilletons*: the eponymous secret sect recalls, at least iconographically, the Sicilian-based "Beati Paoli," described by Luigi Natoli in his historic serial novel *I Beati Paoli* (1909). Whereas the "Beati Paoli" acted as a secret society against the Church and the State, the Red Monks appear to be simply old-style Devil worshippers. They are indeed an impressive sight, with their crimson hoods and robes looking a bit like the mysterious killer in *Der Mönch mit der Peitsche* (a.k.a. *The College Girl Murders*, 1967, Alfred Vohrer), but are given very little to do except move in unison while handling swords, while Martucci's camera films them in menacing wide-angle shots.

Despite the director's visual tricks to establish a Gothic mood, such as the use of mirrors to reflect characters and avoid a shot/counter-shot routine, the scant budget penalizes the result heavily. "Being a horror movie, it needed many more special effects, and better cared for," Martucci admitted. "There was a scene, for instance, where you could see a knife hovering in mid-air, which I had to cut because you could see the wires. In order to achieve special effects you have to bear special costs, and on that film we had no money."[4] The gory effects, limited to a couple of severed heads, are embarrassing, and so is the patently fake tarantula which pops up in a couple of scenes, and which looks suspiciously like one of those seen in *L'aldilà*— the same prop, perhaps?

The ridiculous hangs over the movie like Damocles' sword. Not only is the story completely incoherent, but some plot points are never cleared (whose is the unknown hand that murders the housemaid?), and several scenes defy suspension of disbelief, such as when Ramona is sexually assaulted by a mysterious young man, an incident that is forgotten with no explanation whatsoever: was it a restaging of the assault her gypsy ancestor suffered centuries earlier, and a necessary step to have her become aware of her true identity? One can only guess.... Later she and Roberto find a severed head in the picnic basket, but this incident as well is quickly dismissed as Gherghi pretends to have talked to the police—but no policeman ever shows up at the villa to investigate! Inconsistencies abound, especially in the Middle Age flashback. And, last but not least, the hooded "Red Monks," whom Gherghi incongruously hosts in the subterraneans of his castle, warn him not to deflower his bride, just like the spirit of the Arab warrior did with Renato Pozzetto in *La casa stregata*.

During post-production, after finishing the mixing, Martucci was told that the movie was too short for exportation: he therefore had to re-edit it and add several minutes, by re-envisioning the whole story as a flashback,

with a newly-shot opening scene set in the present in which the last descendant of the Gherghi family (Gaetano Russo) wanders in the park around the house and meets a veiled female violinist; then, in the villa, he spots a beautiful naked lady and follows her in the crypt, where she decapitates him with a sword. The addition destroys whatever suspense the original story might have had, since it blatantly gives away the final twist. It was likely added after the movie had been submitted to the rating board, since the original copy was 2290 meters long (83 minutes and 30 seconds), while the version currently available runs 85 minutes and 17 seconds at 25fps (that is, about 89 minutes).

I frati rossi was briefly released theatrically in August 1989, nine months after obtaining the visa, and then quickly resurfaced on home video. On the cover of the Italian VHS, on the Playtime label, one could read: "*Un film di Lucio*

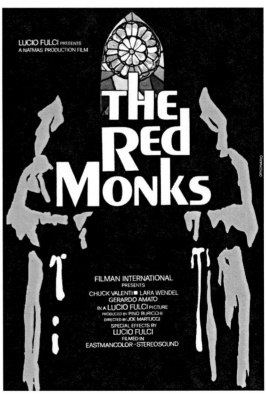

International press sheet for *I frati rossi* (1988, Gianni Martucci), featuring Lucio Fulci's name in evidence-even going so far as listing "a Lucio Fulci picture" and crediting him also for the special effects—even though in fact Fulci had nothing to do with the film. Martucci is credited as "Joe Martucci."

Fulci" ("A film by Lucio Fulci"). This led to a controversy, with Fulci threatening to sue, and the fake credit was obscured by way of a sticker which reported the name of Martucci as director. However, the same stunt was employed in other home video editions throughout the globe. As of today, some still believe it to be a Lucio Fulci film.

NOTES

1. Albiero and Cacciatore, *Il terrorista dei generi*, 361.
2. Eugenio Ercolani, "Gianni Martucci, un intellettuale al servizio del cinema di genere," *PaperBlog*, September 22, 2013 (http://it.paperblog.com/gianni-martucci-un-intellettuale-al-servizio-del-cinema-di-genere-prima-parte-1999579/).
3. *Ibid.*
4. *Ibid.*

Paganini Horror (Paganini Horror)

D: Luigi Cozzi. *S*: Raimondo Del Balzo; *SC*: Luigi Cozzi, Daria Nicolodi; *DOP*: Franco Lecca (Telecolor); *M*: Vince Tempera (Ed. DEAF); *E*: Sergio Montanari; *PD, ArtD*: Marina Pinzuti Ansolini; *CO*: Donatella Cazzola; *SPFX*: Casagni e Prestopino [Franco Casagni, Rosario Prestopino]; *MU*: Franco Casagni; *AMU*: Luigi Ciminelli; *Hair*: Piero Cucchi; *AD*: Marilena Cavola; *AE*: Paolo Lanzani; *2ndAE*: Gianni Pallotto; *C*: Arcangelo Lannutti; *AC*: Enzo Carpineta; *2ndAC*: Carlo Lannutti; *ChEl*: Ennio Di Stefano; *KG*: Sergio Fabbriani; *SE*: Paolo Ricci; *SO*: Mauro Lazzaro; *PrM*: Osvaldo Monaco; *SP*: Antonio Benetti; *SS*: Maria Luisa Merci; *Set technician*: Ugo Tucci; *G*: Claudio Fabriani; *El*: Michele Pellegrini; *W*: Damiana Celletti. *Cast*: Daria Nicolodi (Sylvia Hackett), Jasmine Main [Jasmine Maimone] (Kate), Pascal Persiano (Daniel), Maria Cristina Mastrangeli (Lavinia), Michele Klippstein (Elena), Pietro Genuardi (Mark Singer), Luana Ravegnini (Rita), Giada Cozzi (Sylvia as a child), Elena Pompei (Sylvia's mother), Roberto Giannini, Perla Costantini, Donald Pleasence (Mr. Pickett). *PROD*: Fabrizio De Angelis for Fulvia Film (Rome); *PM*: Gian Maria Vismara Currò; *PS*: Giorgio Padoan; *PSe*: Andrea Usai. *Country*: Italy. Filmed on location in Venice, and at R.P.A. Elios Studios (Rome). *Running time*: 82 minutes (m. 2250). Visa n. 84385 (1.24.1989); *Rating*: V.M.14. *Release dates*: 6.6.1989 (Italy), 1.19.119 (Japan); *Distribution*: Fulvia Film. *Domestic gross*: n.a. *Also known as*: *Paganini Horror—Der Blutgeiger von Venedig* (West Germany—home video), *Melodía de horror* (Argentina), *Partitura mortal* (Portugal).

Kate, the lead singer of a rock group, receives from her drummer Daniel an unpublished piece of music by Niccolò Paganini, which Daniel purchased from the enigmatic Mr. Pickett in Venice. The band rearrange it and make it their next single. It is said that Paganini used that music to evoke the devil, to whom he sold his soul in exchange for fame; but the devil then forced the musician to kill his wife. Kate and the band's producer Lavinia hire renowned horror filmmaker Mark Singer to shoot a horror-inspired music video in Paganini's house in Venice. There, they are welcomed by Silvia, the current owner. Shooting for the video starts, but in the evening Rita and Daniel disappear, then Mark too is killed by a figure which appears to be the ghost of Paganini. Lavinia, Kate and her bandmate Silvia realize that they can't leave the house as it is surrounded by an invisible shield. They try to exorcise the curse by playing Paganini's piece on violin, but to no avail. Eventually, just as Kate—now the only survivor—is about to be killed, the sun rises, striking the ghost with its rays and pulverizing it. But the nightmare is not over...

As Luigi Cozzi recalled, *Paganini Horror* was born in a manner worthy of the glorious golden age of Italian genre cinema. The starting point was to draw on the expected success of Klaus Kinski's pet project *Paganini*, which the actor had been trying to mount since the early 1980s. Finally, *Paganini* was screened in a rough cut at the 1989 Cannes Film Festival. As had happened in the 1960s and 1970s, the news of important and potentially successful films was enough to start production with a series of rip-offs centered on the same theme.

Cozzi came up with the title, producer Ugo Valenti (who had co-financed *Contamination*) liked it and commissioned artist Enzo Sciotti to draw a poster. Sciotti came up with a striking, comic book-like and almost Surrealist image: a ghastly skeletal figure in a tuxedo and with incongruous long white hair—Paganini resurrected from the grave?—is playing the violin, its bow dripping blood. Below, a pair of teenagers, a girl and a boy, are standing under the moonlight before an eerie house which looks very much like Norman Bates' abode in *Psycho* (and its many surrogates seen in Italian posters for the *La casa* series). The teenagers are surrounded by music sheets, menacingly floating around them. These too are stained in blood. Then, once the poster was ready, all that was left to do was to write the script.

Cozzi, who had just finished penning a screenplay on Paganini for producer Nat Wachsberger, recycled a few notions on the famous violinist and, being an avid science fiction fan, threw in many elements and themes from his favorite genre. The result was a story about a haunted house where "time killed you, making you age or rejuvenate suddenly, turning you into a newborn child and then an egg cell,"[1] and originally it was to be shot in Colombia, like *Contamination*.[2] Valenti didn't like the script, though. He had Cozzi rewrite it drastically and add splatter scenes in the process to make it more marketable. But after vainly trying to sell the project, the producer just gave up the film industry and left for Santo Domingo where, according to Cozzi, he set up a successful prawn factory business.

Italian poster for Luigi Cozzi's *Paganini Horror* (1989) (art by Enzo Sciotti).

The director then teamed up with Daria Nicolodi, who around that time was working with him also on what became *De Profundis— The Black Cat*, to crank out a new script. According to Cozzi, "she wrote all the esoteric scenes, like the one about the pact with the Devil."[3] The director also recycled and developed some ideas from a couple of episodes of the TV series "Turno di notte," broadcast on Rai Due between late 1987 and early 1988 in the TV show "Giallo" and on which he shared directing credits with Lamberto Bava—namely *Delitto in rock* (broadcast on December 4, 1987) and *La casa dello Stradivari* (broadcast on December 18, 1987).

Cozzi got in touch with several producers and eventually set up a deal with Fabrizio De Angelis of Fulvia Film, the financer of several Lucio Fulci films. But the director's ambitions were soon to be frustrated. For one thing, De Angelis made last-minute demands which caused Cozzi to rewrite the script all over again: "A few days before filming started, in order to cut costs, he told me to discard all the splatter sequences, and so I tried to rebalance the script by reinserting some of the weirdest and more fantasy-oriented things from my previous version.... The result was definitely not a horror movie but a fantasy or a *fantastique* with lots of irony and lots of theories on music and time,"[4] as the director summed it up. The lack of money proved a decisive factor, too. "There I was with this beautiful, ambitious script and they handed me a 16mm camera, which was broken, gave me a villa to set the story in, and said, 'Start shooting!' In conditions like these, not even the best film director in the world could have done any better."[5]

Shot in three and a half weeks, *Paganini Horror*[6] may not be "the poorest film in the history of cinema" as the director labeled it, but its low budget is evident throughout, as is its haphazard nature. Still, the experience on the set of *Nosferatu a Venezia* proved fruitful when it came to shoot on location in Venice, as the director found a couple of interesting locations for the scene where a music sheet with a composition penned by Paganini, and kept inside a suitcase whose combination is 666, is purchased from the mysterious Mr. Pickett. As the film's guest star and main selling point for the foreign markets, Donald Pleasence (another survivor from the exhausting experience of *Nosferatu a Venezia*) has very little to do, except looking British and devilish. He has the most amusing scene, though, throwing a handful of bills from a Venice bell tower, mumbling about "little devils."

The opening scenes, which follow a little girl (Cozzi's own daughter, Giada) coming home after her violin lessons through the Venice canals and indifferently electrocuting her mother while she's taking a bath, bring to mind the domestic horrors of *Shock* and *Macabro*, for the casual transition from everyday family life to horror; but they also underline the shoestring budget, with the electrocuting effect rendered through cheap optical effects worthy of the laser battle in Roger Corman's *The Raven*. Then the film changes tone dramatically and takes us to a studio were a mostly female rock band (well, sort of) is recording what sounds like a bad rip-off of Bon Jovi's "You Give Love a Bad Name" and "Livin' on a Prayer," complete with awful 1980s keyboards all over the place. The scene is very similar to the opening sequence in *Delitto in rock*, about the search for a valuable tape with a lost Jim Morrison song.

The inclusion of pop-rock tracks (again, sort of) and visuals which ape music videos—an element in common with Fragasso's *Monster Dog*—gives an idea of the makers' view of the decade's music. It also gives away the attempt at jumping on the notorious rock/horror association that was so popular in the period, from the notion of Satanic back-masking in heavy metal songs to the nefarious influence of rock music on teenagers' minds. The growing popularity of hard rock and heavy metal even spawned a horror subgenre which dated back to *Terror on Tour*, and Cozzi certainly knew *Trick or Treat* (1986, Charles Martin Smith), which had been released theatrically in Italy as well.

Paganini, with the many legends surrounding his existence, was the perfect figure to incarnate the pact with the Devil. The script mentions Paganini's "secret music which he used to summon Satan," even though the references to the present are debatable to say the least: instead of mentioning the Rolling Stones' "Sympathy for the Devil" or other famous tunes connected with the Horned One, the characters finds nothing better than name-dropping Michael Jackson's "Thriller." In a scene, Silvia recalls the violinist's devilish pact as follows: "He signed the deal in a Venetian house and then he killed Antonia, his wife, and from her intestines he made the strings of that gilded violin which since then was always his own. An instrument which emitted unique notes when played, probably because its strings contained the soul and the desperation of that poor woman." The only true bit of information here is the name of Paganini's wife, Antonia Bianchi, while the rest is the fruit of Cozzi and Nicolodi's imagination. Namely, the story of the cursed violin is lifted from *La casa dello Stradivari*, which revolved around a Paganini piece (*Le streghe*), a priceless Stradivari violin and took place in a music school called Casa del Sol, like the villa in the film.

On the other hand, for the idea of turning a piece of classical music into a pop tune—not an uncommon occurrence in pop music, starting with, say, Procol Harum's "A Whiter Shade of Pale," with its Bach-derived melody—Cozzi possibly had in mind the Italian/Swiss combo Rondò Veneziano. Emerging in 1979 from a notion by Freddy Naggiar and Gian Piero Reverberi, Rondò Veneziano played 18th century-inspired tunes (written by Reverberi) in baroque pop arrangements. Their debut album was a Top Ten hit, and the covers of their records featured surreal, sci-fi oriented illustrations with spaceships and automatons playing strings in the Venice canals. For the occasion, Vince Tempera didn't go back as far as the 18th century for the supposedly Paganini-penned piece which the band rearranges into a would-be hit: the piano-based melody played by Daniel (Pascal Persiano) blatantly rips off Electric Light Orchestra's "Twilight," included in their 1981 album *Time*.

In one of Cozzi's recurring nods to his friend Dario Argento, the band hires "the world's most famous horror movie director" to shoot the video for the song. The in-joke possibly refers to *Opera*, where Ian Charleson played a horror filmmaker called to direct Verdi's *Macbeth* on stage, an occurrence in turn inspired by Argento's own unfortunate experience when in 1985 he was hired to direct the *Rigoletto* for the Sferisterio theater in Macerata, which he attempted to turn into a Grand Guignol opera, with gimmicks worthy of William Castle. Eventually his idea was discarded, causing him to resign[7] and turn

Opera into some sort of cinematic revenge. But when the renowned Mark Singer (Pietro Genuardi, looking like a distant relative of Urbano Barberini's character in *Opera*) shows up to shoot the allegedly expensive video all by himself, with no crew and just a hand-held 16mm camera, it is hard to keep a straight face—and perhaps Cozzi was just putting on screen what was happening to him on *Paganini Horror*, saddled with a villa and a (broken) 16mm camera. Likewise, the would-be trendy visual style of the music video sequence clashes against lack of means and looks very much like the work of Al Festa (*Gipsy Angel*, 1990; *Fatal Frames—Fotogrammi mortali*, 1996), all wide-angle shots, cheap filters and dry ice.

The more its story develops, the more *Paganini Horror* reveals its slapdash nature. There are too many ideas, some of them half-baked, others which would have been better discarded, and the paucity of means just cannot sustain such a muddled plot. We have a masked, black-gloved figure stalking the corridors that looks like it was lifted from an Argento film, gorily stabbing its victims with a blade coming out of a violin. There are the nods to Mario Bava (directly or by way of Argento's *Inferno*), such as mannequins wearing multi-colored veils, and rooms lighted with bright reds and blues (a suitably eerie scene involves a cobweb-ridden hourglass which has seemingly stopped). There is also room for assorted borrowings: a sheet of music flying away by itself as if animated by a spiteful force recalls Tourneur's *Curse of the Demon* (1957). And, finally, there are the remnants of Cozzi's original idea of a time loop, which the director had toyed with in his film debut *Il tunnel sotto il mondo* (1969) and which was also a recurrent element in Italian Gothic (think of *Danza macabra*). Such a concept is the basis for some of the most bizarre bits: a room whose walls are covered with Einstein's relativity equations; a straight tunnel which nevertheless leads a character back to the starting point; and an invisible barrier which prevents the protagonists from leaving the house, causing a runaway car to explode and crushing someone to death in the film's goriest scene.

The director does his best to enliven the proceedings with weird shots, the camera tilting and rotating, and he tries to milk the suspense for what it's worth; but he can do little to improve upon the horrible acting on the part of most cast members, especially Jasmine Mai-

mone—the role was originally to be played by Cinzia Farolfi.[8] Overall, though, the story never really adds up, at least in the Italian theatrical cut. At dawn the masked stalker dissolves into ashes—shaped, in one of the film's most demented ideas, as a treble clef!—like Nosferatu, but it remains unclear who it really is. Similarly, a character wondering whether the house is actually hell is met elusively by the one who might be the most suited to answer, Mr. Pickett. And despite the circular ending, with a new group of unfortunate victims entering Paganini's house and heading for (presumably) another night of horror, the whole discourse about time and music just sounds like mumbo-jumbo.

The alternate version (included on the German DVD) is more interesting in this respect, as it includes bits and scenes that make Cozzi's claims about the film's science fiction core more coherent and clear. Before the opening credits, in fact, we see shots of a planet and an hourglass floating in space; the latter, a surreal image in tune with Cozzi's most personal efforts such as the two Hercules movies, introduces the theme of warped time right at the start, and it will be reprised near the end. Similarly, inserts of planets rotating in space are interspersed with the scene of the victims hearing a mysterious sound: Sylvia's monologue about the "harmony of the spheres" becomes more clearly linked with the plot, as does the connection between the harmony of the universe and the disruption of time and space coordinates inside the haunted house. The original ending also reveals the nature of the masked Paganini killer: after the new tenants have entered the house, Mr. Pickett dons the same costume as the killer and starts playing the violin.

Released in June 1989, *Paganini Horror* predictably did badly at the box-office, but carved a niche for itself in the Italian home video market, no doubt because of its good distribution (on the Avo Film label) and impressive cover art. It became some sort of cult movie over the years: most viewers approached it as an Ed Wood–style extravaganza, but there were even some serious attempts at re-evaluation. Soon Cozzi would return behind the camera for *De Profundis*, which became *The Black Cat*, but his activity as a filmmaker waned, not least because of the ongoing crisis of the Italian film industry. Meanwhile, in 1989 he started a new commercial venture: he and Argento opened a shop in Rome dedicated entirely to horror in all its forms, the aptly named "Profondo Rosso," which soon became a reference point for film buffs all over the country.

NOTES

1. Matteo Contin, "Intervista con Luigi Cozzi," in Gordiano Lupi, *Cozzi Stellari. Il cinema di Lewis Coates* (Rome: Profondo Rosso, 2009), 281.
2. Luca Cirillo, "Intervista a Luigi Cozzi," www.palcoweb.net (http://www.palcoweb.net/Interviste/Luigi-Cozzi/Index.asp).
3. Palmerini and Mistretta, *Spaghetti Nightmares*, 64.
4. *Ibid.*
5. *Ibid.*
6. The film is sometimes mentioned with the a.k.a. *Il violino che uccide* (The Killing Violin), which nevertheless doesn't appear in the credits nor in ministerial papers.
7. [ANSA agency] "Argento dice "no" alla regia di Rigoletto," *Corriere della Sera*, April 24, 1985.
8. The Milan-born Farolfi was a singer who achieved popularity in the 1990s with the band Cattivi Pensieri. She had appeared in an episode of the TV series "Turno di notte," *Delitto in rock.*

Streghe (Witch Story) (Superstition 2)

D: Alessandro Capone. *S*: Alessandro Capone; *SC*: Rosario Galli, Alessandro Capone; *Adaptation*: Maura Vespini; *M*: Carlo Maria Cordio; *DOP*: Roberto Girometti (Eastmancolor, Technicolor); *E*: Franca Silvi; *Casting*: Bill Williams; *ArtD*: David Minichiello; *SE*: Rick Gonzales; *AD*: Mike Kirton; *AE*: Rosalba Giacobbe, Roberto Amicucci; *SS*: Laura Curreli; *Dial*: Mary Lynn Clemente; *C*: Roberto Brega; *1stAC*: Maurizio Piano; *2ndAC*: Andy Fisher; *SP*: Gianni Caramanico; *SE*: Mike Davy, Mike Ornelas, Dan Bedell, Dave Katz, David Blood, Jesús Martinez; *B*: Maurizio Merli; *CO*: Vera Cozzolino; *ACO*: Rita Cecconi; *W*: Connie Pierce, Beverly Frisz, Maria Pia Boccia; Hair: Anna Chiodi, Pat Patton; *MU*: Amedeo Alessi; *AMU*: Mario Di Salvio, Selena Miller, Victoria Stewart; *KG*: Elio Bosi; *G*: Pietro D'Antoni, Piero Bosi, Cecil Stone, Jorge Frier; *ChEl*: Furio Rocchi; *El*: Italo Di Steffano, Marcello Perricone, Cragg Richards, Jeff Morriss, Don Lamont; *Generator driver*: Claudio Cartocci; *Driver*: Claudio Menchini; *Weapons*: J.R. Johnson; *Press attache*: Kim Gatti, Paola Papi; *SOE*: Alvaro Gramigna, Fernando Caso; *Mix*: Danilo Moroni. *Cast*: Amy Adams (Susan), Jeff Bankert (Michael), Ian Bannen (Father Matthew), Charon Butler (Gloria), Todd Conatser [Conner] (Virgil), John Freda (Alex Hayes), Peter Gold [Pierre Agostino] (Father Gabriel), Kirk Green (Young Father Matthew), Cecil Hawkins (Sheriff), Elise Hirby (Maria Hayes), Gary Kerr (Ed Hayes), Suzanne Law (Rachel Hayes), Deanna Lund (Helena), Jason F. Lefkowitz (Paul), Christopher Peacock (Ken), Stewart Penn (Bus Driver), Richard Powell (Cop), Nancie Sanderson (Simona), Michele Vannucchi [Michele Peacock] (Carol Hayes), Bob Bouchard (Yokel), John Boyd (Yokel), Kevin Kirton (Yokel), Mario Millo (Yokel), Fred 'Big' Price (Yokel). *PROD*: Alessandro Capone, Mauro Morigi, Giuseppe Pedersoli for United Entertainment Corporation, Numero Uno International (Rome); *EP*: Claudio Bonivento; *PS*: Roberto Allocca; *PM*: Ricky Sacco; *PSe*: Antonio Mammolotti; *Location manager*: Stewart Smith; *PAss*: Jeff Lupton, Suzanne Rust; *ADM*: Pasquale Manzollino. *Country*: Italy. Filmed on location in Mount Dora and Winter Garden Groveland (Florida). *Running time*: 90 minutes (m. 2472). Visa n. 84646 (4.28.1989); *Rating*: V.M.14. *Release date*: 5.26.1989 (Italy); *Distribution*: Titanus. *Domestic gross*: n.a. *Also known as*: Witch Story (UK), Tanz der Hexen Teil 2 (Germany), Pesadilla (Spain)

Note: The songs "Down the Highway" (Jones/Cordio) and "Reflex" (Jones/Cordio) are sung by Karen Jones.

Florida, 1927. A young woman, Helena, is lynched by an angry mob for being a witch. A little girl, Rachel, whom the woman took care of as governess, watches in horror as Helena is burnt alive, and commits suicide by jumping from a window of their house. The present: Ed and Carol, two teenage siblings who recently lost their parents in a car accident, move from New York to Florida with a group of friends to the country house they inherited. The house—the same where Helena and Rachel lived—is dilapidated, and the teenagers set out to restore it. But starting on the first night of their stay, strange things happen in there, and the new inhabitants experience nightmares and hallucinations. It turns out that the house is cursed, and Rachel's ghost appears. The teenagers are possessed by the evil entity and are pushed to murder each other in gruesome ways. Ed and Carol find out that Helena had seduced the local priest, Father Michael, which caused the mob to revolt against her. They locate the elderly priest, now defrocked, who faces Helena's undead spirit and attempts to exorcise her. The curse seemingly abates but, as Ed and Carol will find out, evil never dies...

The feature film debut of the then 34-year-old Alessandro Capone is emblematic in its approach to the Gothic genre, a wild mixture of

Italian and U.S. movie references that give away from the very beginning *Streghe*'s composite nature. Capone had started as a screenwriter in the late 1970s, and among his early work there are a couple of horror movies, Gianni Martucci's *Trhauma* and Ruggero Deodato's *Camping del terrore* (1987), which both drew liberally from the American slasher film and its conventions. As Capone explained,

> I was always fond of horror cinema, and I tried for years to make my debut in the genre. Since nobody allowed me to showcase my passion, I decided to set up a company, I produced my first film and of course I made a horror movie! ... We managed to convince an international distributor, Manolo Bolognini, to give us a guaranteed minimum, and then Claudio Bonivento, whom I met in New York for another project, associated with another quote.[1]

Streghe puts on the table a wider variety of references. The plot draws from the Canadian horror film *Superstition*, from which it reprises not only the theme of the vengeful witch, but also the central character of a priest, as well as the presence of a crucifix which plays a crucial role in the story. As for the body count, some of the murders—such as the chainsaw slashing in the pool—try hard to be original, but the notion of Helena's possessed *succubi* attacking the other victims looks very much like what Sam Raimi did in *The Evil Dead* minus the gruesome facial make-up. Capone claimed he took inspiration from Carpenter (even in the use of the scope format), Raimi and Craven, but there are also much more familiar references for fans of Italian Gothic horror films. The opening scenes set in the late 1920s recall the prologue of *L'aldilà*, while the character of Rachel, the little girl with a white ball who asks people to "play with her," is a blatant nod to *Operazione paura*.

But the important thing to Capone was to disguise and conceal the Italian identity, to the point that the film doesn't even include the opening credits, except for the title *Streghe (Witch Story)*—note the fake English title in brackets. It is a chameleon-like game of subtraction that goes in a different direction than the gory fireworks of the early 1980s, where the way to excess was the trick to bite away bigger slices of pie in the chaotic horror market. The setting and context try hard to convince us that we are watching a 1980s American body count flick, starting with the parade of annoying teenagers who joke, bicker and hump each other for the entire duration before being mercilessly exterminated in graphic (but not overly gory) ways.

As often in Italian horror films of the period, the depiction of American teenagers results in involuntary parody, and the characters look like larger-than-life walking stereotypes: an anorexic black girl who boasts she is used to vomiting after eating; a bitchy bimbo who is so proud of her perfect ass that she strips off in front of everybody on the living room table; and a fatso who sports a t-shirt of the female pop/rock band Heart, claims that his only passion in life is eating and swallows handfuls of jam directly from a jar with his bare hands, in what is perhaps an ill-fated homage to John Belushi's unforgettable stint as "Bluto" Blutarsky in John Landis' *Animal House* (1978). In some 1970s horror film such a grotesquely stereotyped slice of humanity would have had perhaps a metaphoric value; here, they simply represent the naïve vision of a different culture and society, which the filmmakers are shaping through their own cinephile experience. Naturally, these teenagers are film buffs too: "He has seen *The Exorcist* one time too many!" someone says when a weird-looking priest shows up on their bus; later they hum the theme song for *The Twilight Zone*, and upon exploring a sinister country mansion someone jokingly mentions Mrs. Bates and her son Norman.

The story moves predictably along the expected horrific events and deaths. Some touches, such as the protagonists' dead father returning from the grave to torment his offspring—possibly another nod to an Italian horror classic, namely *La maschera del demonio*—hint at themes of incest and Catholic guilt which are merely played for their superficial value. Ditto for the expected Gothic trappings, such as the "return of the past" of the curse plaguing generation after generation. For the climax, Capone relies heavily on slow-motion shots of people jumping in the air or through windows, but he fails to generate any suspense. And the twist ending doesn't really make much sense.

Filmed partly in Rome (in November 1988) but mostly in Florida[2] over the course of five weeks, on a budget of about one million dollars,[3] *Streghe* looks very much like Massaccesi's Filmirage productions of the period. Still, the higher amount of money involved results in a suitably professional *mise-en-scène*, with dolly shots, careful lighting schemes, passable special effects (courtesy of Rick Gonzales), and at least one interesting set piece, the tunnel-like underground passage which allows director of photography Roberto Girometti some suitably eerie light/ shadows effects. The cast comprises a number of nondescript young actors, mostly in their first movie role. The only familiar faces in the cast are Deanna Lund (best known for her participation in the TV series *Land of the Giants*) as the evil Helena, and Ian Bannen (in place of Capone's original choice for the role, Donald Pleasence), who turns up an hour into the film for a less-than-inspired special appearance, sporting a blatantly fake-looking wig and cheap make-up. But Z-movie devotees will be thrilled to spot Pierre Agostino, the lead in a couple of Ray Dennis Steckler's most demented efforts, *The Hollywood Strangler Meets the Skid Row Slasher* (1979) and its sequel, *Las Vegas Serial Killer* (1986), here hiding under the a.k.a. Peter Gold.

The Italian distribution through the historical Titanus allowed the film a theatrical release, with a V.M.14 rating.[4] Predictably, it collected harsh reviews: "The usual inventory of coarse special effects," labeled it the *Corriere della Sera*, noting the "slapdash editing, full of inconsistencies" and the "amateur cast (except for a bored-looking Ian Bannen) in a cumbersome parade of grimaces."[5] *Streghe* soon resurfaced on the national home video market. It was sold well abroad, however, allowing Bolognini to recover the advance. Overseas it was advertised—not surprisingly, given the aforementioned similarities—as a sequel to *Superstition*, whereas in Germany it was passed off as *Tanz der Hexen Teil 2*, a sequel to Larry Cohen's horror comedy *Wicked Stepmother* (1989), re-

leased there as *Tanz der Hexen*. As the director recalled, "I remember that during the screening in New York there was an applause, when one of the girls comes out of the pool handling a chainsaw. In Italy people criticized it, because of course you can't start a chainsaw underwater, but once the joke was evident, the American audiences applaud and laugh, whereas the Italians criticize. It's a matter of approach."[6]

Capone (who dedicated the film to his family) moved on to television in the following decade, directing episodes of the TV series *Detective Extralarge*, starring Bud Spencer (whose son Giuseppe co-produced *Streghe*), and sporadically returned to the big screen with an adaptation of his own play *Uomini sull'orlo di una crisi di nervi* (1995). In the 2000s he worked mainly for the small screen, directing TV series such as *Distretto di polizia* (2007–2008), *I delitti del cuoco* (2010) and *I segreti di Borgo Larici* (2014). In 2014 he helmed the sci-fi thriller *2047: Sights of Death*, featuring an astonishing quintet of has-beens: Danny Glover, Daryl Hannah, Michael Madsen, Stephen Baldwin, and Rutger Hauer.

NOTES

1. Taccini, *Stracult horror*, 276.
2. Giovanna Grassi, "Cinema e gente," *Corriere della Sera*, November 18, 1988.
3. Taccini, *Stracult horror*, 279.
4. In 1993 the rating was turned to "all audiences allowed" after some cuts were performed for its TV broadcast (visa n. 87861, 3.22.1993) for a total of 48 meters (about 1 minute and 43 seconds).
5. L.A. [Leonardo Autera], "La casa disabitata nella radura," *Corriere della Sera*, May 26, 1989.
6. Taccini, *Stracult horror*, 279.

Appendix 1:
Direct-to-Video Releases

Entries are arranged in chronological order,
according to their shooting dates

"I maestri del thriller," a.k.a. *"Lucio Fulci presenta"*

PROD: Luigi Nannerini and Antonino Lucidi for Cine Duck (Rome), Alpha Distribuzione Cinematografica (Rome); *PM*: Marco Alfieri, Silvano Zignani, Stefano Trani; *UPM* (*Le porte dell'inferno*): Bruno Bagella, Maurizio Mattei.

Hansel e Gretel

D: Giovanni Simonelli [additional scenes: Lucio Fulci]. *S and SC*: Giovanni Simonelli; *DOP*: Silvano Tessicini; *M*: Lanfranco Perini (Ed. Artem Publishing); *E*: Luigi Gorini; *CO*: Cinzia Milani; *MU*: Pino Ferrante; *Hair*: Maria Teresa Carrera; *AD*: Michele De Angelis; *C*: Luca Alfieri; *AC*: Rolando Stefanelli; *PM*: Vincenzo Lozzi; *B*: Aristide Bagliocchi; *SO*: Davide Magara, Giulio D'Angeli; *Mix*: Claudio Oliviero; *SE*: Gino Vagniluca; *G*: Nino Magostini, Gaetano Barbera; *El*: Massimo Rocchi, Marcello Tallone; *W*: Mirella Pedetti; *SS*: Camilla Fulci; *Generator operator*: Roberto Stiffi. *Cast*: Elisabete Pimenta Boareto (Silvia), Lucia Prato (Lina), Ronald [Gaetano] Russo (Fred), Giorgio Cerioni (Mario), Mario Sandro De Luca, Renzo Robertazzi, Silvia Cipollone (Gretel), Massimiliano Cipollone (Hansel), Paul Muller (Procurer), Maurice Poli (Commissioner Roy); *uncredited*: Brigitte Christensen (Solange), Zora Kerova [Zora Keslerová] (Woman in bath), Roberta Orlandi (Rosi).

Running time: 86 minutes. Also known as: *Hansel and Gretel* (International title); *Die Saat des Teufels* (Germany).

Bloody Psycho

D: Leandro Lucchetti. *S and SC*: Giovanni Simonelli, Leandro Lucchetti; *DOP*: Silvano Tessicini; *M*: Lanfranco Perini; *E*: Luigi Gorini; *CO*: Cinzia Milani; *MU*: Pino Ferrante; *Hair*: Maria Teresa Carrera; *AD*: Michele De Angelis; *C*: Luca Alfieri; *AC*: Rolando Stefanelli; *PM*: Valentino Salvati; *B*: Aristide Bagliocchi; *SO*: Davide Magara, Giulio D'Angeli; *Mix*: Claudio Oliviero; *SE*: Gino Vagniluca; *G*: Gaetano Barbera, Nino Magostini, Armando Salino; *El*: Massimo Rocchi, Marcello Tallone; *W*: Cinzia Reggiani; *SS*: Camilla Fulci. *Cast*: Peter Hintz (Dr. Werner Vogler), Loes Kamma [Louise Kamsteeg] (Micaela di Saint-Bon), Brigitte Christensen (Mrs. Rezzori), Sacha Darwin (Sasha), Nubia Martini (Simona), Any Cerreto (Mary Cohen), Marco Di Stefano (Priest), Alessandra Massari (Micaela as a child), Marco Massari (Werner as a child), Vassili Karis [Vassili Karamenisis] (Tramp/Dr. Williamson), Paul Muller (Lawyer Cohen); *uncredited*: Leandro Lucchetti (Gamekeeper's son).

Running time: 90 minutes. *Also known as*: *The Snake House* (International title); *Bloody Psycho—Lo specchio*; *Nel nido del serpente* (Italian alternate titles); *Pesadilla sangrienta* (Spain); *Snake House* (Germany).

Massacre

D: Andrea Bianchi. *S and SC*: Andrea Bianchi; *DOP*: Silvano Tessicini; *M*: Luigi Ceccarelli (Ed. Creamus); *E*: Vincenzo Tomassi; *CO*: Cinzia Milani; *MU*: Pino Ferrante; *Hair*: Maria Teresa Carrera; *AD*: Michele De Angelis; *C*: Luca Alfieri; *AC*: Rolando Stefanelli; *1stAE*: Paola Tomassi; *2ndAE*: Sergio Fraticelli; *PM*: Vincenzo Luzzi; *B*: Aristide Bagliocchi; *SO*: Davide Magara, Giulio D'Angeli; *Mix*: Claudio Oliviero; *SE*: Gino Vagniluca; *G*: Nino Magostini, Armando Salino; *El*: Massimo Rocchi, Marcello Tallone; *W*: Cinzia Reggiani; *SS*: Camilla Fulci; *Generator operator*: Roberto Stiffi. *Cast*: Gino Concari (Walter), Patrizia Falcone (Jennifer), Silvia Conti (Liza), Pier Maria Cecchini (Robert), Robert

Egon (Jean), Danny Degli Esposti (Adrian), Marcello Furgiuele (Gordon), Lubka Lenzi (Mira), Anna Maria Placido (Madam Yurich), Maria Grazia Veroni, Cristina Lynn, Piero Pieri, Paul Muller (Commissioner), Maurice Poli (Frank Brennan).

Running time: 90 minutes. *Also known as*: *La morte della medium* (TV version, cut).

Luna di sangue

D: Enzo Milioni. *S and SC*: Enzo Milioni, Giovanni Simonelli; *DOP*: Silvano Tessicini; *M*: Paolo Gatti, Alfonso Zenga (Ed. Tangram); *E*: Vincenzo Tomassi; *CO*: Francesco Sforza; *MU*: Pino Ferrante; *AD*: Michele De Angelis, Enzo Rossi; *PrM*: Vincenzo Luzzi; *SO*: Davide Magara; *B*: Aristide Bagliocchi; *Foley artist*: Giulio D'Angeli; *SE*: Gino Vagniluca; *C*: Luca Alfieri; *AC*: Rolando Stefanelli; *G*: Gaetano Barbera, Nino Magostini, Armando Salino; *El*: Massimo Rocchi, Marcello Tallone; *W*: Mirella Pedetti; *SS*: Camilla Fulci; *Generator operator*: Roberto Stiffi. *Cast*: Jacques Sernas (Dr. Marc Duvivier), Zora Kerova [Zora Keslerová] (Mary), Barbara Blasco (Ann Moffet), Alex Berger [Alessandro Freyberger] (Larry Moffet), Jessica Moore [Luciana Ottaviani] (Tania), Giuseppe Morabito (Solly), Pamela Prati (Mirella Alfonsi), Annie Belle [Annie Brillard] (Brigitte Garré).

Running time: 95 minutes. *Also known as*: *Escape from Death* (International title).

Non avere paura della zia Marta

D: Mario Bianchi. *S and SC*: Mario Bianchi. *DOP*: Silvano Tessicini; *M*: Gianni Sposito (Ed. Artem Publishing); *E*: Vincenzo Tomassi; *CO*: Cinzia Milani; *MU*: Pino Ferrante; *Hair*: Maria Teresa Carrera; *AD*: Michele De Angelis; *C*: Luca Alfieri; *AC*: Rolando Stefanelli; *PM*: Vincenzo Lozzi; *B*: Aristide Bagliocchi; *SO*: Davide Magara, Giulio D'Angeli; *Mix*: Claudio Oliviero; *SE*: Gino Vagniluca; *G*: Nino Magostini, Gaetano Barbera; *El*: Massimo Rocchi, Marcello Tallone; *W*: Mirella Pedetti; *SS*: Camilla Fulci; *Generator operator*: Roberto Stiffi. *Cast*: Adriana Russo (Nora Hamilton), Gabriele Tinti (Richard Hamilton), Anna Maria Placido (Richard's mother), Jessica Moore [Luciana Ottaviani] (Georgia Hamilton), Maurice Poli (Thomas the caretaker), Massimiliano Massimi (Charles Hamilton), Edoardo Massimi (Maurice Hamilton), Sacha M. Darwin (Aunt Martha).

Running time: 88 minutes. *Also known as*: *The Murder Secret*; *Don't Be Afraid of Aunt Martha*; *The Broken Mirror* (International titles); *El espejo roto* (Spain).

Sodoma's Ghost (*The Ghosts of Sodom*)

D: Lucio Fulci. *S and SC*: Lucio Fulci, Carlo Alberto Alfieri; *DOP*: Silvano Tessicini; *M*: Carlo Maria Cordio; *E*: Vincenzo Tomassi; *MU*: Pino Ferrante; *Hair*: Maria Teresa Carrera; *AD*: Michele De Angelis; *SO*: Roberto Barbieri; *Foley artist*: Giulio D'Angeli; *SE*: Gino Vagniluca; *C*: Luca Alfieri; *AC*: Rolando Stefanelli; *KG*: Umberto Magostini; *El*: Massimo Rocchi; *W*: Mirella Pedetti; *SS*: Camilla Fulci; *Generator operator*: Roberto Stiffi. *Cast*: Claudio Aliotti (Paul), Maria Concetta Salieri (Celin), Robert Egon (Willi), Luciana Ottaviani (Maria), Teresa Razzaudi (Anne), Sebastian Harrison (Jean); *uncredited*: Pierluigi Conti (Drunken Nazi), Joseph Alan Johnson (Mark), Zora Kerova [Zora Keslerová] (Succubus).

Running time: 84 minutes. *Also known as*: *Los fantasmas de Sodoma* (Spain); *Les fantômes de Sodome* (France); *Sodoma's tödliche Rache* (Germany)

Quando Alice ruppe lo specchio (*Touch of Death*)

D: Lucio Fulci. *S and SC*: Lucio Fulci; *DOP*: Silvano Tessicini; *M*: Carlo Maria Cordio; *E*: Vincenzo Tomassi; *ArtD*: Franco Vanorio; *E*: Vincenzo Tomassi; *MU*: Pino Ferrante; *Hair*: Maria Teresa Carrera; *AD*: Michele De Angelis; *SO*: Roberto Barbieri; *Foley artist*: Giulio D'Angeli; *SE*: Angelo Mattei; *C*: Luca Alfieri; *AC*: Rolando Stefanelli; *KG*: Umberto Magostini; *El*: Massimo Rocchi; *W*: Mirella Pedetti; *SS*: Camilla Fulci; *Generator operator*: Roberto Stiffi. *Cast*: Brett Halsey (Lester Parson), Ria De Simone (Alice Shogun), Pierluigi Conti (Randy), Sacha Darwin (Margie MacDonald), Zora Kerova [Zora Keslerová] (Virginia Field), Marco Di Stefano (The Tramp); *uncredited*: (Guest at Randy's Poker Table), Maurice Poli (TV Newscaster #1).

Running time: 86 minutes. *Also known as*: *La sombra de Lester* (Spain), *Soupçons de mort* (France); *When Alice Broke the Mirror* (Germany).

Le porte dell'inferno

D: Umberto Lenzi. *S*: Umberto Lenzi; *SC*: Olga Pehar; *DOP*: Sandro Mancori; *M*: Piero Montanari; *E*: Vanio Amici; *SE*: Giovanni Corridori; *ArtD*: Dario Micheli; *CO*: Giovanna Deodato; *MU*: Gabriella Trani; *Hair*: Maura Turchi; *Casting*: Werner Pochath; *SO*: Francesco Zannoni, Franco Borni; *B*: Marco Di Biase: *Foley artist*: Giulio De Angeli; *STC*: Franco Fantasia; *C*: Luca Alfieri; *AC*: Davide Mancori; *ChEl*: Fabrizio Faitanini; *KG*: Giovanni Savini; *Generator operator*: Roberto Stiffi; *SS*: Olga Pehar. *Cast*: Barbara Cupisti (Erna), Pietro Genuardi (Paul Brandini), Lorenzo Majnoni (Manfred), Giacomo Rossi Stuart (Dr. Jones), Gaetano Russo (Maurizio Fesner), Andrea Damiano (Laura Benson), Mario Luzzi (Teo), Paul Muller (Simone di Reims).

Running time: 90 minutes. *Also known as*: *Gates of Hell*; *The Hell's Gate* (International titles); *Las puertas del infierno* (Spain).

By the second half of the 1980s, the crisis of the Italian film industry was no more an open secret which everyone knew about but most pretended was untrue, but a harsh reality. Theatrical distribution was becoming more and more difficult, with the disappearance of many venues of the second and third run circuit. Selling films to foreign markets was still an option, although this mostly meant straight to home video releases. But even with regards to the national market, it was inevitable for producers to try and sell their products to television or home video: renouncing to submit a film to the rating board for a theatrical screening certificate meant also saving money, as films released straight-to-video did not need an official rating.

"*I maestri del thriller*" was a project born specifically with the aim of television and home video destination. According to producer Carlo Alberto Alfieri, who claimed that the idea for the series (initially to be called *Il cinema italiano del terrore*) was his own, the main concept was to have several new authors or scriptwriters write and direct their own films. "We started looking for scriptwriters with a great experience in the specific field of horror movies: the basic idea was to put them in a position to realize their vision, but with their own means. This, because scriptwriters complain very often that their scripts are distorted and altered, thus losing their original momentum. We precisely wanted to exploit the desire, the creativity and the unvoiced strength of these authors."[1]

Alfieri presented the project to Luciano Martino, who rejected it, and eventually he set a deal with Augusto Caminito's Scena Internazional, who was attempting to exploit the horror fad of the period (see also *Nosferatu a Venezia*). Caminito then contracted Distribuzione Alpha

Cinematografica and Cineduck, owned by Luigi Nannerini and Antonio "Antonino" Lucidi, and pre-sold the television rights to Reteitalia.

The original project for the series comprised ten films, but eventually, because of Reteitalia refusing to buy all of them, only eight were made: *Hansel e Gretel* (Giovanni Simonelli), *Bloody Psycho* (Leandro Lucchetti), *Massacre* (Andrea Bianchi), *Luna di sangue* (Enzo Milioni), *Non avere paura della zia Marta* (Mario Bianchi), *Sodoma's Ghost* and *Quando Alice ruppe lo specchio* (both directed by Lucio Fulci) and *Le porte dell'inferno* (Umberto Lenzi).[2] The whole series was made with very little money: according to Alfieri, the budget for each film was about 300–350 million *lire*, whereas production manager Silvano Zignani recalled an even smaller sum, about 207 million, and Fulci himself talked of "200–300 million."[3] The films were shot in 16mm and then blown up to 35mm, on tight schedules (three to four weeks each) and with the same crews and several recurring cast members. Another trick to save money would be to shoot some of the films at the producers' own villas, in order to save the rental money. With such premises, it is hard to believe that anyone expected the results to be any good.

Things started out badly with *Hansel e Gretel*. Despite the title, the film is not a modern-day version of the celebrated Grimm fairy tale, as the only element in common is given by the children's names, but merely a tiresome revenge-from-beyond-the-grave plot about a couple of children kidnapped and killed by organ traffickers. The story is as dull as it gets, with sequences stretched to reach an acceptable running time (a case in point is the kidnappers' car driving across country roads and being followed by barking dogs), and the ridiculous is always around the corner.

Hansel e Gretel was Giovanni Simonelli's only movie as a director. The son of director Giorgio Simonelli, and an experienced scriptwriter who had worked among others with Antonio Margheriti, the then 62-year-old debuting filmmaker was not a beginner, and was one of the series' regular contributors, having penned the scripts for *Bloody Psycho* and *Luna di sangue* as well. Soon, however, it became apparent that directing was not his forte. Michele De Angelis (who was the assistant director on all films except Lenzi's) recalls a significant episode in this regard. One day the crew was ready to shoot, but the director was nowhere to be found. The crew was filming in a villa, and the young a.d. finally found Simonelli in the wine cellar. "When he saw me, he told me, 'Look at this beautiful must … now they're making wine out of it…' He didn't even think about the film!"[4]

At the end of the scheduled three weeks' shoot Simonelli had filmed footage for approximately 50 minutes, with whole chunks of the story missing. Shooting went on for the other films in the series, but several weeks later the producers called Lucio Fulci behind the camera to supervise an additional week's shoot, in an attempt to salvage the film. As De Angelis points out, this "supervision" was actually much more than that: "Lucio shot everything. Simonelli stayed by his side, just watching…."[5]

Fulci shot several additional scenes to reach feature length, namely the one in which an elderly woman has her skull transfixed by a wood splinter which gouges out her eye, as in *L'aldilà*; a woman (Zora Kerova) taking off her clothes and having a bubble bath while giving instructions to a pair of thugs; the same woman being dispatched by the ghosts of the two children in the bathtub; the two goons falling into a canal and being torn apart by the dewatering pump; and some scenes which according to De Angelis were shot in a hotel—possibly the love scene between Lina (Lucia Prato) and Fred (Gaetano Russo), and Silvia (Elisabete Pimenta Boareto) relaxing in her bedroom.[6] However, even Fulci's intervention was not enough to make the product marketable, and Andrea Bianchi was reportedly recruited as well. With such a troubled production history, it's not surprising that *Hansel e Gretel* is the lowest point in a series which had hardly any peaks to begin with.

The theme of innocence betrayed and the insistence on violence toward minors are akin to Fulci's work (see *Non si sevizia un paperino*, *Quella villa accanto al cimitero*, and *Voci dal profondo*), and the image of children as revenants is a constant in Italian Gothic, from Bava's *I tre volti della paura* and *Operazione paura* to *La notte dei diavoli* (1972, Giorgio Ferroni)—and one of Fulci's additional scenes even reprises the image of the two children looking eerily from outside a window, featured in Bava and Ferroni's films. Yet Simonelli never goes beyond cut-rate shock value. The gore bits are crude in an H.G. Lewis way, and special effects are as cheap as they come, with plenty of animal entrails and quarters of beef taken from the nearest abattoir making up for body organs and human torsos.

Besides Pimente Boareto, in her only film role, the cast includes regulars of the series such as Brigitte Christensen (as the evil Solange), Maurice Poli and Paul Muller. The acting—including that of the two children—is atrocious, but lines of dialogue such as "You're half-Brazilian, so you should know that the most poisonous snakes are undoubtedly the ones with the most beautiful colors" are beyond redemption. Worst of all, Simonelli's direction is perfunctory and haphazard to the point of amateurishness, with jumbled camera set-ups and plenty of continuity errors: for instance, the kidnappers sedate Hansel and Gretel with chloroform and put them in the car trunk, but in a following scene we see them chatting with the children, who are sitting in the back set of the car; later in the film a man sinks in a pit of quicksand-like manure and in the next scene is found dead on top of it. Post-production is evidently careless. A laughable blooper has the police listening to a tape recording of Solange's death, which even includes a bit of the score from said scene as well.

The second in the series, and the closest to the tradition of Italian Gothic cinema was Leandro Lucchetti's *Bloody Psycho*. Born in Trieste in 1944, the then 43-year-old director had worked on television during the previous decade, with such programs as *Per conoscere Pasolini* (1978), a documentary which included excerpts of the poet's last interview with Enzo Biagi and Alberto Moravia's speech at Pasolini's funeral. This was his third film, after the little-seen *Maledetta Euridice* (1986) and *Mercenari dell'apocalisse* (a.k.a. *Apocalypse Mercenaries*, 1987), the latter featuring most of the same cast as *Bloody Psycho*. It was Alfieri who asked Lucchetti to come aboard the project: "I took it for what it was—an adventure,"[7] the director points out. The film was initially to be directed by Simonelli, who had written the basic scenario. "I changed, adapted and invented as best as I could to put together something that looked like a film. Simonelli hadn't written a real script, but rather a long synopsis or a more or less substantial treatment."

Shot in November 1987, in three weeks, in the villages of Castelnuovo di Porto and Magliano Romano, *Bloody Psycho* features a cast led by German actor Peter Hintz and including other recurring faces in low-budget horror movies of the period, namely Brigitte Christensen, Sacha Darwin (also in *Non avere paura della zia Marta* and *Quando Alice ruppe lo specchio*), Marco Di Stefano (*Quando Alice ruppe lo specchio, Blood Delirium*), plus guest stars Vassili Karis and Paul Muller.

"I'm some kind of medium," says Dr. Vogler (Hintz) to a drunkard (Karis) in the film's opening scene, a line of dialogue which recalls a notorious one in Bava's *Operazione paura*— which Bava himself had mentioned as an example of embarrassment when discussing his mixed feelings toward his own work. There are many such lines in Lucchetti's film, which draws openly from classical Gothic not only in the setting (a medieval village, a creepy castle and a moldy cemetery) but also in its plot about ghosts and *Doppelgängers*. As in *La maschera del demonio*, here as well a female ancestor is trying to take the place of her young descendant who looks just like her (both are played by the same actress); and, like so many Gothic heroes before him, Vogler goes to bed with a reincarnated ghost, who then bares her putrefied breast and asks, "Do I disgust you? And yet I know you like my body…," in yet another mixture of fear and desire, attraction and repulsion. But Vogler the psychic is also a male version of Jennifer O'Neill's character in *Sette note in nero*, as he is shocked and disturbed by visions whose meaning he cannot grasp until the very end. Other scenes solicit weird cinephile references: the one in which a wheelchair-bound zombie falls down a flight of stairs looks like a horror remake of a celebrated moment in *Kiss of Death* (1947, Henry Hathaway), while the same zombie killing a victim (Paul Muller) by trampling over him on the wheelchair comes closer to the sheer delirious insanity of Polselli's *Mania* (1974).

Lucchetti added some dollops of eroticism to the mix as well, as in the glory days of 1970s Gothic. It is soon clear that the relationship between the wheelchair-bound Mrs. Rezzori (Christensen) and her sexy housemaid (Nubia Martini) is a barely disguised sado-masochistic liaison, as the lady of the house throws a cup of tea on the floor and then forces the servant to kneel down "like a whore" to clean it. Soon after, the maid shows up in Vogler's room to provide vital bits of information as well as sexual advances. "Hey, but I'm even better than you with hands! I feel I can make things grow" she says while caressing his crotch, yet another line of dialogue which would have made Bava blush. A sex scene between Hintz and Micaela (Louise Kamsteeg, credited as Loes Kamma)

even features a use of yogurt as an erotic stimulant in a blatant rip-off of the notorious "food scene" in *9½ Weeks*. Overall the plot doesn't really add up, as even the characters admit. "This is really an incredible story," a female reporter named Sacha (Darwin) notes. "So incredible that, if I write it down in the newspaper, they will think I'm mad." To which Micaela replies, "But it would make for a beautiful film … a perfect thriller!"

Besides the nudity, crude splatter scenes and demented dialogue, Lucchetti (who even turns up in a brief cameo role) conveys a passable Gothic mood by way of wide, low-angle camera set-ups and eerie lighting. He is helped in the process by Silvano Tessicini's photography, replete with color filters, silhouettes and dry ice, and definitely better than the d.o.p.'s work in the other films in the series. "Tessicini understood perfectly the mood and lighted the scenes masterfully, making the best of the sets I had chosen," the director noted. "I'm not a big fan of Bava, and even less of Argento. Actually, I admired Hammer's Dracula films."

Lucchetti even attempts some personal touches. In a scene, Vogler and Sacha walk along a path outside a cemetery which is gradually filled with scattered debris of contemporary society, from plastic bottles to ceramic toilet seats, from dolls to broken TV sets, and which leads them to a tomb in a desecrated ground. It's a surreal moment that looks as if it belongs in a Ferreri film, and it sounds strangely out of place, almost like an attempt at claiming ambitions which cannot be fulfilled in such a cheap and clumsy little movie. "It was an inspiration of the moment, as many others in the film, linked to extemporaneous things I discovered on set," Lucchetti recalls.

Overall, although modest, *Bloody Psycho* fares better than the others in the series. It was definitely the one Alfieri was happy with the most, so much so that he even considered submitting it to the board of censors to obtain a visa for theatrical release.[8] It was eventually released to home video just like the other titles, and the English language version features a superimposed credit of Lucio Fulci as supervisor, even though Fulci never showed up on the set nor did he discuss anything about the film with Lucchetti. After *Bloody Psycho*, Alfieri offered the director to make another cheap horror movie for the series, which he refused. "One was enough. The story level was what it was and shooting in three weeks was quite a stress. The game was not worth the candle for me, but it was for Nannerini and Lucidi, who sold this notorious series all over the world!" Lucchetti went on to direct some more low-budget films in the following years, including the W.I.P. *Caged—Le prede umane* (1991) and *La ragnatela del silenzio–A.I.D.S.* (a.k.a. *Web of Silence*, 1994). In 2016 he debuted as a novelist with *Amorosi sensi*, set during the Resistance, followed by a mammoth three-tome work, *Bora scura*.

Some entries in the series feature only sparse Gothic elements. That is the case with Andrea Bianchi's *Massacre*, set during the shooting of a horror movie: the director (Maurice Poli) attempts to inject some frisson into the film by hiring a psychic (Maria Letizia Placido) to perform a séance on the set, resulting in the spirit of Jack the Ripper possessing one of the participants, who starts killing the others one by one. Besides the opening sequence of the film-within-a-film (titled *Dirty Blood*) in which a woman is terrorized in a cemetery by some monstrous figures, and the séance scene, complete with a prowling camera, Sam Raimi–style, the rest of the film works as a gory body count whodunit, long on gore but short on cinematic value. Despite the dialogue name-dropping Anaximenes and Jung's collective unconscious, the attempts at self-reflexiveness are ill-fated, with Poli's character delivering a pompous monologue on the nature of horror cinema: "Films of this type can no longer be dealt with in the spirit of the 1930s, and this because our generation knows what horror means. In fact, besides the atrocities of war and its horrors, cinema introduced us to zombies and other monstrous creatures, so that today even an illiterate knows everything about terror and horror. So, if we still want to frighten the audience, I think we must stick to reality. It's useless to rely on imagination because fantasy will never be reality." He claims he wants to "draw from the faithful reproduction of man's primordial fear," before concluding: "And even in this type of film I want to apply Neorealism."

Enzo Milioni's *Luna di sangue* (also known as *Fuga dalla morte*) is some sort of a mystery with supernatural undertones. Told in flashback by a dying man, in would-be *film noir* style, the incoherent plot deals with a woman (Barbara Blasco) who discovers her husband Larry's dead body, but the corpse disappears, and no one believes her; one year later she is visited by a man who claims to be Larry. The direction and acting are worthy of a South American soap opera, and the story is overly talky and hopelessly boring. Milioni and scriptwriter Giovanni Simonelli try to revive the proceedings with some sex and gore extravaganza, with bullets to the face, a decapitation by scythe (the victim is played by Annie Belle), and a notorious scene where a young mute woman (Jessica Moore) is shot in the head while performing fellatio on her incestuous father, and the killer's second bullet strikes the man's erect member (the scene was shot in two versions, a more explicit one for the foreign markets). It's a moment worthy of Milioni's trashy *giallo*, *La sorella di Ursula* (1978).

The fifth in the series, Mario Bianchi's *Non avere paura della zia Marta* (known abroad as *The Murder Secret*) works for much of its running time as a gory thriller about a family's visit to a country house where the titular aunt Martha is about to return, released after 30 years in a psychiatric hospital. The woman, like Beckett's Godot, doesn't show up though, and while everyone is waiting for her the main characters end up killed one by one in gory ways: a shower murder quotes *Psycho*, and the most gruesome bit has an admittedly obnoxious kid being decapitated with a chainsaw *à la Murder Obsession*. However, the final ten minutes push Bianchi's film right into Gothic territory, with the introduction of a supernatural twist that rips off the evergreen *An Occurrence at Owl Creek Bridge*, redone in a similar way as Herk Harvey's *Carnival of Souls* (1962) and Kevin Billington's *Voices* (1973), and in turn reprised in Fulci's *Le porte del silenzio* (1991) as well as in Jean-Baptiste Andrea and Fabrice Canepa's *Dead End* (2003).

Bianchi was rather pleased with *Non avere paura della zia Marta* ("There was quite some atmosphere, and even some twists") but found the experience of working with Nannerini and Lucidi to be a letdown: "It seemed we'd go on [with this series] for our whole life, with the producer telling me, 'Look, if it goes well we'll never stop!' … and then I found out it was all a scam set up to divide the cake…."[9] Alfieri was less enamored of the result: "Even though the original ideas were good, on many occasions there were disappointments. For instance, with Bianchi. Since he could make films at a very low cost, on a shoestring, once he had the opportunity to put more care and attention on the project, on paper he could achieve interesting results. Whereas he filmed a three-week movie in just two, perhaps he was put under pressure.... Fact is, he worked in haste just like with the films he usually made, so he ended up making a pretty bad movie."[10]

Non avere paura della zia Marta is hardly distinguishable from the others in the series, with crude gore effects, a suitably creepy synth-driven score by ex prog-musician Gianni Sposito, and some nudity courtesy of Adriana Russo and the stunning Jessica Moore (real name Luciana Ottaviani). The 21-year-old actress had debuted in Aristide Massaccesi's *La monaca nel peccato* (1986) and starred in a couple more of Massaccesi's classy soft porn flicks, the 9½ *Weeks* rip-off *Eleven Days, Eleven Nights: 11 giorni, 11 notti* (1987) and *Top Model* (1988), but her career was short-lived. *Non avere paura della zia Marta* was one of Gabriele Tinti's last films. The actor, a former beau of Italian cinema in the 1950s and later a regular of Joe D'Amato films, being Laura Gemser's partner, was already very ill (he would die of cancer in 1991), although he still looks younger than his age (he was 56 at the time of the shooting). Speaking of which, a blatant inconsistency turns up in the narrative: in the flashbacks, when Aunt Martha is hospitalized, Richard is a 10-year-old boy, so at the time of the events in the film, with Marta being released from the asylum "after 30 years," he should be 40, whereas according on the gravestone in the cemetery scene he is 55.

It was d.o.p. Silvano Tessicini who involved Lucio Fulci in "*I maestri del thriller*." Near the end of the 1980s, the director was in rather dire straits. He had moved from Rome to Castelnuovo di Porto, had experienced serious health issues and was back from the unfortunate experience of *Zombi 3*, which the producer completed with additional scenes shot by Bruno Mattei and Claudio Fragasso (but approved by Fulci), with an extra ten days' shoot in the Philippines, without the main actors and with only a minimal crew. Tessicini lived in Morlupo, near Castelnuovo di Porto, and started calling on the director, helping him in some practical matters. "Lucio had just returned from the Philippines, he was not well, and had a huge belly," he recalled. The inflated belly was a consequence of the liver disease which plagued him during the shooting of *Zombi 3*.

The producers accepted Tessicini's suggestion, even though initially Fulci was to act merely as supervisor, but he submitted an idea for another film to direct on his own, namely *Quando Alice ruppe lo specchio*. But when one of the directors backed out, he offered to replace him, and that's how *Sodoma's Ghost*—a script Fulci had co-written with Roberto Gianviti and dated back at least four years—took form. It was the first to go into production, with the working title *Ghost Light*. Filming lasted four weeks, starting May 30, 1988, and took place at the Castel di Decima castle, just outside Rome (the exterior shots portrayed a different villa, though). The film was plagued by production troubles, and it was also the only one of the series to go over budget.[11]

Sodoma's Ghost is basically a ghost story set in a haunted house—a villa in France where in 1943 a group of Nazi officers were killed by a bomb while having a wild party, and one of them was filming the orgy. Forty-four years later, a group of teens end up lost, stumble upon the abandoned villa and spend the night there. But the Nazi ghosts appear and seduce their victims, materializing their passions and desires. Fulci called it his worst film[12] and on one occasion he even claimed he had left the set.[13] According to some sources, Mario Bianchi shot the remaining scenes after his departure, but Bianchi himself explained: "Fulci didn't leave the set, absolutely. He finished the film."[14] In fact, Bianchi—who had just finished filming *Non avere paura della zia Marta*[15]—was recruited at some point during the shooting by production manager Silvano Zignani, upon Fulci's request, to film some scenes as second unit.

> Fulci told me, "Look, do me a courtesy, shoot some connecting scenes for me...." He asked me because he was probably a bit behind schedule. It was he who told me what to shoot: the boys' arrival at the house on a jeep, the various bits. Moral of the story: by saying "Shoot this, shoot that," from three short bits I ended up shooting much more footage, several scenes. Meanwhile he completed the movie, shooting other scenes. If I happened to have the four or five leads, he would film other scenes, but most times I had to wait until he finished working with them and then I could shoot.[16]

In the same interview, Bianchi claimed that "I wouldn't say I shot half the film, but almost," and complained that Fulci never even thanked him. However, Michele De Angelis pointed out that Bianchi was on the set for only a couple of days,[17] which would obviously reduce greatly his contribution to the film.

In a French interview, Fulci described the

film as follows: "It's as if a bomb exploded in Pasolini's film *Salò o le 120 giornate di Sodoma*,"[18] but the most obvious connection is with the Nazisploitation thread of the mid–1970s. The script borrows ideas from other sources as well: the scene where the protagonists vainly try to escape from the villa but always find themselves back in front of its castle is lifted from *The Legacy*. That said, the result is less than mediocre. Fulci belabors one of his favorite themes, that of time, albeit in a much less successful way than in his subsequent made-for-TV film, *La casa nel tempo*, and he throws away the most interesting idea, about the curse having to be broken only by means of an old film reel (a concept reprised also in Lamberto Bava's *A cena col vampiro*). The dialogue is awful, especially the phony lingo spoken by the young protagonists (who are headed to Paris but have surf boards atop their jeep!), the actors are atrocious, and the low budget is painfully evident in the ridiculous special effects.

In accordance with one of Italian Gothic's main topics, Fulci's ghosts are an embodiment of the main characters' hidden desires and obsessions, but this results in bargain-basement erotic scenes, filmed like a cheap soft porn flick. The most bizarre bit has a Nazi officer playing pool while a girl is lying with her legs spread on the billiard table and preparing to shoot a cue ball right into her crotch. It's unlikely Fulci knew Alberto Cavallone's 1977 surrealist drama *Spell—Dolce mattatoio*, which features a similar scene, but Cavallone's version is much more powerful than his cheap attempt at transgression. The director had some problems with an actress, Teresa Razzaudi, who at first refused to perform nude scenes, much to Fulci's displeasure. After many discussions, the scene of her being seduced by a Nazi ghost was partially shot with a body double.

Filming for *Quando Alice ruppe lo specchio*—with the working title *Licia ha rotto lo specchio* (Licia Has Broken the Mirror)—started just three days after finishing *Sodoma's Ghost* and went on for four weeks, starting on June 22, 1988, around Rome and at Vides studios.[19] To save on the budget, some interiors were shot in Nannerini's own villa. This time Fulci approached the project with much more care, even though the resort to long takes (such as the opening scene, which amusingly references to *Citizen Kane*) must not be seen as a stylistic choice but rather as a cost-cutting gimmick, as

the director pointed out: "Have you ever thought why there are so many useless shots in *Quando Alice ruppe lo specchio* or *Sodoma's Ghost*...? So as to get to the minimum running time of one hour and 22 minutes ... there were not enough money to shoot more scenes (and anyway, it was a bet with myself)!"[20]

But the budget constraints were once again overwhelming. The story takes place in an unlikely, depopulated America which looks very much like Italian suburbia, and according to Michele De Angelis many extraordinary ideas in the script didn't come out well on screen or were simply discarded for lack of time and money. Fulci eventually got fed up, and during shooting he had many arguments with the producers, who on the other hand were unhappy with the director being constantly behind schedule (and not helped in this regard by his d.o.p. Silvano Tessicini, who was good but quite slow).

As with other films in the late phase of Fulci's career, *Quando Alice ruppe lo specchio* has a literary, philosophical core to it. Despite the over-the-top gory scenes (with the most gruesome one placed near the beginning, as if to fool the audience into thinking they are watching a brain-dead splatterfest), it is an original meditation on the theme of the double and identity. The director's open dislike toward psychoanalysis notwithstanding, the idea of a man suffering a split personality and becoming dissociated with his own shadow seemingly draws from Otto Rank's study *The Double*, who had discussed the way "primitive man considers his shadow as something real, as a being attached to him, and he is confirmed in his view of it as a soul by the fact that the dead person ... simply no longer casts a shadow,"[21] and to Jung's concept of the shadow as the hostile double, "that hidden, repressed, for the most part inferior and guilt-laden personality"[22] which stands in opposition to the rationally-governed ego. *Aenigma* featured a scene in which a narcissistic gym teacher is attacked and strangled by his own mirror image, a moment which vaguely recalls Giacomo Rossi Stuart's encounter with his evil double in *Operazione paura*. Here, Lester Parsons—a modern-day Bluebeard who seduces, kills, robs of their wealth and sometimes *eats* rich women—is framed by his own shadow, who leaves vital clues for the police to identify him.

The main problem is that the concept doesn't stand up for the entirety of a feature film, hence the many stretched out sequences of Lester seducing his horrid victims (who all have physical defects, a nod to Siodmak's *The Spiral Staircase*, 1946) and dispatching their cadavers, which are filled with a grotesque humor not unlike Buñuel's *Ensayo de un crimen*, well-served by Brett Halsey's spot-on, self-ironic performance. If anything, the film shows Fulci's growing interest toward the abstract and the metaphysical, which clashes jarringly with his habit of indulging in hyperviolent scenes: it is not particularly good, but it's undoubtedly personal.

Umberto Lenzi's *Le porte dell'inferno* was the last to be made. As the Tuscan director recalled,

> Fulci was contacted by Dania to direct two films of the series "*Le case maledette*," and after shooting *Il fantasma di Sodoma* and *Quando Alice ruppe lo specchio* he gave up and left the project. Then the executive producer, Alfieri, called me and offered me to make the two films that Lucio would have to shoot. I accepted out of friendship, but I suggested a story of mine. I was to direct two films for them. The first was *Le porte dell'inferno*, while the second was *Paura nel buio* which eventually I made with Massaccesi.[23]

Lenzi also realized immediately that the budget was too scant, in his words "not enough even for a one-hour TV movie." However, there is little to salvage in the story about a group of speleologists (including Barbara Cupisti and Giacomo Rossi-Stuart, the latter in his last movie role) who descend into a cave to help their wounded colleague (Gaetano Russo) and find out that the place is haunted by the spirits of seven monks burnt at the stake 700 years before, who swore to take their revenge. Lenzi's script (credited to his wife Olga Pehar) does little to establish a convincing Gothic mood, and stumbles upon laughable ideas, such as a copy of Umberto Eco's best-selling mystery *Il nome della rosa* showing up in a couple of scenes to provide a cultural basis for the plot's references to heresies. Ditto for the resort to numerology to spice up the medieval prophecy which provides the excuse for the graphic deaths that follow. The story proceeds with the expected gory body count, as the speleologists are offed one by one while wandering around the labyrinthine caves and tunnels: one scene featuring poisonous spiders even pays reference to Fulci's *L'aldilà* (and Lenzi would reprise a similar moment in *La casa delle anime erranti*). However, the result comes

closer to *Alien 2—Sulla Terra* (1980, Ciro Ippolito) than to *La chiesa*, with a final twist borrowed from *Rats—Notte di terrore*, before Lenzi reprises the "it-was-all-a-dream" circular ending of his own *Incubo sulla città contaminata*.

Unbeknownst to Alfieri, Fulci, in accordance with Nannerini and Lucidi, made another film, *Il gatto nel cervello*, assembling most of the gory footage from the other titles in the "*I maestri del thriller*" series and adding new scenes in which he played himself, a horror film director who suffers from nightmares and goes to a psychiatrist, unaware that the latter is a serial killer. It was some sort of revenge against Alfieri, who had given him an advance to make two more low-budget movies. The producer sued him and won the trial, but Fulci was already dead by then.

The eight films were released to home video as "*Lucio Fulci presenta*" (Lucio Fulci Presents) on the label Formula Home Video. Alfieri sued the company too, since he owned the rights to the home video market. Formula went bankrupt and Avo Film purchased the rights and rereleased them to VHS and DVD. Since none of them had been submitted to the rating board, any theatrical release was out of the question.

NOTES

1. Albiero and Cacciatore, *Il terrorista dei generi*, 362.

2. The chronology is confirmed by Michele De Angelis, who points out that after *Massacre* the crew did minor reshoots (two or three days) for *Bloody Psycho*, and that after *Luna di sangue* a whole week was spent shooting additional scenes for *Hansel e Gretel* under Fulci's supervision. Michele De Angelis, email interview with the author, May 2018.

3. Romagnoli, *L'occhio del testimone*, 35.

4. Albiero and Cacciatore, *Il terrorista dei generi*, 365.

5. De Angelis, email interview with the author.

6. Albiero and Cacciatore, *Il terrorista dei generi*, 365.

7. Leandro Lucchetti, email interview with the author, November 2017. All the quotes from Lucchetti come from this interview.

8. Even though Alfieri claimed that *Bloody Psycho* was submitted to the rating board to obtain a regular certificate for theatrical distribution, there is no record of this in ministerial papers.

9. Stefano Ippoliti and Matteo Norcini, "Mario Bianchi. 'Il mio cinema pizza e fichi,'" *Cine70 e dintorni* #5, Summer 2004, 29.

10. Albiero and Cacciatore, *Il terrorista dei generi*, 362.

11. *Ibid.*, 366.

12. Romagnoli, *L'occhio del testimone*, 35.

13. Marcello Garofalo, "Uno, nessuno, centofulci," *Segnocinema* #65, January/February 1994.

14. Albiero and Cacciatore, *Il terrorista dei generi*, 366.

15. Ippoliti and Norcini, "Mario Bianchi. 'Il mio cinema pizza e fichi,'" 29.

16. *Ibid.*

17. De Angelis, email interview with the author.

18. Maccaron and Nadjar, "Lucio Fulci: 'Je suis un monstre,'" 55.

19. Albiero and Cacciatore, *Il terrorista dei generi*, 369.

20. Romagnoli, *L'occhio del testimone*, 35.

21. Otto Rank, *The Double. A Psychoanalytic Study* (Chapel Hill: University of North Carolina Press, [1914] 2012), 83.

22. Carl Gustav Jung, *Memories, Dreams, Reflections* (New York: Pantheon Books, 1963), 417.

23. Gomarasca, *Umberto Lenzi*, 260.

Appendix 2
Made-for-TV Films

"Brivido giallo"
(Giallo Thrill)

D: Lamberto Bava. *DOP*: Gianlorenzo Battaglia, Gianfranco Transunto; *M*: Simon Boswell, Mario Tagliaferri; *E*: Mauro Bonanni, Daniele Alabiso; *PD, ArtD*: Antonello Geleng; *CO*: Valentina Di Palma; *AD*: Fabrizio Bava, Franco Fantasia; *MU*: Fabrizio Sforza, Luigi Ciminelli, Barbara Morosetti; *SPFX*: Fabrizio Sforza, Rosario Prestopino; *Hair*: Giancarlo Marin; *PrM*: Roberto Ricci, Romano Renzi; *SO*: Giuliano Piermarioli; *Mix*: Alberto Doni, Romano Checcacci; *SE*: Angelo Mattei, Paolo Ricci; *AC*: Enzo Frattari, Giancarlo Battaglia; *ChEl*: Domenico Cauli, Franco Rachin, Stefano Marinoi; *KG*: Franco Micheli, Luigi Orso; *SP*: Roberto Nicosia Vinci, Francesco Narducci; *W*: Mirella Pedetti, Anna Cirilli; *AE*: Carlo Bartolucci, Rossana Cingolani, Mario Cinotti, Silvana Di Legge; *SS*: Paola Bonelli.

PROD: Dania Film (Rome), Reteitalia (Milan). *EP*: Massimo Manasse, Marco Grillo Spina; *PS*: Francesco Fantacci, Renato Fié; *PSe*: Alberto Brusco; *ADM*: Anna de Pedys; *DubD*: Gianni Giuliano.

Episodes from "Brivido giallo" are arranged in chronological order according to their original air dates

Una notte al cimitero (*Graveyard Disturbance*)
S: Dardano Sacchetti; *SC*: Dardano Sacchetti, Lamberto Bava. *Cast*: Gregory Lech Thaddeus (Robin), Lea Martino (Tina), Beatrice Ring (Micky), Gianmarco Tognazzi (Gianni), Karl Zinny (David), Lino Salemme (Tavern Keeper), Gianpaolo Saccarola (Man at Tavern), Fabrizio Bava (Shop Assistant), Mirella Pedetti (Shop Assistant); *uncredited*: Lamberto Bava (Shop Keeper).

Running time: 93 minutes. Aired on August 8, 1989. *Also known as*: *Zombies des Grauens* (West Germany)

Per sempre (a.k.a. ***Fino alla morte***) (*Until Death*)
S: Elisa Briganti, Dardano Sacchetti; *SC*: Dardano Sacchetti, Lamberto Bava. *Cast*: Gioia Scola [Gioia Maria Tibiletti] (Linda), David Brandon (Carlo), Giuseppe [Stefano] De Sando (Carabinieri Marshall), Roberto Pedicini (Luca), Marco Vivio (Alex), Urbano Barberini (Marco).

Running time: 93 minutes. Aired on August 15, 1989.

La casa dell'orco (*Demons III: The Ogre*)
S: Dardano Sacchetti; *SC*: Dardano Sacchetti, Lamberto Bava. *Cast*: Virginia Bryant (Cheryl), Paolo Malco (Tom), Sabrina Ferilli (Anna), Patrizio Vinci (Bobby), Stefania Montorsi (Maria), Alice Di Giuseppe (Young Cheryl), David Flosi (The Ogre), Alex Serra (Dario, the Artist); *uncredited*: Lamberto Bava (Man in Bar), Roberto Dell'Acqua (Man in Bar).

Running time: 96 minutes. Aired on August 22, 1989. *Also known as*: *The Ogre* (International English language title); *Demons 3; The Ogre* (UK); *Ghost House II* (Germany); *El ogro* (Spain); *Una extraña casa macabra* (Argentina).

A cena col vampiro (*Dinner with the Vampire*)
S: Luciano Martino; *SC*: Dardano Sacchetti, Lamberto Bava; *SVFX*: Sergio Stivaletti. *Cast*:

George Hilton (Jurek), Patrizia Pellegrino (Rita), Riccardo Rossi (Gianni), Isabel Russinova, Valeria Milillo (Sasha), Yvonne Sciò (Monica), Daniele Aldrovandi (Gilles), Igor Zalewsky (Gilles), Roberto Pedicini, Letizia Ziaco (Nadia), Stefano Sabelli (Matteo).

Running time: 92 minutes. Aired on August 29, 1989.

When discussing his move from the big to the small screen, Lamberto Bava explained:

> People in the movie industry, up to a certain point, thought of television as an adversary. Whereas I made some assessment.... Looking at the TV ratings, back then, you could see that those products that did badly were seen by at least two million viewers. Far more people could see your work on television, and so a genre which has always been very important to me, the Fantastic—I'm not just speaking about horror, but Fantastic, which is a wider genre—could reach a much wider audience.[1]

Silvio Berlusconi's company Reteitalia was willing to invest in horror after the huge commercial success of *Dèmoni* and *Dèmoni 2*, not to mention the many foreign films released theatrically in Italy. The home video market as well showed that the genre was among the most popular among consumers, and several companies had a large part of their catalog devoted to horror and the *fantastique*. Berlusconi's TV network was quick to follow the trend, and horror movies became a staple of its schedule, especially on the channel "Italia 1," aimed specifically at younger audiences.

News that Reteitalia would be financing "*Brivido giallo*," a series of five made-for-TV films directed by Lamberto Bava, came in July 1986. "These will be low-budget products, signed by young authors who should be able to rejuvenate the movie business," Reteitalia's executive for Italian productions Massimiliano Fasoli commented when announcing the new films and telefilms to be produced by the company.[2] In addition to "*Brivido giallo*," another significant investment was the TV comedy series *I ragazzi della 3°C* (The Boys in Class 3C), set in a high school and directed by Dino Risi's son Claudio—a clear sign of the target audience these products would be aimed at.

The series, which eventually comprised four (instead of five) films co-written by Dardano Sacchetti and produced by Luciano Martino's Dania Film, was shot between 1987 and 1988. The four TV movies—*Una notte al cimitero, Per sem-pre, La casa dell'orco,* and *A cena col vampiro*—dealt with characters and themes typical of the Gothic genre: the vampire (*A cena col vampiro*), the haunted house (*La casa dell'orco*), the ghost story in different forms (*Per sempre, Una notte al cimitero*), all revised through the parameters of contemporary taste. The music scores were written by Simon Boswell. It took a couple of years before they were eventually aired during prime time in August 1989, on Italia 1.

Una notte al cimitero—Bava's original title was *Dentro il cimitero* (Inside the Cemetery)—was the first to be aired, and it came as a shock for those who had in mind the savage bloodshed of the *Dèmoni* films. The story, about five teenagers (including Beatrice Ring, Karl Zinny, and Gianmarco Tognazzi), who steal goods from a store and then make a bet to stay a night in a cemetery inside a cursed crypt, to collect a treasure, relied heavily on humor. Bava defended this choice, explaining that first and foremost the products "had to avoid being too "heavy," and should not be exceedingly gory; at the same time, they had to have a somewhat relaxed approach, with some tongue-in-cheek moments. I'm not saying "comic," but something that would release tension—which, however, you never get to find on television...."[3]

The film had received its baptism of fire a couple of years earlier, in October 1987, at the Sitges Film Festival in Spain. It was introduced by the director himself, who warned the audience that what they were going to see was not supposed to be a picture for theatrical release. It didn't help much, as *Una notte al cimitero* was heavily booed, with a pale-faced Bava sitting in the audience. The Catalonian newspaper *La Vanguardia* commented the memorable screening as follows:

> Rarely we have seen the audience scream for a film's heroes' death, but this is what happened. During the screening of *Graveyard Disturbance* by Lamberto Bava, a sector bawled, another was outraged and the other threw down the simultaneous translation equipments. The five oh-so-very-cute young Italian fashion models spent over one hour inside a crypt lit like a carnival, repeating the same dialogue over and over, getting lost without moving from the site and not believing at all (thank goodness) their misadventure. The dead (whose faces are the only—badly—made-up part) run away from them, and every now and then a silly joke comes up, pretending (?) to be parody. Luckily, the detestable protagonists end up arrested by the "carabinieri," an experience that many

wished for the director, invited by the festival together with one of the "actors," Ugo Tognazzi's son.[4]

The second episode, *Per sempre* was another old script by Sacchetti, about a pregnant woman, Linda (Gioia Scola), who kills her husband with the help of her lover, Carlo (David Brandon). Eight years later an unknown drifter named Marco (Urbano Barberini) stops at Linda and Carlo's inn by the lake and asks for a job. But he seems to know far too many things about Linda's dead husband. As Bava noted, scriptwise, it had the most cinematic strength and impact of the four. It starred Gioia Scola, Urbano Barberini and David Brandon.

The episode caused some controversy, for Lucio Fulci claimed the original idea was his own:

> One day I told (Dardano) the story of *Evil Comes Back*, a sequel on a fantastic note to *The Postman Always Rings Twice*, and he wrote it up and proposed it several times over to producers with my name on it as director, and then, one day, he registered it with his name on it! (laughs) I later found out that he'd sold it to a friend of mine—[Luciano] Martino—but in view of our past friendship I decided not to sue him. I just broke off all relations with him.[5]

Sacchetti's version of the story goes as follows:

> It is one of the most painful moments in my relationship with Fulci. We hadn't been speaking to each other for some years. Then one day he called me. He and Roberto Gianviti were trying to put together a story about sex and ghosts … they were both very confused, because they didn't know whether to emphasize the sex or the ghosts. I attended meetings with them for about a week. I told them I didn't like their story, and Fulci asked me what I was working on. I told him I had written a sort of sequel to *The Postman Always Rings Twice*. Fulci read it and liked it very much. He found a producer who bought the story and commissioned me and Elisa Briganti to write the script…. After I delivered the screenplay, the producer didn't pay me and said he was not able to make the film…. Fulci brought the script to another producer, who … went around for some time trying to make it into a film, but to no avail. The magic moment of Italian horror film had waned, and so had Fulci's, after the financial catastrophe of *Conquest* and other mistakes. Fulci kept on carrying the script around, which was beautiful. I was against this … unbeknownst to me, he had an English translation done by Brett Halsey, promising him the leading role. I got angry and finally broke off my relationship with Lucio. A couple of years later, working on the "*Brivido giallo*" series, we needed one more script to complete the series. Lamberto, who knew about the

project, asked me if it was still available. I said yes and gave it to him. Fulci, who was jealous about Lamberto (whom he didn't hold in any esteem) making a film he cared a lot about, came out saying that the project was his·…. Fact is, in that moment he was ill, in disgrace, with money problems, and back from very bad experiences such as *Zombi 3*.[6]

Next was *La casa dell'orco*, starring Virginia Bryant (seen in *Dèmoni 2*, and Fulci's original choice for the leading role in *Aenigma*), Paolo Malco, Sabrina Montorsi and Sabrina Ferilli (the latter soon to become one of Italy's top actresses). The story bore more than passing similarities to *Quella villa accanto al cimitero*, which Bava Jr. at a certain point was slated to direct. In fact, as the director himself explained, the script for *La casa dell'orco* was based on Sacchetti's original one for *Quella villa accanto al cimitero*, which had been liberally altered by Fulci. But Sacchetti had a different version:

> *Quella villa accanto al cimitero* and *La casa dell'orco* are not the same story, but they are part of my poetics regarding home and children: a recurring theme which I have explored several times with different shades, but also with assonances. These are stories that came from my own life in this great country house that had a strange fame and was inhabited by a disturbing presence. So, let's say that the feeling behind these movies is the same … the house had a first cellar, from which a staircase leading to a second cellar came down for more than fifteen meters, dug into rock. After the electrical system was interrupted, that staircase and that second cellar remained in darkness for eternity. No one knew what was below. Only my grandmother dared go down those stairs. I stayed on the first steps handing a lit candle and saw her disappear in the dark. I only heard noises. So the films are different, but behind them there is the same emotion I experienced at different moments and with different moods.[7]

The last in the series, *A cena col vampiro*, was openly parodistic, and packed full of movie references, starring George Hilton as the suave director-cum-vampire Jurek, who stays young like Dorian Gray while his ageing self is trapped in an old black-and-white film. It was also the only one shot in a typical Gothic location, the Moorish-style Castle Sammezzano near Florence.

The very title itself, "*Brivido giallo*" (Giallo Thrill), which presents the four films as *gialli*, not as Gothics, is significant. By targeting the four films as sticking to the *giallo* tradition, the producers showed no trust in the Gothic as a marketing factor, which is understandable. But even the promised thrills were few and far between.

From a narrative point of view, pastiche and in-jokes aimed at film buffs are the norm. In *La casa dell'orco* Bava and Sacchetti reprise almost to the letter the scene of the underwater room in *Inferno*, while *Una notte al cimitero* and especially *A cena col vampiro* feature a plethora of references and self-references that range from Mario Bava to Murnau's *Nosferatu* and *The Fearless Vampire Killers*—not forgetting the director's own *Dèmoni*, with the idea of the film-within-a-film.

Predictably, the most disturbing elements, such as the visionary and violent excesses and the themes related to transgression (especially sexual) were absolutely precluded. For instance, as Bava explained, *La casa dell'orco* suffered a lot from self-censorship. "An issue in the script was when the ogre showed up. What could we do with it? Had it been a movie ... the ogre would eat children, but on TV you couldn't do that. So we settled for a "symbolism" of the ogre, with people disappearing."[8] The odd gory scene, such as a heart ripped from a chest by invisible hands in *A cena col vampiro*, could be acceptable if inserted in an openly humorous context: "I had the alibi of comedy,"[9] the director commented.

Visually, the results display the serial approach to the product. A case in point is the recycling of Antonello Geleng's set-pieces to save on budget: the crypt seen in *Una notte al cimitero* was turned into the ogre's subterranean lair in *La casa dell'orco*. On the other hand, the films show a quick disinterest in reimagining and portraying the Gothic genre beyond the mere playful and postmodernist rereading of clichés.

This is primarily a sign of the new way audiences dealt with the genre. Young viewers developed a film buff mentality, and welcomed cinephile homages, a recurring element in the highly popular *Dylan Dog* comics. Horror and the Fantastic were now being perceived as a universe formed by bits and pieces of old and new movies, some sort of a representation which recombined the same elements in different variations. But such a choice shows also a two-faced relationship with the genre's archetypes. On the one hand it is parasitic, because TV audiences need stereotyped and easily recognizable references; on the other, it is detached if not openly mocking. The Gothic tradition is represented as

a dusty inventory, which *can* and *must* be laughed at. Moreover, the gags are littered with references to the small screen: for instance, the hunchbacked and idiotic servant in *A cena col vampiro* is not so much a reworking of Marty Feldman's Igor in *Young Frankenstein*, as of Isaia, a recurring character in the TV sketches starring the comic duo Zuzzurro & Gaspare (Andrea Brambilla and Nino Formicola), one of the most popular acts in the TV show *Drive In*,[10] also broadcast on Italia 1. In fact, the actor playing both characters is the same.

In short, the Gothic emerges from these films as a heritage of the past, serviceable as a background and little more. "We're at the end of the 20th century, the age of electronics. The world is full of stuff to be afraid of: pollution, atomic warfare, AIDS ... but not this! It's all papier-maché," the vampire's assistant explains to a girl who was frightened by the sight of severed limbs, skulls and assorted body parts in *A cena col vampiro*. Later, the vampire himself says: "Nowadays vampires hold a controlling interest in large corporations, they fly the Concorde, as evolution has been good to us we have the world at our feet...." Despite the appearances, this is not a discourse similar as that of Freda's *I vampiri* or Corrado Farina's *...hanno cambiato faccia*. The updating of the times has a metafilmic angle (the vampire is a famous horror movie director), but this is not a trick to reflect on the present, and not even to renovate the genre's archetypes in an effective way. It is simply a joke, a step behind, a way for the makers to distance themselves from what is being told. When Hilton's character complains, "You can't imagine how boring a vampire's life can be," the nod to the eternal sadness of the bloodsucker as portrayed in Herzog's version of *Nosferatu* is immediately turned into a joke, as he concludes: "Always in bed before sunrise, never getting up before sunset, always sleeping in the same old coffin...." His would-be-victims are not much impressed either. "Don't you have a vampires' union?" the skeptical Gianni (Riccardo Rossi) asks.

The Gothic is presented in its playful and more superficial aspects. Despite the odd literary reference (such as *The Picture of Dorian Gray*, which provides the key to the solution in *A cena col vampiro*) the real blueprints are Halloween parties and amusement parks. Significantly, Antonello Geleng's impressive set-pieces in *Una notte al cimitero* look less like horror movie material than funhouse paraphernalia.

A compulsory choice, given the average target audience: "Up to the 1980s moviegoers were usually older than 16," as Sacchetti pointed out. "I remember that going to the movies alone was almost a male initiation, a sort of rite of passage to adult age. After the 1980s, especially in America, cinema became a matter of consumption for kids who were 16 or younger, and so you'd have to make films that would satisfy the tastes of this type of moviegoer."[11]

Another sign of the times is the depiction of the male and female protagonists. Italian Gothic was connected since the beginning to the portrayal of femininity as a perturbing element and has always drawn from fetishistic images of strong, distant, unreachable heroines, whether they be the alluring characters played by Barbara Steele or the naked *ingénues* of the following decade. In the 1980s the new prototype was deeply linked with what commercial television offered, and not surprisingly "*Brivido giallo*" features in the casts such female icons as Patrizia Pellegrino and Isabel Russinova, familiar faces (and bodies) for the Italian public thanks to their appearances on the small screen.

Likewise, the lack of strong male figures is noticeable and in stark contrast with the 1970s, where television offered several memorable heroes, starting with Ugo Pagliai's character in *Il segno del comando*. Instead, the will to have the audience identify with the main characters had Bava opt for teenage stereotypes, inherited from U.S. teen horror flicks: the juvenile delinquents of *Una notte al cimitero* and the young actors looking for movie roles of *A cena col vampiro* look no less phony and ridiculous than the unlikely thugs in *Katarsis/Sfida al diavolo* (1963). And they show a similar inadequacy on the part of the makers to read the present in a critical manner. Rather than an attempt to disguise a product by sticking to the American standard, as in the action and war movies made for foreign consumption during the decade, this is the umpteenth sign of a cultural capitulation which will have devastating effects, far beyond the cinematic field.

There is an exception, though. In *Per sempre*, Bava and Sacchetti managed to find room for a more personal product. The provincial setting, an inn on the Lake Bolsena, is a far cry from the Gothic castles and mansions, and is closer to the Italian sensibility, recalling the likes of *Malombra* (1942) and *Un angelo per Satana* (1966, Camillo Mastrocinque), as well as Bava's

own *Macabro*. Moreover, with *Per sempre* Lamberto Bava reconnects with his father's cinema, most notably *Shock*.

Here, however, "the re-emerging of Bava's staples doesn't look like a silly citationist operation right off the table. Rather, it is an unconscious resurfacing from memory, a reconnecting to a poetry … recreated in a low-key, almost domestic dimension."[12] In *Per sempre*, the reworking of the genre tradition is barely conditioned by commercial needs—there is not a single positive character, and humor is absent—and the few narrative compromises are far less intrusive than usual. As a result, the film is by far the most original and successful of the lot. With regards to eroticism, it is also a notable exception to the bland and sexless proceedings of the "*Brivido giallo*" series, thanks to the slovenly and sweaty sexuality embodied by the stunning-looking Gioia Scola, who in a scene confesses: "I can't live without love," a line of dialogue very much like the one uttered by Barbara Steele's character in *Danza macabra*. She's not a noble and haughty ghost, though, just a desperate housewife in search of the right man.

"*Brivido giallo*" was a critical and audience flop, resulting in Bava's subsequent series "*Alta tensione*," shot between late 1988 and Spring 1989, being shelved. "*Alta tensione*" consisted of four films, with horror elements but closer to the thriller genre: *Il maestro del terrore* (a.k.a. *The Prince of Terror*), *L'uomo che non voleva morire* (a.k.a. *The Man Who Didn't Want to Die*, based on a short story by Giorgio Scerbanenco), *Testimone oculare* (a.k.a. *Eyewitness*) and *Il gioko* (a.k.a. *School of Fear*). Apart from the self-referential *Il maestro del terrore*—the story of a scriptwriter's revenge against a conceited horror movie director (and which Dardano Sacchetti claimed to be his own retaliation on Bava, Jr.)—which was released to home video in the early 1990s, they remained unseen for a decade, and were broadcast on the Mediaset network only in 1999 (except for the ultraviolent *L'uomo che non voleva morire*, broadcast in 2007 on the satellite channel Fantasy TV).

Lamberto Bava's next project would be a made-for-TV remake of *La maschera del demonio* (on which he initially wanted Barbara Steele to play a minor role[13]), as part of a European television series (*Sabbath*) on the theme of witchery produced between 1989 and 1990—cofinanced by the Spanish TVE, the Portuguese RTP, France 3, Silvio Berlusconi's Reteitalia, and the companies SFP and Betafilm. The new version of *La maschera del demonio* had a disastrous premiere in June 1990, at Rome's Fantafestival. Bava eventually found his dimension on the small screen with the fairy tale miniseries *Fantaghirò* (1991) and its many sequels.

The four "*Brivido giallo*" films had a different destiny outside Italy and surfaced on home video. A couple of them, *Una notte al cimitero* and *Per sempre*, were accordingly released on tape in Germany more than a year before their airing on Italian television. *Per sempre* was released on video as a sequel to *The Changeling* (1980, Peter Medak), while *La casa dell'orco* was released abroad as *Demons III: The Ogre* and advertised as the third chapter in the *Dèmoni* saga. A German DVD release, bearing the title *Ghost House II*, confused matters even further, relating Bava's film to Umberto Lenzi's *La casa 3—Ghosthouse*.

NOTES

1. Gomarasca, "Intervista a Lamberto Bava," 42.
2. "Berlusconi a capofitto nel cinema," *La Stampa*, July 17, 1986.
3. Gomarasca, "Intervista a Lamberto Bava," 42.
4. Félix Flores, "Un filme húngaro contempla Sitges a vista de pájaro," *La Vanguardia*, October 8, 1987.
5. Palmerini and Mistretta, *Spaghetti Nightmares*, 87.
6. Dardano Sacchetti interviewed, in www.davinotti.com (http://www.davinotti.com/index.php?option=com_content&task=view&id=58).
7. Dardano Sacchetti interviewed, in www.davinotti.com (http://www.davinotti.com/index.php?option=com_content&task=view&sectionid=3&id=59).
8. Gomarasca, "Intervista a Lamberto Bava," 43.
9. *Ibid.*, 44.
10. *Drive In* was one of the cornerstones of Silvio Berlusconi's TV empire and imagery as well: its mixture of gross comedy and scantily-dressed babes—a provincial rendition of an imaginary American drive-in populated with stand-up comedians and cheerleading types—proved immensely successful. It ran for five years, from 1983 to 1988, and launched many of the most popular Italian comedians of the decade, such as Ezio Greggio and Giorgio Faletti (who went on to become a singer-songwriter and best-selling mystery novelist). Significantly, in 1989 and 1990, during summer months, "Italia 1" broadcast the popular "Zio Tibia Picture Show," a weekly program where a puppet modeled upon the character of Uncle Creepy presented a series of horror films, engaging in macabre jokes. The show was broadcast on Friday nights, at prime time: after the Mammì law, it would be out of the question to show a horror movie at prime time, if not previously cut to obtain a new "all audiences" certificate.
11. Paolo Fazzini, *Gli artigiani dell'orrore. Mezzo secolo di brividi dagli anni '50 ad oggi* (Rome: Un mondo a parte, 2004), 132.
12. Alberto Pezzotta, "Per sempre," in *Genealogia del delitto. Guida al cinema di Mario e Lamberto Bava*, 59.
13. Grassi, "Vi preparo quattro serate horror."

"*Le case maledette*"
(Houses of Doom)
PROD: Massimo Manasse, Marco Grillo Spina for Dania Film (Rome), Reteitalia; *PM*: Renato Fiè; *PS*: Alessandro Loy; *PAcc*: Massimo Massimi.

Films from "Le case maledette" are arranged in chronological order according to their shooting date

La casa del sortilegio (*The House of Witchcraft*)
D: Umberto Lenzi. *S*: Gianfranco Clerici, Daniele Stroppa; *SC*: Umberto Lenzi; *DOP*: Giancarlo Ferrando; *M*: Claude King [Claudio Simonetti]; *E*: Alberto Moriani; *CO*: Valentina Di Palma; *Hair*: Maria Teresa Carrera; *SE, SPFX*: Giuseppe Ferranti; *AD*: Alessandra Lenzi; *SD*: Sandro Velchi; *PrM*: Roberto Granieri; *SO*: Giuliano Piermarioli; *Foley artist*: Enzo Diliberto; *C*: Bruno Cascio; *AC*: Alessandro Capuccio; *KG*: Matteo Giordano; *GA*: Armando Moreschini; *SP*: Maria Rosa Messori; *W*: Mirella Pedetti; *SS*: Olga Pehar. *Cast*: Andy J. Forest (Luca Balmas), Sonia Petrovna (Marta Balmas), Susanna Martinková (Elsa Balmas), Marina Giulia Cavalli (Sharon Mason), Maria Stella Musy (Debora Balmas), Paul Muller (Andrew Mason), Alberto Frasca (Steven), Maria Clementina Cumani Quasimodo (Witch); *uncredited*: Tom Felleghy (Police Inspector).

Running time: 86 minutes. *Also known as*: *La casa dei sortilegi* (Alternate Italian title); *Ghosthouse 4: Haus der Hexen*; *Totentanz der Hexen II* (Germany).

La casa delle anime erranti (*The House of Lost Souls*)
D: Umberto Lenzi. *S and SC*: Umberto Lenzi; *DOP*: Giancarlo Ferrando; *M*: Claude King [Claudio Simonetti]; *E*: Alberto Moriani; *CO*: Valentina Di Palma; *Hair*: Maria Teresa Carrera; *SPFX*: Giuseppe Ferranti; *AD*: Alessandra Lenzi; *SD*: Francesco Cuppini; *ASD*: Marco Marcucci; *PrM*: Roberto Granieri; *SO*: Giuliano

Piermarioli; *SOE*: Tullio Arcangeli, Gjka Sodir, Roberto Sterbini; *C*: Bruno Cascio; *AC*: Luigi Conversi; *KG*: Matteo Giordano; *GA*: Armando Moreschini; *SP*: Maria Rosa Messori; *W*: Mirella Pedetti; *1stAE*: Ernesto Triunvieri; *2ndAE*: Nicoletta Leone; *SS*: Olga Pehar. *Cast*: Joseph Alan Johnson (Kevin), Stefania Orsola Garello (Carla), Matteo Gazzolo (Massimo), Laurentina Guidotti (Mary), Gianluigi Fogacci (Guido), Yamanouchi Haruhiko (Buddhist Monk), Licia Colò (Daria), Costantino Meloni (Gianluca), Charles Borromel (Hotel Owner), Dino Iaksic (Ghost Child), Marina Reiner (Ghost), Benny Cardoso (Ghost), Fortunato Arena (Ghost), Massimo Sarchielli (Cemetery Caretaker), Fabio Branchini, Giulio Massimini (Librarian), Vincenzo Menniti.

Running time: 89 minutes.

La casa nel tempo (*The House of Clocks*)

D: Lucio Fulci. *S*: Lucio Fulci; *SC*: Daniele Stroppa, Gianfranco Clerici; *DOP*: Nino Celeste; *M*: Vince Tempera; *E*: Alberto Moriani; *CO*: Valentina Di Palma, Cinzia Milani; *Hair*: Maria Teresa Carrera; *AD*: Michele De Angelis, Camilla Fulci; *PrM*: Vincenzo Luzzi; *SD*: Elio Micheli; *ASD*: Paolo Faenzi; *SO*: Giuliano Piermarioli; *SPFX*: Giuseppe Ferranti; *C*: Sandro Grossi; *AC*: Francesco Damiani, Camillo Sabatini; *SP*: Romolo Eucalitto; *KG*: Tarcisio Diamanti; *GA*: Armando Moreschini; *W*: Milena Pintus; *AE*: Rosaria Bellu, Nicoletta Leone; *SS*: Egle Guarino; *Set technician*: Elio Terribili. *Cast*: Keith Van Hoven (Tony), Karina Huff (Sandra), Paolo Paoloni (Vittorio Corsini), Bettine Milne (Sara Corsini), Peter Hintz (Paul), Al Cliver [Pierluigi Conti] (Peter), Carla Cassola (Maria), Paolo Bernardi (The Nephew), Francesca DeRose (The Niece), Massimo Sarchielli (Storekeeper); *uncredited*: Vincenzo Luzzi (Policeman #1).

Running time: 84 minutes. *Also known as*: *Die Uhr des Grauens* (Germany); *A Casa do Tempo* (Portugal).

La dolce casa degli orrori (*The Sweet House of Horrors*)

D: Lucio Fulci. *S*: Lucio Fulci; *SC*: Vincenzo Mannino, Gigliola Battaglini; *DOP*: Nino Celeste; *M*: Vince Tempera; *E*: Alberto Moriani; *CO*: Valentina Di Palma; *PD*: Giacomo Calò Carducci; *Hair*: Maria Teresa Carrera; *AD*: Michele De Angelis, Camilla Fulci; *SD*: Antonello Geleng; *ASD*: Paolo Faenzi; *PrM*: Vincenzo Luzzi; *C*: Sandro Grossi; *AC*: Francesco

Damiani, Luigi Conversi; *SP*: Romolo Eucalitto; *KG*: Tarcisio Diamanti; *GA*: Armando Moreschini; *W*: Milena Pintus; *AE*: Rosaria Bellu; *SS*: Egle Guarino; *Set technician*: Elio Terribili. *Cast*: Jean-Christophe Brétignière (Carlo), Cinzia Monreale (Marcia), Lubka Cibulova (Mary Valdi), Lino Salemme (Guido), Franco Diogene (Mr. Oppidi), Alexander Vernon Dobtcheff (The Exorcist), Giuliano Gensini (Marco), Ilary Blasi (Sarah), Dante Fioretti (Priest), Pascal Persiano (Roberto Valdi).

Running time: 84 minutes. *Also known as*: *Das Haus des Bösen* (Germany), *A Doce Casa dos Horrores* (Portugal).

Soon after finishing "*Brivido giallo*," producer Luciano Martino set up another horror series destined to Reteitalia. This time it was centered on the common theme of haunted houses, and appropriately titled "*Le case maledette*" (Houses of Doom). Developed for Dania Film by Gianfranco Clerici, Daniele Stroppa and Vincenzo Mannino, the project was inspired by the success of Sam Raimi's *The Evil Dead*, which resulted in many rip-offs sporting the Italian title *La casa*.[1] Reteitalia participated as co-producer with Dania National Cinematografica and secured the TV rights to the films.

Originally the series was to comprise six titles, to be directed by Lucio Fulci, Umberto Lenzi and Lamberto Bava, but due to other working commitments Bava was replaced by Marcello Avallone. Fulci approached the project enthusiastically and asked to substitute two of his own stories for the ones he had been assigned, and Lenzi did the same with one of his own invention, *La casa delle anime erranti*. But a last-minute budget cut on the part of Reteitalia and Avallone's commitments had the series resized to four titles only, namely *La casa nel tempo* (script by Stroppa and Clerici, from a story by Fulci), *La dolce casa degli orrori* (scripted by Mannino and his wife, Gigliola Battaglini, also from a story by Fulci), *La casa delle anime erranti* (written by Lenzi) and *La casa del sortilegio* (scripted by Lenzi, from a story by Clerici and Stroppa). The remaining two titles to be directed by Avallone, *La casa del nano deforme* (The House of the Deformed Dwarf), then retitled *La casa dell'amico del cuore* (The Best Friend's House), and *La casa della bambola con i capelli che crescono* (The House of the Doll with Growing Hair), were left in the drawer. "It's a real shame, because the two films Marcello Avallone would direct were really good," Stroppa recalled. "We had written those scripts with lots of passion and interest, trying to blend the Fantastic and contemporary issues. In fact, *La casa dell'amico del cuore*, written by me and Clerici … treated the issue of organ transplants in an original way," the scriptwriter explained (thus revealing a passing similarity with Giovanni Simonelli's *Hansel e Gretel*, in the "*I maestri del thriller*" series), adding that "the story devised by Mannino and Battaglini for *La casa della bambola con i capelli che crescono* centered on abortion."[2]

The four films were shot on 16mm, outside Rome (in order to be able to work six days a week, which wouldn't have been possible otherwise), with a filming schedule of four weeks each, starting with the ones directed by Lenzi, which were made between October and December 1988. The budget was around 900 million *lire* each. *La casa del sortilegio*[3] (a.k.a. *The House of Witchcraft*) is the story of a man, Luca (Andy J. Forest), who suffers from a recurring nightmare in which he is persecuted and decapitated by a witch who puts his severed head in a cauldron. As a way of relief from the stress, he and his estranged, occult-obsessed wife Marta (Sonia Petrovna) move to a country house inhabited by a blind pianist (Paul Muller) and his niece Sharon (Maria Giulia Cavalli), which turns out to be the same as in Luca's nightmare. Soon horrific events ensue, and Luca begins to suspect that Marta is actually the witch of his dreams…

Shot in the Tuscan countryside, in a villa owned by Daria Nicolodi's uncle and surrounded by a beautiful park, the film benefits from an interesting and typically Italian atmosphere and turns out as another variation on a Gothic staple, the theme of seduction and repulsion. Despite psychiatrist Elsa (Susanna Martinková) claiming that witches are only "the outside projection of our secret obsessions," the witch in the film is very much real. As with Argento's *Suspiria* and *Inferno*, *La casa del sortilegio* conveys a dark fairy-tale like mood: the initial appearance of the ugly hag, cooking a gruesome meal in a boiling cauldron in the villa's kitchen, is an image reminiscent of the Grimm Brothers' fables, and the sorceress can even turn into a black cat. The script makes use of the genre's tropes (the return of the past, the mysterious portrait and the ineluctability of fate) and plays on the ambiguity of the witch's identity in a way akin to what Mastrocinque's *La cripta e l'incubo* did with its female vampire, amassing clues that lead to the ambiguous Marta—who in one scene is seen walking in her sleep in the park like a 1960s Gothic heroine—only to come out with a predictable twist ending.

The final revelation and the circular ending are in tune with the genre's staples (the protagonist is seduced and defeated by an evil creature hiding behind a seemingly innocent façade), and the idea of a marriage crisis paving the way for a man's irrational obsession is an interesting starting point. A line of dialogue even mentions Marco Bellocchio's film *La visione del sabba*, where witchcraft is openly linked with sexual repression. The plot has its share of inconsistencies (not to mention a ridiculous car accident near the beginning) but compared with Lenzi's horror films of the late 1980s the direction is less ham-fisted, with some oddly surreal moments, such as the scene of the snowfall in the cellar.

La casa delle anime erranti (a.k.a. *The House of Lost Souls*) fares much worse. It is the story of six students on vacation who stop by an old abandoned hotel in the Alps, where a massacre happened many years earlier. The ghosts of the victims still haunt the place and seek revenge on the teenagers, who find out they cannot leave the building…. Despite the attempt at making a ghost story in an Italian setting, Lenzi bluntly described the result as "downright crap" and complained he hadn't found the right setting for the movie, which was shot in the region of Marche, in Central Italy, with a Fascist summer camp made to pass as an old hotel. Moreover, there were issues during filming—such as the art director abandoning the set after an argument with the production manager, and the cast and crew having to shoot amid cold weather and snow.

The story soon turns into a series of gory deaths, with plenty of decapitations (including one by washing machine), severed limbs, bodies hung in cold cells and spiders crawling into their victims' mouths (yet another nod to *L'aldilà*). The debts to *The Shining* are blatant to the point of plagiarism: one character, Carla (Stefania Orsola Garello), is a psychic who "sees" the gruesome events in the past. As with Lamberto Bava's "*Brivido giallo*" films, the story revolving around a group of teenagers is further evidence of the genre's adherence to the standards of 1980s American horror films. The cast of unknowns—save for a couple of familiar faces in Italian genre cinema, such as Haruhiko "Hal" Yamanouchi and Charles Borromel, while Licia Colò, soon to become a noted TV presenter, has a small role as a reporter—doesn't help either. Both films were scored by Claudio Simonetti, hiding behind the a.k.a. Claude King and recycling themes from *Dèmoni* and *Opera*.

Lucio Fulci talked about the experience with "*Le case maledette*" in very positive terms: "Fantastic! Excellent filmmaking! Nino Celeste is a splendid cameraman. They're two of the best films I've made. I wrote both the stories for *La casa nel tempo* and *La dolce casa degli orrori* and I'm very pleased with them."[4] Indeed the two movies revolved around more personal themes than the ones he had helmed for Nannerini and Lucidi, and the director worked on the projects carefully. *La casa nel tempo*—shot with the working title *La casa degli orologi*, the literal translation of the international title *The House of Clocks*—was filmed in a villa in Torgiano, near Perugia, between January 31 and February 25, 1989[5]; immediately after Fulci set out to work on *La dolce casa degli orrori*, wrapping it in March. His daughter Camilla was the a.d. on both films. According to those on the set, the director was much more energetic and motivated than on his latest works, a sign that Fulci believed in the projects, especially *La casa nel tempo*.

"I hate time: it's our slavery," Fulci once claimed. "We are crushed by time; it can't be stopped. I hate the idea that tomorrow will come, and what the fuck do I care about tomorrow... If I could, I would master time and move it at my will. Stop it when I feel like it, go on, go back...."[6] The film marks the director's most explicit reflection on the theme. Opening with a quote by Honoré de Balzac ("If time turned back, our sins would also have to start anew"), *La casa nel tempo* introduces us to an elderly couple, Paolo and Sara Corsini (Paolo Paoloni and Bettine Milne), who live in a luxurious villa with a housekeeper (Carla Cassola) and a sinister-looking one-eyed gardener (Al Cliver), surrounded by a multitude of clocks of all sizes and shapes. The Corsinis are in fact homicidal maniacs who have killed their nephews and keep their rotten bodies in the family chapel, and when the housekeeper discovers it, she too is dispatched by Sara by way of a spiked pole in the groin, in a scene that openly quotes the climax of *Paura nella città dei morti viventi*. A trio of young thugs—Tony (Keith Van Hoven), his girlfriend Sandra (Karina Huff) and their friend Paul (Peter

Hintz)—sneak into the villa to steal their jewels, but they end up killing the owners and the gardener. Immediately all the clocks stop and start going backwards: as time regresses, the dead return to life and act their revenge upon their murderers.

Fulci was very proud of the result, but even at a little over 80 minutes the plot seems overly stretched, with lengthy introductory sequences (including one in which the trio goes shoplifting at a local store) that take up almost half of the running time. Moreover, the destination for the small screen explains some rushed scenes, while the gore effects are rather crude and the acting ranges from passable to awful, with the trio of young protagonists faring the worst. But this time, unlike in *Sodoma's Ghost* and *Quando Alice ruppe lo specchio*, the director's visual style is remarkable, with ample use of tracking shots and dollies, turning the titular "house of clocks" into a fascinating haunted mansion, amid eerie light and shadow games.

The main themes, typical of the last phase of Fulci's filmography—the persistence of guilt,

Karina Huff and Paolo Paoloni in a scene from Lucio Fulci's made-for-TV film *La casa nel tempo* (1989).

the damnation of sin, the obsession of death—are also more lucidly developed than in his other works of the period. On top of that, *La casa nel tempo* sports a chilling, nihilistic vision of humanity, that makes it one of Fulci's darkest films. In his gallery of human monsters, the Corsinis are among the most unpleasant and horrible ever, as amiable on the surface as they are viciously violent and selfish, but the other characters are no better, even though, as in *Sodoma's Ghost*, the depiction of the younger generation is far from convincing. The appearance of a black cat, in what at first looks like a gratuitous depiction of (simulated) cruelty upon animals, seems just a passing reference to the director's 1981 film. But in the denouement—which blends together a circular "dream" ending borrowed straight from *Dead of Night* (1945) and a sneering sting in the tail that vaguely recalls *Le salaire de la peur* (a.k.a. *The Wages of Fear*, 1953, Henri-Georges Clouzot)—the feline becomes an agent of arbitrary justice and moral retribution, in a world dominated by cruelty and madness. In fact, the only ones who benefit from an enigmatic happy ending are the original victims of the Corsinis, who are seen having breakfast together in the villa, in an image of new-found familiar serenity. But once again, this idyllic sight hides a dark, horrible truth: the situation has reversed, and now it's the revived nephews who keep their aunt and uncle's dead bodies as trophies. Obviously, they are just as mad as their predecessors.

Shot in Ponte Pattoli, near Perugia, with a small cast that included Cinzia Monreale, Franco Diogene, Lino Salemme, Pascal Persiano, and Alexander Vernon Dobtcheff (a last-minute replacement for Cosimo Cinieri), *La dolce casa degli orrori* opens with yet another quote (this time by Nathaniel Hawthorne: "…when I try to imagine the impossible, I would like to return to childhood. Only children can reach the impossible"). The film focuses on one of Fulci's favorite themes, the inner violence of childhood, which imbued the last part of his work as well, as proven by several of the short stories included in the collection *Le lune nere* as well as by his second-to-last work, *Voci dal profondo* (1990). Here, the script borrows from Bava as well as from *Poltergeist*, and pits two orphan siblings, Sarah and Marco,[7] against the world of adults. After their parents have been horribly killed by a thief (who turns out to be the caretaker), the children keep living in the villa where the mur-

ders took place with their aunt and uncle; the building is still haunted by the souls of the departed, and Sarah and Marco (who are able to see their dead parents, like Marco did in *Shock*) become the instruments of their revenge.

Fulci's idea was to meditate on death from the children's innocent point of view. Horror takes the form of a child's game—as shown by Sarah and Marco's laughter at the adults, after the latter fall victim to gruesome accidents and deaths, and their total lack of surprise before supernatural events (as Tommy's in *Manhattan Baby*). But there's more: the scenes of the happy family virtually reunited, the children playing with the ghost of their parents (and the dog!) in the villa's garden, shot in slow motion and in soft-focus as if they belonged to some 1970s tearjerker, convey a sense of regret and loss that turns these mawkish and potentially ridiculous bits into some of the most personal and open-hearted material in Fulci's late career.

The mixture of horror, grotesque and sentiment is often uneasy, in an attempt at creating a harsh fairytale where innocence and cruelty are inextricably blended. In a way, *La dolce casa degli orrori* is the opposite of *Quella villa accanto al cimitero*, which featured a monster who fed on childish fears and cried like a baby; here the ghosts are benevolent presences who protect children against adults who are either stupid, cruel, or just plain ugly. Interestingly, keeping a child's point of view, unappealing or ugly characters are also mean, such as the fat real estate dealer (Franco Diogene) who is nicknamed "the infamous Sausage." The same can be said about the exorcist, Teufel (Alexander Vernon Dobtcheff), who claims he is not afraid of ghosts but despises them. His characterization—thin, black-dressed, with a ridiculous red beard—is like that of a stern and obtuse teacher who takes a perverted pleasure in punishing weaker creatures, such as children and ghosts.

La dolce casa degli orrori shows that Fulci was still willing to experiment. He had his d.o.p. use a very bright, soft-focus photography, with blinding whites and fog filters, to create a dreamy mood which would enhance the story's absurdist twists. Several sequences, such as the long take in the cemetery during the funeral, portraying Sarah and Marco's point-of-view (as if they were one entity, thus enhancing their distance from adulthood), or the children's magic rite, are indeed worthy of his best material. But ultimately the clashing mixture of extreme graphic violence and fairy tale falters, and some scenes—such as the ending featuring a bulldozer going on a rampage, which is played for laughs like some sort of a silent movie gag—just don't work. Moreover, the gore is unconvincing and crude, and the score by Vince Tempera is best forgotten.

Eventually, "*Le case maledette*" suffered a sad fate in its home country, resulting in the series being shelved, possibly because of the gory content, which was likely to have put off TV execs: in the opening scenes of *La dolce casa degli orrori*, a man has his head repeatedly bashed against a column and an eye gouged out, and a woman has her face reduced to a gory mess with a meat grinder. It was too much, considering the protests that Dario Argento's silly short films in the TV program *Giallo* had caused among the public due to their violent content.

In the early 1990s, when asked when the films would be broadcast, Fulci gave a disillusioned reply:

> "You'll have to ask Reteitalia, because, although the series has already been sold all over the world, nobody knows when *Le case del terrore* [*sic*] will be broadcast in Italy. I'd be pleased if someone rings these people up and ask about the program; it might get things moving a bit. It all ends up in the grinder—television manages to devour and soak up everything…. Television should be re-examined at some point and the right amount of time dedicated to watching it; it's a very important means of communication, though it's used unwisely—always in a transient, changeable way."[8]

Looking back on the experience, Lenzi was adamant:

> "I must say that back then I was very inexperienced regarding television…. My colleagues and I were not the only ones though, but even the producers were, and they completely messed up the series. They didn't consider that the horror genre couldn't be accepted by TV sponsors…. I wasn't an expert and I made those films as I would have made them for a theatrical release. I didn't realize that this way I was precluding myself from a career on television…. It was the wrong project: we'd have had to make thrillers, whereas the stories that were proposed to us were all centered on witches, enchanted forests and so on."[9]

In Italy, the four films were eventually released directly on VHS only in 2000, thanks to the efforts of the magazine *Nocturno Cinema*, and surfaced on Italian satellite TV in 2006, whereas abroad they found their way to the home video market.

NOTES

1. Raimi's *Evil Dead II* (a.k.a. *La casa 2*) was also popular in Italy, and excerpts of it even turned up in a box-office comedy hit, *Vacanze di Natale 90* (1990), starring comedians Massimo Boldi and Christian De Sica.
2. Manlio Gomarasca and Davide Pulici, booklet for the VHS release of *La casa del sortilegio*.
3. The on-screen title reads *La casa dei sortilegi*.
4. Palmerini and Mistretta, *Spaghetti Nightmares*, 87
5. Albiero and Cacciatore, *Il terrorista dei generi*, 375.
6. Romagnoli, *L'occhio del testimone*, 13.
7. The two children were Giuliano Gensini and Ilary Blasi. The latter became a well-known showgirl and the wife of soccer player Francesco Totti.
8. Palmerini and Mistretta, *Spaghetti Nightmares*, 87
9. Gomarasca, *Umberto Lenzi*, 262–263.

Bibliography

On the Gothic Genre in Fiction

Amigoni, Ferdinando. *Fantasmi nel Novecento*. Turin: Bollati Boringhieri, 2004.

Anselmi, Gian Mario (ed.), *Mappe della letteratura europea e mediterranea: Dal Barocco all'Ottocento*. Milan: Paravia—Bruno Mondadori, 2000.

Bordoni, Carlo. *Del soprannaturale nel romanzo fantastico*. Cosenza: Pellegrini, 2004.

Botting, Fred, *Gothic*. London/New York: Routledge, 1996.

Burke, Edmund. *A Philosophical Inquiry into the Origin of Our Ideas of the Sublime and Beautiful*. New York: Digireads.com, 2009.

Calvino, Italo (ed.). *Fantastic Tales: Visionary and Everyday*. New York: Penguin Books, 2001/2009.

Ceserani, Remo, Lucio Lugnani, Gianluigi Goggi, Carla Benedetti and Elisabetta Scarano (eds.). *La narrazione fantastica*, Pisa: Nistri-Lischi, 1983.

Foucault, Michel. *Language, Counter-Memory, Practice: Selected Essays and Interviews*. Ithaca NY: Cornell University Press, 1980.

Freud, Sigmund, "The Uncanny," in Freud, Sigmund. *Writings on Art and Literature*. Redwood City, CA: Stanford University Press, 1997.

Fruttero, Carlo, and Franco Lucentini (eds.) *Storie di fantasmi. Racconti del soprannaturale*. Turin: Einaudi (1960) 1984.

Hogle, Jerrold E. (ed.). *The Cambridge Companion to Gothic Fiction*. Cambridge: Cambridge University Press, 2002.

Lévy, Maurice. *Le Roman gothique anglais 1764–1824*. Paris: Albin-Michel, 2001 (1968).

Punter, David. *The Literature of Terror: A History of Gothic Fictions from 1765 to the Present Day, Vol. 1: The Gothic Tradition*. New York: Routledge, 1996.

_____. *The Literature of Terror: A History of Gothic Fictions from 1765 to the Present Day, Vol. 2: The Modern Gothic*. New York: Routledge, 1996.

Todorov, Tzvetan. *The Fantastic: A Structural Approach to a Literary Genre*. Ithaca: Cornell University Press, 1975.

Varma, Devendra P. *The Gothic Flame: Being a History of the Gothic Novel in England: Its Origins, Efflorences, Disintegration, and Residuary Influences*. London: Scarecrow, (1957) 1987.

Vax, Louis. *La natura del fantastico*. Rome-Naples: Theoria, 1987.

Žižek, Slavoj. *Looking Awry: An Introduction to Jacques Lacan Through Popular Culture*. Cambridge MA: MIT Press, 1992.

On Fantastic, Gothic and Horror Cinema

Hardy, Phil (ed.). *The Aurum Film Encyclopedia: Horror*. London: Aurum Press, 1993.

Hogan, David J. *Dark Romance. Sexuality in the Horror Film*. Jefferson NC: McFarland, 1997.

Leutrat, Jean-Louis. *La vie des fantômes: le fantastique ai cinéma*. Paris: Cahiers du Cinéma—Collection essais, 1995.

Navarro, Antonio José (ed.). *Pesadillas en la oscuridad. El cine de terrór gotico*. Madrid: Valdemar, 2010.

Pirie, David. *A New Heritage of Horror. The English Gothic Cinema*. London: I.B. Tauris, 2008.

Rigby, Jonathan. *Euro Gothic. Classics of Continental Horror Cinema*. Cambridge: Signum Books, 2016.

Silver, Alain and Ursini, James (eds.) *Horror Film Reader*. New York: Limelight, 2000.

Williams, Charles P. *The Complete H.P. Lovecraft Filmography*. Westport, CT: Greenwood Publishing, 2001.

On Italian Cinema and Italian Gothic Horror of the 1980s

BIOGRAPHIES, AUTOBIOGRAPHIES, INTERVIEW BOOKS

Argento, Dario. *Paura*. Turin: Einaudi, 2014.

Avati, Pupi. *Sotto le stelle di un film*. Trento: Il Margine, 2008.

Faldini, Franca, and Goffredo Fofi (eds.). *Il cinema italiano d'oggi, 1970–1984 raccontato dai suoi protagonisti*. Milan: Mondadori, 1984.

Fazzini, Paolo. *Gli artigiani dell'orrore. Mezzo secolo di brividi dagli anni '50 ad oggi*. Rome: Un mondo a parte, 2004.

Fidani, Demofilo. *Il medium esce dal mistero*. Trento: Luigi Reverdito Editore, 1986.

Freda, Riccardo. *Divoratori di celluloide*. Milan: Edizioni del Mystfest, Il Formichiere, 1981.

Gomarasca, Manlio. *Umberto Lenzi*. Milan: Nocturno Libri, 2001.

Gomarasca, Manlio, and Davide Pulici. *99 donne. Stelle e stelline del cinema italiano*. Milan: MediaWord Production, 1999.

Martino, Sergio. *Mille peccati... nessuna virtù?* Milan: Bloodbuster, 2017.

Palmerini, Luca M., and Gaetano Mistretta. *Spaghetti Nightmares*. Rome: M&P edizioni, 1996.

Poindron, Éric. *Riccardo Freda. Un pirate à la camera*. Lyon-Arles: Institute Lumière/Actes Sud, 1994.

Tornatore, Giuseppe. *Il quarto moschettiere. Quattro chiacchiere con Riccardo Freda*. Taormina: TaorminaFilmFest, 2007.

DICTIONARIES, REFERENCE BOOKS AND ACADEMIC STUDIES

Abramovit, Ruggero, and Claudio Bartolini. *Il gotico padano. Dialogo con Pupi Avati*. Genoa: Le Mani, 2010.

Abramovit, Ruggero, Claudio Bartolini and Luca Servini. *Nero Avati. Visioni dal set*. Genoa: Le Mani, 2011.

Aguilar, Carlos, and Anita Haas. *John Phillip Law. Diabolik Angel*. Pontevedra/Bilbao: Scifiworld/Quatermass, 2008.

Albiero, Paolo, and Giacomo Cacciatore. *Il terrorista dei generi. Tutto il cinema di Lucio Fulci—Seconda edizione aggiornata*. Palermo: Leima (2004) 2015.

Bruschini, Antonio, and Antonio Tentori. *Operazione paura: i registi del gotico italiano*. Bologna: Puntozero, 1997.

Comotti, Davide, and Vittorio Salerno. *Professione regista e scrittore*. Salerno: Booksprint, 2012.

Costantini, Daniele, and Francesco Dal Bosco. *Nuovo cinema inferno. L'opera di Dario Argento*. Parma: Pratiche Editrice, 1997.

Curti, Roberto. *Fantasmi d'amore*. Turin: Lindau, 2011.

Curti, Roberto. *Italian Gothic Horror Films, 1957–1969*. Jefferson, NC: McFarland, 2015.

Curti, Roberto. *Italian Gothic Horror Films, 1970–1979*. Jefferson, NC: McFarland, 2017.

Curti, Roberto. *Mavericks of Italian Cinema. Eight Unorthodox Filmmakers. 1940s–2000s*. Jefferson NC: McFarland, 2018.

Curti, Roberto. *Riccardo Freda: The Life and Works of a Born Filmmaker*. Jefferson, NC: McFarland, 2017.

Curti, Roberto, and Alessio Di Rocco. *Visioni proibite—I film vietati dalla censura italiana (dal 1969 a oggi)*. Turin: Lindau, 2015.

Della Casa, Stefano, and Bruno Piazza. *Il cinema secondo Mario Bava*. Turin: Movie Club, 1984.

Giovannini, Fabio. *Il libro dei vampiri: dal mito di Dracula alla presenza quotidiana*. Bari: Dedalo (1985) 1997.

Gomarasca, Manlio, and Davide Pulici. *Io Emanuelle. Le passioni, gli amori e il cinema di Laura Gemser*. Milan: Media Word Publications 1997.

Howarth, Troy. *The Haunted World of Mario Bava—Revised and Expanded Edition*. Baltimore: Midnight Marquee Press, 2014.

Howarth, Troy, and Mike Baronas. *Splintered Visions: Lucio Fulci and His Films*. Baltimore: Midnight Marquee Press, 2015.

Kezich, Tullio. *Il nuovissimo Millefilm. Cinque anni al cinema, 1977–1982*. Milan: Mondadori, 1983.

Koven, Mikel J. *La Dolce Morte: Vernacular Cinema and the Italian Giallo*. Lanham, MD: Scarecrow, 2006.

Lafond, Frank (ed.). *Cauchemars Italiens. Volume 1: Le cinéma fantastique*. Pris: L'Harmattan, 2011.

_____ (ed.). *Cauchemars Italiens. Volume 2: Le cinéma horrifique*. Pris: L'Harmattan, 2011.

Loparco, Stefano. *Klaus Kinski. Del Paganini e dei capricci*. Piombino: Il Foglio, 2015.

Lucas, Tim. *Mario Bava: All the Colors of the Dark*. Cincinnati OH: Video Watchdog, 2007.

Lupi, Gordiano. *Cozzi Stellari. Il cinema di Lewis Coates*. Rome: Profondo Rosso, 2009.

Maiello, Fabio. *Dario Argento. Confessioni di un maestro dell'horror*. Milan: Alacran, 2007.

McDonagh, Maitland. *Broken Mirrors/Broken Minds. The Dark Dreams of Dario Argento*. London: Sun Tavern Fields, 1991.

Miller, David. *The Complete Peter Cushing*. Richmond, Surrey: Reynolds & Hearn, 2005.

Navarro, Antonio José (ed.). *El giallo italiano. La oscuridad y la sangre*. Nuer, Madrid 2001.

Newman, Kim. *Nightmare Movies*. London: Bloomsbury, 1988/2011.

Pezzotta, Alberto. *Mario Bava*. Milan: Il Castoro, (1995) 2013.

_____. *Regia Damiano Damiani*. Udine: Centro Espressioni Cinematografiche—Cinemazero, 2004.

Poppi, Roberto. *Dizionario del cinema italiano. I registi*. Rome: Gremese, 2002.

Poppi, Roberto, and Mario Pecorari. *Dizionario del cinema italiano. I film (1980–1989)* (Rome: Gremese, 1991.

Pugliese, Roberto. *Dario Argento*. Milan: Editrice Il Castoro (1986) 2011.

Romagnoli, Michele. *L'occhio del testimone. Il cinema di Lucio Fulci*. Bologna: Granata Press, 1992.

Taccini, Brando. *Stracult Horror. Guida al meglio (e al peggio) del cinema horror italiano anni '80*. Rome: Quintilia Edizioni, 2012.

Tentori, Antonio, and Luigi Cozzi (eds.). *Guida al cinema horror Made in Italy*. Rome: Profondo Rosso, 2007.

Thrower, Stephen. *Beyond Terror. The Films of Lucio Fulci*. Godalming, Surrey: FAB Press (1999) 2016.

Zagarrio, Vito (ed.). *Argento vivo. Il cinema di Dario Argento tra genere e autorialità*. Venice: Marsilio, 2008.

ESSAYS IN VOLUMES

Hunt, Leon. "A (Sadistic) Night at the Opera," in Ken Gelder (ed.). *The Horror Reader*. New York: Routledge, 2000.

Mora, Teo. "Mario Bava. Il visionario filmico," in Bertieri, Claudio and Salotti, Marco (eds.). *Genova in celluloide. I registi liguri*. Genoa: Comune di Genova—Assessorato alla cultura, 1984, p. 204

Paniceres, Ruben. "El gotico italiano. Fantastico y ciencia ficcion," in Palacios, Jesus and Paniceres, Ruben (eds.). *Cara a cara. Una mirada al cine de genero italiano.* Gijon: Semana Negra, 2004.

PERIODICALS—SPECIAL ISSUES

Bava, Lamberto, and Grazia Fallucchi. "Omaggio a Mario Bava." *La Lettura,* September 1980.

Della Casa, Stefano (ed.). "Speciale fantastico italiano." *Cineforum* #299, November 1990.

Fassone, Riccardo (ed.). *La stagione delle streghe. Guida al gotico italiano. Nocturno Dossier* #80, March 2009.

Gomarasca, Manlio, and Davide Pulici (eds.). *Eroi & antieroi del cinema italiano. Nocturno Dossier* #10, April 2003.

_____ and _____ (eds.). *Genealogia del delitto. Il cinema di Mario e Lamberto Bava. Nocturno Dossier* #24, July 2004.

_____ and _____ (eds.). *Il punto G. guida al cinema di Enzo G. Castellari. Nocturno Dossier* #66, January 2008.

_____ and _____ (eds.). *Il sopravvissuto. Guida al cinema di Bruno Mattei. Nocturno Dossier* #45, April 2006

_____ and _____ (eds.). *Joe D'Amato. Guida al cinema estremo e dell'orrore. Nocturno Dossier* #78, January 2009.

_____ and _____ (eds.), *L'opera al nero. Il cinema di Lucio Fulci. Nocturno Dossier* #3, September 2002.

_____ and _____ (eds.). *Le sorelle di Venere 2. Nocturno Dossier* #59, June 2007.

_____ and _____ (eds.). *Le tre madri. Guida alla trilogia di Dario Argento. Nocturno Dossier* #64, November 2007.

Monell, Robert. *Riccardo Freda. European Trash Cinema Special* #2, 1997.

Morsiani, Alberto (ed.). *Rosso italiano (1977/1987). Sequenze* #7, March 1988.

Romero, Javier G. (ed.). *Antología del cine fantástico italiano. Quatermass* #7, November 2008.</BIB>

PERIODICALS AND WEBZINES— MONOGRAPHIES, INTERVIEWS, REVIEWS

Berger, Howard "Claudio Fragasso's Gore Wars," *Fangoria* #163, June 1997.

Caddeo, Federico, and Lopéré, Laurent. "Passion devoreuse." *Mad Movies* #175, May 2005. Interview with Claudio Fragasso)

Castoldi, Gian Luca. "Riccardo Freda o del decadentismo dell'orrore." *Amarcord* #8–9, May–August 1997.

Codelli, Lorenzo. "Entretien avec Pupi Avati. Zeder." *L'Écran fantastique* #36, July/August 1983.

Ercolani, Eugenio. "Gianni Martucci, un intellettuale al servizio del cinema di genere." *PaperBlog,* September 22, 2013.

_____. "Tra cinema e cavalli: Intervista a Marcello Avallone." *PaperBlog,* January 17, 2014.

Gans, Christophe. "Les deux nouveaux films de Lucio Fulci." *L'Écran fantastique* #21, November 1981.

_____. "La maison pres du cimetière." *L'Écran fantastique* #22, January 1982.

Garofalo, Marcello. "Uno, nessuno, centofulci." *Segnocinema* #65, January/February 1994.

Gires, Pierre. "Frayeurs." *L'Écran fantastique* #16, January 1981.

Gomarasca, Manlio. "Claudio Lattanzi. La verità secondo Claude Milliken," in Davide Pulici (ed.), *Misteri d'Italia 3. Guida ai film rari e scomparsi. Nocturno Dossier* #70, May 2008.

_____. "Saprofito. Intervista con Al Cliver," *Nocturno Cinema* #3, June 1997.

Ippoliti, Stefano, and Norcini, Matteo. "Mario Bianchi. 'Il mio cinema pizza e fichi,'" *Cine70 e dintorni* #5, Summer 2004.

_____ and _____. "Una favola chiamata cinema. Intervista a Martine Brochard." *Cine70 e dintorni* #6, 2004.

Lavagnini, Massimo F. "Sergio Bergonzelli. Una cinepresa in pugno al diavolo." *Nocturno Cinema* #2, December 1996.

Lucas, Tim. "Looking with Averted Eyes: The Terror of Pupi Avati." *Video Watchdog* #3, January/February 1991.

Maccaron, Bruno, and Patrick Nadjar. "Lucio Fulci: 'Je suis un monstre!' Le grand retour du maître Italien de l'horreur." *L'Écran fantastique* #116, October 1990.

Martin, John. "Lucio Fulci: L'Edgar Poe du 7e art." *L'Écran fantastique* #149, May 1996.

Padovan, Igor Molino, Giorgio Navarro and Luca Rea. "Dagmar Lassander, il rosso segno della bellezza." *Amarcord* #13, May–June 1998.

Pezzotta, Alberto. "Dèmoni." *Filmcritica* #368, October 1986.

Pulici, Davide, and Gomarasca, Manlio. "Il dolce mattatoio. Incontro con Alberto Cavallone." *Nocturno Cinema* #4, September 1997.

Ruocco, Luca. "Discutendo con Marco Antonio Andolfi [Eddy Endolf] dell'importanza di avere uno pseudonimo e delle molteplici forme del demonio," *Rapporto Confidenziale* #10, December 2008.

_____. "Riassumendo Marco Antonio Andolfi," *Rapporto Confidenziale* #10, December 2008.

Salza, Giuseppe. "Le retour de Lucio Fulci." *L'Écran fantastique* #44, April 1984.

Schlockoff, Alain, and Robert Schlockoff. "Entretien avec Lamberto Bava." *L'Écran fantastique* #16, January 1981.

Schlockoff, Robert. "Entretien avec Lucio Fulci." *L'Écran fantastique* #16, January 1981.

_____. "Entretien avec Lucio Fulci," *L'Écran fantastique* #22, January 1982.

Záccaro, Samuele. "Intervista esclusiva a Rossella Drudi." www.darkveins.com, 21 March 2009.

Index

215